AF814433

QUE Bee

From Doubts to Distinction

Your ICSE 2026 Exams Partner

GIST OF THE TEXTBOOK
Crisp & Complete Theory - No need to go back to textbooks!

ALL TYPES OF LATEST PATTERN QUESTIONS
MCQs | Case-based | Assertion-Reason | Fill-ups; All in one place!

KEY WORDS HIGHLIGHTED
Important points and formulae neatly highlighted never miss what matters

COUNCIL-STYLE ANSWERS
Write responses like an examiner expects

SAMPLE PAPER
Practice in real-exam mode. Perfect your timing, strategy and confidence.

arihant
SUCCESS AND NOTHING LESS

ARIHANT PRAKASHAN
(School Division Series)

ADMINISTRATIVE & PRODUCTION OFFICES
Regd. Office
'Ramchhaya' 4577/15, Agarwal Road, Darya Ganj, New Delhi -110002
Tele: 011- 47630600, 43518550; Fax: 011- 23280316

Head Office
Kalindi, TP Nagar, Meerut (UP) - 250002, Tel: 0121-7156203, 7156204

SALES & SUPPORT OFFICES
Agra, Ahmedabad, Bengaluru, Bareilly, Chennai, Delhi, Guwahati, Hyderabad, Jaipur, Jhansi, Kolkata, Lucknow, Nagpur & Pune.

PO No : TXT-XX-XXXXXXX-X-XX

Published By Arihant Publications (India) Ltd.

For further information about the books published by Arihant, log on to www.arihantbooks.com or e-mail at info@arihantbooks.com

Follow us on

PRICE ₹225.00

PRODUCTION TEAM

Publishing Manager
Keshav Mohan

Project Head
Yojna Sharma

Cover Designer
Bilal Hashmi

Inner Designer
Ankit Tyagi

Page Layouting
Subhash Chaprana

Proof Reader
Mansi, Ishan

QUE Bee

ICSE
PHYSICS
Class 9

Types of Questions & their Respective Number

Type of Questions	Total Number
Multiple Choice Questions (MCQs)	156
Assertion-Reason (A-R)	56
Fill-ups	73
Very Short Answer Questions (VSA)	154
Short Answer Type Questions (SA)	90
Long Answer Type Questions (LA)	57
Case Based Questions	38
Numericals	168
TOTAL NO. OF QUESTIONS	**792**

Created by
Nitin Goel
20 Yrs. Experienced
PGT, ST. Francis Convent School, Meerut

Contributor
Sayonika Jana

From Learner to Leader

Step-Into the Spotlight

QUE Bee is more than just a book - it's a platform for young achievers like you to guide future toppers. If you've cracked the code to smart study or have insights that can make learning easier for others, this is your moment to shine!

What Can You Share?

- Your study techniques, time management tips, or motivation hacks
- Feedback or suggestions to make QUE Bee even better
- Real experiences that can guide other students through the exam maze

What's in It for You?

- Your name will be featured in our exclusive Student Panel in the next edition
- Win exciting & surprise rewards for impactful suggestions
- **Get published** - your photo, Ideas-or even interviews can be featured in the book
- **Become a student icon** - recognized and followed by peers across schools

Let your learning become someone else's ladder.
Be remembered. Be featured. Be the guide.

SCAN TO SHARE YOUR IDEA

QUE Bee

Index

Latest
Course Structure

There will be one paper of **two hours** duration carrying 80 marks and Internal Assessment of practical work carrying 20 marks.

Note: Unless otherwise specified, only S I. Units are to be used while teaching and learning, as well as for answering questions.

Measurements and Experimentation

(i) International System of Units, the required SI units with correct symbols are given at the end of this syllabus. Other commonly used system of units - fps and cgs.

(ii) Measurements using common instruments, Vernier callipers and micro-metre screw gauge for length, and simple pendulum for time.

Measurement of length using, Vernier callipers and micro-metre screw gauge. Decreasing least-count leads to an increase in accuracy; least-count (LC) of Vernier callipers and screw gauge), zero error (basic idea), (no numerical problems on callipers and screw gauge), simple pendulum; time period, frequency, graph of length l vs. T^2 only; slope of the graph. Formula $T=2\pi\sqrt{l/g}$ [no derivation]. Only simple numerical problems.

Motion in One Dimension

Scalar and vector quantities, distance, speed, velocity, acceleration; graphs of distance-time and speed-time; equations of uniformly accelerated motion with derivations.

Examples of Scalar and vector quantities only, rest and motion in one dimension; distance and displacement; speed and velocity; acceleration and retardation; distance-time and velocity-time graphs; meaning of slope of the graphs; [Non-uniform acceleration excluded].

Equations to be derived: $v = u + at$; $S = ut + \frac{1}{2}at^2$; $S = \frac{1}{2}(u+v)t$; $v^2 = u^2 + 2aS$. [Equation for S_n^{th} is not included].

Simple numerical problems.

Laws of Motion

(i) Contact and non-contact forces; cgs & SI units.

Examples of contact forces (frictional force, normal reaction force, tension force as applied through strings and force exerted during collision) and non-contact forces (gravitational, electric and magnetic). General properties of non-contact forces. cgs and SI units of force and their relation with Gravitational units.

(ii) Newton's First Law of Motion (qualitative discussion) introduction of the idea of inertia, mass and force.

Newton's first law; statement and qualitative discussion; definitions of inertia and force from first law, examples of inertia as illustration of first law. (Inertial mass not included).

(iii) Newton's Second Law of Motion (including F=ma); weight and mass.

Detailed study of the second law. Linear momentum,

$p = mv$; change in momentum $\Delta p = \Delta(mv) = m\Delta v$ for mass remaining constant, rate of change of momentum;

$\Delta p/\Delta t = m\Delta v/\Delta t = ma$ or

$$\{\frac{p_2 - p_1}{t} = \frac{mv - mu}{t} = \frac{m(v-u)}{t} = ma\};$$

Simple numerical problems combining $F = \Delta p/\Delta t = ma$ and equations of motion. Units of force - only cgs and SI.

(iv) Newton's Third Law of Motion (qualitative discussion only); simple examples.

Statement with qualitative discussion; examples of action - reaction pairs, (F_{BA} and F_{AB}); action and reaction always act on different bodies.

(v) Gravitation

Universal Law of Gravitation. (Statement and equation) and its importance. Gravity, acceleration due to gravity, free fall. Weight and mass, Weight as force of gravity comparison of mass and weight; gravitational units of force, (Simple numerical problems), (problems on variation of gravity excluded)

Fluids

(i) Change of pressure with depth (including the formula $p=h\rho g$); Transmission of pressure in liquids; atmospheric pressure.

Thrust and Pressure and their units; pressure exerted by a liquid column $p = h\rho g$; simple daily life examples, (i) broadness of the base of a dam, (ii) Diver's suit etc. some consequences of $p = h\rho g$; transmission of pressure in liquids; Pascal's law; examples; atmospheric pressure; common manifestation and consequences.. Variations of pressure with altitude, (qualitative only); applications such as weather forecasting and altimeter. (Simple numerical problems)

(ii) Buoyancy, Archimedes' Principle; floatation; relationship with density; relative density; determination of relative density of a solid.

Buoyancy, upthrust (F_B); definition; different cases, F_B>, = or < weight W of the body immersed; characteristic properties of upthrust; Archimedes' principle; explanation of cases where bodies with density ρ >, = or < the density ρ' of the fluid in which it is immersed.

Relative Density (RD) and Archimedes' principle. Experimental determination of RD of a solid and liquid denser than water. Floatation: principle of floatation; relation between the density of a floating body, density of the liquid in which it is floating and the fraction of volume of the body immersed; ($\rho_1/\rho_2 = V_2/V_1$); apparent weight of floating object; application to ship, submarine, iceberg, balloons, etc.

Simple numerical problems involving Archimedes' principle, buoyancy and floatation.

Heat and Energy

(i) Concepts of heat and temperature.

Heat as energy, SI unit – joule,

1 cal = 4.186 J exactly.

(ii) *Anomalous expansion of water; graphs showing variation of volume and density of water with temperature in the 0° to 10°C range. Hope's experiment and consequences of Anomalous expansion.*

(iii) Energy flow and its importance:

Understanding the flow of energy as Linear and linking it with the laws of Thermodynamics- 'Energy is neither created nor destroyed' and 'No Energy transfer is 100% efficient.

(iv) Energy sources.

Solar, wind, water and nuclear energy (only qualitative discussion of steps to produce electricity). Renewable *versus* non-renewable sources (elementary ideas with example).

Renewable energy: biogas, solar energy, wind energy, energy from falling of water, run-of-the river schemes, energy from waste, tidal energy, etc. Issues of economic viability and ability to meet demands.

Non-renewable energy – coal, oil, natural gas. Inequitable use of energy in urban and rural areas. Use of hydro electrical powers for light and tube wells.

(v) Global warming and Green House effect:

Meaning, causes and impact on the life on earth. Projections for the future; what needs to be done. Energy degradation –meaning and examples.

Light

(i) Reflection of light; images formed by a pair of parallel and perpendicular plane mirrors; .

Laws of reflection; experimental verification; characteristics of images formed in a pair of mirrors, (a) parallel and (b) perpendicular to each other; uses of plane mirrors.

(ii) Spherical mirrors; characteristics of image formed by these mirrors. Uses of concave and convex mirrors. (Only simple direct ray diagrams are required).

Brief introduction to spherical mirrors - concave and convex mirrors, centre and radius of curvature, pole and principal axis, focus and focal length; location of images from ray diagram for various positions of a small linear object on the principal axis of concave and convex mirrors; characteristics of images.

f = R/2 (without proof); sign convention and direct numerical problems using the mirror formulae are included. (Derivation of formulae not required)

Uses of spherical mirrors.

Scale drawing or graphical representation of ray diagrams not required.

Sound

(i) Nature of Sound waves. Requirement of a medium for sound waves to travel; propagation and speed in different media; comparison with speed of light.

Sound propagation, terms – frequency (f), wavelength (λ), velocity (v), relation v = fλ. (Simple numerical problems) effect of different factors on the speed of sound; comparison of speed of sound with speed of light; consequences of the large difference in these speeds in air; thunder and lightning.

(ii) Infrasonic, sonic, ultrasonic frequencies and their applications.

Elementary ideas and simple applications only. Difference between ultrasonic and supersonic.

Electricity and Magnetism

(i) Simple electric circuit using an electric cell and a bulb to introduce the idea of current (including its relationship to charge); potential difference; insulators and conductors; closed and open circuits; direction of current (electron flow and conventional)

Current Electricity: brief introduction of sources of direct current - cells, accumulators (construction, working and equations excluded); Electric current as the rate of flow of electric charge (direction of current - conventional and electronic), symbols used in circuit diagrams. Detection of current by Galvanometer or ammeter (functioning of the meters not to be introduced). Idea of electric circuit by using cell, key, resistance wire/resistance box/rheostat, qualitatively.; elementary idea about work done in transferring charge through a conductor wire; potential difference V = W/q.

(No derivation of formula) simple numerical problems.

Social initiatives: Improving efficiency of existing technologies and introducing new eco-friendly technologies. Creating awareness and building trends of sensitive use of resources and products, e.g. reduced use of electricity.

(ii) Induced magnetism, Magnetic field of earth. Neutral points in magnetic fields.

Magnetism: magnetism induced by bar magnets on magnetic materials; induction precedes attraction; lines of magnetic field and their properties; evidences of existence of earth's magnetic field, magnetic compass. Uniform magnetic field of earth and non-uniform field of a bar magnet placed along magnetic north-south; neutral point; properties of magnetic field lines.

(iii) Introduction of electromagnet and its uses.

Internal Assessment of Practical Work

Candidates will be asked to carry out experiments for which instructions are given. The experiments may be based on topics that are not included in the syllabus but theoretical knowledge will not be required. A candidate will be expected to be able to follow simple instructions, to take suitable readings and to present these readings in a systematic form. He/she may be required to exhibit his/her data graphically. Candidates will be expected to appreciate and use the concepts of least count, significant figures and elementary error handling.

A set of 6 to 10 experiments may be designed as given below or as found most suitable by the teacher. Students should be encouraged to record their observations systematically in a neat tabular form - in columns with column heads including units or in numbered rows as necessary. The final result or conclusion may be recorded for each experiment. Some of the experiments may be demonstrated (with the help of students) if these cannot be given to each student as lab experiments.

1. *Determine the least count of the Vernier callipers and measure the length and diameter of a small cylinder (average of three sets) - may be a metal rod of length 2 to 3 cm and diameter 1 to 2 cm.*
2. *Determine the pitch and least count of the given screw gauge and measure the mean radius of the given wire, taking three sets of readings in perpendicular directions.*
3. *Measure the length, breadth and thickness of a glass block using a metre rule (each reading correct to a mm), taking the mean of three readings in each case. Calculate the volume of the block in cm^3 and m^3. Determine the mass (not weight) of the block using any convenient balance in g and kg. Calculate the density of glass in cgs and SI units using mass and volume in the respective units. Obtain the relation between the two density units.*

4. *Measure the volume of a metal bob (the one used in simple pendulum experiments) from the readings of water level in a measuring cylinder using displacement method. Also calculate the same volume from the radius measured using Vernier callipers. Comment on the accuracies.*

5. *Obtain five sets of readings of the time taken for 20 oscillations of a simple pendulum of lengths about 70, 80, 90, 100 and 110 cm; calculate the time periods (T) and their squares (T^2) for each length (l). Plot a graph of l vs. T^2. Draw the best - fit straight - line graph. Also, obtain its slope. Calculate the value of g in the laboratory. It is 4p² x slope.*

6. *Take a beaker of water. Place it on the wire gauze on a tripod stand. Suspend two thermometers - one with Celsius and the other with Fahrenheit scale. Record the thermometer readings at 5 to 7 different temperatures. You may start with ice cold water, then allow it to warm up and then heat it slowly taking temperature (at regular intervals) as high as possible. Plot a graph of T_F vs. T_C. Obtain the slope. Compare with the theoretical value. Read the intercept on T_F axis for $T_C = 0$.*

7. *Using a plane mirror strip mounted vertically on a board, obtain the reflected rays for three rays incident at different angles. Measure the angles of incidence and angles of reflection. See if these angles are equal.*

8. *Place three object pins at different distances on a line perpendicular to a plane mirror fixed vertically on a board. Obtain two reflected rays (for each pin) fixing two pins in line with the image. Obtain the positions of the images in each case by extending backwards (using dashed lines), the lines representing reflected rays. Measure the object distances and image distances in the three cases. Tabulate. Are they equal? Generalize the result.*

9. *Obtain the focal length of a concave mirror (a) by distant object method, focusing its real image on a screen or wall and (b) by one needle method removing parallax or focusing the image of the illuminated wire gauze attached to a ray box. One could also improvise with a candle and a screen. Enter your observations in numbered rows.*

10. *Connect a suitable dc source (two dry cells or an acid cell), a key and a bulb (may be a small one used in torches) in series. Close the circuit by inserting the plug in the key. Observe the bulb as it lights up. Now open the circuit, connect another identical bulb in between the first bulb and the cell so that the two bulbs are in series. Close the key. Observe the lighted bulbs. How does the light from any one bulb compare with that in the first case when you had only one bulb? Disconnect the second bulb. Reconnect the circuit as in the first experiment. Now connect the second bulb across the first bulb. The two bulbs are connected in parallel. Observe the brightness of any one bulb. Compare with previous results. Draw your own conclusions regarding the current and resistance in the three cases.*

11. *Plot the magnetic field lines of earth (without any magnet nearby) using a small compass needle. On another sheet of paper place a bar magnet with its axis parallel to the magnetic lines of the earth, i.e. along the magnetic meridian or magnetic north-south. Plot the magnetic field in the region around the magnet. Identify the regions where the combined magnetic field of the magnet and the earth is (a) strongest, (b) very weak but not zero, and (c) zero. Why is neutral point, so called?*

12. *Using a spring balance obtain the weight (in N) of a metal ball in air and then completely immersed in water in a measuring cylinder. Note the volume of the ball from the volume of the water displaced. Calculate the upthrust from the first two weights. Also calculate the mass and then weight of the water displaced by the bob M=V.r, W=mg). Use the above result to verify Archimedes principle.*

01

MEASUREMENTS AND EXPERIMENTATION

Physical Quantities and Units

- **Measurement** is defined as the process of comparison of an unknown quantity with a known or standard quantity.
- All those quantities which can be defined and measured directly or indirectly are called **physical quantities**.
  e.g. Length, time, mass, force, etc.
- Those physical quantities which are independent of other physical quantities are called **fundamental quantities** or **base quantities.**
- Those quantities which can be derived from the fundamental quantities are called **derived quantities.**
  e.g. Velocity, acceleration, linear momentum, etc.
- To measure a physical quantity, a standard is needed which is called **unit** of that physical quantity.
- The result of a measurement of a physical quantity is expressed by a **number** (numerical value) accompanied by a unit. i.e

  Physical quantity = Magnitude × Unit

  or

  $$Q = n \times u$$

  where, *n* represents the numerical value and *u* represents the unit.
- The units of fundamental quantities or base quantities, i.e. length, mass and time are called **fundamental units** or **base units**.
- The units of measurement of all other physical quantities which can be obtained from fundamental units are called **derived units.**

  e.g.
  $$\text{Speed} = \frac{\text{Distance}}{\text{Time}} = \frac{\text{m}}{\text{s}} = \text{ms}^{-1}$$

System of Units

(i) **FPS System** It is the British engineering system of units, which uses **foot** as the unit of length, **pound** as the unit of mass and **second** as the unit of time.

(ii) **CGS System** It is based on Gaussian system of units, which uses **centimetre, gram** and **second** for length, mass and time, respectively.

(iii) **MKS System** It uses **metre, kilogram** and **second** as the fundamental units of length, mass and time, respectively.

(iv) **International System of Units (SI Units)** The system of units, which is accepted internationally for measurement is the System Internationaled Units (French for International System of Units) abbreviated as SI.

This system consists of seven fundamental units and two supplementary units which are abbreviated as shown in table below

Base Quantities and their SI Units

Quantity	Unit	Symbol
Length	Metre	m
Mass	Kilogram	kg
Time	Second	s
Electric current	Ampere	A
Thermodynamic temperature	Kelvin	K
Amount of substance	Mole	mol
Luminous intensity	Candela	cd

Supplementary Quantities and their SI Units

Quantity	Unit	Symbol
Plane angle	Radian	rad
Solid angle	Steradian	Sr

Some Examples of Derived SI Units Expressed in Terms of Base Units

Derived Quantity	Definition	Derived Units	Symbol
Area	Length × Breadth	Metre × Metre	m^2
Volume	Length × Breadth × Height	Metre × Metre × Metre	m^3
Density	$\frac{\text{Mass}}{\text{Volume}}$	$\frac{\text{Kilogram}}{(\text{Metre})^3}$	kg-m^{-3}
Speed/Velocity	$\frac{\text{Distance}}{\text{Time}}$	$\frac{\text{Metre}}{\text{Second}}$	ms^{-1}
Acceleration	$\frac{\text{Velocity}}{\text{Time}}$	$\frac{\text{Metre / Second}}{\text{Second}}$	ms^{-2}
Force	Mass × Acceleration	Kilogram × $\frac{\text{Metre}}{(\text{Second})^2}$	kg-ms^{-2} or N
Momentum	Mass × Velocity	Kilogram × $\frac{\text{Metre}}{\text{Second}}$	kg-ms^{-1} or N-s
Work/Energy	Force × Displacement	Kilogram × $\frac{\text{Metre} \times \text{Metre}}{(\text{Second})^2}$	kg-m^2s^{-2} or J
Power	$\frac{\text{Work}}{\text{Time}}$	Kilogram × $\frac{(\text{Metre})^2}{(\text{Second})^2}$ / Second	kg - m^2s^{-3} or Js^{-1} or W
Electric charge	Current × Time	Ampere × Second	A-s or C
Pressure	$\frac{\text{Force}}{\text{Area}}$	Newton/$(\text{Metre})^2$	Nm^{-2} or Pa
Frequency	$\frac{1}{\text{Time period}}$	$\frac{1}{\text{second}}$ or Hz	s^{-1} or Hz

Some Other Important Units for Length

(i) **Centimetre (cm)** 1 cm = 10^{-2} m

(ii) **Millimetre (mm)** 1 mm = 10^{-3} m

(iii) **Micron or Micrometre** 1 μm = 10^{-6} m

(iv) **Nanometre (nm)** 1 nm = 10^{-9} m, **Kilometre (km)** 1 km = 10^3 m

Non-metric units of length

Bigger units

(i) **Astronomical Unit** It is the mean distance of the earth from the sun.

$$1 \text{ AU} = 1496 \times 10^{11} \text{ m}$$

(ii) **Light Year** It is the distance travelled by light in vacuum in one year.

$$1 \text{ ly} = 9.46 \times 10^{15} \text{ m}$$

(iii) **Parallactic Second** It is the distance at which an arc of length 1 astronomical unit subtends an angle of 1s of arc.

$$1 \text{ parsec} = 3.084 \times 10^{16} \text{ m} = 3.26 \text{ ly}$$

Smaller units

(i) **Angstrom Unit** This unit is used for interatomic and intermolecular separation.

$$1 \text{Å} = 10^{-10} \text{m} = 10^{-1} \text{ nm} = 10 \text{ Å}$$

(ii) **Fermi** This unit is used for measuring nuclear sizes.

$$1 \text{ fm} = 10^{-15} \text{m}$$

Some Important Units for Mass

(i) Gram (g), $1 \text{ g} = 10^{-3} \text{ kg}$
(ii) Milligram (mg), $1 \text{ mg} = 10^{-6} \text{ kg}$
(iii) Quintal (q), $1 \text{q} = 100 \text{ kg}$
(iv) Metric tonne (t), $1\text{t} = 1000 \text{ kg}$
(v) 1 Solar mass $= 2 \times 10^{30}$ kg
(vi) 1 u or (amu) $= 1.66 \times 10^{-27}$ kg

Smaller Units of Time

(i) Millisecond (ms) $1 \text{ ms} = 10^{-3} \text{ s}$
(ii) Microsecond (μs) $1 \ \mu\text{s} = 10^{-6} \text{ s}$
(iii) $1 \text{ shake} = 10^{-8} \text{ s}$
(iv) Nanosecond (ns) $1 \text{ ns} = 10^{-9} \text{ s}$

Bigger Units of Time

$1 \text{ min} = 60 \text{ s}$, $\quad 1 \text{h} = 3600 \text{ s}$

$1 \text{ day} = 86400 \text{ s}$, $\quad 1 \text{ year} = 365 \text{ days} = 3.153 \times 10^7 \text{ s}$

$1 \text{ decade} = 10 \text{ years} = 3.1536 \times 10^8 \text{ s}$

Measurement of Length using Vernier Calliper

Vernier calliper is a device used to measure accurately upto $\left(\frac{1}{10}\right)$th of a millimetre.

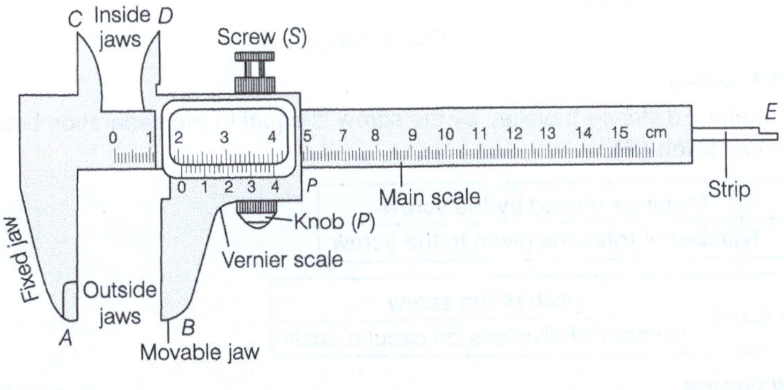

Principle of Vernier Calliper

In the vernier calliper, 10 divisions of vernier scale coincide with 9 divisions of main scale.

$\therefore$ | 10 VSD (Vernier Scale Division) = 9 MSD (Main Scale Division) |

$$\therefore \quad 1 \text{ VSD} = \frac{9}{10} \text{ MSD}$$

$$1 \text{ VSD} = \frac{9}{10} \text{ mm} \qquad (\because 1 \text{ MSD} = 1 \text{mm})$$

Thus, the difference between one main scale division and one vernier scale division is 1 mm − 0.9 mm = 0.1 mm.

So, **vernier calliper can measure length accurately upto 0.1 mm.**

Least Count (LC) of Vernier Calliper

- The minimum measurement that vernier calliper can take is called its least count. It is also known as the **vernier constant.**

$$\therefore \quad \text{Least Count (LC)} = \frac{\text{Value of one of the smallest divisions on main scale}}{\text{Total number of small divisions on the vernier scale}}$$

∴ When the number of small divisions on the vernier scale increases, LC decreases which in turn increases the accuracy of measurement by the instrument.

Zero Error in Vernier Callipers

- If the instrument is perfect, the zero mark of the vernier scale should coincide with the zero mark of the main scale, when the jaws *C* and *D* are made to touch each other.
- If the zero marks do not coincide, then vernier calliper said to have zero error. Zero error can be of two types
  - (i) **Positive Zero Error** When the zero mark of the vernier scale lies towards the right side of the zero of the main scale, when jaws *C* and *D* are made to touch each other, then the zero error is called positive zero error.
  - (ii) **Negative Zero Error** When the zero mark of the vernier scale lies towards the left side of the zero of the main scale, when jaws *C* and *D* are in contact with each other, then the zero error is called negative zero error.
- Correct reading = Observed reading − Zero error (with sign)

Screw Gauge

- It is an instrument used for measuring very small lengths such as diameters of wires or thickness of a paper.

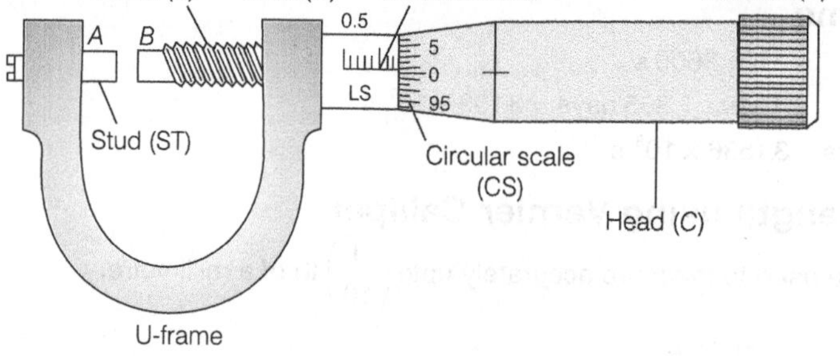

Screw gauge

Least Count of a Screw Gauge

- During one complete rotation, distance travelled by the screw is equal to the separation between two consecutive threads which is known as **pitch (*P*)**.

Therefore, $$\text{Pitch} = \frac{\text{Distance moved by the screw}}{\text{Number of rotations given to the screw}}$$

and $$\text{Least count} = \frac{\text{pitch of the screw}}{\text{Number of divisions on circular scale}}$$

Zero Error in a Screw Gauge

- When the end of screw *B* and the surface of the stud *A* come in contact, then the zero marks of the linear scale and the main scale should coincide with each other. If it is not so, then the screw gauge is said to have zero error.
- There are two types of zero error occurs
  - (i) **Positive Zero Error** In this case, the zero of the circular scale is below the line of graduation as the gap between *A* and *B* is reduced to zero. Since, the zero of the circular scale lies to the right hand side of the zero of the pitch scale, the error is called positive zero error.

REVISION NOTES

(ii) **Negative Zero Error** In this a case, the zero of the circular scale lies above the line of graduation, when the gap between A and B is reduced to zero.

Under this condition, the edge of the circular scale lies to the left hand side or above the zero of the pitch scale. This is why, the zero error is called negative zero error.

- Correct Reading = Observed Reading − Zero Error (with sign).
- **Backlash Error** Error due to wear and tear of the screw is called backlash error.

Simple Pendulum

A heavy object (bob), suspended from a rigid support, by an inextensible and light string set to oscillate freely due to gravity is called a simple pendulum.

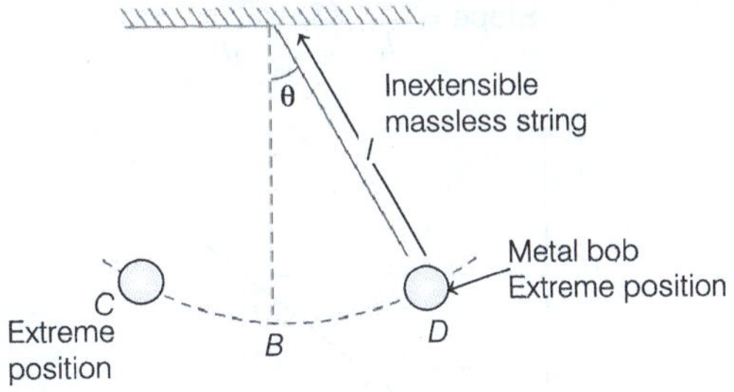

Terms Related to Simple Pendulum

(i) **Oscillation** One complete cycle of to and fro motion of the pendulum is known as one oscillation.

(ii) **Time Period** (period of oscillation) The time taken to complete one oscillation is called time period. It is denoted by T and its SI unit is second (s).

(iii) **Frequency of Oscillation** The number of oscillations in one second is known as frequency of oscillation. It is denoted by (f) and its SI unit is hertz (Hz).

(iv) **Amplitude** It is the maximum displacement of simple pendulum from its mean position. Its SI unit is metre (m).

(v) **Effective length of a pendulum** It is the distance of the point of oscillation (i.e. the centre of gravity of the bob) from the point of suspension. It is shown by l.

Relation between l and T

- Length of a pendulum (l) and its time period (T) are related to each other by the given relation $T = 2\pi\sqrt{\frac{l}{g}}$, where g is acceleration due to gravity.

Graph of Length l *versus* T^2

- As $T = 2\pi\sqrt{\frac{l}{g}}$, $T^2 \propto l$

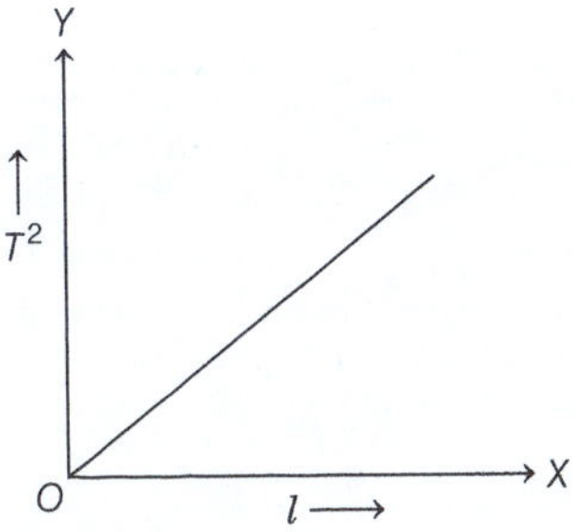

Hence, graph between l and T^2 will be a straight line starting from origin as shown above.

Factors affecting the time period of a simple pendulum

(i) The time period of oscillation is directly proportional to the square root of its effective length i.e. $T \propto \sqrt{l}$

(ii) The time period of oscillation is inversely proportional to the square root of acceleration due to gravity i.e. $T \propto \frac{1}{\sqrt{g}}$.

(iii) The time period of oscillation does not depend on the mass or material of the body suspended (i.e., the bob)

(iv) The time period of oscillation does not depend on the extent of swing on either side (i.e, on amplitude).

Slope of T^2 *versus* l graph

The slope of T^2 *versus* l graph is constant at a given place and is given by

$$\text{Slope} = \frac{T_1^2 - T_2^2}{l_1 - l_2} = \frac{4\pi^2}{g}$$

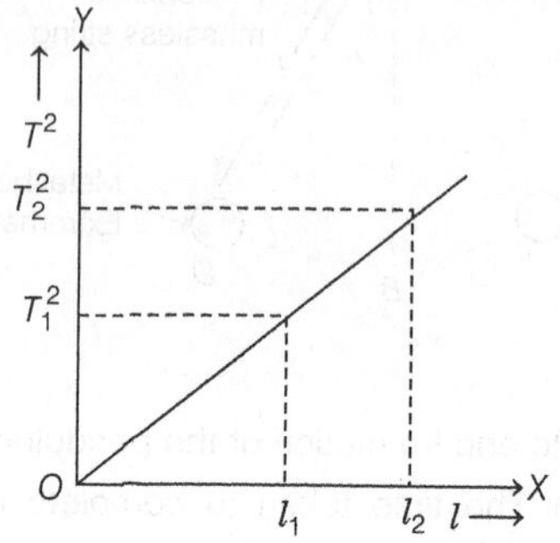

Second's Pendulum

A pendulum with a time period of oscillation equal to **two seconds** is known as a second's pendulum. It is used in clocks.

EXAM ORIENTED QUESTIONS

TYPE - 1 01 Mark

Multiple Choice Questions

Q.1 Which of the following is a fundamental unit?
(a) Newton (b) Pascal
(c) Hertz (d) Second

Ans. (d) Second is the fundamental unit of time, while newton, pascal and hertz are derived units of force, pressure and frequency, respectively.

Q.2 Which of the following has a derived unit?
(a) Mass (b) Length
(c) Volume (d) Temperature

Ans. (c) Volume has the derived unit which is derived from fundamental unit of length, i.e. metre.
Unit of volume = metre × metre × metre = $(\text{metre})^3$

Q.3 The least count of a vernier calliper is
(a) 1 cm (b) 0.001 cm (c) 0.1 cm (d) 0.01 cm

Ans. (d) The least count of a vernier calliper is obtained by dividing the value of one division of main scale by the total number of divisions on vernier scale. The value of least count of vernier calliper is 0.01 cm.

Q.4 If the zero of the vernier scale is ahead of the main scale zero, the error is
(a) negative zero error
(b) positive zero error
(c) No zero error
(d) systematic error

Ans. (b) When the zero of the vernier scale is ahead of the main scale zero, it indicates overestimation, leading to positive zero error.

Q.5 Identify the function of thimble in screw gauge.
(a) To mark circular scale.
(b) To mark main scale and base line.
(c) To read length correct upto 1 mm.
(d) Helps to read length correct upto 0.01 mm.

Ans. (a) The hollow cylinder in screw gauge is known as thimble. Its function is to mark the circular scale.

Q.6 The diameter of a thin wire can be measured by a
(a) vernier calliper (b) metre rule
(c) screw gauge (d) None of these

Ans. (c) A screw gauge is used to measure the diameter of a thin wire because the least count of screw gauge is 0.001cm. However, the least count of a micrometer screw gauge is 1 μm (0.0001 cm).

Q.7 Choose the correct option about the time period of a simple pendulum.
(a) The time period of oscillation is directly proportional to the effective length of pendulum.
(b) The time period of oscillation depends on the mass of the body suspended.
(c) When the time period of pendulum decreases, its effective length increases.
(d) Decrease in the value of g, increase the time period of oscillations.

Ans. (d) A pendulum clock goes slow, i.e. the time period increases, when the value of g decreases because time period of pendulum is inversely proportional to the square root of acceleration due to gravity.

Q.8 An oscillation of a swinging pendulum occurs when the bob moves from X to Y and back to X again.

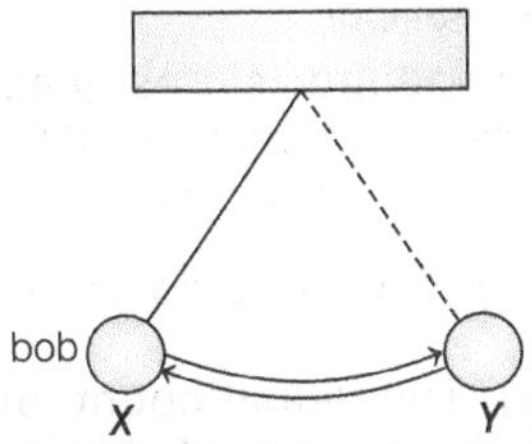

Using a stopwatch, which would be the most accurate way to measure the time for one oscillation of the pendulum?
(a) Time 20 oscillations and multiply by 20.
(b) Time 20 oscillations and divide by 20.
(c) Time one oscillation.
(d) Time the motion from X to Y, and double it.

Ans. (b) It is more accurate to measure a longer period of time. The time for one oscillation is the time taken for the bob to swing from X to Y and back to X.

Q.9 The length of a second's pendulum is nearly
(a) 0.5 m (b) 9.8 m
(c) 1.0 m (d) 2.0 m

Ans. (c) The effective length of the second's pendulum, at a place where $g = 9.8 \text{ m/s}^2$ is nearly 1 m.

TYPE - 2 01 Mark

Assertion-Reason Type Questions

Directions (Q. Nos. 1-5) In the following questions two statements are given as Assertion and Reason.
(a) Both A and R are true and R is the correct explanation of A.

(b) Both A and R are true but R is not the correct explanation of A.
(c) A is true but R is false.
(d) A is false but R is true.

Q.1 Assertion (A) The prefix 'milli' is used to denote 10^{-3}.
Reason (R) The prefix 'milli' is commonly used in measurements like millimetres and milligrams.

Ans. (a) Milli represents 10^{-3} and it is widely used for small measurements like millimetres (mm) and milligrams (mg).

Q.2 Assertion (A) A vernier calliper can measure more accurately than a meter scale.
Reason (R) A vernier calliper has a least count of 0.1 mm, which is smaller than that of a meter scale.

Ans. (a) The least count determines the accuracy of an instrument. Vernier callipers is designed for finer measurements.

Q.3 Assertion (A) A micrometer screw gauge is used to measure the diameter of a wire accurately.
Reason (R) A screw gauge has a lower least count than a vernier calliper.

Ans. (a) A screw gauge is designed for very small measurements (least count of 0.01 mm), making it suitables for measuring thin wires.

Q.4 Assertion (A) The least count of screw gauge is 1 mm.
Reason (R) The least count of an instrument depends on the number of divisions on its circular scale and the pitch.

Ans. (d) The least count of a screw gauge is generally 0.01 mm. It is calculated as

$$\text{Least count} = \frac{\text{Pitch}}{\text{Number of divisions on the circular scale}}$$

Q.5 Assertion (A) The time period of a simple pendulum is independent of its mass.
Reason (R) The time period of a simple pendulum depends only on the length of the pendulum and the acceleration due to gravity.

Ans. (a) The formula $T = 2\pi\sqrt{\frac{l}{g}}$ shows that the mass of the pendulum does not affect its time period. Only the length of the pendulum and the value of g determine the time period.

TYPE - 3 — 01/02 Marks

Fill in the Blanks

Q.1 The time period of a simple pendulum is the time taken to complete one .... [oscillation/revolution] **[1]**

Ans. oscillation

Q.2 The length of the pendulum is the distance from the point of suspension to the ...... [bottom/centre] of the bob. **[1]**

Ans. centre

Q.3 If the length of the pendulum increases, the time period .... [increases/remains the same] **[1]**

Ans. increases

Q.4 The relationship between frequency and time period is .... [directly/inversely] proportional. **[1]**

Ans. inversely

Q.5 The time period of a simple pendulum is directly proportional to the square root of its ...... [mass/length] **[1]**

Ans. length

Q.6 The T^2 *versus* L graph is a .... [curved/straight] line from origin.

Ans. straight

Q.7 To calculate g from the slope of T^2 *versus* L, the formula is $g = \frac{4\pi^2}{\text{slope}}$. This shows g is .... [directly/inversely] proportional to the slope. **[1]**

Ans. inversely

Q.8 The unit of .... [mass/length] in the CGS system is gram and the unit of .... [length/mass] in the FPS system is pound. **[2]**

Ans. mass, mass

Q.9 The least count of a vernier calliper depends on the .... [vernier/main] scale division and the number of .... [main/vernier] scale divisions. **[2]**

Ans. main, vernier

Q.10 The pitch of a screw gauge is defined as the distance moved by the screw in one .... [rotation/division] and is measured in ....[Centimetres/millimetres] **[2]**

Ans. rotation, millimetres

TYPE - 4 — 02 Marks

Very Short Answer Type Questions

Q.1 Define the term fundamental unit. Name fundamental units of current and temperature. **[2]**

Ans. Those physical quantities which can neither be derived from other units, nor be further resolved into more simpler units are called fundamental units.
Current → Ampere (A)
Temperature → Kelvin (K)

Q.2 Write the fundamental units along with their symbols. **[2]**

Ans. There are seven fundamental units as given below
(i) Metre (m) — Unit of length

(ii) Kilogram (kg) — Unit of mass
(iii) Second (s) — Unit of time
(iv) Kelvin (K) — Unit of temperature
(v) Ampere (A) — Unit of electric current
(vi) Candela (cd) — Unit of luminous intensity
(vii) Mole (mol) — Unit for amount of substance

Q.3 How are the following derived units related to the fundamental units?
(i) newton (ii) joule [1]
(iii) watt (iv) pascal [1]

Ans. (i) Newton (N) = $kg - ms^{-2}$
(ii) Joule (J) = $kg - m^2s^{-2}$
(iii) Watt (W) = $kg - m^2s^{-3}$
(iv) Pascal (Pa) = $kg - m^{-1}s^{-2}$

Q.4 Name the three convenient units used to measure very long distance and relate it to its SI unit.

Ans. Astronomical unit (AU), light year (ly) and parsec are three units used to measure very long distances.

$1\text{ AU} = 1.496 \times 10^{11}\text{ m}$
$1\text{ ly} = 9.46 \times 10^{15}\text{ m}$
$1\text{ parsec} = 3.084 \times 10^{16}\text{ m}$

Q.5 How can we convert the following units to m?
(i) light year (ii) Å
(iii) micron (iv) fermi

Ans. (i) 1 light year = 9.46×10^{15} m
(ii) 1Å = 10^{-10}m
(iii) 1 micron = 10^{-6} m
(iv) 1 fermi = 10^{-15} m

Q.6 Express each of the following in terms of kilogram.
(i) 1 g (ii) 1 mg (iii) 1 quintal (iv) 1 amu

Ans. (i) 1 g = 10^{-3} kg
(ii) 1mg = 10^{-6} kg
(iii) 1 quintal = 100 kg
(iv) 1 amu = 1.66×10^{-27} kg

Q.7 Name the physical quantities which are measured in the following units.
(i) ly (ii) nm
(iii) kg (iv) µs

Ans. (i) distance (ii) length
(iii) mass (iv) time

Q.8 What is meant by zero error of vernier calliper? [2]

Ans. If the zero of vernier scale and zero of the main scale do not coincide, when the external jaws of vernier are closed, then the vernier is said to have zero error.

Q.9 Explain.
(i) Positive zero error [1]
(ii) Negative zero error. [1]

Ans. (i) **Positive Zero Error** The zero error is said to be positive when the zero mark of the vernier scale lies towards the right side of the zero of the main scale when the jaws are in contact.

(ii) **Negative Zero Error** The zero error is said to be negative when the zero mark of the vernier scale lies towards the left side of the zero mark of the main scale when jaws are in contact.

Q.10 State the purpose of ratchet in a screw gauge.

Ans. In a screw gauge, the circular scale is attached with a ratchet by a spring. The purpose of ratchet in a screw gauge is to advance the screw by turning it till the object is gently held between the stud and spindle of the screw.

Q.11 Mention the relation between frequency and time period of a simple pendulum. What is the SI unit of frequency?

Ans. Frequency of a simple pendulum (f) is equal to reciprocal of its time period (T), i.e. $f \propto \frac{1}{T}$.

The SI unit of frequency is hertz (Hz).

Q.12 What will be the frequency of oscillation of a simple pendulum in a cabin that is falling freely under acceleration due to gravity?

Ans. If a cabin is falling freely, acceleration due to gravity $g = 0$.

Since, $f = \frac{1}{2\pi}\sqrt{\frac{g}{l}}$

$\therefore$ $f = 0$, if $g = 0$

Q.13 Two pendulums P and Q of lengths 4 m and 8 m are made to oscillate. Which pendulum will make more oscillations and why?

Ans. The time period of a pendulum is given by the expression $T = 2\pi\sqrt{\frac{l}{g}}$. Since, it depends directly on the square root of length, therefore pendulum Q will have more time period than pendulum P. Hence, in the same time, pendulum P will make more oscillations than pendulum Q.

Q.14 How is the length of a simple pendulum related to acceleration due to gravity for a constant time period?

Ans. Time period of a simple pendulum is given by

$$T = 2\pi\sqrt{\frac{l}{g}} \Rightarrow T\sqrt{g} = 2\pi\sqrt{l}$$

i.e., $\sqrt{l} = \frac{T}{2\pi}\sqrt{g}$

As T is constant, therefore

$$\sqrt{l} \propto \sqrt{g}$$

i.e. $l \propto g$

TYPE - 5 03 Marks

Short Answer Type Questions

Q.1 State the difference between derived and fundamental units with examples. **[3]**

Ans.

	Fundamental Units	Derived Units
(i)	A fundamental unit is a unit which is independent of any other unit.	Derived units are those which depend upon the fundamental units and can be expressed in terms of the fundamental units.
(ii)	They cannot be changed or related to any other fundamental units.	These units can also be expressed with respect to other derived units.
(iii)	e.g. Mass, Length, Time.	e.g. Force, Pressure, Acceleration.

Q.2 Write the derived units of the following:

(i) Momentum
(ii) Work/Energy
(iii) Pressure
(iv) Force
(v) Power
(vi) Density

Ans. (i) Momentum-kg ms^{-1}or N-s.
(ii) Work/Energy-kg m^2s^{-2} or J
(iii) Pressure-Nm^{-2} or Pa
(iv) Force-kg ms^{-2} or N
(v) Power-kg $m^2 s^{-3}$or W
(vi) Density-kg m^{-3}

Q.3 Define the following units
(i) Leap year **[1]**
(ii) Lunar month **[1]**
(iii) Decade **[1]**

Ans. (i) **Leap year** A leap year is considered as the year in which the month of February is of 29 days.
1 leap year = 366 days.
(ii) **Lunar month** A lunar month is of 29.5 days and 12 lunar months are of 354.37 days.
(iii) **Decade** One decade has 10 years.
1 decade = 3.1536×10^8 s

Q.4 (i) What is meant by Least Count (LC) of a measuring device? **[1]**
(ii) What is the least count of vernier calliper? **[1]**
(iii) What is vernier constant? **[1]**

Ans. (i) The least count of a measuring device is the smallest value of physical quantity which can be measured accurately by the instrument.
(ii) Least count of vernier calliper,

$$LC = 1\,MSD - 1\,VSD = 1\,MSD - \frac{9}{10}\,MSD$$

$$LC = \frac{1}{10}\,MSD$$

Usually, MSD = 0.1 cm

$\therefore$ LC = 0.01 cm

(iii) Vernier constant is the least count of vernier calliper.

Q.5 (i) A screw gauge may be considered as the advancement of vernier calliper, explain. **[1]**
(ii) Will a pendulum gain or lose time, when taken to a mountain? **[1]**
(iii) Why does simple pendulum eventually stop? **[1]**

Ans. (i) A screw gauge is an instrument used for measuring very small lengths such as diameters of wires which cannot be accurately measured by vernier calliper. It is because the least count of screw gauge is smaller than the least count of a vernier calliper.
(ii) When a pendulum is taken to the top of a mountain, g will decrease. Therefore, T will increase i.e., the pendulum will take more time to complete one oscillation. In other words, it will lose time.
(iii) Due to frictional resistance between air and bob, the amplitude of oscillation of the pendulum gradually decreases and eventually the pendulum stops.

Q.6 Name the instrument you would use to measure the following
(i) Diameter of a ball pen
(ii) Diameter of a pencil
(iii) External/internal diameter of a calorimeter
(iv) Diameter of a metal ball (ball bearings)
(v) Internal diameter of a test tube
(vi) Width of a desk

Ans. (i), (ii) are measured by micrometer screw gauge while (iii), (iv), (v) are measured by vernier calliper and (vi) is measured by meter scale.

Q.7 Answer the following
(i) Will the time period of pendulum increase or decrease, when taken to a mountain? **[1]**
(ii) The bob of a simple pendulum is made of ice. How will the time period be affected, if the ice starts melting? **[2]**

Ans. (i) At the top of mountain, the value of g decreases, as $T \propto \frac{1}{\sqrt{g}}$. Thus, the time period increases, when g is decreased.
(ii) The time period of the pendulum is independent of the mass of the bob. So, the time period is unaffected, if ice melts.

Q.8 (i) What do you mean by effective length of a simple pendulum? **[1]**

(ii) Draw graphs of l *versus* T^2 and l *versus* T for a simple pendulum. **[2]**

Ans. (i) Effective length of a simple pendulum is the distance between the point of suspension and the centre of the bob shown in diagram.

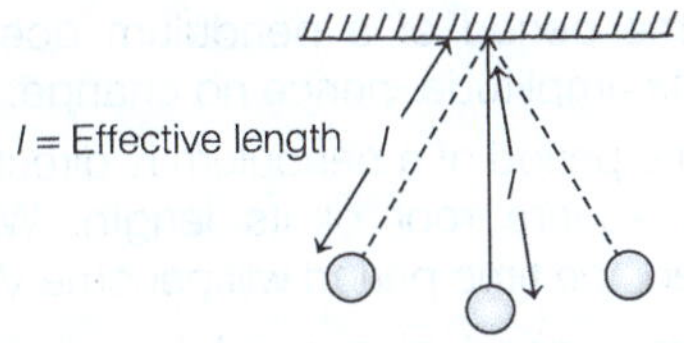

(ii) The graphical representation of l *versus* T^2 and l *versus* T are shown below

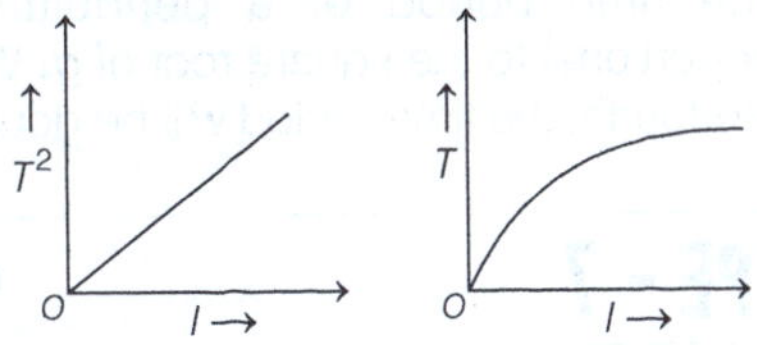

TYPE - 6 04 Marks

Long Answer Type Questions

Q.1 (i) What is the need for measuring lengths with vernier callipers? **[2]**

(ii) How do you show by a labelled diagram, the positions of the main scale and the vernier scale in case of two types of zero error? **[2]**

Ans. (i) The distance less than a millimetre could be only approximated as the ordinary scales cannot be marked in sub parts of millimetre. Thus, in order to measure the small distance accurately for precision machinery, vernier callipers was invented.

(ii) Zero error is of two types

1. **Positive Zero Error** The zero error is said to be positive, if on contacting both the jaws together, the zero mark of the vernier is on the right side of the zero mark of the main scale.

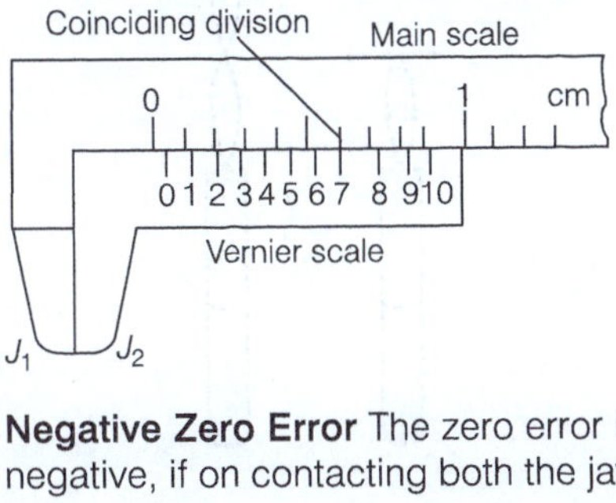

2. **Negative Zero Error** The zero error is said to be negative, if on contacting both the jaws together, the zero mark of the vernier is on the left side of the zero of the main scale.

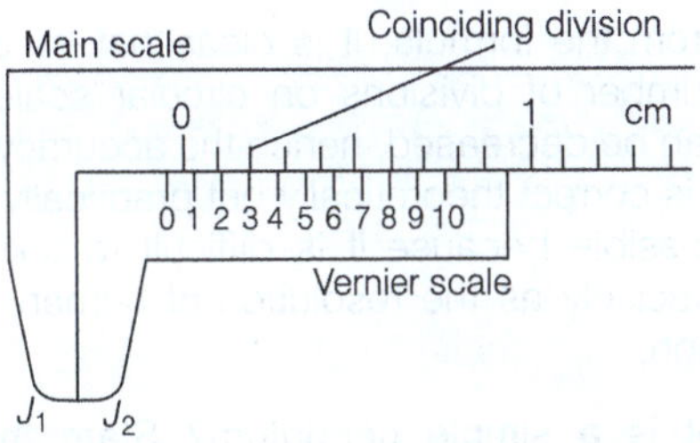

Q.2 How will you measure the diameter of a wire by screw gauge?

Ans. The following steps to be taken in order to find the diameter of a wire by screw gauge

(i) Calculate the least count of screw gauge, i.e.

Least Count (LC)

$$= \frac{\text{Pitch}}{\text{Number of divisions on circular scale}}$$

(ii) Calculate zero error (if any).

(iii) Place the given wire in between stud and movable screw and turn the ratchet till it becomes free.

(iv) Note Main Scale Reading (MSR).

(v) Note Circular Scale Reading (CSR).

(vi) Use the formula of diameter = MSR + (CSR × LC)

(vii) The correct diameter will be obtained by correcting the zero error.

The correct diameter is the final measurement of the diameter of wire (given).

Q.3 Answer the following

(i) You are given a thread and a meter scale. How will you estimate the diameter of the thread? **[2]**

(ii) A screw gauge has a pitch of 1.0 mm and 200 divisions on the circular scale. Do you think, it is possible to increase the accuracy of the screw gauge arbitrarily by increasing the number of divisions on the circular scale? **[2]**

Ans. (i) The diameter of a thread is so small that it cannot be measured using a meter scale. To measure the diameter of the thread, we find the number of turns of the thread on the meter scale, so that the turns are closely touching one another. Count the number of turns n and measure the length l of the coiled thread using the meter scale.

$$\text{Diameter of thread} = \frac{\text{Length of coiled thread } (l)}{\text{Number of turns } (n)}$$

(ii) Yes, the accuracy of the screw gauge can be increased by increasing the number of divisions on the circular scale as the least count of the screw gauge is given by

$$\text{Least count} = \frac{\text{Pitch}}{\text{Number of divisions on circular scale}}$$

From the formula, it is clear that by increasing the number of divisions on circular scale, least count can be decreased, hence the accuracy will increase. It is correct theoretically but practically it may not be possible because it is difficult to take the reading precisely as the resolution of human eye is not so high.

Q.4 **What is a simple pendulum? State the factors on which time period of a simple pendulum depends.**

Ans. A simple pendulum is a device which contains a heavy point mass called bob, suspended from a rigid support by an inextensible and massless string. Its effective length is taken from the point of suspension to the centre of the bob.

The period of oscillation (T) is

(i) directly proportional to the square root of length l i.e. $T \propto \sqrt{l}$.

(ii) inversely proportional to the square root of acceleration due to gravity (g)

i.e. $T \propto \frac{1}{\sqrt{g}}$

$$T = \text{constant} \sqrt{\frac{l}{g}}$$

Thus, $T = 2\pi \sqrt{\frac{l}{g}}$

Q.5 Define the following terms related to simple pendulum.

(i) Oscillation (ii) Amplitude

(iii) Time period (iv) Frequency

Ans. (i) When the bob moves from its mean position to the extreme right, then from the extreme right to extreme left and finally back to the mean position, it completes one **oscillation**.

(ii) **Amplitude** is the maximum displacement of the bob from its mean position on either side.

(iii) **Period of oscillation** (or the **time period**) is the time taken to complete one oscillation. It is denoted by T and its SI unit is second.

(iv) **Frequency** of oscillation of a simple pendulum is the number of oscillations made in one second. It is denoted by ν or n or f. Its SI unit is per second or hertz (Hz).

Q.6 How is the time period of a simple pendulum affected in the following situations?

(i) Amplitude of a pendulum is increased. **[1]**

(ii) The length of a pendulum is doubled. **[1]**

(iii) The brass bob is replaced with an identical aluminium bob. **[1]**

(iv) The value of g is made one-fourth. **[1]**

Ans. The time period of a pendulum is given by the expression, $T = 2\pi \sqrt{\frac{l}{g}}$

(i) The time period of a pendulum does not depend upon its amplitude, hence no change.

(ii) The time period of a pendulum is directly proportional to the square root of its length. When length is doubled, the time period will become $\sqrt{2}$ times.

(iii) The time period of a pendulum does not depend upon its mass, hence no change.

(iv) The time period of a pendulum is inversely proportional to the square root of g. When g is made one-fourth, the time period will be doubled.

TYPE - 7 — 03/04 Marks

Case Based Questions

Q.1 Raju and Ravi fight frequently over who is taller. They decide to measure their heights by standing next to a wall and marking their heights.

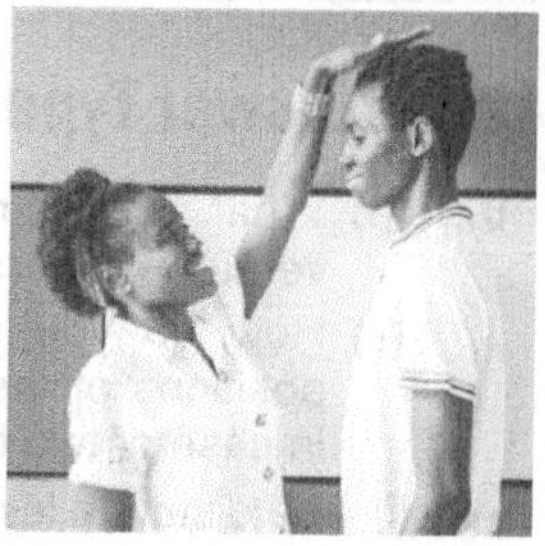

They measure the height of each mark by using a gilli-danda to measure the distance between the foot of the wall and their respective marks.

It is found that Raju's height is equal to two dandas and one gilli, whereas that of Ravi is equal to two dandas and two gillis. Hence, Ravi is taller than Raju.

(i) What is the main problem with using a gilli-danda for measuring height? **[1]**

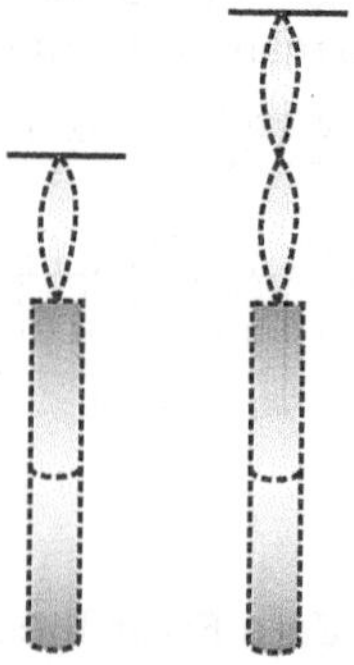

(ii) Suppose a danda is approximately 60 cm and a gilli is 10 cm. Convert Raju's and Ravi's heights into centimetres. **[1]**

(iii) How does this case study highlight the importance of standardization in measurement? **[1]**

Ans. (i) The gilli-danda is not a standard unit of measurement and its length may vary. This leads to inaccurate and inconsistent results.

(ii) Raju's height $= (2 \times 60) + 10$

$= 120 + 10 = 130$ cm

Ravi's height $= (2 \times 60) + (2 \times 10)$

$= 120 + 20 = 140$ cm

Since, 140 cm > 130 cm.

(iii) This case shows that using non-standard units (gilli-danda) leads to inconsistencies and errors. Standardized units like metres and centimetre provide accurate and universally accepted measurements.

Q.2 If the bob of a vibrating simple pendulum is made of ice, then the period of swing of the simple pendulum will remain unchanged till the location of centre of gravity of the ice bob left after melting the ice remains at a fixed distance from the point of suspension. If the centre of a gravity of an ice bob after melting is raised upwards, then the effective length of a pendulum decreases and start time period of the swing decreases. If the centre of gravity shifts on the lower side, the time period of the swing increases.

(i) What will happen to the time in a pendulum clock at hills or inside the mines?

(ii) Length of a simple pendulum is infinite then why is time not infinite?

(iii) If the mass of the pendulum is increased two-fold, then what will be the effect on the periodic time of the pendulum?

Ans. (i) As time is inversely proportional to the square root of gravity, time period will decrease with the value of g. The value of acceleration due to gravity is less at hills or in the mines than that of on the surface of earth, the time period of simple pendulum increases at hills or inside the mines. Hence, the pendulum clock will be slowed down which means it will be losing time.

(ii) The relation of time period for a simple pendulum is not valid if the effective length of a simple pendulum is more than the radius of the earth. This means that, T increases up to a certain limit only.

(iii) There will be no change in the periodic time because the periodic time is independent of the mass but depends upon the length of the pentagon and the acceleration due to gravity, which will not be affected if the mass of the pendulum is increased.

Q.3 A tennis ball suspended from a rigid support by an inextensible and light string set to oscillate freely as shown in the figure below.

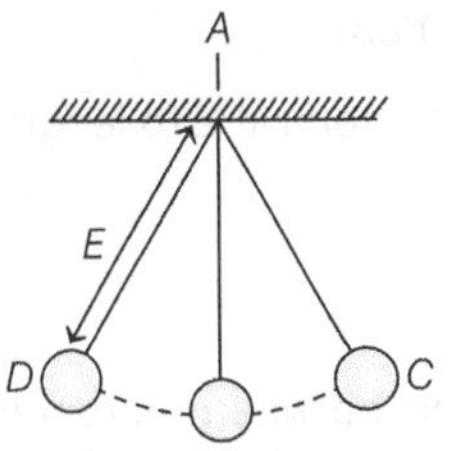

Complete the table, using the labels from the figures. The first label is done for you.

Sr. No.	Description	Label
a	Point of suspension	A
b	Extreme position of ball	
c	Equilibrium position	
d	Effective length	

Ans.

Sr. No.	Description	Label
a	Part of suspension	A
b	Extreme position of ball	C and D
c	Equilibrium position	B
d	Effective length	E

TYPE - 8

Numerical Questions

Q.1 The value of gravitational constant G in SI system is 6.67×10^{-11} N-m^2 kg^{-2}. What will be its value in CGS? **[2]**

Sol. Given, $G = 6.67 \times 10^{-11}\,\text{N-m}^2\,\text{kg}^{-2}$

$= 6.67 \times 10^{-11}\ (\text{kg - ms}^{-2})\ \text{m}^2\text{kg}^{-2}$

$= 6.67 \times 10^{-11}(\text{m}^3)\ (\text{s}^{-2})\ (\text{kg}^{-1})$

$= 6.67 \times 10^{-11}\ (100\ \text{cm})^3\ (\text{s})^{-2}\ (10^3\text{g})^{-1}$

$= 6.67 \times 10^{-8}\,\text{cm}^3\ \text{g}^{-1}\ \text{s}^{-2}$

Q.2 Convert 25 nm in metres and micron. **[2]**

Sol. $1\ \text{nm} = 10^{-9}$ m

$\therefore$ $25\ \text{nm} = 25 \times 10^{-9}$ m

Now, $1\ \text{micron} = 10^{-6}$ m

$\therefore$ $1\ \text{nm} = 10^{-3}$ micron

$\therefore$ $25\ \text{nm} = 25 \times 10^{-3}$ micron

Q.3 **The size of a bacteria is 2 μm. Find the number of bacteria in 2 m length.** **[2]**

Sol. $1\mu m = 10^{-6} m$

$\Rightarrow \quad 1 m = 10^{6} \mu m$

$\therefore$ Number of bacteria in 2 m length $= \dfrac{2 m}{2 \mu m}$

$= \dfrac{2 \times 10^{6} \mu m}{2 \mu m} = 10^{6}$

Q.4 **Deduce relation between astronomical unit, light year and parsec. Arrange them in decreasing order of their magnitudes.** **[3]**

Sol. We know that, $1 AU = 1.496 \times 10^{11} m$

$1 ly = 9.46 \times 10^{15} m$

$1 parsec = 3.084 \times 10^{16} m$

$\therefore \quad \dfrac{1 ly}{1 AU} = \dfrac{9.46 \times 10^{15}}{1.496 \times 10^{11}} = 6.32 \times 10^{4}$

$1 ly = 6.32 \times 10^{4} AU$

Now, conversion of light year into parsec,

i.e. $\dfrac{1 parsec}{1 ly} = \dfrac{3.084 \times 10^{16}}{9.46 \times 10^{15}} = 3.26$

$\therefore \quad 1 parsec = 3.26 ly$

On comparing above results, we get

$1 parsec > 1 ly > 1 AU$

Q.5 **How many kilometres are there in 1 AU and 1 light year?** **[2]**

Sol. $1 AU = 1.496 \times 10^{11} m$

$1 AU = 1.496 \times 10^{11} \times 10^{-3} km$

$= 1.496 \times 10^{8} km$

$\therefore 1.496 \times 10^{8}$ km are in 1 AU.

$\because$ 1 light year $= 9.46 \times 10^{15} m = 9.46 \times 10^{12} km$

Q.6 **Calculate the number of light years in one metre.** **[2]**

Sol. We know that, $1 ly = 9.46 \times 10^{15} m$

or $\quad 9.46 \times 10^{15} m = 1 ly$

$\therefore \quad 1 m = \dfrac{1}{9.46 \times 10^{15}} ly = 1.057 \times 10^{-16} ly$

Q.7 **Write the following quantities in their respective SI unit.**

(i) 3.2 ly **(ii) 4 parsec**

(iii) 2.3 Å **(iv) 1.5× 10⁻³ fm** **[2]**

Sol. (i) $1 ly = 9.46 \times 10^{15} m$

$\therefore 3.2 ly = 3.2 \times 9.46 \times 10^{15} m = 3.02 \times 10^{16} m$

(ii) $4 parsec = 4 \times 3.084 \times 10^{16} m$

$= 1.233 \times 10^{17} m$

(iii) $2.3 Å = 2.3 \times 10^{-10} m$

(iv) $1.5 \times 10^{-3} fm = 1.5 \times 10^{-3} \times 10^{-15} m$

$= 1.5 \times 10^{-18} m$

Q.8 **What do you understand by the statement, the density of mercury is 13.6 g/cm³? Convert this value into SI unit.** **[2]**

Sol. The above statement means that the mass volume of $1 cm^{3}$ of mercury is 13.6 g.

$13.6 g/cm^{3} = \dfrac{13.6 g}{1 cm^{3}} = \dfrac{13.6 \times 10^{-3} kg}{(10^{-2})^{3} m^{3}}$

$= 13.6 \times 10^{3} kg/m^{3}$

$= 13600 kg m^{-3}$

The SI unit of density is $kg m^{-3}$.

Q.9 **The mass of a 8 cm cube is 4096 g. Calculate its density in**

(i) SI system **(ii) CGS system**

Sol. Mass of the cube $= \dfrac{4096}{1000} kg$

Each side of the cube = 8 cm

$= \left(\dfrac{8}{100}\right) m$

$\therefore$ Volume $= \left(\dfrac{8}{100}\right)^{3} m^{3}$

Now, density $= \dfrac{mass}{volume} = \dfrac{4096}{1000} \times \dfrac{10^{6}}{512}$

$= 8000 kg m^{-3}$

$\therefore$ (i) In SI system, density $= 8000 kg m^{-3}$

(ii) In CGS system, density $= \dfrac{4096}{8^{3}} = 8 g cm^{-3}$

Q.10 **Two balls A and B of different materials has same mass. Their volumes are 200 cm³ and 400 cm³, respectively. Compare their densities.** **[3]**

Sol. Let the masses of each ball be *m* grams.

$\therefore$ Density of ball A $(D_A) = \dfrac{Mass}{Volume}$

$= \dfrac{m}{200} g cm^{-3}$

Density of ball B $(D_B) = \dfrac{m}{400} g cm^{-3}$

$\therefore \quad \dfrac{D_A}{D_B} = \dfrac{\frac{m}{200}}{\frac{m}{400}} = \dfrac{2}{1}$

$\Rightarrow \quad D_A : D_B = 2:1$

Q.11 **The diameter of a ball is 20 cm. If the mass of the ball is 528 g, then calculate its density in SI units.** **[3]**

Sol. Diameter of the ball = 20 cm

$\therefore$ Radius of the ball $= \dfrac{20}{2} = 10 cm$

$\therefore$ Volume $= \dfrac{4}{3}\pi(10)^{3} cm^{3}$

$$= \frac{\frac{4\pi}{3} \times 1000}{10^6} m^3$$

$$\text{Mass} = 528 \text{ g} = \frac{528}{1000} \text{ kg}$$

$$\Rightarrow \text{Density} = \frac{\text{Mass}}{\text{Volume}}$$

$$= \frac{528}{1000} \times \frac{10^6}{\frac{4 \times 22}{3 \times 7} \times 1000}$$

$$= \frac{528}{1000} \times \frac{10^6 \times 21}{88 \times 1000}$$

$$= 126 \text{ kg m}^{-3}$$

Q.12 The wavelength of light is 589 nm. What is its wavelength in Å and μm? **[2]**

Sol. $1 \text{ nm} = 10^{-9}$ m and $1 \text{ Å} = 10^{-10}$ m

So, $1 \text{ nm} = 10 \text{Å}$

$\therefore$ Wavelength of light = 589 nm = 5890 Å

$= 0.589 \times 10^{-6} \text{m} = 0.589 \mu\text{m}$

Q.13 The wavelength of light of a particular green colour is 5000 Å. Express it in

(i) nanometre (ii) micrometre

(iii) metre (iv) centimetre **[2]**

Sol. (i) $5000 \text{ Å} = 5.0 \times 10^2$ nm (nanometre)

(ii) $5000 \text{ Å} = 5.0 \times 10^{-1}$ μm (micrometre)

(iii) $5000 \text{ Å} = 5.0 \times 10^{+3}$ Å

$= 5.0 \times 10^3 \times 10^{-10} \text{ m} = 5.0 \times 10^{-7}$ m

(iv) $5000 \text{ Å} = 5.0 \times 10^{-7} \times 10^{+2} \text{ cm} = 5.0 \times 10^{-5}$ cm

Q.14 How many protons would make 1 g, if the mass of a proton is 1.67×10^{-27} kg? **[2]**

Sol. $$\text{Number of protons in 1 g} = \frac{\text{Total mass}}{\text{Mass of one proton}}$$

$$= \frac{1 \text{ g}}{1.67 \times 10^{-27} \text{ kg}} = \frac{1 \text{ g}}{(1.67 \times 10^{-27} \times 10^3) \text{ g}}$$

$$= 5.99 \times 10^{23}$$

Q.15 (i) Distance of the nearest star (other than sun) alpha centauri is 4 light year. Express it in km. **[1]**

(ii) 1 gigagram makes how many metric tonne? **[1]**

Sol. (i) As we know that, $1 \text{ ly} = 9.46 \times 10^{15}$ m

$\therefore$ $4 \text{ ly} = 4 \times 9.46 \times 10^{15} \text{m} = 37.84 \times 10^{15}$ m

Distance $= 3.784 \times 10^{13}$ km

(ii) $$\frac{1 \text{ gigagram}}{1 \text{ metric tonne}} = \frac{10^9 \text{ g}}{10^3 \text{ kg}} = \frac{10^6 \text{ kg}}{10^3 \text{ kg}} = 10^3$$

$\therefore$ 1 gigagram = 1000 metric tonne

Q.16 The mass of Earth is 6×10^{24} kg. Calculate the number of atoms present in Earth, if average mass of an atom of Earth is 80 u. **[2]**

Sol. Mass of 1 atom $= 80 \text{u} = 80 \times 1.6 \times 10^{-27}$ kg

$$\therefore \text{Number of atoms} = \frac{6 \times 10^{24}}{80 \times 1.6 \times 10^{-27}}$$

$= 4.68 \times 10^{49}$ atoms

Q.17 (i) Express 0.01 mm in micron. **[1]**

(ii) Calculate the number of seconds in 365 days. **[1]**

Sol. (i) $1 \text{ mm} = 10^{-3}$ m and $1 \text{ micron} = 10^{-6}$ m

$\Rightarrow 1 \text{ mm} = 10^3$ micron

$\therefore 0.01 \text{ mm} = 0.01 \times 10^3 \text{ micron} = 10$ micron

(ii) Number of seconds in 365 days

$\Rightarrow 365 \times 24 \times 60 \times 60$

(days) (hours) (minutes) (seconds)

$= 365 \times 86400 \text{ s} = 31536000 \text{ s} = 3.15 \times 10^7$s

Q.18 Find the time period of a simple pendulum of length 90 cm at a place where $g = 10 \text{ ms}^{-2}$. (Take, $\pi = 3.142$) **[2]**

Sol. Given, $l = 90$ cm = 0.9 m, $g = 10 \text{ ms}^{-2}$, $T = ?$

We know that, $$T = 2\pi\sqrt{\frac{l}{g}} = 2 \times 3.142\sqrt{\frac{0.9}{10}}$$

$\Rightarrow T = 1.88 \simeq 1.9$ s (approx)

Q.19 Find the length of a pendulum which completes 6 oscillations in 15 s. (Take, $g = 9.8 \text{ ms}^{-2}$, $\pi = 3.14$) **[2]**

Sol. Given, $g = 9.8 \text{ ms}^{-2}$,

$$T = \frac{15 \text{ s}}{6} = 2.5 \text{ s}, l = ?$$

$$\therefore T = 2\pi\sqrt{\frac{l}{g}}$$

$$\Rightarrow \frac{T}{2\pi} = \sqrt{\frac{1}{g}} \Rightarrow \left(\frac{T}{2\pi}\right)^2 = \frac{1}{g}$$

$$\Rightarrow l = \frac{gT^2}{4\pi^2} = \frac{(9.8 \text{ ms}^{-2}) \times (2.5 \text{ s})^2}{4 \times (3.14)^2} = 1.55 \text{ m}$$

Q.20 Time periods of two pendulums are in ratio of 1.28 : 0.32. Calculate the ratio of lengths. **[2]**

Sol. Given, $T_1 = 1.28$, $T_2 = 0.32$, $l_1 = ?$, $l_2 = ?$

As, $$T = 2\pi\sqrt{\frac{l}{g}} \Rightarrow T \propto \sqrt{l}$$

$$\therefore \frac{T_1}{T_2} = \sqrt{\frac{l_1}{l_2}} \text{ or } \frac{T_1^2}{T_2^2} = \frac{l_1}{l_2}$$

$$\therefore \frac{l_1}{l_2} = \frac{(1.28)^2}{(0.32)^2} = \frac{16}{1} \Rightarrow l_1 : l_2 = 16 : 1$$

Q.21 A pendulum whose length is 36 cm has time period 1.2 s. Find the time period of another pendulum whose length is 81 cm. **[2]**

Sol. Given,

$l_1 = 36$ cm, $T_1 = 1.2$ s,
$l_2 = 81$ cm, $T_2 = ?$

We know that, time period of a simple pendulum is given by

$$T = 2\pi\sqrt{\frac{l}{g}}$$

$$\because \quad \frac{T_2}{T_1} = \sqrt{\frac{l_2}{l_1}} \text{ or } \frac{T_2}{12} = \sqrt{\frac{81}{36}} = \frac{9}{6}$$

$$\therefore \quad T_2 = 12 \times \frac{9}{6} = 18 \text{ s}$$

Q.22 **The length of a pendulum is decreased by 5%. What effect does it have on the time period of a pendulum?** **[3]**

Sol. Let the length of a pendulum be l.

i.e. $l_1 = l$, $l_2 = l - 5\%$ of $l = l - \frac{5}{100} \times l = 0.95\,l$

We know that, time period, $T \propto \sqrt{l}$

$$\therefore \quad \frac{T_2}{T_1} = \frac{\sqrt{l_2}}{\sqrt{l_1}} = \sqrt{\frac{0.95\,l_1}{l_1}}$$

$$\Rightarrow \frac{T_2}{T_1} = \sqrt{0.95} = 0.97$$

$$T_2 = 0.97\,T_1 = (1 - 0.03)\,T_1 = T_1 - 0.03\,T_1$$

i.e. $T_2 = T_1 - 3\%\,T_1$

So, the time period will decreased by 3%, if length is decreased by 5%.

Q.23 **Find the length of a simple pendulum whose time period of oscillation is 2.8 s.**
(Take, $g = 9.8$ ms^{-2}) **[2]**

Sol. Given, time period of a pendulum, $T = 2.8$ s

Acceleration due to gravity, $g = 9.8$ ms^{-2}

We know that, $T = 2\pi\sqrt{\frac{l}{g}}$

$$\Rightarrow \quad l = \frac{T^2 g}{4\pi^2} = \frac{(2.8)^2 \times 9.8}{4 \times (3.14)^2} = 1.94 \text{ m}$$

So, length of a simple pendulum = 1.94 m

Q.24 **Suppose the length of a simple pendulum is tripled. Then, how will the**

(i) time period be affected? **[1]**

(ii) frequency be affected? **[2]**

Sol. (i) We know that, time period,

$$T = 2\pi\sqrt{\frac{l}{g}}$$

$\therefore$ When the length is tripled, the new time period becomes

$$T' = 2\pi\sqrt{\frac{3l}{g}} = \sqrt{3}\left(2\pi\sqrt{\frac{l}{g}}\right) = \sqrt{3}\,T$$

$\therefore$ The new time period increases $\sqrt{3}$ times.

(ii) Also, $T = \frac{1}{f}$

$$\therefore \quad T' = \frac{1}{f'}$$

$$\Rightarrow \quad \sqrt{3}\,T = \frac{1}{f'}$$

$$\Rightarrow \quad \frac{\sqrt{3}}{f} = \frac{1}{f'}$$

$$\Rightarrow \quad f' = \frac{f}{\sqrt{3}}$$

$\therefore$ The frequency reduces $\sqrt{3}$ times.

Q.25 **(i) A pendulum is moved to a planet M where the acceleration due to gravity is one-ninth of that of the earth. How will the time period be affected?** **[2]**

(ii) Suppose the length of the string is 10 m, then calculate the time period of the pendulum on the planet M. [Take, $g = 10$ m/s^2] **[2]**

Sol. Time period of the pendulum on earth $(T) = 2\pi\sqrt{\frac{l}{g}}$

When the pendulum is taken to a new planet M, g becomes $\frac{g}{9}$.

$$\text{Then, } T' = 2\pi\sqrt{\frac{l}{\left(\frac{g}{9}\right)}} = 2\pi\sqrt{\frac{9l}{g}}$$

$$= 3\left(2\pi\sqrt{\frac{l}{g}}\right) = 3T$$

$\therefore$ The time period becomes three times to that of the earth.

(ii) Given that, $\quad l = 10$ m, then

$$T' = 3 \times 2\pi\sqrt{\frac{l}{g}} = 3 \times 2 \times 3.14 \times \sqrt{\frac{10}{10}}$$

$$\Rightarrow \quad T' = 18.84 \text{ s}$$

Q.26 **Suppose we have a simple pendulum of length l. It has a time period of 4 s on earth (provided g on earth is 10 ms^{-2} approx). What will be the time period of a simple pendulum on any planet which has $g = 40$ ms^{-2}?** **[4]**

Sol. As, l is same.

Thus, $\quad T \propto \frac{1}{\sqrt{g}}$

Given, $g_e = 10$ ms^{-2}, $g_p = 40$ ms^{-2},
$T_e = 4$ s
and $\quad T_p = ?$

$$\therefore \quad \frac{T_e}{T_p} = \sqrt{\frac{g_p}{g_e}}$$

$$\Rightarrow \quad \frac{T_e}{T_p} = \sqrt{\frac{40}{10}} \Rightarrow \frac{T_e}{T_p} = 2$$

where, g_e = acceleration due to gravity on earth,

T_e = time period on earth,

g_p = acceleration due to gravity on planet

and T_p = time period on planet.

Thus, $T_e = 2\,T_p$ or $T_p = \frac{1}{2}T_e$

Hence, time period of a simple pendulum on planet will be $\frac{1}{2}T_e$.

$$\therefore \quad T_p = \frac{4}{2} = 2\text{ s}$$

Q.27 Length of second's pendulum is 100 cm. Find the length of another pendulum whose time period is 2.4 s. **[3]**

Sol. We know that, the time period of the second pendulum is 2s.

$\therefore$ $T_1 = 2\text{s}, l_1 = 100\text{ cm}$

$T_2 = 2.4\text{s}, l_2 = ?$

As, $T = 2\pi\sqrt{\frac{l}{g}} \Rightarrow T^2 = 4\pi^2\frac{l}{g}$

Let T_1 = Time period of second's pendulum

and T_2 = Time period of another pendulum.

$\Rightarrow$ $T^2 \propto l$

$\therefore$ $\frac{T_1^2}{T_2^2} = \frac{l_1}{l_2} \Rightarrow \frac{2^2}{(2.4)^2} = \frac{100}{l_2}$

$\Rightarrow$ $l_2 = \frac{(2.4)^2}{2^2} \times 100$

$\Rightarrow$ $l_2 = \frac{5.76}{4} \times 100 = 144\text{cm}$

Q.28 What is the effective length of a second's pendulum?

Sol. Time period of a second's pendulum is 2 s. **[2]**

As, $T = 2\pi\sqrt{\frac{l}{g}} \Rightarrow l = \frac{1}{4\pi^2}gT^2$

$l = \frac{1}{4\pi^2} \times 9.8 \times (2)^2$ $\quad (\because g = 9.8\text{ ms}^{-2})$

$= \frac{1}{4\times\left(\frac{22}{7}\right)^2} \times 9.8 \times 4$ $\quad \left(\because \pi = \frac{22}{7}\right)$

$= 0.99\text{ m} \simeq 1\text{m}$

$\therefore$ The effective length of a second's pendulum is about 1 m.

Q.29 Calculate the length of second's pendulum on the surface of moon, when acceleration due to gravity on moon is 1.63 ms^{-2}. **[3]**

Sol. Given, $T = 2$ s, $g = 1.63\text{ ms}^{-2}$ and $L = ?$

We know that, the time period of a simple pendulum is given by

$$T = 2\pi\sqrt{\frac{L}{g}}$$

$$\therefore \quad 2 = 2 \times \frac{22}{7}\sqrt{\frac{L}{1.63}}$$

Squaring on both sides, we have

$$4 = 4 \times \frac{484}{49} \times \frac{L}{1.63}$$

$$\therefore \quad L = \frac{4 \times 49 \times 1.63}{4 \times 484} = 0.165\text{ m.}$$

02

MOTION IN ONE DIMENSION

Scalar and Vector Quantities

- The physical quantities which can be expressed only by their magnitude are called **scalar quantities**. e.g. Mass, time, distance, speed, etc.
- The physical quantities which require magnitude as well as direction for their representation are called **vector quantities**. e.g. Weight, displacement, velocity, etc.
- A vector quantity is represented by using an arrow over its symbol, e.g. $\vec{a}, \vec{v}$ etc, or by putting the symbol in bold (e.g. **v**, **a**)

Motion in one Dimension

- When the motion of a body is along a straight line, then it is said to be in **one-dimensional motion.** e.g., the motion of a train on a straight track, a stone falling vertically downwards, etc. One-dimensional motion is also known as **rectilinear** or **translatory motion**.

Rest and Motion

- If a body changes its position with respect to time and its surroundings, then the body is said to be in **motion**.
- In the same way, if the position of an object does not change with time and w.r.t. its surroundings, then it is said to be in **rest**.
- **Motion and rest are always relative to each other** i.e., an object in motion with respect to another object can be in rest with respect to other.

Various Terms Related to Motion

Position

- The location of an object with respect to a particular point is known as the position of the object. The particular point about which the position of the object is defined, is called **reference point** or **origin**.

Distance

- The distance travelled by a body is the actual length of the path covered by it, irrespective of the direction in which the body travels. It is a **scalar quantity**. Its SI unit is **metre** (m).

Displacement

- The displacement of an object is the change in the position of the object in a particular direction when it moves from a given position to another position.
- It is equal to the length of the shortest path measured in the direction from the initial position to the final position of the object.
- It is a **vector quantity**. Its SI unit is also **metre (m)**.
- **Distance *versus* Displacement**

  (i) Displacement of a moving object can never be greater than the distance travelled by it.

  $\therefore$ Displacement $\leq$ Distance

  $$\Rightarrow \quad \frac{\text{Displacement}}{\text{Distance}} \leq 1$$

  i.e. Ratio of displacement and distance is always less than or equal to 1.

REVISION NOTES

(ii) If a body moves along a straight line (only in one direction), then distance and displacement will be equal.

(iii) Displacement of the object can be positive, negative or zero but distance cannot be negative or zero.

Speed

- The speed of an object is defined as the distance travelled by it per unit time.

$$\text{Speed of an object } (v) = \frac{\text{Distance } (s)}{\text{Time } (t)}$$

- Speed is a **scalar quantity**. The SI unit of speed is **metre per second** (m/s).
- The distance travelled by an object is either positive or zero, so the speed of that object may be positive or zero but never be negative.
- The various types of speed are as given below

  (i) **Uniform Speed** If a moving body covers equal distances in equal intervals of time throughout its motion, then the speed of the body is said to be uniform, i.e. constant speed.
  e.g. Motion of a ball in a frictionless plane surface.

  (ii) **Non-uniform (variable) Speed** If a moving body covers unequal distances in equal intervals of time, then the speed of the body is said to be non-uniform or variable speed.

  e.g. Motion of a car in a crowded street.

  (iii) **Average Speed** It is defined as the total distance travelled by a body divided by the total time taken. It is expressed as

$$\text{Average speed} = \frac{\text{Total distance travelled}}{\text{Total time taken}}$$

  (iv) **Instantaneous Speed** The speed of an object at any particular instant of time or at a particular point of its path is called the instantaneous speed of the object.

Velocity

- Velocity is the speed of an object moving in a definite direction. Velocity of an object is defined as the displacement of the body per unit time.
  It is expressed as

$$\text{Velocity of an object } (v) = \frac{\text{Displacement } (d)}{\text{Time } (t)}$$

- It is numerically equal to the displacement of a body in 1s.
- Velocity is a **vector quantity**. The SI unit of velocity is **metre per second** (m/s) and the CGS unit is **centimetre** per second (cms^{-1}).
- Velocity of an object can be **positive, zero** or **negative.**
- The various types of velocity are as given below

  (i) **Uniform Velocity** If an object covers equal displacements in equal intervals of time without changing direction, then its velocity is known as uniform velocity, i.e. constant velocity.

  e.g. Rain drops reaching on earth's surface.

  (ii) **Non-uniform (variable) Velocity** If an object covers unequal displacements in equal intervals of time, then its velocity is known as non-uniform velocity, i.e. variable velocity. e.g. Motion of a body in circular path.

  (iii) **Average Velocity** It is defined as the ratio of total displacement of the object to the total time taken.

  It is expressed as

$$v_{av} = \frac{\text{Total displacement}}{\text{Total time taken}}$$

  (iv) **Instantaneous Velocity** The velocity of an object at a particular instant of time or at a particular point of its path is called its instantaneous velocity.

Note
- **Speedometer** is a device which is used to measure instantaneous speed of a moving body.
- If a body is moving in a straight line, then the magnitude of its speed and velocity will be equal.
- Average speed of a moving object can never be zero but the average velocity of a moving object can be zero.

Acceleration

- It is defined as the rate of change of velocity with respect to time.

$$\text{Acceleration } (a) = \frac{\text{Change in velocity}(\Delta v)}{\text{Change in time}(\Delta t)}$$

- In a given time interval t, the velocity of a body changes from u to v, then acceleration a is expressed as

$$a = \frac{\text{Final velocity }(v) - \text{Initial velocity }(u)}{\text{Time interval }(t)}$$

- The SI unit of acceleration is **metre per second square** ($m\ s^{-2}$) and CGS unit is centimetre per second (cms^{-1}) It is a **vector quantity**.
- The acceleration is taken to be **positive**, if it is in the direction of velocity, **negative** if it is opposite to the direction of velocity and **zero** when a body is moving with a constant velocity.
- If velocity of an object decreases with time, then it is said to have **negative acceleration**. Negative acceleration is also called **deceleration** or **retardation**.
- The various types of acceleration are as given below

(i) **Uniform acceleration** If an object travels in a straight line and its velocity increases or decreases by equal amounts in equal intervals of time, then the object is said to be in a uniform acceleration.

e.g. (a) The motion of a freely falling body. (b) The motion of a ball rolling down on an inclined plane.

(ii) **Non-uniform acceleration** If velocity of an object increases or decreases by unequal amounts in equal intervals of time, then the object is said to be in a non-uniform acceleration.

e.g. (a) The movement of a car on a crowded city road.
(b) The motion of the train leaving or entering the platform.

Graphical Representation of Motion

1. Distance-Time Graph

- The change in the position of an object with respect to time can be represented on the distance-time graph by adopting a convenient scale of choice.
- The slope of the distance-time graph gives the speed of the body.
- Distance-time graphs under various conditions are explained below

Case I When the object is at rest

If the position of the object does not change with time, then the object is said to be at rest.

The distance-time graph for an object at rest is a straight line parallel to the time axis which is shown in figure.

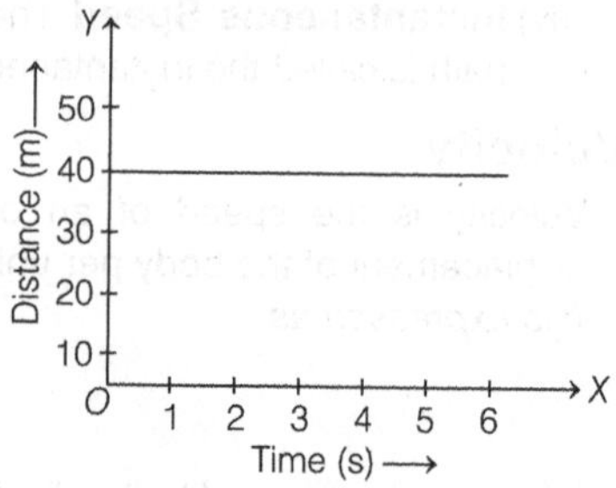

Distance-time graph for an object is at rest

Case II If the object is moving with uniform speed, then it travels equal distance in equal interval of time. For uniform speed, a graph of distance travelled against time is a straight line as shown in the figure given below

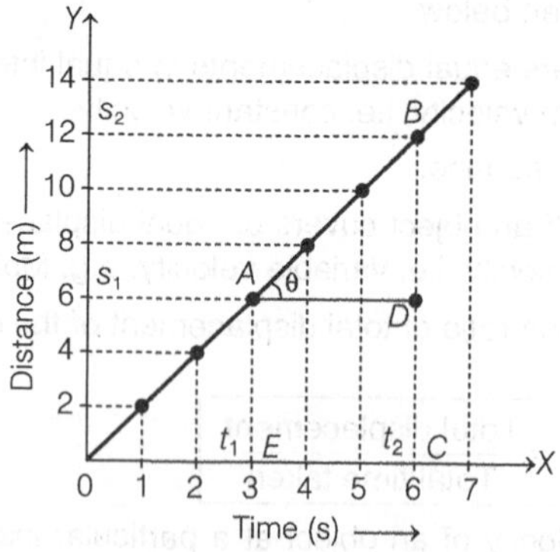

Distance-time graph for uniform motion

Now,
$$\text{slope} = \tan\theta = \frac{BD}{AD} = \frac{s_2 - s_1}{t_2 - t_1}$$

- **Displacement-time graph with positive and negative slopes**

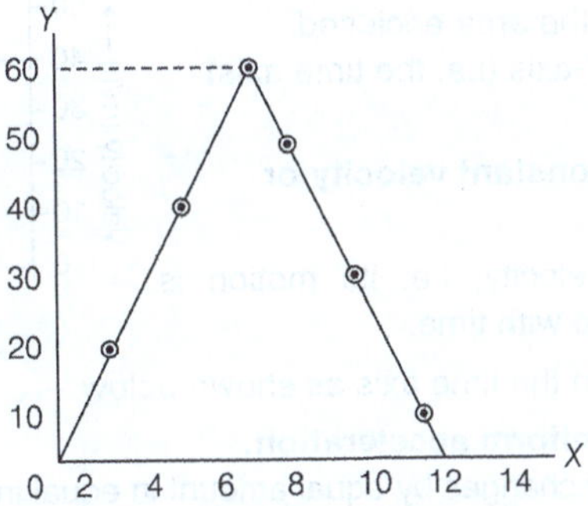

Thus slope of line *OA* is positive. (away from the starting point)

And slope *AB* is negative. (Which represent uniform motion in opposite direction i.e. towards the starting point).

Note The displacement time graph can never be a straight line parallel to the displacement axis because such a line would mean that the distance covered by the body in a certain direction increases. without any increase in time (i.e. the velocity of the body is infinite) Which is impossible.

Case III When the object is moving with variable velocity or uniform acceleration then it covers unequal distances in equal interval of time (non-uniform motion), it means graph is not a straight line but it is a curve.

This non-uniform motion due to uniform acceleration is of two types such as

(a) **When the speed of the body increases with passage of time,** then the distance-time graph will be a curve with positive slope as shown below

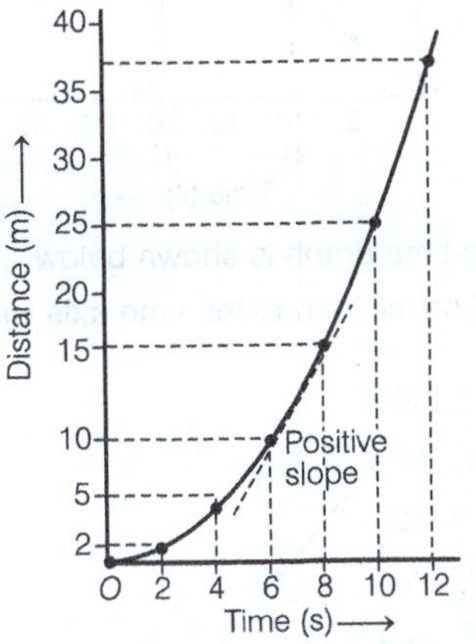

(b) **When the speed of the body decreases with passage of time,** then the distance-time graph will be a curve with negative slope as shown below

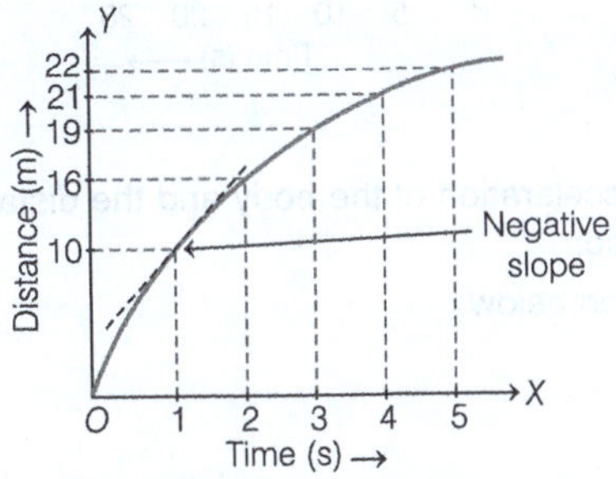

The velocity at any instant can be obtained by finding the slope of the tangent drawn on the curve at that instant of time.

2. Velocity-Time Graph

- Velocity-time graph shows how the velocity of a body changes with the passage of time.
- The slope of the velocity-time graph gives the acceleration of the body.

- Velocity-time graph various conditions are explained below.
- Since, velocity × time = displacement, the area enclosed, between the velocity-time curve and X-axis (i.e. the time axis) gives the displacement of the body.

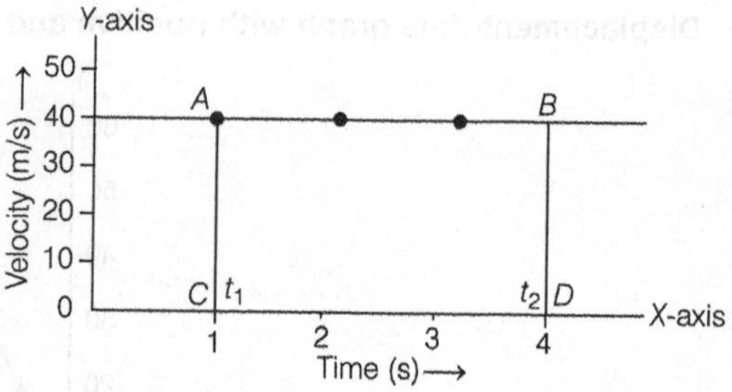

Case I When a body is moving with constant velocity or uniform velocity

When a body moves with constant velocity, i.e. its motion is uniform, then its velocity does not change with time.

The graph will be a straight line parallel to the time axis as shown below.

Case II When a body is moving with uniform acceleration.

In uniform accelerated motion, the velocity changes by equal amount in equal interval of time. So, the velocity-time graph is a straight line.

Velocity-time graph will be a straight line inclined to the time axis

(a) **For uniform acceleration**, velocity-time graph is shown below

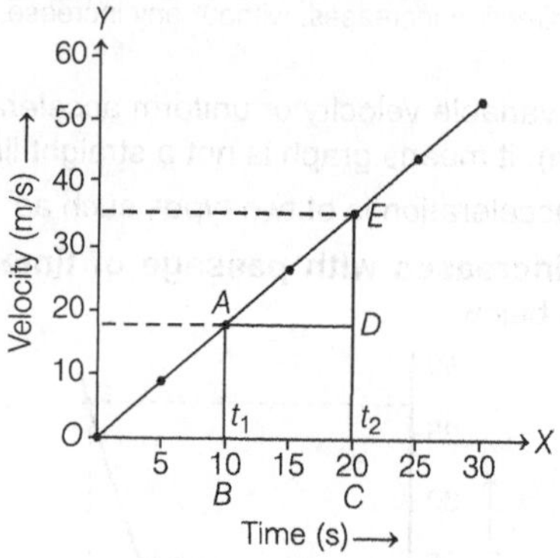

(b) **For uniform retardation**, the velocity-time graph is shown below

Velocity-time graph will be a straight line inclined to the time axis with a negative slope.

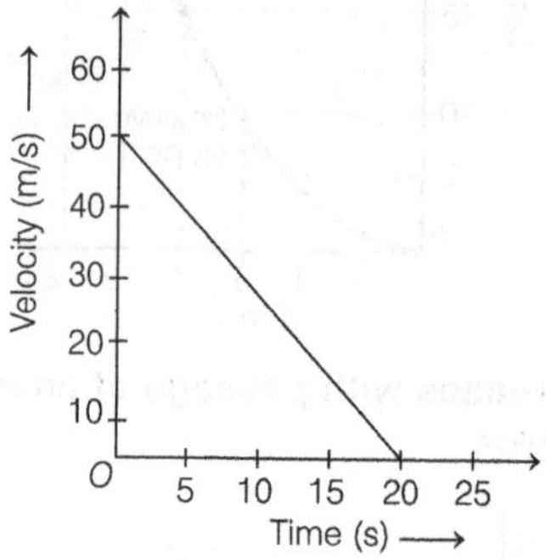

Equations of Motion

Relation between velocity of the body, acceleration of the body and the distance travelled by the body in a particular time interval is known as equation of motion.

The three equations of motion are as given below

(i) $v = u + at$

(ii) $s = ut + \frac{1}{2}at^2$

(iii) $v^2 - u^2 = 2as$

where, u is the initial velocity of the body, a is the uniform acceleration of the body, v is the final velocity of the body after t second and s is the distance travelled in this time.

Note When the body is undergoing a uniform retardation, then the acceleration a is considered to be negative.

EXAM ORIENTED QUESTIONS

TYPE - 1

01 Mark

Multiple Choice Questions

Q.1 The numerical ratio of displacement and distance for a moving object is

(a) always less than 1 (b) always equal to 1

(c) always more than 1 (d) equal to or less than 1

Ans. (d) Displacement of an object can be less than or equal to the distance covered by the object, because the magnitude of displacement is equal to the straight line distance between the initial and the final position of the object irrespective of the path length which it covers. However, it can be equal to distance if the motion is along a straight line without any change in direction.

Q.2 Which of the following figures represents uniform motion of a moving object correctly?

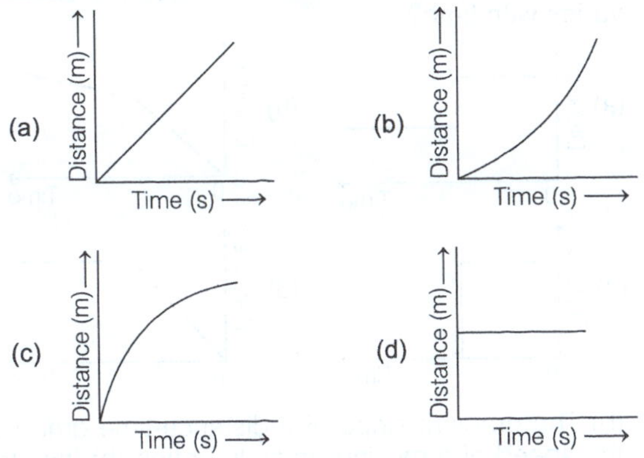

Ans. (a) For uniform motion, the distance-time graph is a straight line passing through origin inclined at an angle of 45° with both the axes. (because in uniform motion, object covers equal distance in equal interval of time).

Q.3 Speedometer is a device which is used to measure

(a) average speed

(b) average acceleration

(c) instantaneous speed

(d) instantaneous acceleration

Ans. (c) Speedometer is used to measure instantaneous speed.

Q.4 A truck takes 20 s to travel the first 80 m, and another 10 s to travel a further 70 m. What is the average speed?

(a) 0.20 m/s (b) 2.3 m/s

(c) 4.0 m/s (d) 5.0 m/s

Ans. (d) Average speed $= \dfrac{\text{Total distance}}{\text{Total time}}$

$$= \frac{80+70}{20+10}\ \text{m/s} = 5\ \text{m/s} \qquad \left(\text{Average speed} \neq \frac{\frac{80}{20}+\frac{70}{10}}{2}\right)$$

Q.5 A car driver takes a total of 2 hours to make a journey of 75 km. She has a coffee break of half an hour and spends a quarter of an hour stationary in a traffic jam. At what average speed must she travel during the rest of the time if she wants to complete the journey within two hours?

(a) 38 km/h (b) 50 km/h

(c) 60 km/h (d) 75 km/h

Ans. (c) Since, average speed $= \dfrac{\text{total distance}}{\text{total time}}$

The required speed for the rest of the journey

$$= \frac{75}{2-0.5-0.25}\ \text{km/h}$$

$$= 60\ \text{km/h}$$

Q.6 A lorry takes 15 minutes to travel along the path *PQRS*.

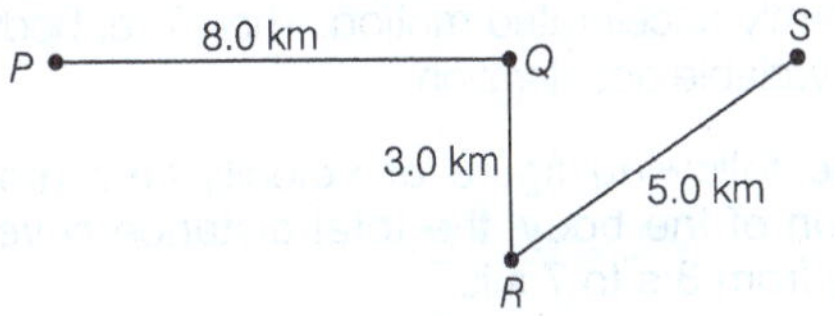

What is the average speed of the lorry?

(a) 4.0 km/h (b) 22 km/h

(c) 48 km/h (d) 64 km/h

Ans. (d) Average speed $= \dfrac{\text{Total distance}}{\text{Total time}}$

$$= \frac{16\ \text{km}}{0.25\ \text{hour}}$$

$$= 64\ \text{km/h}$$

Q.7 A car begins to move. It speeds up until it reaches a constant speed. It continues to travel at this constant speed for the rest of the journey. What happens to the acceleration and what happens to the velocity of the car during the journey?

(a) Both the acceleration and the velocity change.

(b) Only the acceleration changes.

(c) Only the velocity changes.

(d) Neither the acceleration nor the velocity changes.

Ans. (a) The graph shows the motion of a car

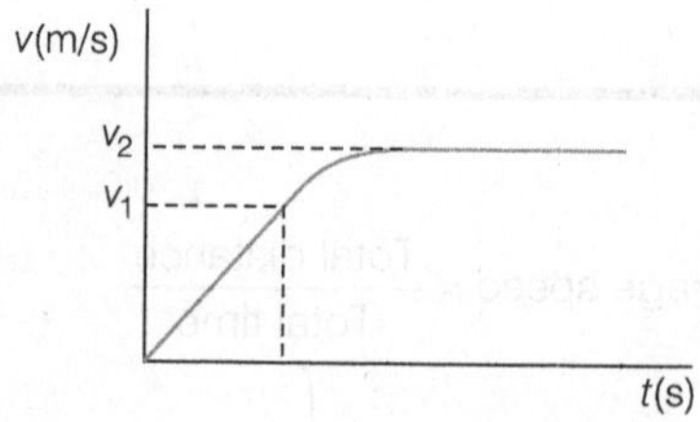

It shows that the car accelerates untill it reaches the velocity v_1 after which it starts retarding and when it reaches the maximum velocity v_2, the acceleration of the car becomes zero and it moves with the constant velocity v_2.

Q.8 What must change when a body is accelerating?

(a) The force acting on the body
(b) The mass of the body
(c) The speed of the body
(d) The velocity of the body

Ans. (d) Since acceleration is rate of change of velocity, a body is accelerating when the velocity of the body is changing.

Q.9 Velocity-time graph for a moving object is found to be curved line, then its acceleration is

(a) constant (b) variable
(c) zero (d) None of these

Ans. (b) Since, velocity-time graph for a moving object is curved line, this means that object is moving with non-uniformly accelerated motion. Therefore, body is moving with variable acceleration.

Q.10 In the following figure of velocity-time graph for the motion of the body, the total distance covered by the body from 3 s to 7 s is

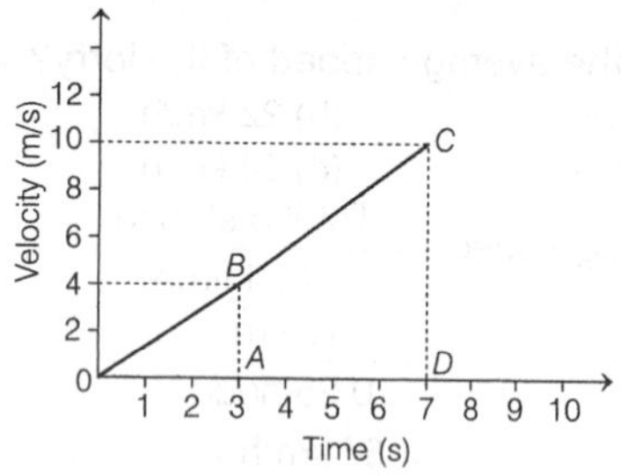

(a) 28 m (b) 56 m (c) 14 m (d) 35 m

Ans. (a) Total distance covered by the body from 3s to 7s

$$s = \text{Area of trapezium } ABCD = \frac{(AB + DC) \times AD}{2}$$

From given graph, we have

$AB = 4$ m/s

$DC = 10$ m/s

$AD = (7 - 3) = 4$ s

$$\therefore \quad s = \frac{(4 + 10)(7 - 3)}{2} = \frac{14 \times 4}{2} = 28 \text{ m}$$

Q.11 The velocity-time graph for one-dimensional motion is shown in the figure.

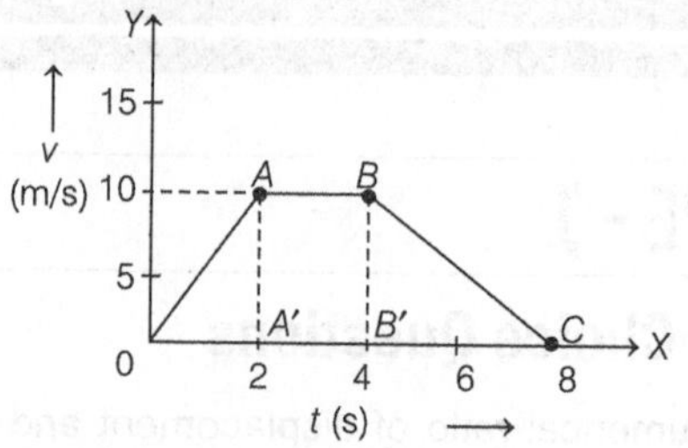

The acceleration of the body from point B to point C is

(a) -2.5 m/s^2 (b) 5 m/s^2 (c) 0 (d) 2.5 m/s^2

Ans. (a) From point B to C, the body undergoes uniform retardation.

Time taken by the body = 8 − 4 = 4s

Now, acceleration of body = slope of line BC

$$= \frac{0 - 10}{4} = -\frac{10}{4} = -2.5 \text{ m/s}^2$$

Q.12 A free-fall parachutist falls at a constant speed and then he opens his parachute and continues to fall with a lower but a constant speed. Which diagram shows how the distance fallen by the parachutist varies with time?

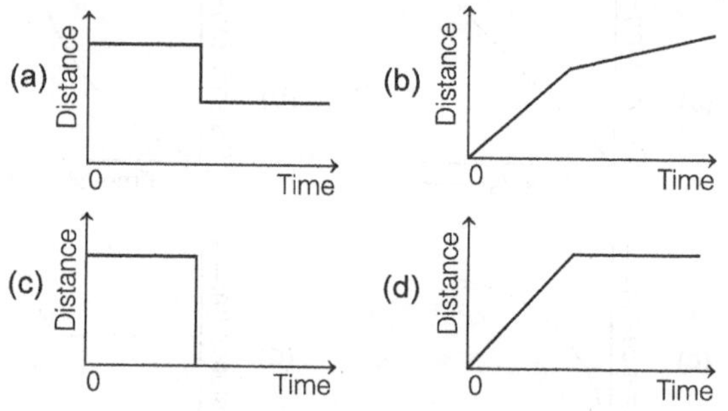

Ans. (b) The gradient slope of a distance-time graph gives the speed of a moving body. In option (b) the straight line with a greater slope shows the greater constant speed followed by the straight line with lesser slope showing the lower constant speed.

Q.13 A student walk at a constant speed for a distance of 50 m in a time of 40s. The students rests for a time of 10s and then walks back to the starting point at a constant speed in a time of 30s .

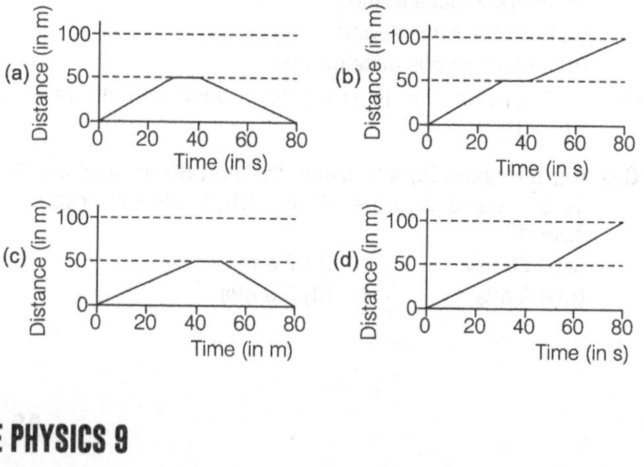

Ans. (a) The student moves 50 m in 40s (upward slope), rests for 10s (horizontal line), and returns in 30s (downward slope).

Q.14 A parachutist falls from a stationary balloon at time $t = 0$. The velocity-time graph for the parachutist from time $t = 0$ untill the time when he is just above the ground is shown.

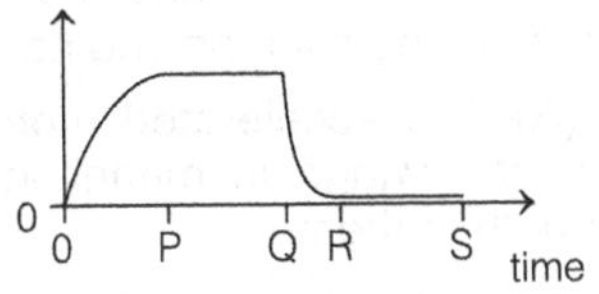

Which graph best shows the variation with time of the acceleration of the parachutist?

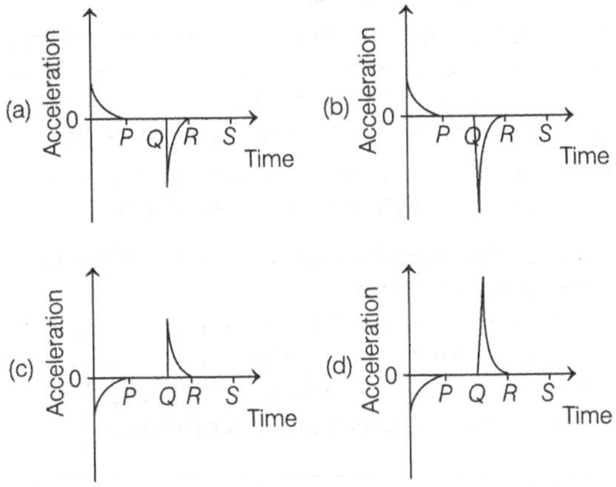

Ans. (c) Initially, acceleration is g (free fall). As velocity increases, air resistance reduces acceleration to zero. When the parachute opens, there is a sudden negative acceleration, then it gradually approaches zero.

Q.15 A train starting from rest attains a velocity of 90 km/h in 2 min, then the distance travelled by the train for attaining this velocity is

(a) 1.5 km (b) 2 km

(c) 2.5 km (d) 1.2 km

Ans. (a) Given, initial velocity, $u = 0$,

Final velocity, $v = 90\text{ km/h} = 90 \times \frac{5}{18} = 25\text{ m/s}$

Time, $t = 2\text{ min} = 2 \times 60 = 120\text{ s}$

From the equation of motion,

$$v = u + at$$

$$\Rightarrow \quad a = \frac{v}{t} \qquad (\because u = 0)$$

$$= \frac{25}{2 \times 60} = \frac{5}{24}\text{ m/s}^2$$

Distance covered,

$$s = ut + \frac{1}{2}at^2 = 0 + \frac{1}{2} \times \frac{5}{24} \times (120)^2$$

$$= \frac{1}{2} \times \frac{5}{24} \times 120 \times 120 = 1500\text{ m} = 1.5\text{ km}$$

Q.16 Which car moving from rest, has an average acceleration of 2.0 m/s^2?

(a) A car reaching a speed of 10 m/s in 2 s.

(b) A car reaching a speed of 20 m/s in 5 s.

(c) A car reaching a speed of 30 m/s in 10 s.

(d) A car reaching a speed of 40 m/s in 20 s.

Ans. (d) A car from rest reaching a speed of 40 ms^{-1} in 20 s.

$$\because \quad v = u + at \Rightarrow v = 0 + 2 \times 20 = 40\text{ m/s}$$

Q.17 An object moves from P to Q in 10 s with uniform acceleration.

Velocity at $P = 5$ m/s

Velocity at $Q = 12$ m/s

What is the acceleration?

(a) 0.5 m/s^2 (b) 0.7 m/s^2

(c) 1.2 m/s^2 (d) 1.7 m/s^2

Ans. (b) $a = \frac{v - u}{t}$

$$\therefore \quad a = \frac{12 - 5}{10} = 0.7\text{ m/s}^2$$

Q.18 If the displacement of an object is proportional to square of time, then the object moves with

(a) uniform velocity

(b) uniform acceleration

(c) increasing acceleration

(d) decreasing acceleration

Ans. (b) Let object start from rest, i.e. initial velocity $u = 0$ and let the acceleration be a at time t.

From second equation of motion,

$$s = ut + \frac{1}{2}at^2$$

Then, $s = 0 \times t + \frac{1}{2}at^2$

$$\Rightarrow \quad s = \frac{1}{2}at^2$$

$$s \propto t^2, \text{ if } a = \text{constant}$$

Thus, displacement s of an object is proportional to square of time t, when the object moves with constant or uniform acceleration.

Q.19 An astronaut on the moon, where there is no air resistance, throws a ball vertically upward. The initial velocity of the ball is 8 ms^{-1} and the acceleration due to gravity on the moon is 1.60 ms^{-2}. What is the speed of the ball 9 s after being thrown?

(a) 6.4 ms^{-1}

(b) 10.6 ms^{-1}

(c) 12.8 ms^{-1}

(d) 3.2 ms^{-1}

Ans. (a) Let us consider that the ball is thrown from a point A. and it reaches its highest point at O shown in figure.

Let us first consider the upward motion of the ball.

Initial velocity $(u) = 8\text{ ms}^{-1}$

Acceleration due to gravity (g_M) = 1.60 ms^{-2}.

∴ Time taken for upward journey = $\frac{u}{g_M}$ = 5 s.

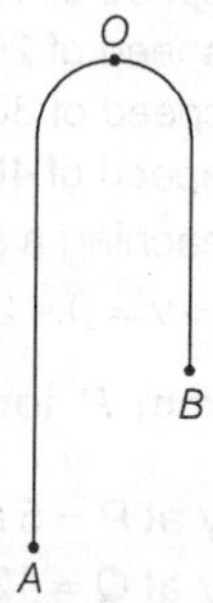

∴ Time taken for downward journey = 5 s.

Now, during the 9th second the ball is in its downward journey and it is at point *B*.

∴ Time taken for the ball to reach point *B* from point *O* = 4 s.

∴ Speed of the ball at point *B* = $g_M \times 4 = 1.6 \times 4$
= 6.4 ms^{-1}

TYPE - 2 — 01 Mark

Assertion-Reason Type Questions

Directions (Q. Nos. 1-6) In the following questions two statements are given as Assertion and Reason.

(a) Both A and R are true and R is the correct explanation of A.

(b) Both A and R are true but R is not the correct explanation of A.

(c) A is true but R is false.

(d) A is false but R is true.

Q.1 Assertion (A) Displacement of a body may be zero when distance travelled by it is not zero.

Reason (R) The displacement is the shortest distance between initial and final positions.

Ans. (a) The displacement is the shortest distance between initial and final position. When final position of a body coincides with its initial position, displacement is zero, but the distance travelled is not zero.

Q.2 Assertion (A) The displacement of an object can be either positive, negative or zero.

Reason (R) Displacement has both the magnitude and direction.

Ans. (a) Displacement may be positive, negative or zero as displacement is a vector quantity.

Q.3 Assertion (A) The speedometer of a car or a motorcycle measures its average speed.

Reason (R) Average velocity is equal to total displacement divided by total time taken.

Ans. (d) Speedometer measures the speed of the vehicle at every moment and not the average speed.

Q.4 Assertion (A) Motion with uniform velocity is always along a straight line path.

Reason (R) In such a motion, speed is the magnitude of the velocity and is equal to the instantaneous velocity.

Ans. (b) Because the Assertion can be explained on the basis of Newton's first law and the Reason is just a consequence of the Assertion and not its explanation.

Q.5 Assertion (A) The accelerated motion of an object may be due to change in magnitude of velocity or direction or both of them.

Reason (R) Acceleration can be produced only by change is magnitude of the velocity. It does not depend on the direction.

Ans. (c) Change in the direction of the velocity also produces acceleration as in the case of circular motion. So, the change in the magnitude or direction of the velocity, both can produce acceleration.

Q.6 Assertion (A) Acceleration and displacement are in the opposite direction during retardation.

Reason (R) Acceleration is given as the change in velocity per unit time.

Ans. (b) Both Assertion and Reason are true but Reason is not the correct explanation of Assertion because Assertion is an independent fact and Reason just gives the correct definition of acceleration.

TYPE - 3 — 01/02 Marks

Fill in the Blanks

Q.1 When an object covers unequal distances in equal intervals of time, it is said to be ...... [uniform motion/non-uniform motion]

Ans. non-uniform motion

Q.2 The physical quantities that have both magnitude and direction are .... [scalar quantities/vector quantities].

Ans. vector quantities

Q.3 The acceleration is taken to be......... [positive/negative] when velocity of a body increases with time and ...... [positive/negative] when the velocity of the body decreases with time.

Ans. positive, negative

Q.4 If the velocity of an object decreases with time, then the acceleration is .... [zero/positive/negative] in nature.

Ans. negative

Q.5 Velocity-time graph represents .... (change in velocity/change in position) of an object with respect to time.

Ans. change in velocity

Q.6 A graph of velocity *versus* time for a uniformly accelerated motion is a .... (horizontal/ vertical /straight sloping) line.

Ans. straight sloping

Q.7 The equation of motion $v = u + at$ can be used to calculate .... (displacement/velocity/distance)

Ans. velocity

Q.8 The slope of a distance-time graph gives ...... (speed/acceleration).

Ans. speed

TYPE - 4 — 02 Marks

Very Short Answer Type Questions

Q.1 What do you mean by motion in one direction? Give example.

Ans. When a body moves along a straight line, then the motion of body is said to be in one direction.
e.g. A car moving on a long and straight road.

Q.2 How can we describe the location of an object?

Ans. To describe the position of an object, we need to specify a reference point called the origin.

e.g., Suppose that a library in a city is 2 km North of the railway station. We have specified the position of the library with respect to the railway station, i.e., in this case, the railway station acts as the reference point.

Q.3 Differentiate between distance and displacement.

Ans. Differences between distance and displacement are

Distance	Displacement
It is the length of the actual path travelled by object irrespective of its direction of motion.	Displacement is the shortest distance between the initial and final positions of an object in a given direction.
Distance is a scalar quantity.	Displacement is a vector quantity.
Distance covered can never be negative. It is always positive or zero.	Displacement may be positive, negative or zero.
Distance is always greater than or equal to the magnitude of displacement.	Displacement is always less than or equal to the magnitude of distance.

Q.4 Two trains A and B start moving at the same time. The distances travelled by them in given intervals of time are shown below.

Time	Distance travelled by train A (in km)	Distance travelled by train B (in km)
6.00 pm	0	0
6.15 pm	10	15
6.30 pm	20	24
6.45 pm	30	32
7.00 pm	40	38
7.15 pm	50	42
7.30 pm	60	47

State which train has uniform motion and which train has non-uniform motion.

Ans. Since, train A travels equal distances in equal intervals of time of 15 min, so the motion of train A is uniform motion.

On the other hand, train B travels unequal distances in equal intervals of time of 15 min, so the motion of train B is non-uniform motion.

Q.5 A scooter is moving along a straight line AB covers a distance of d m in t_1 seconds and returns back from B to C and coveres d' m in t_2 seconds. Find the total path length travelled by the scooter.

Ans. From the above question, we draw the following figure.

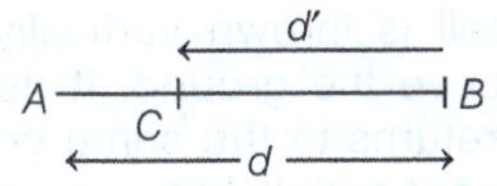

Hence, to find out the total path length it does not matter what is the time taken by a scooter to reach at B and the time taken to return to C.

Total path length = $AB + BC = d + d'$

Q.6 How are the distance travelled by an object related to the time taken when an object travels equal distances in equal intervals of time?

Ans. In this case, distance travelled by the object is directly proportional to the time taken. As the time increases, the distance travelled by the object also increases linearly.

Q.7 Which is smaller, distance or displacement? Is the displacement of an object dependent on the choice of the position of origin of the coordinate system?

Ans. Displacement of a moving object is always smaller than the distance travelled by it. No, the displacement of the object does not depend on the choice of the position of the origin.

Q.8 A honey bee travels from A to B and then moves from B to C (as shown in the figure). Show resultant displacement in the diagram.

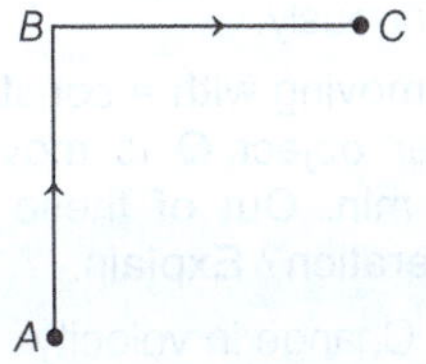

Ans. Since, displacement is the shortest distance between two points, so AC as shown in the figure will be the resultant displacement.

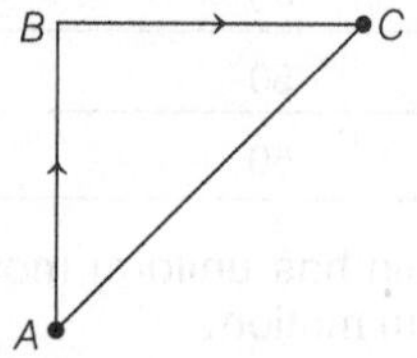

Q.9 If the displacement of a body is zero, is its distance travelled necessarily zero? Answer with a suitable example.

Ans. No, because the distance covered by an object is the actual length of the path covered by the object and the displacement of an object is given by the straight line distance between the initial position and final position.

e.g. A boy starts from his home and moves towards market along a straight path. Then, he returns to home along the same path. Here, displacement is zero but distance travelled is non-zero.

Q.10 Suppose a ball is thrown vertically upwards from a position *P* above the ground. It rises to the highest point *Q* and returns to the same point *P*. What is the net displacement and distance travelled by the ball?

Ans. The net displacement is zero. The distance travelled by the ball is twice the distance between position P and Q.

Q.11 Suppose a boy is enjoying a ride on a merry-go-round which is moving with a constant speed of 10 ms^{-1}. What does it imply?

Ans. In merry-go-round, the speed is constant but velocity is not constant because its direction goes on changing, i.e., there is an acceleration in the motion. So, we can say that the boy is in a uniformly a accelerated motion.

Q.12 Can an object be accelerated, if it is moving with constant speed? Justify your answer with an example.

Or **Can a body have constant speed and still be accelerating? Give an example.**

Or **Explain how is it possible for an object to move with a constant speed but with uniform acceleration?**

Ans. An object moving with constant speed can be accelerated, if its direction of motion changes. e.g., An object moving with a constant speed in a circular path has an acceleration because its direction of motion changes continuously.

Q.13 An object *P* is moving with a constant velocity for 5 min. Another object *Q* is moving with a variable velocity for 5 min. Out of these two objects, which one has acceleration? Explain. **[2]**

Ans. $\text{Acceleration} = \dfrac{\text{Change in velocity}}{\text{Time taken}}$

Since, the velocity of object P is not changing or change in velocity of the object is zero, therefore object P has no acceleration. On the other hand, there is change in velocity for the object Q. So, it has acceleration.

Q.14 The graph between total path length and time for a particle moving along a straight line as shown in figure is not possible. Explain why?

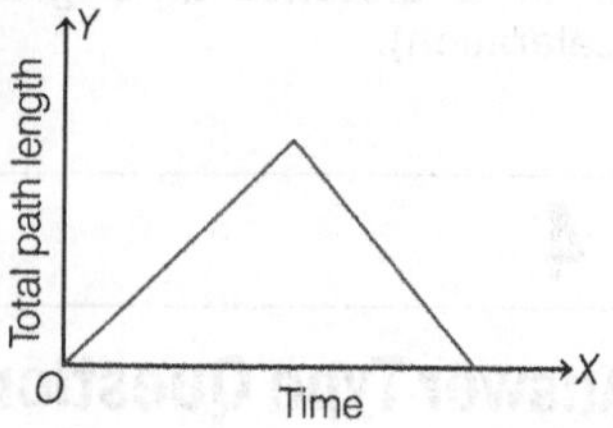

Ans. The graph shows that with the passage of time, total path length first increases and then decreases.The path length always increases or remains constant with passage of time but it cannot decrease with time as shown in given figure. Thus, this graph is not possible.

Q.15 From the given velocity-time graph (see figure), what can be concluded?

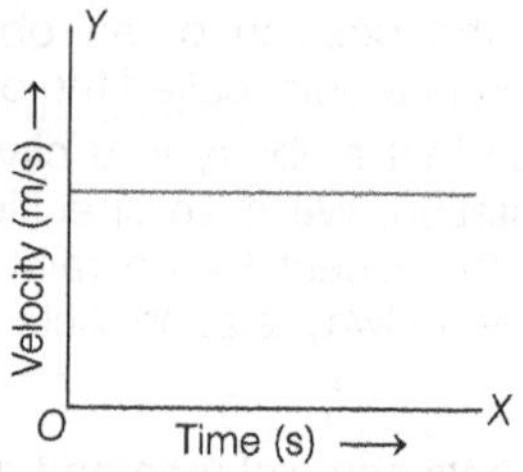

Ans. From the given velocity-time graph, it is clear that the velocity of the object is not changing with time, i.e., the object is in uniform motion.

Q.16 The distance-time graph for motion of Ram and Shyam is shown below.

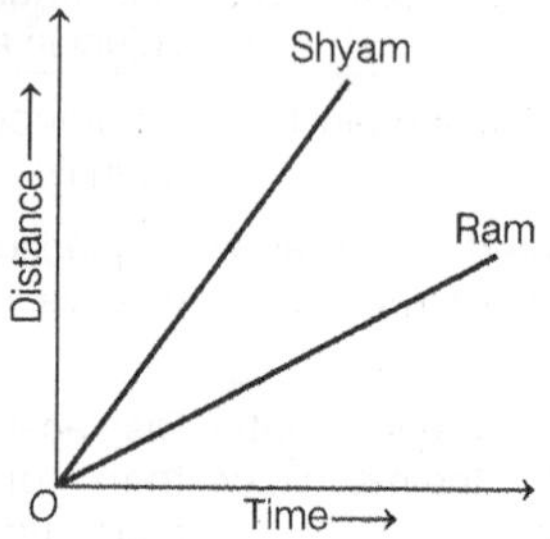

Which of them has greater acceleration? Justify your answer.

Ans. Both Ram and Shyam have zero acceleration as they are moving with constant velocity. Since, distance-time graph is a straight line.

Q.17 Study the given velocity-time graph of two bodies *M* and *N* and answer the following questions.

(i) Which body starts from rest and which body has some initial velocity? **[1]**

(ii) Which body is having lesser acceleration? **[1]**

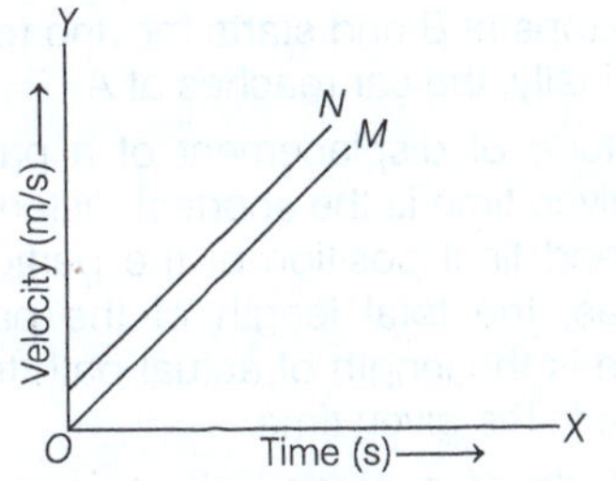

Ans. (i) Body *M* starts from rest, as $t = 0$, $v = 0$ but body *N* has some initial velocity as $v \neq 0$.

(ii) Both have the same acceleration because lines *N* and *M* are parallel to each other and hence, have a same slope.

Q.18 What do the graphs (i) and (ii) shown here indicate? **[2]**

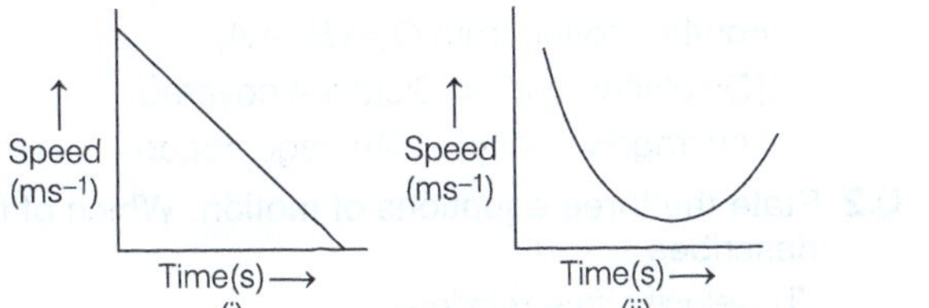

Ans. Graph (i) indicates that a body has certain initial speed and then undergoes a uniform retardation untill its speed becomes zero.

Graph (ii) shows that a body first retards and then accelerates non-uniformly.

Q.19 Out of the following, identify the graph which corresponds to a motion with (i) uniform retardation and (ii) zero acceleration. **[1+1=2]**

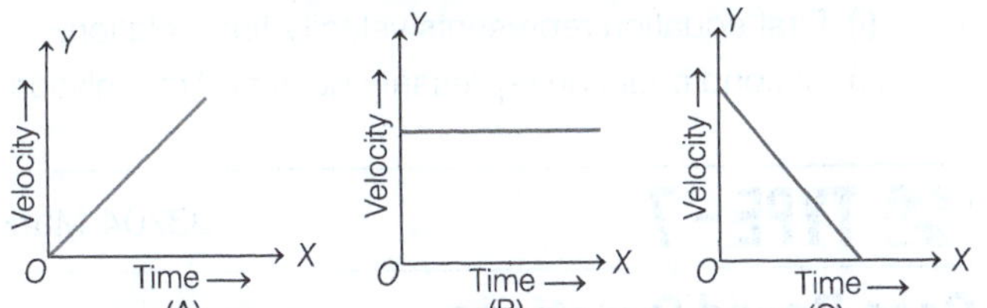

Ans. (i) The graph with uniform retardation is shown in graph (C), since in this graph, the velocity of the object decreases uniformly.

(ii) The graph (B) corresponds to the zero acceleration because the velocity of body does not change with time.

TYPE - 5   03 Marks

Short Answer Type Questions

Q.1 State which of the following situations are possible and give an example for each of these.

(i) An object with a constant acceleration but with zero velocity. **[1]**

(ii) An object moving in a certain direction with an acceleration in the perpendicular direction. **[2]**

Ans. (i) When an object is thrown vertically upward, then at highest point its velocity is zero but it has constant acceleration 9.8 ms^{-2} (acceleration due to gravity).

(ii) An aeroplane flies in horizontal direction but the acceleration due to gravity is in vertically downward direction, i.e., along the direction perpendicular to the direction of motion.

Q.2 Figure shows the displacement-time graph of four children *A, B, C* and *D*. Which child has the

(i) highest velocity and lowest velocity **[1]**

(ii) Compare the velocities of *A* and *C*. **[2]**

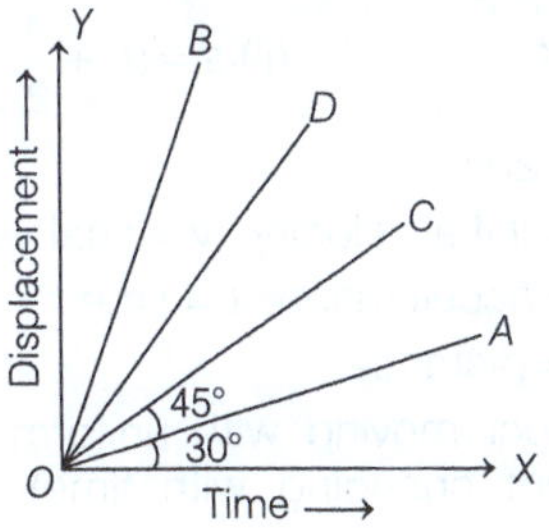

Ans. (i) Velocity = Slope of displacement-time

Since, slope of child *B* is greater than all other children, hence child *B* has the highest velocity.

Similarly, the slope of child *A* is smallest, so it has the lowest velocity.

(ii) v_c = slope of $c = \tan 45° = 1$

v_A = slope of $A = \tan 30° = 1/\sqrt{3}$

$\therefore \; v_c : v_A = 1 : (1/\sqrt{3}) = \sqrt{3} : 1$

Q.3 Draw a velocity *versus* time graph of a stone thrown vertically upward and then coming downwards after attaining the maximum height.

Ans. When a stone is thrown vertically upwards, it has some initial velocity *u*. As, the stone goes vertically upwards, its velocity goes on decreasing

($\because$ it is moving against the gravity) and at the highest point, (i.e. maximum height) its velocity becomes zero.

Let the stone take time *t* seconds to reach at the highest point. After that stone begins to fall (with zero initial velocity), its velocity goes on increasing

($\because$ it is moving along the gravity) and it reaches its initial point of projection with the velocity *u*, with which it was thrown in the same time.

So,

Velocity	u	0	$-u$
Time	0	t	$2t$

The velocity-time graph for the whole journey is shown below

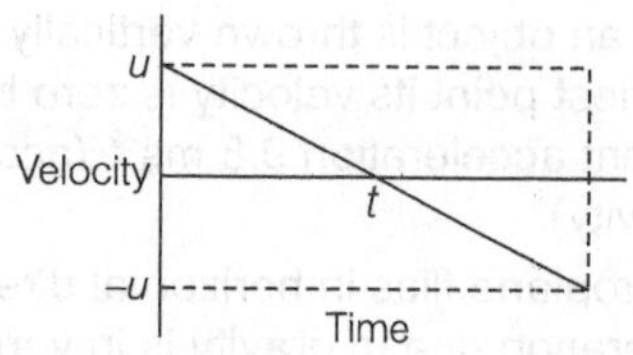

Since, velocity is a vector quantity and for the upward and downward journey, the direction of velocity is opposite so the negative value of v is consider.

Q.4 How will the equations of motion for an object moving with a uniform velocity change?

Ans. We know that the equations of uniformly accelerated motion are

(i) $v = u + at$ (ii) $s = ut + \frac{1}{2}at^2$

(iii) $v^2 = u^2 + 2as$

where, u = initial velocity, v = final velocity, a = acceleration, t = time and s = distance

For an object moving with uniform velocity (velocity which is not changing with time), the acceleration $a = 0$.

So, equations of motion will become (putting $a = 0$ in above equations)

(i) $v = u$ (ii) $s = ut$ (iii) $v^2 = u^2$

TYPE - 6 — 04 Marks

Long Answer Type Questions

Q.1 Explain clearly with examples, the distinction between

(i) magnitude of displacement (sometimes called distance) over an interval of time and the total length of the path covered by a particle over the same interval. [2]

(ii) magnitude of average velocity over an interval of time and the average speed over the same interval. [2]

Show in both (i) and (ii) that the second quantity is either greater than or equal to first. When is the equality sign true? (for simplicity, consider one-dimensional motion only).

Ans. Let us consider an example.

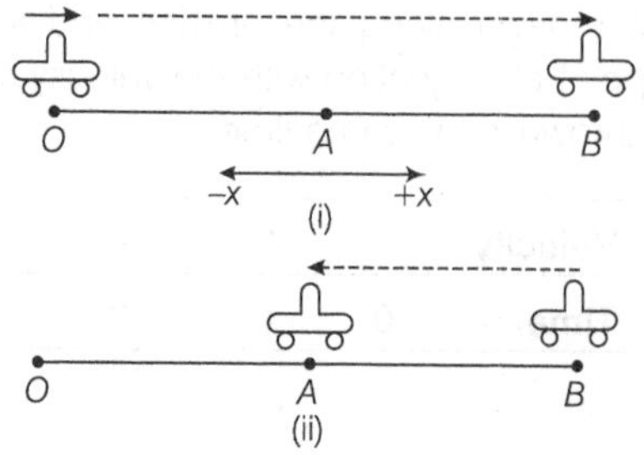

A car starts from O and moves along positive X-axis. The car stops at B and starts moving towards negative X-axis. Finally, the car reaches at A.

(i) Magnitude of displacement of a particle in motion for a given time is the shortest distance between the initial and final position of the particle in that time, whereas, the total length of the path covered by particle is the length of actual path traversed by the particle in the given time.

(ii) Magnitude of average velocity over an interval of time is equal to the magnitude of displacement divided by time interval, whereas the average speed is the total path length divided by the time interval.

For the motion from O to B,

$|\text{Displacement}|$ = Distance covered

$|\text{Average velocity}|$ = Average speed

For the motion from $O \to B \to A$,

$|\text{Displacement}| <$ Distance covered

$|\text{Average velocity}| <$ Average speed

Q.2 State the three equations of motion. Which of them describes

(i) velocity-time relation? [2]

(ii) position-time relation? [2]

Ans. For a body moving along a straight line at velocity u and accelerating uniformly with acceleration a for time t to attain a velocity v and cover displacement s. Thus, the three equations of motion are as

First equation, $v = u + at$ ...(i)

Second equation, $s = ut + 1/2at^2$ ...(ii)

Third equation, $v^2 = u^2 + 2as$ ...(iii)

(i) First equation represents velocity-time relation.

(ii) Second equation represents position-time relation.

TYPE - 7 — 03/04 Marks

Case Based Questions

Q.1 Distance and displacement are two quantities that seem to mean the same but different with different meanings of definitions. Distance is the measure of "how much distance an object has covered during its motion" while displacement refers to the measure of "how far the object actually is from initial place.

(i) Rahul travels 20 km North but then comes back South for 40 km to pick up a friend. What is Rahul's total distance? [1]

(ii) Akash travels 20 km East but then comes back West for 10 km. Find displacement. [2]

(iii) Define distance and displacement of a particle. [1]

Ans. (i) The total distance travelled is the sum of the distances travelled in both directions

Distance travelled due to North= 20 km

Distance travelled due to South= 40 km

Total distance = 20 km + 40 km

= 60 km

So, total distance travelled by Rahul is 60 km.

(ii) Akash travels 20 km East and then comes back 10 km West.

Displacement = 20 km (East) −10 km (West)

= 10 km (East)

So, displacement of Akash is 10 km East.

(iii) The actual length of the path covered by a body in a certain interval of time is called the distance travelled by a body.

The shortest distance from the initial to the final position of the body is called displacement.

Q.2 A body is said to have uniform motion, if it travels equal distances in equal intervals of time, no matter how small these intervals may be. The distance travelled by an object in uniform motion increases linearly.

A train travels from one station to the next. The driver of train *A* starts from rest at time $t = 0$ and accelerates uniformly for the first 20s. At time $t = 20$ s, train reaches its top speed of 25 ms^{-1} , then travels at this speed for further 30s before decelerating uniformly to rest. Total time for the journey of train *A* is 60 s.

Another train *B* is travelling parallel to train *A* has zero speed at $t = 0$ and then accelerates uniformly for first 10 s.

At time $t = 10$ s it reaches its top speed of 30 ms^{-1}, then travels at this speed for further 20s, before decelerating uniformly to rest. Total time for the journey of train *B* is 80 s.

(i) What is the deceleration of the train *A* as it comes to rest ? **[2]**

(ii) In which time interval, speed of train *B* is constant? **[1]**

(iii) What is the initial speed of trains *A* and *B*? **[1]**

Ans. (i) Deceleration $= \dfrac{\text{Change in velocity}}{\text{Time}}$

$= \dfrac{25}{10} = 2.5 \text{ m/s}^2$

(ii) Speed of train *B* is constant during the time interval 10 s to 30 s.

(iii) Initial speed of train *A* and *B* is zero as both trains start from rest.

Q.3 Imagine a car with a leaky engine that drips oil at a regular rate of 50 drops per second. As the car travels through town, it would leave a trace of oil on the street that would reveal information about the motion of the car. The trace of the oil in four different situations are shown. (The positions are given in centimetres).

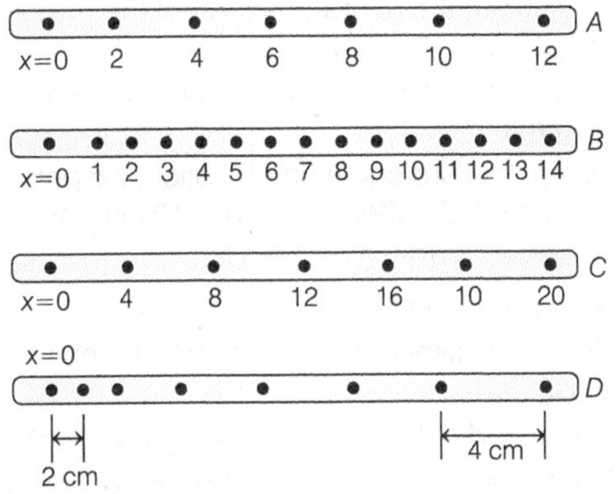

(i) Identify the type of motion by the car in situations *A*, *B*, *C* and *D*. **[1]**

(ii) What is the ratio of speed of the car in situations *A*, *B* and *C* ? **[1]**

(iii) What is the acceleration of the car in situation *D* ? **[2]**

Ans. (i) *A*, *B* and *C* show uniform motion.

D shows non-uniform velocity/uniform by accelerated motion.

(ii) 2:1:4

(iii) Time between each drop = 1/ 50 = 0.02 s

$$u = \frac{0.02}{0.02} = 1 \text{ m/s}, \quad v = \frac{0.04}{0.02} = 2 \text{ m/s}$$

$$t = 7 \times 0.02 = 0.14 \text{ s}$$

$$a = \frac{v-u}{t} = 7.14 \text{ m/s}^2$$

Q.4 John is doing an experiment at the rooftop of a building. He throws an eraser upwards and lets it fall to the ground. The eraser reaches its highest point at a height of 5 m measuring from the rooftop and takes 4s to reach the ground from the moment it leaves John's hand.

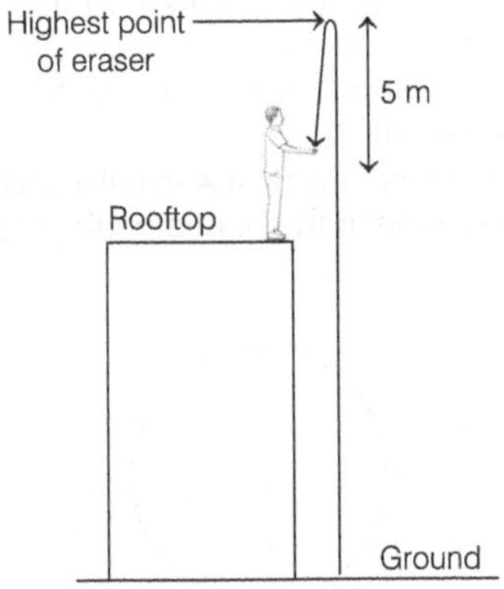

(i) Find the maximum speed of the eraser the moment it leaves John's hand. **[1]**

(ii) What is the eraser's speed at its highest point? Is the acceleration of the ball zero at that point ? **[1]**

(iii) Calculate the average speed of the eraser. [Take, $g = 10\ ms^{-2}$] **[1]**

Ans. (i) Let the speed with which John throws a ball be $u\ ms^{-1}$.

Using the third equation of motion, we get

$v^2 = u^2 - 2gh$, where $v = u$, $g = 10\ ms^{-2}$ and $h = 5$ m

$\therefore\ u^2 = 2 \times 10 \times 5 = 100$

$\Rightarrow\ u = 10\ ms^{-1}$

So, the maximum speed with which John throws the eraser is $10\ ms^{-1}$.

(ii) The speed of the eraser at its highest point is zero.

No, the acceleration of the ball is not zero because even though the speed becomes zero, the body still experiences the acceleration due to gravity in the downward direction.

(iii) Time taken by the ball to reach the highest point,

$$t = \frac{u}{g} = \frac{10}{10} = 1\ s$$

$\therefore$ Total time taken by the eraser to reach the ground from its highest point $(t_2) = (4 - 1) = 3$ s.

$\therefore$ Distance travelled by the eraser during its downward motion,

$$d = \frac{1}{2} g \times t_d^2 = \frac{1}{2} \times 10 \times 3 \times 3 = 45\ m$$

$$\therefore\ \text{Average speed} = \frac{\text{Total distance travelled}}{\text{Total time taken}}$$

$$= \frac{5 + 45}{4} = \frac{50}{4} = 12.5\ ms^{-1}$$

TYPE - 8

Numerical Type Questions

Q.1 **An insect moves along a circular path of radius 10 cm with a constant speed. It takes 1 min to move from a point on the path to the diametrically opposite point. Find (i) the distance covered, (ii) the speed and (iii) the displacement.** **[1 + 1 + 1 = 3]**

Ans. Suppose the insect was at A initially and it moves along ACB to reach the diametrically opposite point B in 1 min.

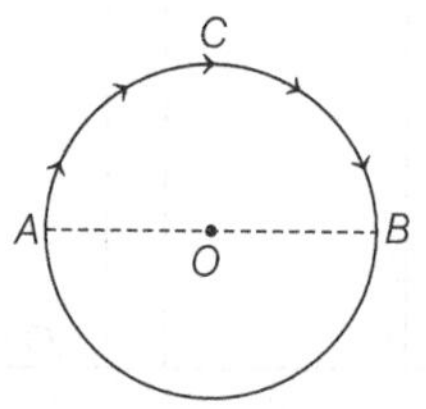

(i) $\therefore$ The distance moved in 1 min $= \pi r$

$= 3.14 \times 10 = 31.4$ cm

(ii) $\therefore$ Speed $= \dfrac{\text{Distance}}{\text{Time}} = \dfrac{31.4}{1} = 31.4$ cm/min

(iii) $\therefore$ Displacement, $AB = 2r = 2 \times 10 = 20$ cm

Q.2 **An ant climbs up five stairs, each of width 20 cm and height 20 cm. Find the distance covered and displacement of ant.** **[2]**

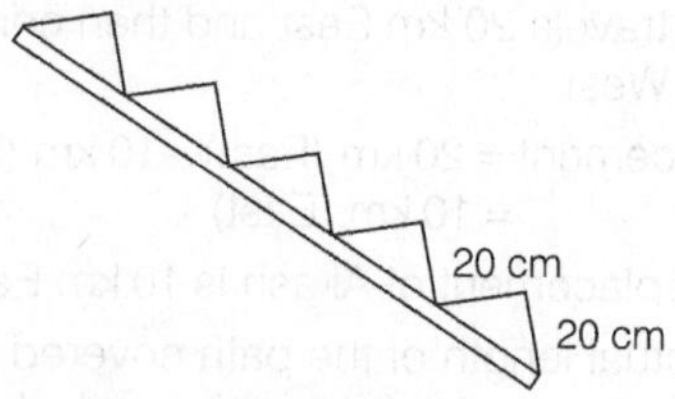

Sol. Distance covered by ant $= 5 \times (20\ cm + 20\ cm)$

$= 5 \times 40\ cm = 200$ cm

Displacement $= 5 \times \sqrt{(20)^2 + (20)^2}$

i.e., Sum of all hypotenuse of the right triangles

$= 5 \times \sqrt{800} = 100\sqrt{2}$ cm

Q.3 **An object travels 14 m in 4s and then another 16 m in 2s. What is the average speed of the object?** **[2]**

Sol. According to question, first distance, $s_1 = 14$ m

second distance, $s_2 = 16$ m,

Time, $t_1 = 4$ s, $t_2 = 2$ s

$$\therefore\ \text{Average speed} = \frac{\text{Total distance}}{\text{Total time}} = \frac{s_1 + s_2}{t_1 + t_2}$$

$$= \frac{14 + 16}{4 + 2} = \frac{30}{6} = 5\ m/s$$

Therefore, the average speed of an object is 5 m/s.

Q.4 **A train travels at a speed of 60 km/h for 0.5 h, 24 km/h for next 0.25 h and then at 72 km/h for the next 0.75 h. Calculate the distance travelled by train and its average speed.** **[2]**

Sol. Total time = 0.5 h + 0.25 h + 0.75 h = 1 .5 h

Total distance $= v_1t_1 + v_2t_2 + v_3t_3$

$= (60)\ (0.5) + (24)\ (0.25) + (72)\ (0.75)$

$= 90$ km

$$\text{Average speed} = \frac{\text{Total distance}}{\text{Total time}} = \frac{90\ km}{1.5\ h} = 60\ km/h$$

Q.5 **A car moves with a speed of 30 km/h for half an hour, 25 km/h for one hour and 40 km/h for two hours. Calculate average speed of the car.** **[2]**

Sol. Time taken to travel,

$t_1 = 0.5$ h, $t_2 = 1$ h, $t_3 = 2$ h

$t = t_1 + t_2 + t_3 = 0.5 + 1 + 2 = 3.5$ h

Speeds, $v_1 = 30$ km/h, $v_2 = 25$ km/h, $v_3 = 40$ km/h

Distances, $s_1 = v_1t_1 = 30 \times 0.5 = 15$ km

$s_2 = v_2t_2 = 25 \times 1 = 25$ km

$s_3 = v_3t_3 = 40 \times 2 = 80$ km

$s = s_1 + s_2 + s_3 = 15 + 25 + 80 = 120$ km

$$\text{Average speed} = \frac{\text{Total distance}}{\text{Total time}} = \frac{s}{t} = \frac{120}{3.5}$$
$$= 34.3 \text{ km/h}$$

Q.6 A train starting from a railway station and moving with uniform acceleration attains a speed of 40 km/h in 10 min. Find its acceleration. **[2]**

Sol. Initial velocity of train, $u = 0$

Final velocity of train, $v = 40 \text{ km / h}$

$$= 40 \times \frac{5}{18} = 11.11 \text{ m / s}$$

Time taken, $t = 10\text{min} = 10 \times 60 = 600 \text{ s}$

$$\text{Acceleration, } a = \frac{v - u}{t} = \frac{11.11 - 0}{600}$$
$$= 0.0185 \text{ m/s}^2$$
$$= 1.85 \times 10^{-2} \text{ m/s}^2$$

Hence, acceleration of the train is 1.85×10^{-2} m/s^2.

Q.7 The distance-time graph below shows different kinds of motion of a vehicle at rest, increasing speed, decreasing speed and constant speed.

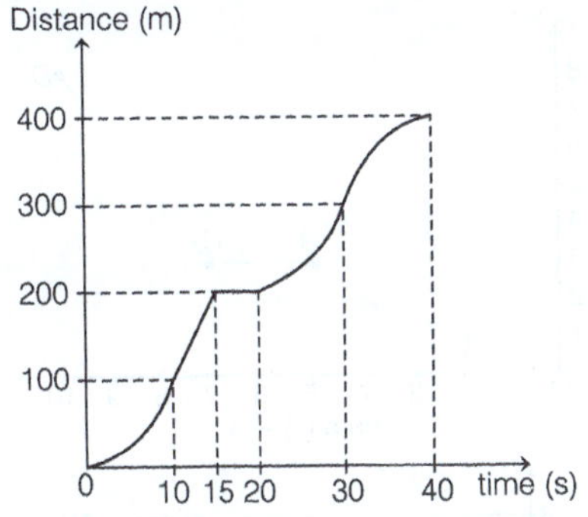

(a) Describe the motion of the vehicle from 0 s to 40 s. **[1]**

(b) (i) Calculate the constant speed from 10 s to 15 s? **[1]**

(ii) What is the total distance travelled? **[1]**

(iii) Find the average speed of the vehicle. **[1]**

Sol. (a) 0 s to 10 s, increasing speed

10 s to 15 s, constant speed

15 s to 20 s, at rest

20 s to 30 s, increasing speed

30 s to 40 s, decreasing speed

(b) (i) Constant speed from 10 s to 15 s

$$= \frac{200 - 100}{15 - 10}$$
$$= \frac{100}{5} = 20 \text{ ms}^{-1}$$

(ii) 400 m

(iii) $\text{Average speed} = \dfrac{400}{40} = 10 \text{ ms}^{-1}$

Q.8 Find the displacement of a body whose velocity-time graph is shown as below. **[2]**

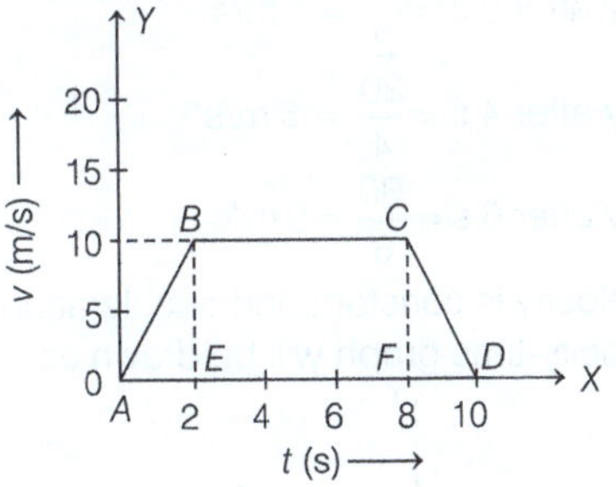

Sol. Displacement = Area under velocity- time curve

$$= \frac{1}{2} \text{(sum of parallel sides)} \times \text{height}$$
$$= \frac{1}{2}(AD + BC) \times CF = \frac{1}{2}(10 + 6) \times 10 = 80 \text{ m}$$

Q.9 The velocity-time graph of a body is shown below.

(i) State the kind of motion represented by *OP* and *PQ*. **[1]**

(ii) Find the velocity of the body after 30 s and 40 s. **[1]**

(iii) What is the negative acceleration of the body. **[1]**

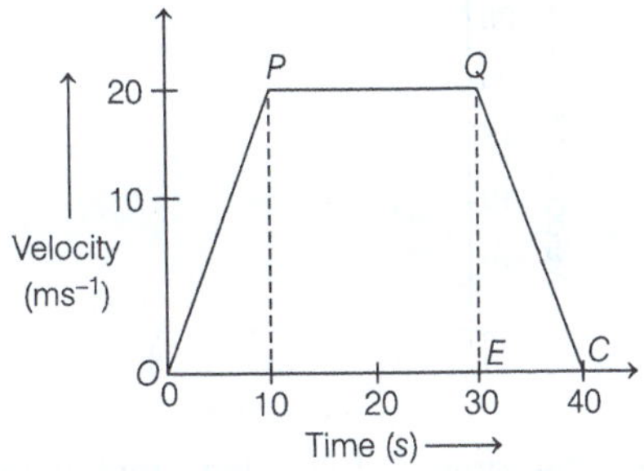

Ans. (i) *OP* represents uniform acceleration,

PQ represents constant velocity.

(ii) Velocity after 30 s = 20 ms^{-1}

Velocity after 40s = zero

(iii) Negative acceleration = Slope of *QC*

$$= \frac{0 - 20}{40 - 30} = -2 \text{ ms}^{-2}$$

Q.10 Make a velocity-time graph from the following displacement-time graph. **[2]**

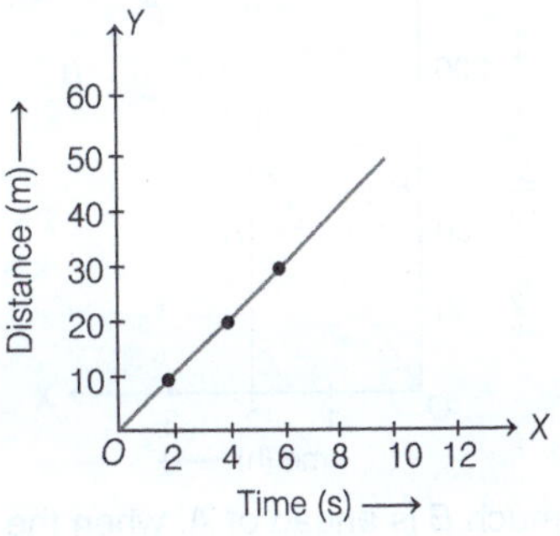

Sol. From the graph,

Velocity after 2 s $= \frac{10}{2} = 5$ m/s

Velocity after 4 s $= \frac{20}{4} = 5$ m/s

Velocity after 6 s $= \frac{30}{6} = 5$ m/s

e.g., Velocity is constant and acceleration = 0.

So, velocity-time graph will be drawn as

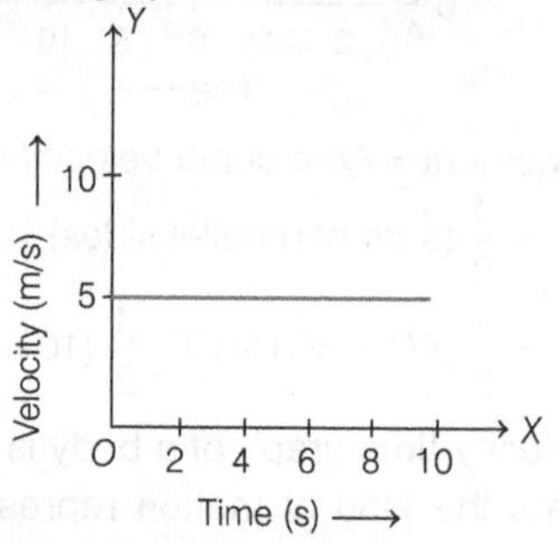

Q.11 The velocity-time graph (see figure) shows the motion of a cyclist. Find (i) its acceleration (ii) its velocity and (iii) the distance covered by the cyclist in 15 s. **[1 × 3]**

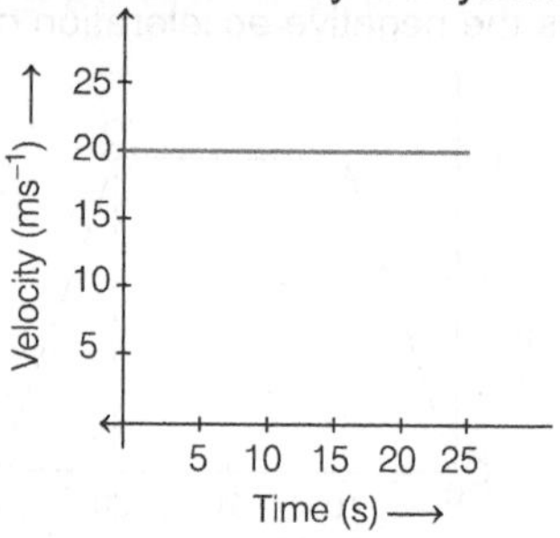

Sol. (i) From the graph, it is clear that velocity is not changing with time, i.e., acceleration is zero.

(ii) Again from the graph, we can see that there is no change in the velocity with time, so velocity after 15 s will remain same as 20 ms^{-1}.

(iii) Distance covered by cyclist in 15 s = Velocity × Time

$= 20 \times 15 = 300$ m

Q.12 The distance -time graph of two trains *A* and *B* are given below. The trains start simultaneously in the same direction.

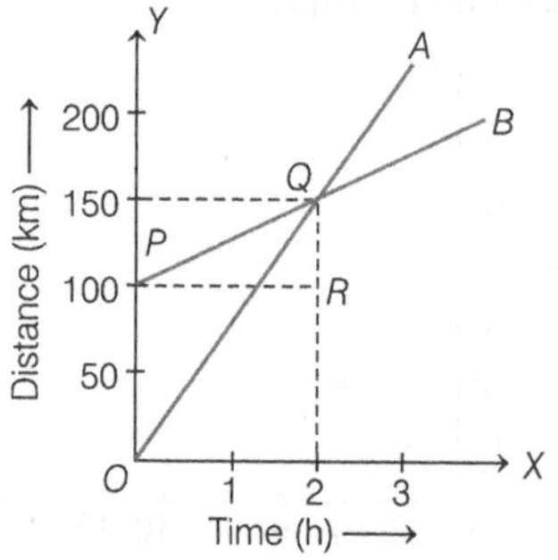

(i) How much *B* is ahead of *A*, when the motion starts?

(ii) What is the speed of *B*?

(iii) When and where will *A* catch *B*?

(iv) What is the difference between speeds of *A* and *B*?

(v) Is the speed of both the trains uniform or non-uniform? Justify your answer. **[4]**

Sol. (i) *B* is ahead of *A* by 100 km as *OP* = 100 km

(ii) Speed of *B* = Slope of $PQ = \frac{150 - 100}{2 - 0} = 25$ km/h

(iii) *A* and *B* meet at *Q*, i.e. 150 km from origin and 2 h after the start.

(iv) Speed of *A* = Slope of $OQ = \frac{150}{2} = 75$ km/h

Difference between speeds = 75 − 25 = 50 km/h

(v) Speed of both the trains is uniform as speed-time graph is a straight line.

Q.13 The graph below shows the positions of a body at different times. Calculate the speed of the body as it moves from (i) *A* to *B*, (ii) *B* to *C* and (iii) *C* to *D*. **[1 × 3]**

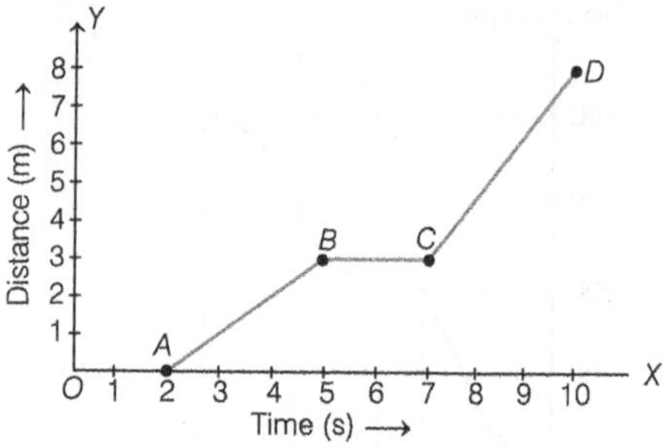

Sol.

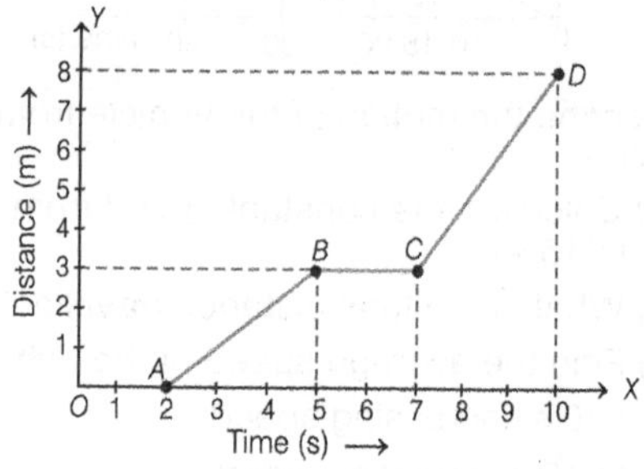

(i) For the motion from point *A* to *B*,

Time taken, $t = 5 - 2 = 3$ s

Distance covered = 3 − 0 = 3 m

∴ Speed during the motion from point,

$$A \text{ to } B = \frac{\text{Distance}}{\text{Time}} = \frac{3}{3} = 1 \text{ m/s}$$

(ii) For the motion from point *B* to *C*,

Time taken, $t = 7 - 5 = 2$ s

Distance covered = 3 − 3 = 0 m

(∵ body does not change its position from point *B* to *C*)

∴ Speed during the motion from point,

$$B \text{ to } C = \frac{\text{Distance}}{\text{Time}} = \frac{0}{2} = 0 \text{ m/s}$$

(iii) For the motion from point C to D,

Time taken, $t = 10 - 7 = 3$ s

Distance covered $= 8 - 3 = 5$ m

$\therefore$ Speed during the motion from point,

$$C \text{ to } D = \frac{\text{Distance}}{\text{Time}} = \frac{5}{3} \text{ m/s}$$

Q.14 **A girl walks along a straight path to drop a letter in the letter box and comes back to her initial position. Her displacement-time graph is shown in figure. Plot a velocity-time graph for the same.** **[3]**

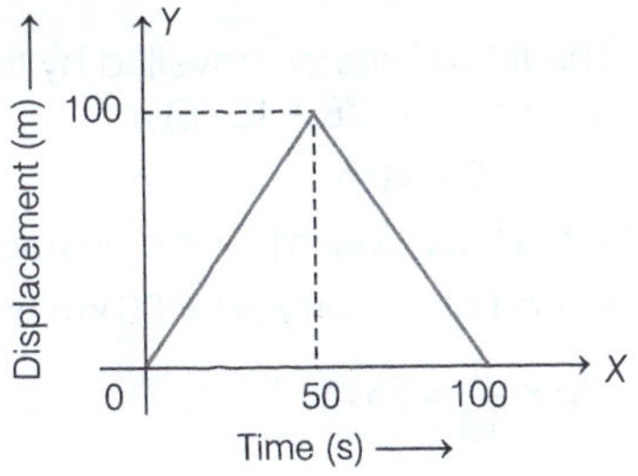

Sol. From the graph,

initial velocity, $u = 0$

velocity after 50 s,

$$v = \frac{\text{displacement}}{\text{Time}} = \frac{100}{50} = 2 \text{ ms}^{-1}$$

Velocity after 100 s,

$$v = \frac{\text{displacement}}{\text{time}} = \frac{0}{100} = 0$$

Therefore,

v (ms^{-1})	0	2	0
t (s)	0	50	100

Velocity-time graph plotted from the above data is shown as below

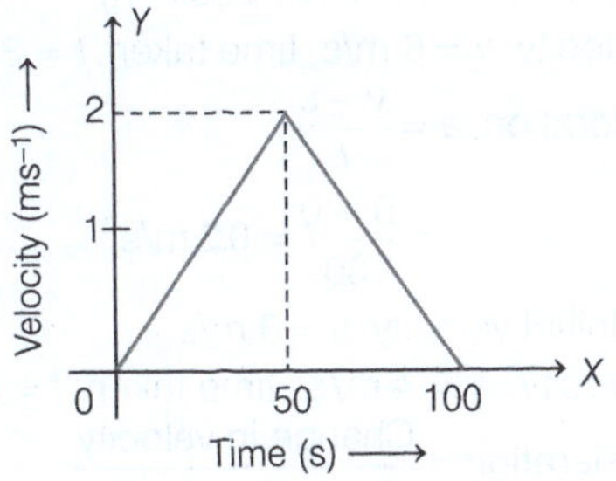

Q.15 **(a) When will you say a body is in (i) uniform acceleration and (ii) non-uniform acceleration?** **[1 + 1 = 2]**

(b) What is the nature of distance-time graphs for (i) uniform motion and (ii) non-uniform motion of an object? **[1 + 1 = 2]**

Sol. (a) (i) A body is in uniform acceleration, when it travels in a straight path with its velocity increases or decreases by equal amount in equal time intervals.

(ii) A body is in non-uniform acceleration, when it travels in a straight path with its velocity increases or decreases by unequal amount in equal time intervals.

(b) (i) The distance-time graph for uniform motion of an object is a straight line.

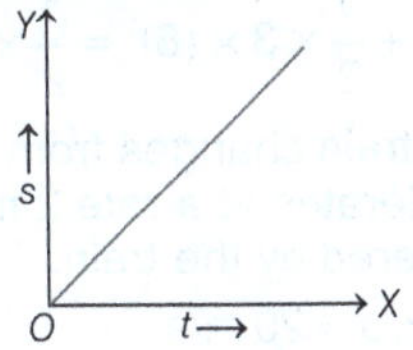

(ii) The distance-time graph for non-uniform motion of an object is a curved line.

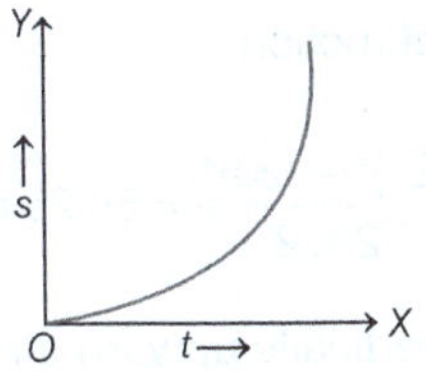

(Speed increases)

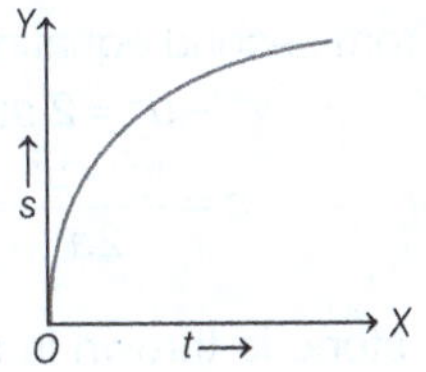

(Speed decreases)

Q.16 **A body is accelerating at a constant rate of 10 m/s². If the body starts from rest, then how much distance will it cover in 2 s?** **[2]**

Sol. Given, $u = 0, a = 10 \text{ m/s}^2, t = 2 \text{ s}, s = ?$

From second equation of motion,

$$s = ut + \frac{1}{2}at^2$$

$$s = 0 \times 2 + \frac{1}{2} \times 10 \times 2 \times 2$$

$$s = 20 \text{ m}$$

The body covers 20 m in 2 s.

Q.17 **Brakes applied to a car produce an acceleration of 6 m/s² in opposite direction to motion. If the car takes 2 s to stop after application of brakes, then calculate the distance it travels during this time.** **[2]**

Sol. Since, car stops after applying the brakes, final velocity, $v = 0$

and $a = -6 \text{ m/s}^2, t = 2$ s

From first equation of motion, $v = u + at$

or $u = v - at = 0 - (-6)(2) = 12$ m/s

From the second equation of motion,

$$s = ut + \frac{1}{2}at^2 = (12)(2) + \frac{1}{2}(-6)(2)^2 = 12 \text{ m}$$

The distance travelled in 2 s is 12 m.

Q.18 A motorboat starting from rest on a lake accelerates in a straight line at a constant rate of 3.0 ms^{-2} for 8.0 s. How far does the boat travel during this time? **[2]**

Sol. The motorboat starts from rest, so initial velocity, $u = 0$

Time taken, $t = 8$ s, acceleration, $a = 3\ ms^{-2}$

Distance covered during the given time,

$$s = ut + \frac{1}{2}at^2 \quad \text{(second equation of motion)}$$

$$= 0 \times 8 + \frac{1}{2} \times 3 \times (8)^2 = \frac{1}{2} \times 3 \times 64 = 96 \text{ m}$$

Q.19 Velocity of a train changes from 20 m/s to 25 m/s when it accelerates at a rate 2 m/s^2. Find the distance covered by the train. **[2]**

Sol. Initial velocity, $u = 20$ m/s

Final velocity, $v = 25$ m/s

Acceleration, $a = 2\ m/s^2$

From second equation of motion,

$$v^2 - u^2 = 2as$$

or $$s = \frac{v^2 - u^2}{2a} = \frac{(25)^2 - (20)^2}{2 \times 2} = 56.25 \text{ m}$$

Q.20 A stone is thrown in a vertically upward direction with a velocity of 5 m/s. If the acceleration of the stone during its motion is 10 m/s^2 in the downward direction, what will be the height attained by the stone and what time will it take to reach there? **[3]**

Sol. Given, $u = 5\ ms^{-1}$

$a = -10\ ms^{-2}$ (negative sign is due to upward direction)

$v = 0$ (at maximum height velocity is zero)

Height attained, $s = ?$

Time taken, $t = ?$

From third equation of motion, $v^2 = u^2 + 2as$

$$0 = (5)^2 + 2 \times -10 \times s$$

$$s = \frac{25}{20} = 1.25 \text{ m}$$

From first equation of motion, $v = u + at$

$$0 = 5 + (-10)t \Rightarrow t = \frac{5}{10} = 0.5 \text{ s}$$

Q.21 On a rainy day, a lorry is travelling at 80 km h^{-1}. The driver sees an obstacle 55 m away and applies the breakes to prevent a collision. His reaction time is 0.35 s.

(i) What is the distance travelled by the lorry while the driver is reacting? **[1]**

(ii) If the maximum deceleration of the lorry is 6 ms^{-2} and the initial speed of the lorry is

(a) 54 km h^{-1} and **[1]**

(b) 90 km h^{-1}, will lorry hit the obstacle? **[1]**

Ans. (i) To convert km h^{-1} to ms^{-1}

$$80 \text{ km h}^{-1} = \frac{80 \times 1000}{60 \times 60} = 22.2 \text{ ms}^{-1}$$

Distance travelled by the lorry during the reaction time = 22.2 × 0.35 = 7.78 m

(ii) Deceleration of the lorry(r) = 6 ms^{-2}

(a) Initial speed of the lorry (u) = 15 km h^{-1}

$$= 54 \times \frac{5}{18} = 15 \text{ ms}^{-1}$$

∴ Distance travelled by the lorry while it decelerates is

$$d = \frac{u^2}{2xr} = \frac{15 \times 15}{2 \times 6} = 18.75 \text{ m}$$

∴ The total distance travelled by the lorry before it stops = (7.78 + 18.75) m

= 26.53 m

So, the lorry doesn't hit the obstacle.

(b) Initial speed of the lorry (u) = 90 km h^{-1}

$$= 90 \times \frac{5}{18} = 25 \text{ ms}^{-1}$$

∴ Distance travelled by the lorry while it decelerates is

$$d = \frac{u^2}{2 \times r} = \frac{25 \times 25}{2 \times 6} = 52.08 \text{ m}$$

∴ The total distance travelled by the lorry before it stops = (7.78 + 52.08) m

= 59.86 m

So, in this case the lorry will hit the obstacle.

Q.22 Starting from a stationary position, a car attains a velocity of 6 m/s in 30 s. Then, the driver of the car applies a brake such that the velocity of the car comes down to 4 m/s in the next 5 s. Calculate the acceleration of the car in both the cases. **[4]**

Sol. Case I Initial velocity of the car, $u = 0$

(∵ It starts from stationary position)

Final velocity, $v = 6$ m/s, time taken, $t = 30$ s

$$\therefore \text{Acceleration, } a = \frac{v - u}{t}$$

$$= \frac{6 - 0}{30} = 0.2 \text{ m/s}^2$$

Case II Initial velocity, $u = 6$ m/s

Final velocity, $v = 4$ m/s, time taken, $t = 5$ s

$$\therefore \text{Acceleration} = \frac{\text{Change in velocity}}{\text{Time}}$$

$$= \frac{\text{Final velocity} - \text{Initial velocity}}{\text{Time}}$$

$$= \frac{v - u}{t}$$

$$\Rightarrow \quad a = \frac{4 - 6}{5}$$

$= -0.4 \text{ m/s}^2$

Thus, the acceleration in the two cases are 0.2 m/s^2 and -0.4 m/s^2.

Q.23 A stone is thrown vertically upwards. The variation with time t of the displacement s of the stone is shown in figure.

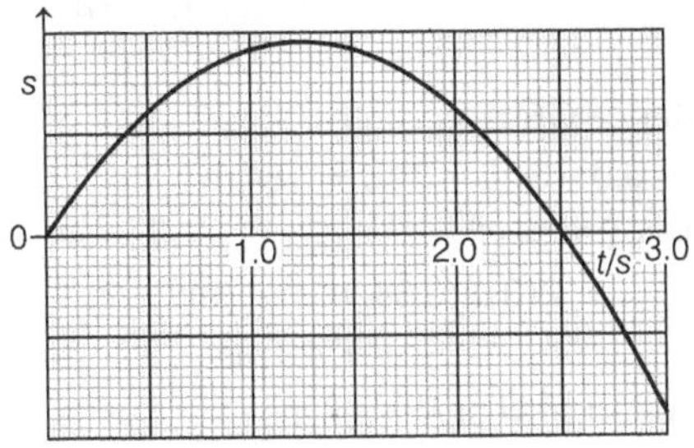

(a) Use figure to describe, without calculation, the speed of the stone from $t = 0$ to $t = 3.0$ s **[1]**

(b) Assume air resistance is negligible and therefore the stone has constant acceleration.

Calculate for the stone,

(i) the speed at 3.0 s. **[1]**

(ii) the distance travelled from $t = 0$ to $t = 3.0$ s **[1]**

(iii) the displacement from $t = 0$ to $t = 3.0$ s. **[1]**

Sol. (a) Speed decreases due to decrease in gradient and becomes zero at $t = 1.25$ s.

It increases in opposite direction after $t = 1.25$ s.

(b) (i) $v = u + at$

$= 0 + (9.81)(1.75)$

$= 17.17 \approx 17.2 \text{ ms}^{-1}$

(ii) Let s_1 be the distance travelled in first 1.25 s and from 1.25 s to 2.50 s.

$$s_1 = ut + \frac{1}{2}at^2$$

$$= (0)(2.50 - 1.25) + \frac{1}{2}(9.81)(2.50 - 1.25)^2$$

$= 7.66$ m

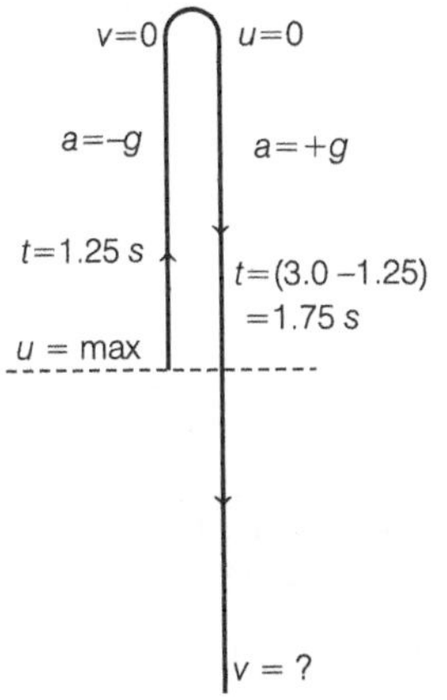

Let s_2 be the distance travelled from 1.25 s to 3.0 s.

$$2as_2 = v^2 - u^2$$

$\Rightarrow \quad 2(9.81)(s_2) = (17.2)^2 - (0)^2$

$\Rightarrow \quad s_2 = 15.1$

$\therefore$ Distance travelled from 0s to 3.0 s

$= s_1 + s_2$

$= 7.66 + 15.1$

$= 22.76$

≈ 22.8 m

(iii) Displacement $= s_2 - s_1$

$= 15.1 - 7.66$

$= 7.44$ m

Direction = Downward

Q.24 A car is travelling along a straight road at speed v. A hazard suddenly appears in front of the car. In the time interval between the hazard appearing and the brakes on the car coming into operation, the car moves forward a distance of 29.3 m. With the brakes applied, the front wheels of the car leave skid marks on the road that are 12.8 m long, as illustrated in figure.

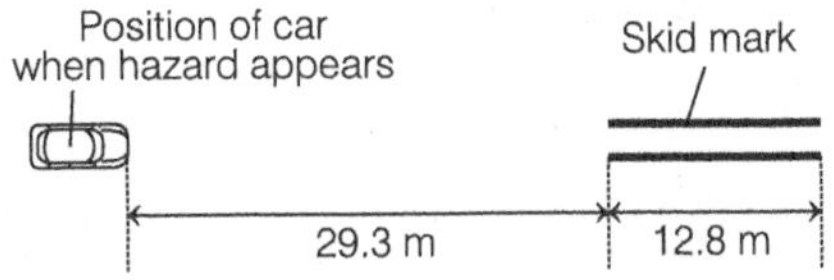

It is estimated that, during the skid, the magnitude of the deceleration of the car is 0.85 g, where g is the acceleration of free fall.

(a) Determine,

(i) the speed v of the car before the brakes are applied. **[1]**

(ii) the time interval between the hazard appearing and the brakes being applied. **[1]**

(b) The legal speed limit on the road is 60 km per hour. Use both of your answers in (a) to comment on the standard of the driving of the car. **[2]**

Sol. (a) (i) $2as = v^2 - u^2$

$2(-0.85g)(12.8) = (0)^2 - (v)^2$

$-2(0.85)(9.81)(12.8) = -v^2$

$v^2 = 213$

$v = 14.6 \text{ ms}^{-1}$

(ii) $s = vt$

$\Rightarrow \quad 29.3 = (14.6)t$

$\Rightarrow \quad t = \frac{29.3}{14.6} = 2.0$ s

(b) Since, $60 \text{ kmh}^{-1} = \frac{60 \times 1000}{60 \times 60} = 16.7 \text{ ms}^{-1}$

So, speed of car is within the speed limit but the reaction time of driver is too long.

Q.25 Figure shows an object M on a slope.

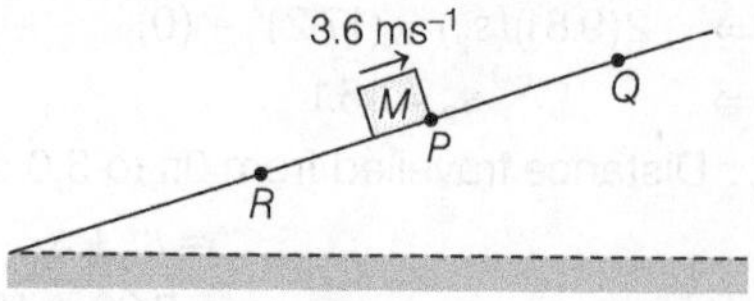

M moves up the slope, comes to rest at point Q and then moves back down the slope to point R.

M has a constant acceleration of 3.0 ms^{-2} down the slope at all times.

At time $t = 0$, M is at point P and has a velocity of 3.6 ms^{-1} up the slope.

The total distance from P to Q and then to R is 6.0 m.

(a) Calculate, for the motion of M from P to Q,

(i) the time taken. **[1]**

(ii) the distance travelled. **[1]**

(b) Show that the speed of M at R is 4.8 ms^{-1}. **[1]**

(c) Draw the variation with time t of the velocity v of M for the motion P to Q to R. **[1]**

Sol. (a) (i) Using, $v = u + at$

$$v_Q = u_P + at$$

$$0 = 3.6 + (-3.0)t$$

$$t = \frac{3.6}{3.0} = 1.2 \text{ s} = 1.2 \text{ s}$$

(ii) Distance travelled, $s = (u_P)t + \frac{1}{2}at^2$

$$= (3.6)(1.2) + \frac{1}{2}(-3.0)(1.2)^2$$

$$= 4.32 - 2.16 = 2.16 \text{ m}$$

(b) Distance QR is

$$s_{QR} = 6.0 - 2.16 - 2.16 = 3.84 \text{ m}$$

Using, $2as = v^2 - u^2$

$$2(3.0)(3.84) = v^2 - (0)^2$$

$$\Rightarrow \quad v = 4.8 \text{ ms}^{-1}$$

$\therefore$ Speed of M at R = 4.8 ms^{-1}.

(c)

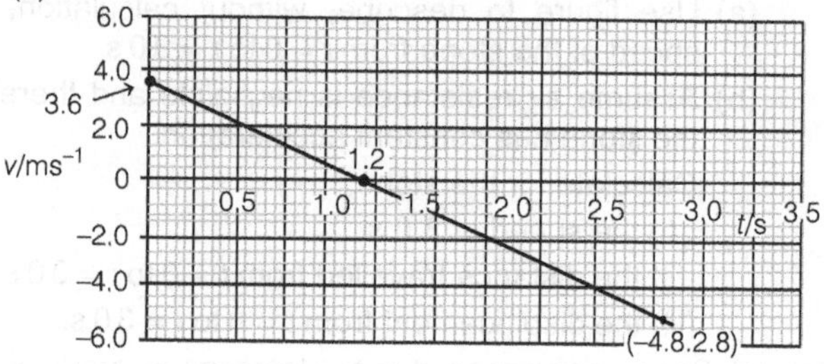

03

LAWS OF MOTION

Force

- A force is that physical cause which changes or tends to change either the size or the shape or the state of rest or of motion of a body.
- Any action which causes **pull, hit or push** on a body is called **force**. It is used in our everyday actions like pushing, pulling, lifting, stretching, twisting and pressing.

  e.g.

  (i) A force is used, when we kick a football.

  (ii) A force is used, when we lift a box from the floor.
- It is a **vector quantity** and its SI unit is **newton (N)** and CGS unit is **dyne**.

Effects of Force

- A force applied on a body can produce **four types of effects** such as

  (i) Force can start or stop a motion.

  (ii) Force can change speed of an object, i.e. making it to move slower or faster.

  (iii) Force can change the direction of motion of an object.

  (iv) Force can change the size and shape of an object.

Types of Forces

- According to the point of view of application, forces are divided into two parts.

1. Contact Forces

The forces that act between two or more bodies, when they are in physical contact with each other, are called contact forces. Some contact forces are discussed below

(i) **Frictional Force** When a body slides (or rolls) over a rough surface, a force acts in opposite direction to the motion of body along the surface in contact, this force is known as frictional force or the force of friction.

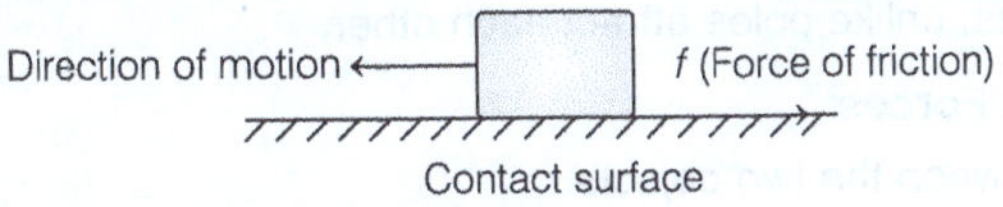

(ii) **Normal Reaction** It is a contact force between two surfaces in contact. It is always perpendicular to the surfaces of contact.

e.g. When a book is kept at a surface, weight of the book acts vertically downward and reaction force of surface is normal reaction which acts vertically upward.

(iii) **Force Exerted by a Spring** When a spring is compressed or extended by an external force, a restoring force is generated, which tries to bring the spring back to its normal position.

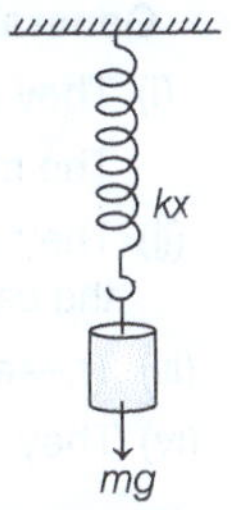

Spring force

REVISION NOTES

(iv) **Tension Force as Applied Through String** When a body is suspended with the string, then the weight of the body acts downward while a force acts just opposite to the downward force for balancing it, this force is called tension.

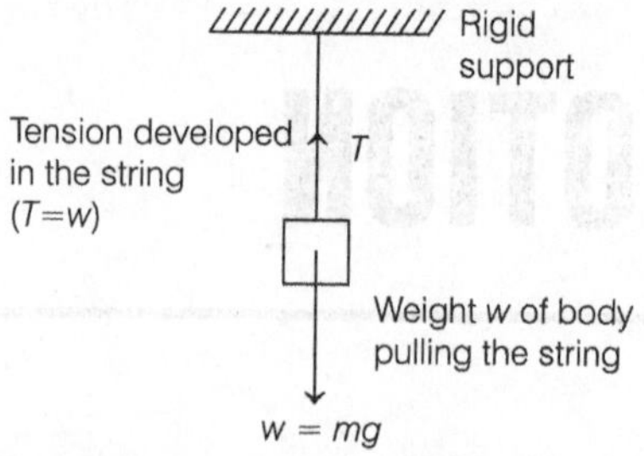

(v) **Force Exerted During Collision** When two bodies collide, they push each other. As a result, equal and opposite forces act on each body.

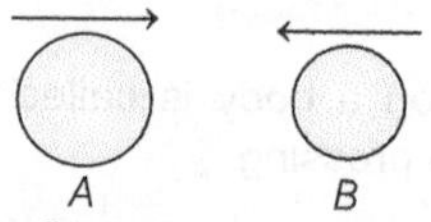

(a) Two bodies moving towards each other

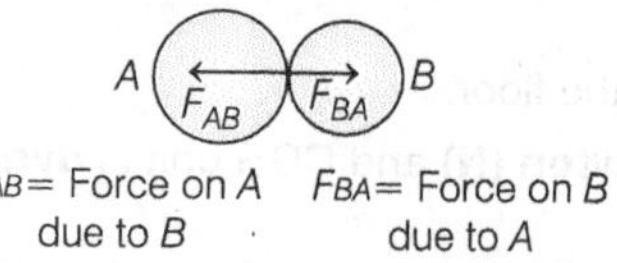

(b) Force exerted during collision

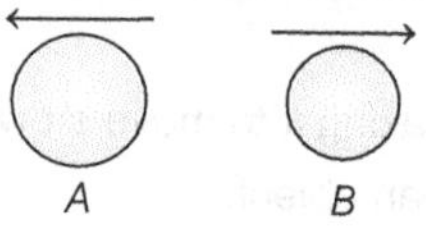

(c) After collision

2. Non-Contact Forces

The forces that act between two or more objects without any physical contact with each other are called non-contact forces. Some non-contact forces are discussed below

(i) **Gravitational Force** The force of mutual attraction between any two objects (without any physical contact) is called gravitational force. The gravitational force is always of attractive nature.

(ii) **Electrostatic Force** The force of attraction or repulsion between two charged particles is called electrostatic force. **Like charges repel** each other while **opposite charges attract** each other.

(iii) **Magnetic Force** The force of attraction or repulsion between two magnetic poles is called magnetic force. Like poles repel each other, whereas, unlike poles attract each other.

- **General Properties of Non-Contact Forces**

(i) They depend upon the distance between the two objects.
The magnitude of force varies inversely as the square of distance of separation.

(ii) They depend upon the medium between the two objects in case of electrical and magnetic forces but not in the case of gravitational force.

(iii) These forces always form an action-reaction pair.

(iv) They are long-range forces and always act along the line joining the centres of the two bodies.

Newton's First Law of Motion

- It states that an object will continue to remain in its state of rest or uniform motion along a straight line path unless an external force acts on it. This means, all objects resist change in their state. First law of motion is also called **law of inertia**.

Inertia

- The tendency of a body to oppose or resist any change in its **state of rest** or of **uniform motion** is called inertia of the body. It is the **inherent property** of all the objects.
- Inertia of an object is measured by its mass. It is directly proportional to the mass. **A heavy object will have more inertia than lighter one.**
- Inertia is divided into **three types** as given below
  (i) **Inertia of Rest** The tendency of a body to resist (oppose) any change in its state of rest is known as inertia of rest.
  (ii) **Inertia of Motion** The tendency of a body to resist (oppose) any change in its state of uniform motion is known as inertia of motion.
  (iii) **Inertia of Direction** The tendency of a body to oppose any change in its direction of motion is known as inertia of direction.

Momentum

- Momentum of a body is the quantity of motion possessed by the body. It is defined as the product of its **mass** (m) and **velocity** v and is denoted by p.

$\therefore$

$$\boxed{\text{Momentum, } p = mv}$$

- SI unit of momentum is kg - m/s or kg - ms^{-1}
- CGS unit of momentum is g - cm/s or g- cms^{-1}
- It is a **vector quantity** and its direction is along the direction of velocity of the body.

Newton's Second Law of Motion

- This law states that the rate of change of momentum of a body is directly proportional to the external force applied on it and the change in momentum takes place in the direction of the applied force.
- Force = Rate of change of momentum $= \dfrac{\text{Change in momentum } (\Delta p)}{\text{Change in time } (\Delta t)}$ or $F = \dfrac{m\Delta V}{\Delta t}$

$$\Delta p = p_2 - p_1 = mv - mu \Rightarrow F = \frac{\Delta p}{\Delta t} = \frac{m(v-u)}{t}$$

$\because$

$$\frac{(v-u)}{t} = a \text{ (accelertion)}$$

$\therefore$

$$\boxed{F = ma}$$

- The SI unit of force is **newton** (N) and CGS unit of force is **dyne**.
- **1 Newton** One newton is the force which when acts on a body of mass 1 kg, produces an acceleration of 1 m/s^2

  i.e. $1 \text{ Newtons} = 1\text{kg} \times 1 \text{m/s}^2$
- **1 dyne** One dyne is the force which when acts on a body of mass 1g produces an acceleration of 1 cm/s^2

  i.e. **1 dyne** $= 1\text{g} \times 1 \text{cm/s}^2$.
- **Relation between newton and dyne**

$$1 \text{ N} = 1 \text{ kg ms}^{-2} = \frac{1000 \text{ g} \times 100 \text{ cm}}{\text{s}^2} = 10^5 \text{ g cms}^{-2}$$

Thus, $1 \text{ N} = 10^5 \text{ dyne}$

Newton's Third Law of Motion

- It states that, whenever an object exerts a force on another object, then the second object exerts an equal and opposite force on the first object. These pair of opposing forces are also known as **action and reaction forces.**
- To every action there is always an **equal** and **opposite** reaction.
- These action and reaction forces are equal in magnitude and opposite in direction.

Some important implications of the Newton's third law of motion are

(i) Newton's third law of motion is applicable irrespective of the nature of the forces.
(ii) Action and reaction always act on two different bodies.
(iii) The force of action and reaction cannot cancel each other.
(iv) No action can occur in the absence of a reaction.

EXAM ORIENTED QUESTIONS

TYPE - 1 01 Mark

Multiple Choice Questions

Q.1 Which of the following force is non-contact force?

(a) Force of reaction (b) Force due to gravity

(c) Tension in string (d) Force of friction

Ans. (b) Force due to gravity is non-contact force. Gravitational force of attraction acts between the two objects due to their masses.

Q.2 The inertia of an object tends to cause the object to

(a) increase its speed

(b) decrease its speed

(c) resists any change in its state of motion

(d) decelerate due to friction

Ans. (c) Inertia is the property of an object by virtue of which it resists any change in its state of motion.

Q.3 An athlete often runs before taking a long jump, which of the following reason?

(a) Running help to apply more force

(b) With running action and reaction forces will increase

(c) He gains energy to take him through the long distance

(d) By running, he gives himself large inertia

Ans. (d) An athlete often runs before taking a long jump because by running he brings his whole body in the state of motion. Due to inertia, when the body is in motion, it becomes easier to take a long jump.

Q.4 In the given figure, a block of weight 45 N is hanging from a rigid support by a string.

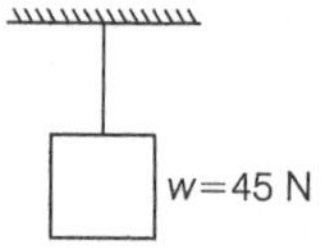

The force exerted by block on the string is

(a) 45 N downward (b) 45 N upward

(c) 90 N downward (d) 90 N upward

Ans. (a) Weight acts in downward direction. Therefore, the block will exert 45 N force downward on the string.

Q.5 Which two forces act on the system of a ball hanged from roof using a string?

(a) Weight and friction

(b) Friction and tension

(c) Tension and normal reaction

(d) Tension and weight

Ans. (d) The forces acting on the system are action-reaction forces. Action force is due to the weight of the ball in downward direction and reaction due to the action force in string, in the form of tension.

Q.6 Which of the following is the correct form of Newton's second law of motion?

(a) $F = p_2 - p_1$

(b) $F = mv$

(c) $F = \dfrac{\Delta p}{\Delta t}$

(d) All of these

Ans. (c) According to Newton's second law of motion, force is defined as the rate of change of momentum, i.e.

$$F = \frac{\Delta p}{\Delta t}$$

Q.7 Two forces F_1 and F_2 are acting on a body as shown in the figure, then acceleration in the body is

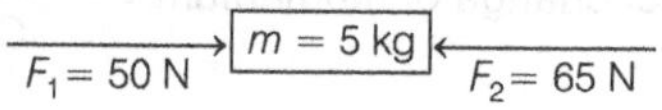

(a) 23 m/s² (b) 3 m/s² (c) 2 m/s² (d) 22 m/s²

Ans. (b) Resultant force on a body,

$$F = F_2 - F_1 = 65 - 50 = 15 \text{ N}$$

By Newton's second law of motion,

$$F = ma$$

$\Rightarrow$ $15 = 5a$

$\Rightarrow$ $a = 3 \text{ m/s}^2$

Q.8 A force of 1600 N accelerates a car, of mass 800 kg, from rest. What is the car's acceleration and its velocity after 4.0 s?

	Acceleration (m/s²)	Velocity (m/s)
(a)	0.50	0.13
(b)	0.50	0.50
(c)	2.0	2.0
(d)	2.0	8.0

Ans. (d) A constant force produces a constant acceleration.

$\therefore$ $a = \dfrac{F}{M} = \dfrac{1600}{800} = 2.0 \text{ m/s}^2$

Also, $a = \dfrac{v - u}{t}$

$2.0 = \dfrac{v - 0}{4.0}$

$\therefore$ $v = 8.0 \text{ m/s}$

Q.9 Consider two spring balances hooked as shown in the figure below. We pull them in opposite directions. If the reading shown by *A* is 1.5 N, the reading shown by *B* will be

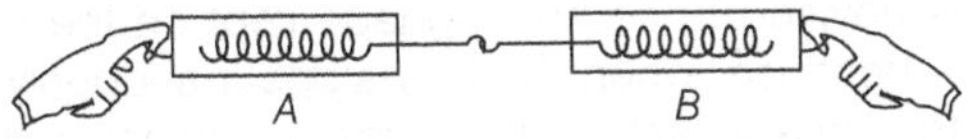

(a) 1.5 N (b) 2.5 N (c) 3.5 N (d) zero

Ans. (a) According to Newton's third law of motion, every action has equal and opposite reaction. Hence, force (action) exerted by *A* on *B* and force (reaction) exerted by *B* on *A* are equal, hence reading shown by *B* will be 1.5 N.

Q.10 A block of weight 15 N is hanged from a rigid support by a string. The force exerted by string on the block is

(a) 150 N upward (b) 15 N downward
(c) 15 N upward (d) 150 N downward

Ans. (c) According to Newton's third law of motion, every action has an equal and opposite reaction. Hence, force exerted by string on the block is same as that of force exerted by block on the string but in opposite direction, i.e. 15 N upwards.

TYPE - 2 — 01 Mark

Assertion-Reason Type Questions

Directions (Q. Nos. 1-5) In the following questions two statements are given as Assertion and Reason.

(a) Both A and R are true and R is the correct explanation of A.
(b) Both A and R are true and R is not the correct explanation of A.
(c) A is true but R is false.
(d) A is false but R is true.

Q.1 Assertion (A) The momentum of a stationary object is zero.

Reason (R) Momentum depends on the velocity of an object.

Ans. (a) Momentum is given by $p = mv$. For a stationary object, $v = 0$, So, $p = 0$

$\therefore$ Momentum depends on the velocity of an object.

Q.2 Assertion (A) A truck and a car moving with the same velocity have the different momentum.

Reason (R) Momentum depends only on the velocity of the object.

Ans. (c) Momentum also depends on mass ($p = mv$).

Since the truck has a greater mass than the car, it will have a larger momentum, even if the velocity is the same.

Q.3 Assertion (A) When a mass of an object is doubled, its acceleration under the same force is halved.

Reason (R) Acceleration is inversely proportional to the mass of the object.

Ans. (a) If the mass of an object is doubled (new mass = $2m$), and the force remains the same, the acceleration becomes

$$a_{new} = \frac{F}{2m} = \frac{1}{2}a \qquad \left[\because \frac{F}{m} = a\right]$$

This means the acceleration is reduced to half its orginal value.

According to Newton's second law of motion,

$$F = ma$$

or $$a = \frac{F}{m}$$

On increasing mass acceleration decreases.

Q.4 Assertion (A) A heavy object is harder to push than a light object.

Reason (R) According to Newton's second law, force is inversely proportional to mass for a given acceleration.

Ans. (c) Newton's second law ($F = ma$) states that the force required to accelerate an object is directly proportional to its mass. Thus, a heavy object is harder to push than a light one because it has a larger mass, required more force to achieve the same acceleration.

According to Newton's second law, force is directly proportional to mass for a given acceleration.

Q.5 Assertion (A) If two persons walking or running in opposite direction collide with each other, then both feel hurt.

Reason (R) To every action, there is an equal and opposite reaction.

Ans. (a) According to Newton's third law of motion, every action has an equal and opposite reaction, but always act on two different bodies.

Therefore, both persons feel hurt after collision.

TYPE - 3 — 01/02 Marks

Fill in the Blanks

Q.1 When a bird pushes air downwards with its wings, the air pushes the bird .... [forward/upward] with an equal force. **[1]**

Ans. upward

Q.2 A horse pulls a cart by exerting force on the ground. The reaction force by the ground moves the horse and cart......... [forward/backward] **[1]**

Ans. forward

Q.3 The force exerted by the rocket's exhaust gases on the rocket is an example of Newton's .... [second/third] law. **[1]**

Ans. third

Q.4 The force applied on an object can compress it, resulting in a change in its ...... [weight/shape] and .... [shape/size] **[2]**

Ans. shape, size

Q.5 The force exerted by a rope during a tug of war is a ......[contact/non-contact] force, while the force of the Earth's pull on the paticipants is a ...... [contact/non-contact] force. **(2)**

Ans. contact, non-contact

Q.6 Earth's force on an apple is the ...... [action/reaction] force and the force exerted by the apple on the earth is the ...... [action/reaction] force. **[2]**

Ans. action, reaction

TYPE - 4

02 Marks

Very Short Answer Type Questions

Q.1 Why do bodies of larger mass require larger initial effort to bring them into motion?

Ans. The inertia of a body is directly proportional to mass, larger the mass, greater will be the inertia. So, larger mass needs larger initial effort to bring it into motion.

Q.2 Which will have greater inertia amongst three balls *A*, *B* and *C* filled with same volume of mercury, water and air, respectively? Give reasons to support your answer.

Ans. Mercury has more inertia than water and air because mercury has greatest density and hence greatest mass. If a body has more mass, it has more inertia and that's why heavier body has more inertia than the lighter body. A mercury ball *A* has more inertia than water ball *B* and air ball *C*.

Q.3 When we shake the branch of a mango tree, the mangoes fall down. Why?

Ans. When we shake the branch of a mango tree, the mangoes fall down due to inertia of rest. The branch moves, but the mangoes tend to remain at rest. As a result, they get detached and fall due to gravity.

Q.4 Why do we fall in the forward direction, when a moving bus suddenly applies brakes and we tend to fall backward, when it suddenly accelerates from rest?

Ans. When a moving bus suddenly applies brakes, due to inertia of motion the upper part of the body of the passengers tend to remain in motion however the feel of the passengers suddenly comes to rest with the bus making them fall in the forward direction.

When a bus suddenly accelerates from rest, due to inertia of rest, the upper part of the body of the passengers tend to remain at rest but the feel of the passengers suddenly goes into motion with the bus making them fall in the backward direction.

Q.5 Why is it advised to tie the luggage kept on the roof of a bus with a rope?

Ans. It is advised to tie any luggage kept on the roof of a bus because, when the bus stops it suddenly comes in the state of rest but the luggage remains in the state of motion, due to inertia of motion, So, the luggage may move forward and fall down from the roof of the bus. It not tied with a rope.

Again if the bus suddenly, starts then the bus comes in the state of motion but luggage remains in the state of rest etc. If due to inertia of rest. So, the luggage move in the backward direction and may fall down.

Q.6 A person driving a car suddenly applies the brakes on seeing a child on the road ahead. If he is not wearing seat belt, he falls forward and his head hits against the steering wheel. Why?

Ans. When a person driving a car suddenly applies brakes, the car suddenly comes to rest and hence the feel of the driver also suddenly comes to rest. However the upper part of the body remains in motion due to inertia of motion which makes the driver fall forward and hit his head against the staring wheel.

Q.7 Why does a coin thrown vertically upward in moving bus come back to the thrower's hand?

Ans. Coin thrown vertically upward in moving bus comes back to the thrower's hand because it remains in the same state of forward motion, as the thrower even during the time it is in the air due to inertia of motion of the coin.

Q.8 How can a small mass such as a bullet kill a person when fired from a gun?

Ans. The mass of the bullet is small. So, it moves out of the gun with a very high velocity, due to which the momentum produced is very high ($p = mv$). This high momentum of the bullet produces a large force in a short span of time which is enough to kill a person.

Q.9 Why a cricket player, while taking a catch always moves his hands backward?

Ans. When a cricket player tries to catch a high speed ball, the momentum of the ball suddenly becomes zero in a very short span of time increasing the force applied by the ball on the palms of the cricket player, which may cause an injury. If the cricketer withdraws his hands, then the time taken by the ball to come to a stop increases, which in turn reduces the force that the ball exerts on the cricket player's hands which reduces the chances of any injury.

Q.10 Glass wares are wrapped in straw during their transportation. Justify giving reason.

Ans. During transportation, the glass wares may break, if they collide with each other in the event of jerks.

When they are wrapped in straw, the force of jerk is transmitted to them through the pieces of straw in a longer period of time. Which reduces the impact of force on the glass waves avoiding the breakage.

Q.11 State Newton's second law of motion. Write its mathematical formulation.

Ans. According to Newton's second law of motion, the rate of change of linear momentum is directly proportional to the force applied on (or by) the object.

Mathematically, it is expressed as

$$F \propto \frac{\Delta p}{\Delta t}$$

$$\therefore \quad F = k\frac{m(v-u)}{t} \text{ or } F = kma \quad \left(\because \frac{v-u}{t} = a\right)$$

As, $\quad k = 1, F = ma$

Q.12 When the glass vessels fall on a hard floor, they break, but when they fall on a carpet (or sand) they do not break. Why?

Ans. When a glass vessel falls from a height on a hard floor, it comes to rest almost instantaneously (i.e. in a very short span of time), so the floor exerts a very large force and thus the vessel breaks.

But if it falls on carpet (or sand), the time duration (for it to come to rest) increases, so force decreases. Thus the vessel does not break.

Q.13 According to the third law of motion, when we push an object, it pushes back with an equal and opposite force. If the object is a massive truck parked along the roadside, it will probably not move. A student justifies this by answering that the two opposite and equal forces cancel each other. Comment on this logic and explain, why the truck does not move?

Ans. The logic given by the student is not correct because two equal and opposite forces cancel each other only if they act on the same body. According to Newton's third law, action and reaction force always act on two different bodies, so they cannot cancel each other.

When a massive truck is pushed, the action force applied by the student on the truck is not sufficient to overcome the force of friction which acts between the road and the wheels of the truck in the opposite direction to the action force and hence the truck remains stationary.

Q.14 Two identical bullets are fired one by one by a light rifle and another by a heavy rifle with the same force, which rifle will hurt the shoulder more and why?

Ans. Since both the bullets are identical and are fired with a same action force so the reaction experienced by both the bullets will be the same. Also, since the time interval of firing of the bullets are same in both cases so the change in momentum of the two bullets are also same. During the recoil of the guns, the rifle with the lighter body will move back with greater velocity as compared to the rifle with heavier body even though the recoil momentum is same for both the cases, because the mass of the lighter rifle is less as compared to the heavier rifle. Hence, the lighter rifle will hurt the shoulders more.

Q.15 Why is it difficult to climb up a greasy pole?

Ans. A man trying to climb up a pole presses the pole downward with his feet and hands which is the action force and the frictional force acting between the feet of the man and the pole acts in the upward direction providing the necessary reaction force. If the pole is greasy, the friction between the hands and feet of the man and the pole reduces, which reduces the amount of reaction force making it difficult for him to climb the pole.

Q.16 On a sail boat, air is blown on the sail from an electric fan attached to the same boat. Will the boat start moving?

Ans. When air is blown on the sail from an electric fan attached to the boat, the air blown by the fan provides the action force to the sail and the sail in turn provides a reaction force on the air around it. But since the sail and the fan are attached to the same boat so the net resultant force acting on the boat as a whole is zero. Hence, the boat doesn't move.

TYPE - 5 — 03 Marks

Short Answer Type Questions

Q.1 What are the differences between contact and non-contact forces?

Ans.

	Contact forces	Non-contact forces
(i)	The forces experienced by a body due to physical contact are called contact forces.	The forces experienced by a body without any physical contact are called non-contact forces.
(ii)	There is no field linked with contact force.	There is always a field linked with non-contact force like electric field, magnetic field etc.
(iii)	**Example** Firction, normal contact force etc.	**Example** Gravitational force, electromagnetic force etc.

Q.2 Which of the following has more inertia?

(i) A stone and a rubber ball of same size. **[1]**

(ii) A bicycle and a train. **[1]**

(iii) A five rupees coin and a one rupee coin. **[1]**

Give reason for your answer.

Ans. Inertia of an object is due to quantity of matter possessed, thus it is the measure of its mass.

(i) A stone of same size as that of rubber ball will have greater mass, so the stone will have more inertia.

(ii) A train has much greater mass than that of a bicycle, so the train will have more inertia.

(iii) A five rupees coin has more mass than a one rupee coin, so five rupees coin will have greater inertia.

Q.3 A stone when thrown on a glass window pane, it smashes the window pane into pieces, but bullet from the gun passes through it making a clean hole, why?

Ans. Speed of stone is small, so it remains in contact with window pane for a longer time. Due to this, it transfers its momentum to window pane and breaks it into pieces. A bullet on the other hand moves with a high speed and hence doesn't get much time to transfer its momentum to the particles of the window pane near the impact of the bullet, just makes a clean hole and passes.

Q.4 State reason for the following questions.

(i) Road accidents occurring due to high speeds are much worse than accidents due to low speeds of vehicles. [1]

(ii) When a motorcar makes a sharp turn at a high speed passengers tend to be thrown to one side. [2]

Ans. (i) Road accidents occurring due to high speeds are much worse than accidents due to low speeds of vehicles. This is because the momentum of high speed vehicles is more than that of the low speeds of vehicles.

(ii) When a motor car makes sharp turn at a high speed, the bodies of the passengers tend to oppose the change in the direction of motion of the motor car due to the inertia of motion which makes them fall in the direction opposite to the direction of turning of the motorcar.

Q.5 Look at the diagram below and answer the following questions.

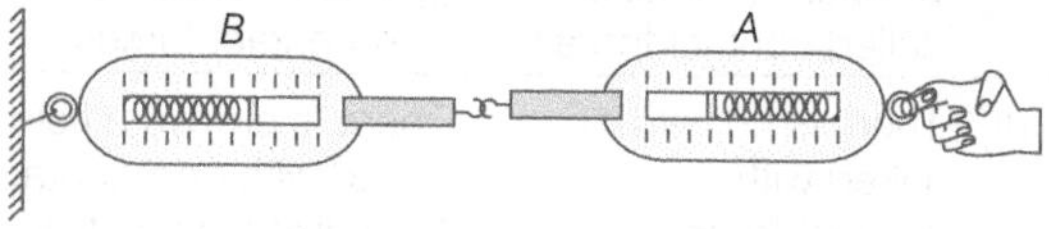

(i) When a force is applied through the free end of the spring balance *A*, the reading on the spring balance *A* is 15 g-wt. What will be the measure of the reading shown by spring balance *B*? [1]

(ii) Write reasons for your answer. [1]

(iii) Name the force which balance *A* exerts on balance *B* and the force of balance *B* on balance *A*. [1]

Ans. (i) The reading shown by the spring balance *B* is 15 g-wt.

(ii) From Newton's third law, the force exerted by *B* on *A* and force exerted by *A* on *B* are equal.

(iii) Force of reaction and force of action.

Q.6 Identify action and reaction forces in the following cases

(i) A book resting on a table. [1]

(ii) A person jumping off the ground. [1]

(ii) A swimmer pushing against the pool wall. [1]

Ans. (i) The weight of the book exerts downward force on the table, this is action. The table exerts an equal and opposite upward force on the book, this is reaction.

(ii) When a person jumps, they push against the ground with their legs (action force applied). The ground responds by exerting an equal and opposite force. which pushes the person upward (reaction force).

(iii) When a swimmer pushes off the pool wall, they push the wall backward (action). In response, the wall pushes the swimmer forward, propelling them through the water (reaction).

TYPE - 6 — 04 Marks

Long Answer Type Questions

Q.1 (i) Two balls of the same size but of different materials, rubber and iron are kept on the smooth floor of a moving train. The brakes are applied suddenly to stop the train. Will the balls start rolling? If so in which direction? Will they move with the same speed? Give reasons for your answer. [2]

(ii) Give two applications of inertia in daily life. [2]

Ans. (i) When the train is stopped suddenly, then it comes in the state of rest but the balls remain in the state of motion. So, due to inertia of motion, the balls move in the forward direction.

As the balls are of same size but of different materials that means their mass will be different. So, both the balls will move with different speeds.

(ii) Applications of inertia in daily life are given below

(a) A carpet is beaten with stick, so that dust particles fall down.

(b) Branches of tree are shaken, so that fruits fall down.

Q.2 State the following cases.

(a) Why are the mudguards provided over the wheels? [1]

(b) Why do the sparks produced during sharpening process of a knife fly-off tangentially? [1]

(c) When a train starts or stops suddenly, sliding doors of some compartments may open or close. Explain. [1]

(d) Why does the electric fan continue to rotate for sometime after the current is switched OFF? [1]

Ans. (a) The rotating wheels of cycle throw out mud sticking to it tangentially due to inertia of direction. This is why mudguards are provided over the wheels to protect the clothes of the cyclist.

(b) When a knife is sharpened against a grinding stone, sparks produced fly-off tangentially due to inertia of direction.

(c) When a train starts or stops suddenly, sliding doors of some compartments may open or close due to inertia of rest and motion.

(d) The electric fan continues to rotate due to inertia of motion until the friction in the bearings and that of the air brings it to state of rest after sometime.

Q.3 A large truck and a car, both moving with speed v, have a head-on collision and both of them come to halt after that. If the collision lasts for 10s.

(i) Which vehicle experiences the greater force of impact? **[1]**

(ii) Which vehicle experiences the greater momentum change? **[1]**

(iii) Which vehicle experiences the greater acceleration? **[1]**

(iv) Why is the car likely to suffer more damage than the truck? **[1]**

Ans. (i) Both the vehicles experience same force of impact as action and reaction are equal and opposite.

(ii) The truck experiences a greater change in momentum an account of its greater mass.

(iii) The car experiences greater change in acceleration as force remaining same, acceleration is inversely proportional to mass.

(iv) Because of greater change in acceleration, the car will suffer more damage.

TYPE - 7 — 03/04 Marks

Case Based Questions

Q.1 A block is moving on the rough surface due to external force acting on it in horizontal direction as shown in the figure below. **[3]**

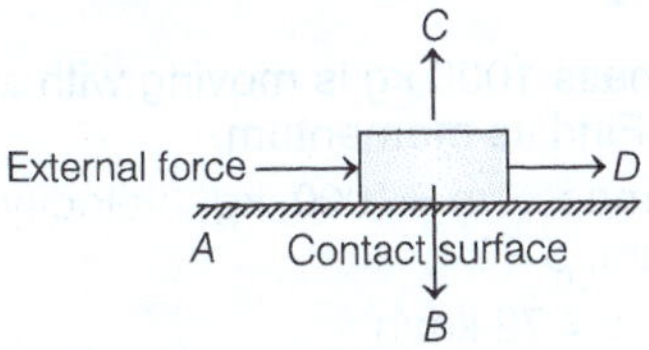

Complete the table using the labels from the figure. The first label is done for you.

Sr. No.	Description	Label
a	Direction of weight	B
b	Normal reaction	
c	Direction of motion	
d	Frictional force	

Ans.

Sr. No.	Description	Label
a	Direction of weight	B
b	Normal reaction	C
c	Direction of motion	D
d	Frictional force	A

Q.2 Varshney sir was demonstrating an experiment in his class with the setup as shown in the figure below.

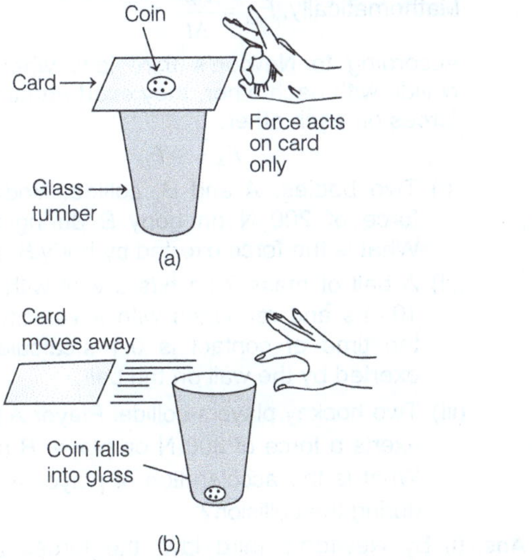

A five-rupee con is set on a stiff card covering an empty glass tumbler standing on a table. He then flicks the card hard with his fingers.

(i) Why does the coin fall into the glass instead of moving with the card? **[1]**

(ii) What will happen it the card is pulled slowly instead of flicked? **[1]**

(iii) If the flicking force is too small, will the coin still fall into the glass? why or why not? **[1]**

(iv) How is this experiment related to Newton's first law of motion? **[1]**

Ans. (i) When the card is flicked hard, the card suddenly comes into motion but it is not able share the motion with the coin due to inertia of rest of the coin & hence the coin stays and fall down due to the gravitational force acting on it.

(ii) If the card is pulled slowly, friction between the coin and the card will acts for a longer duration, causing the coin to move with the card instead of falling into the glass.

(iii) If the flicking force is too small, the card may not move quickly enough to leave the coin behind. In this case, the coin might move with the card due to friction.

(iv) This experiment is a practical application of Newton's first law of motion, which states that an object at rest remains at rest unless acted upon by an external unbalanced force.

Q.3 During a collision, two bodies interact and exert force on each other.

According to Newton's second law, the rate of change in momentum of the body is directly proportional to the force acting on it and the change takes place in the direction of the applied force.

Mathematically, $F_{net} = \frac{\Delta p}{\Delta t}$

According to Newton's third law, when two bodies collide with each other, they exert equal and opposite forces on each other.

$$F_A = -F_B$$

(i) Two bodies, A and B, collide. Body A exerts a force of 200 N on body B during the collision. What is the force exerted by body B on body A? **[1]**

(ii) A ball of mass 2 kg hits a wall with a velocity of 10 m/s and rebounds with a velocity of 8 m/s. If the time of contact is 0.1 s,calculate the force exerted by the wall on the ball. **[1]**

(iii) Two hockey players collide. Player A (mass 60 kg) exerts a force of 300 N on player B (mass 80 kg). What is the acceleration of player A and player B during the collision? **[1]**

Ans. (i) By Newton's third law, the forces are equal in magnitude and opposite in direction.

$$F_B = -F_A = -200 \text{ N}$$

So, body B exerts a force of 200 N (opposite direction).

(ii) Change in momentum,

$$\Delta p = m\,(v_{final} - v_{initial}) = 2\,(8 - (-10)) = 2 \times 18$$
$$= 36 \text{ kg m/s}$$

Force exerted, $F = \frac{\Delta p}{\Delta t} = \frac{36}{0.1} = 360 \text{ N}$

The wall exerts a force of 360 N.

(iii) Force exerted is equal in magnitude but opposite in direction.

For player A, $a_A = \frac{F}{m_A} = \frac{300}{60} = 5 \text{ m/s}^2$

For player B, $a_B = \frac{F}{m_B} = \frac{300}{80} = 3.75 \text{ m/s}^2$

Player A accelerates at 5 m/s^2 and player B accelerates at 3.75 m/s^2.

Q.4 The third law of motion states that when one object exerts a force on another object, The second object instantaneously exerts a force back on the first. The two forces are always equal in magnitude but opposite in direction.

These forces act on different object but never acts on the same object. It is important to note that even though the action and reaction forces are always equal in magnitude, these forces may not produce accelerations of equal magnitudes, this is because each force acts on a different object that may have a different mass. The two opposing forces are also known as action and reaction forces.

(i) A person sitting on a chair pushes a wall with their hands. The chair moves backward. Explain, why this happens. **[1]**

(ii) When a hammer strikes a nail, why does the nail move into the wood instead of hammer moving backward? **[1]**

(iii) Why does a car's exhaust system emit gases while the car moves forward? **[1]**

Ans. (i) According to Newton's third law, when the person pushes the wall, the wall pushes back on the person with an equal and opposite force. Since, the person is sitting on a chair, the reaction force pushes the chair backward, causing it to move.

(ii) The hammer exerts a force on the nail, and the nail exerts an equal and opposite force on the hammer. The hammer has much larger mass as compared to the nail, so the nail accelerates more significantly into the wood while the backward acceleration of hammer is negligible.

(iii) The engine expels exhaust gases backward action and the gases exert an equal and opposite force on the car propelling it forward reaction. The car's movement is a result of this reaction force.

TYPE - 8

Numerical Questions

Q.1 A car of mass 1000 kg is moving with a velocity of 72 km/h. Find its momentum. **[1]**

Ans. Given, mass, $m = 1000$ kg, velocity, $v = 72$ km/h, momentum, $p = ?$

Velocity, $v = 72$ km/h

$$= 72 \times \frac{5}{18} = 20 \text{ m/s} \qquad \left(\because 1\text{km/h} = \frac{5}{18}\text{m/s}\right)$$

Momentum = Mass × Velocity

$\therefore \quad p = m \times v = 1000 \times 20 = 2 \times 10^4$ kg-m/s

Thus, the momentum of the car is 2×10^4 kg-m/s.

Q.2 The mass of a lorry is 4000 kg and the mass of goods loaded on it is 20000 kg. If the lorry is moving with a velocity of 2 m/s, then what will be its momentum? **[2]**

Ans. Given, velocity of lorry, $v = 2$ m/s,

Mass of lorry, $m_1 = 4000$ kg

Mass of goods on the lorry, $m_2 = 20000$ kg,

Momentum, $p = ?$

Total mass in motion = Mass of lorry + Mass of goods

i.e. $m = m_1 + m_2 = 4000 \text{ kg} + 20000 \text{ kg} = 24000 \text{ kg}$

$\therefore$ Momentum = Mass × Velocity

$$p = mv = 24000 \text{ kg} \times 2 \text{ m/s}$$
$$= 4.8 \times 10^4 \text{ kg-m/s}$$

Thus, momentum of the lorry $= 4.8 \times 10^4$ kg-m/s

Q.3 Three blocks *A*, *B* and *C* of masses 4 kg, 2 kg and 1 kg respectively, are in contact on a frictionless surface as shown. **[3]**

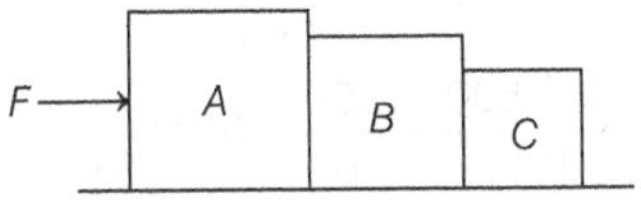

If a force of 14 N is applied on the 4 kg block, then find the contact force between *A* and *B*.

Ans. Given, $m_A = 4$ kg,

$m_B = 2$ kg and

$m_C = 1$ kg

Total mass, $m = m_A + m_B + m_C = 4 + 2 + 1 = 7$ kg

Using newton's second law the acceleration of the system is

$$a = \frac{F}{m_{\text{total}}} = \frac{14}{7} = 2 \text{ m/s}^2$$

The contact force between *A* and *B* is due to the force required to accelerate *B* and *C* together. The combined mass of *B* and *C* is

$$m_{B+C} = m_B + m_C = 2 + 1 = 3 \text{ kg}$$

The force needed to accelerate *B* and *C* is

$$F_{AB} = (m_{B+C}) \cdot a = 3 \times 2 = 6 \text{ N}$$

$\therefore$ The contact force between *A* and *B* is 6 N.

Q.4 A hockey ball of mass 200 g travelling at 10 ms^{-1} is struck by a hockey stick, so as to return it along its original path with a velocity at 5 ms^{-1}. Calculate the change in momentum occurred in the motion of the hockey ball due to the force applied by the hockey stick. **[3]**

Ans. Given, mass of hockey ball, $m = 200\text{g} = 0.2$ kg

Initial velocity, $u = 10 \text{ ms}^{-1}$

Final velocity, $v = -5 \text{ ms}^{-1}$

($\because$ Final velocity of the ball is in the direction opposite to the direction of initial velocity)

Change in momentum of the ball

= Final momentum – Initial momentum

$$= mv - mu = m(v - u) = 0.2(-5 - 10)$$
$$= 0.2 \times (-15) = -3 \text{ kg ms}^{-1}$$

Q.5 If a force of 1000 N is applied over a vehicle of 500 kg, then in how much time the velocity of the vehicle will increase from 2 m/s to 10 m/s? **[2]**

Ans. Given, force, $F = 1000$ N, mass, $m = 500$ kg

Final velocity, $v_2 = 10$ m/s

Initial velocity, $v_1 = 2$ m/s

Time, $t = ?$

From Newton's second law, $F = \dfrac{m(v_2 - v_1)}{t}$

$$\Rightarrow \quad t = \frac{m(v_2 - v_1)}{F} = 500 \times \frac{(10 - 2)}{1000} = 4 \text{ s}$$

Q.6 Two persons manage to push a motorcar of mass 1200 kg at a uniform velocity along a level road. The same motorcar can be pushed by three persons to produce an acceleration of 0.2 ms^{-2}. With what force does each person push the motorcar? (Assume that all persons push the motorcar with the same muscular effort.) **[2]**

Ans. Given, mass of motorcar, $m = 1200$ kg

Acceleration produced, $a = 0.2 \text{ ms}^{-2}$

$\therefore$ Force applied on the car by three persons,

$$F = ma = 1200 \times 0.2$$
$$= 240 \text{ N}$$

Force applied by each person

$$= \frac{F}{3} = \frac{240}{3} = 80 \text{ N}$$

Q.7 A body of mass 0.5 kg is resting on a frictionless surface. When a force of 2000 dyne acts on it for 10 s, then calculate the distance travelled by it in 10 s. **[2]**

Ans. Given, mass, $m = 0.5$ kg

$$F = 2000 \text{ dyne} = 2000 \times 10^{-5} \text{ N}$$
$$= 0.02 \text{ N},$$
$$t = 10 \text{ s}, \quad u = 0$$

$$\therefore \quad F = ma$$
$$0.02 = 0.5 \times a$$
$$\Rightarrow \quad a = \frac{0.02}{0.5} = \frac{2}{50} = \frac{1}{25} \text{ m/s}^2$$

$\therefore$ Distance, $s = ut + \dfrac{1}{2}at^2$

$$= 0 \times 10 + \frac{1}{2} \times \frac{1}{25} \times 10 \times 10$$
$$\Rightarrow \quad s = 2 \text{ m}$$

Q.8 A force of 10 N produces an acceleration of 5 ms^{-2} in mass m_1 and 20 ms^{-2} in mass m_2. What will be the acceleration by this force, if both masses m_1 and m_2 are tied together? **[2]**

Ans. Given, force, $F = 10$ N, $m = m_1, a_1 = 5 \text{ ms}^{-2}, a_2 = 20 \text{ ms}^{-2}$

$$m_1 = \frac{F}{a_1} = \frac{10}{5} = 2 \text{ kg}$$

$$m_2 = \frac{F}{a_2} = \frac{10}{20} = \frac{1}{2} \text{ kg}$$

Therefore, $M = m_1 + m_2$

$$= 2 + \frac{1}{2} = 2.5 \text{ kg}$$

When both m_1 and m_2 are tied together ,

$$a = \frac{F}{M} = \frac{10}{2.5} = 4 \text{ms}^{-2}$$

Q.9 **How much momentum will a dumb-bell of mass 10 kg transfer to the floor, if it falls from a height of 80 cm? Take, its downward acceleration to be 10 ms^{-2}.** **[2]**

Ans. Given, mass of dumb bell, $m = 10$ kg

Initial velocity, $u = 0$ ($\because$ it falls from rest)

Distance covered, $s = 80$ cm $= 0.8$ m

$a = 10 \text{ ms}^{-2}$

From equation of motion, $v^2 = u^2 + 2as$

$$v^2 = 0 + 2 \times 10 \times 0.8 = 16$$

$$v = \sqrt{16} = 4 \text{ ms}^{-1}$$

Momentum of dumb-bell just before it touches the floor, $p = mv = 10 \times 4 = 40$ kg-ms^{-1}

When the dumb-bell touches the floor, its velocity becomes zero and hence the momentum also becomes zero. Thus, the total momentum of the dumb bell is transferred to the floor.

$\therefore$ The momentum transferred to floor is 40 kg ms^{-1}.

Q.10 **A car is moving with a uniform velocity 30 ms^{-1}. It is stopped in 2 s by applying force of 1500 N through its brakes. Calculate**

(i) the retardation produced in car **[1]**

(ii) mass of car **[1]**

(iii) change in momentum of car. **[1]**

Ans. Given, initial velocity, $u = 30 \text{ms}^{-1}$

Final velocity, $v = 0$ (stopped), $t = 2$ s

(i) From first equation of motion, $v = u + at$

$$\Rightarrow \quad 0 = 30 + a \times 2$$

$$a = -15 \text{ms}^{-2}$$

(Negative sign shows retardation)

(ii) As, $F = ma$

$$1500 = m(15)$$

Mass of car, $m = \frac{1500}{15} = 100 \text{kg}$

(iii) Change in momentum of car,

$$\Delta p = p_f - p_i = mv - mu = m(v - u)$$

$$\Delta p = 100\,(0 - 30)$$

$$\Delta p = -3000 \text{ kg ms}^{-1}$$

(Negative sign shows decrease in momentum)

Q.11 **An object of mass 100 kg is accelerated uniformly from a velocity of 5 ms^{-1} to 8 ms^{-1} in 6 s. Calculate the initial and final momentum of the object. Also, find the magnitude of the force exerted on the object.** **[3]**

Ans. Given, mass of an object, $m = 100$ kg , time = 6 s

Initial velocity, $u = 5 \text{ ms}^{-1}$

Final velocity, $v = 8 \text{ ms}^{-1}$

$\therefore$ Initial momentum $= mu = 100 \times 5 = 500$ kg ms^{-1}

and final momentum $= mv = 100 \times 8 = 800$ kg ms^{-1}

Change in momentum $= \Delta p = (800 - 500)$ kg ms^{-1}

$= 300$ kg ms^{-1}

From Newton's second law,

Force exerted on the object

= Rate of change of momentum

$$= \frac{\text{Change in momentum}}{\text{Time}}$$

$$= \frac{\text{Final momentum} - \text{Initial momentum}}{\text{Time}}$$

$$= \frac{800 - 500}{6} = \frac{300}{6} = 50 \text{ N}$$

Q.12 **Two balls A and B of masses $2m$ and $4m$ are in motion with velocities $2v$ and v, respectively. Compare**

(i) their inertia **[1]**

(ii) their momentum **[1]**

(iii) the force needed to stop them in the same time **[1]**

Ans. (i) Mass is the measure of inertia, so

Inertia of A: Inertia of $B = 2\,m : 4\,m$

$\therefore$ Inertia of A : Inertia of $B = 1:2$

(ii) Momentum of A = mass $\times$ velocity

$= 2m \times 2v = 4\,mv$

Momentum of $B = 4m \times v = 4mv$

So, momentum of A: Momentum of $B = 4mv : 4mv$

$\therefore$ Momentum of A: Momentum of $B = 1:1$

(iii) From Newton's second law of motion,

rate of change of momentum is directly proportional to the force applied on it.

Force needed to stop A : Force needed to stop B

$= 1:1$

Q.13 **A bullet train is moving with a velocity of 180 km/h and it takes 5 s to stop after the brakes are applied. Find the force exerted by the brakes on the wheel of train, if its mass with the wagon is 2000 kg.** **[3]**

Ans. Given, initial velocity, $u = 180$ km/h

$$= 180 \times \frac{5}{18} \text{m/s} = 50 \text{ m/s}$$

Final velocity, $v = 0$, time, $t = 5$ s, mass, $m = 2000$kg, force, $F = ?$

From first equation of motion,

$$v = u + at$$

$\Rightarrow \quad u = -at \quad (\because v = 0)$

$\Rightarrow \quad a = \frac{-u}{t} = \frac{-50}{5} = -10\ m/s^2$

Now, force exerted by the brakes on the wheel is given by Newton's second law,

$$F = ma = 2000 \times (-10) = -20000\ N$$
$$= -2 \times 10^4\ N$$

Negative sign shows the direction of force is in opposite to motion of the body.

Q.14 A 500 kg vehicle moving with a speed of 10 m/s is brought to rest at a distance of 50 m.

(i) Find the acceleration and time. [2]

(ii) Calculate unbalanced force acting on it. [2]

Ans. Given, mass, $m = 500$ kg, initial velocity, $u = 10$ m/s, distance, $s = 50$ m, acceleration, $a = ?$ and force, $F = ?$

(i) From third equation of motion, $v^2 = u^2 + 2as$

$\Rightarrow \quad u^2 = -2as \quad (\because v = 0)$

$\Rightarrow \quad a = \frac{-u^2}{2s} = \frac{-100}{2 \times 50} = -1\ m/s^2$

Time taken to stop the vehicle is given by equation of motion.

From first equation of motion,

$$v = u + at$$

$\Rightarrow \quad u = -at \quad (\because v = 0)$

$\Rightarrow \quad t = \frac{u}{-a} = \frac{10}{-(-1)} = 10\ s$

(ii) Now, unbalanced force is given by Newton's second law.

$\therefore \quad F = ma = 500 \times (-1) = -500\ N$

Thus, acceleration, time and unbalanced force are $-1\ m/s^2$, 10 s and -500 N respectively.

Q.15 A force of 5 N gives a mass m_1, an acceleration of $10 m/s^2$ and a mass m_2, an acceleration of $20\ m/s^2$. What acceleration would it give, if both the masses were tied together? [3]

Ans. Given, force, $F = 5$ N

Acceleration in mass m_1, $a_1 = 10\ m/s^2$

Acceleration in mass m_2, $a_2 = 20\ m/s^2$

Acceleration produced when both the masses are tied together, $a = ?$

From Newton's second law of motion,

$$m_1 = \frac{F}{a_1}, m_2 = \frac{F}{a_2}$$

Total mass, $m = m_1 + m_2$

$\therefore \quad m_1 = \frac{5}{10} = 0.5\ kg, \ m_2 = \frac{5}{20} = 0.25\ kg$

$\therefore \quad m = 0.5 + 0.25 = 0.75$ kg

Acceleration produced in combined mass, $a = \frac{F}{m}$

$\therefore \quad a = \frac{5}{0.75} = 6.67\ m/s^2$

Thus, acceleration is $6.67\ m/s^2$ when both the masses were tied together.

Q.16 A truck starts from rest and rolls down a hill with a constant acceleration. It travels a distance of 400 m in 20 s. Find its acceleration. Find the force acting on it, if its mass is 7 tonne. (Take, 1 tonne = 1000 kg) [2]

Ans. The truck starts from rest, so initial velocity, $u = 0$

Distance, $s = 400$ m, Time, $t = 20$ s

Mass, $m = 7$ tonne
$= 7 \times 1000 = 7000$ kg

From second equation of motion,

$$s = ut + \frac{1}{2}at^2$$

$\Rightarrow \quad 400 = 0 \times 20 + \frac{1}{2} \times a \times (20)^2$

$\Rightarrow \quad 400 = 200\ a$

$\Rightarrow \quad a = 2\ ms^{-2}$

From Newton's second law of motion, force acting on the truck,

$$F = ma = 7000 \times 2 = 14000\ N = 1.4 \times 10^4\ N$$

Q.17 A stone of size 1 kg is thrown with a velocity of $20\ ms^{-1}$ across the frozen surface of a lake and comes to rest after travelling a distance of 50 m. What is the force of friction between the stone and the ice? [3]

Ans. Given, mass of stone, $m = 1$ kg

Initial velocity, $u = 20\ ms^{-1}$

Final velocity, $v = 0$ ($\because$ the stone comes to rest)

Distance covered, $s = 50$ m

From third equation of motion,

$$v^2 = u^2 + 2as$$
$$(0)^2 = (20)^2 + 2a\ (50)$$
$$100a = -400$$

$\Rightarrow \quad a = -4\ ms^{-2}$

Here, negative sign shows that there is a retardation in the motion of stone.

Force of friction between stone and ice

= Force required to stop the stone

$= ma = 1 \times 4 = 4$ N

Q.18 A force acts on a body at rest of mass 200 kg for 10 s. When the force stops acting, the body moves through a distance 100 m with a constant velocity in 5 s. Calculate the force. [3]

Ans. When the force is acting, then

initial velocity, $u = 0, m = 200$ kg, $t = 10$s

When force stops

$$s = 100\text{m}, \quad t = 5\text{s}$$

$$v = \frac{s}{t} \Rightarrow v = \frac{100}{5} = 20\,\text{ms}^{-1}$$

v is the final velocity attained by object due to acceleration given by force.

From first equation of motion,

$$v = u + at$$

$$20 = 0 + a \times 10$$

$$\Rightarrow \quad a = 2\,\text{ms}^{-2}$$

$$\therefore \quad F = ma = 200 \times 2 = 400\text{ N}$$

Q.19 A 8000 kg engine pulls a train of 5 wagons, each of 2000 kg, along a horizontal track. If the engine exerts a force of 40000 N and the track offers a friction force of 5000 N, then calculate **[3]**

(i) the net accelerating force

(ii) the acceleration of the train and

(iii) the force of wagon 1 on wagon 2.

Ans. (i) $\because$ Net accelerating force

= Force exerted by engine – Friction force

[here, frictional force is subtracted because it opposes the motion)

$= 40000 - 5000 = 35000$ N

$= 3.5 \times 10^4$ N

(ii) From Newton's second law of motion,

Accelerating force

= Mass of the train × Acceleration of train

$$\Rightarrow \quad a = \frac{F}{m}$$

Mass of train = Mass of engine + Mass of all wagons

$= 8000 + 5 \times 2000 = 8000 + 10000 = 18000$ kg

$$\therefore \quad \text{Acceleration} = \frac{35000}{18000} = \frac{35}{18} = 1.94\,\text{ms}^{-2}$$

(iii) Force of wagon 1 on wagon 2

= Mass of the engine × Acceleration

$= 8000 \times 1.94 = 15520$ N

Q.20 A ball of mass 10 g is moving with a velocity of 60 ms^{-1}. On applying a constant force on ball for 2.0s, it acquires a velocity of 80 ms^{-1}. **[4]**

Calculate

(i) the initial momentum of ball

(ii) the final momentum of ball

(iii) the rate of change of momentum

(iv) the acceleration of ball and

(v) the magnitude of force applied.

Ans. Given, $m = 10\text{ g} = \frac{10}{1000}\text{kg} = 0.01\,\text{kg}$

$u = 60\,\text{ms}^{-1}, \; v = 80\,\text{ms}^{-1}, \; t = 2.0\,\text{s}$

(i) Initial momentum of ball = Mass × Inital velocity

$= mu = 0.01 \times 60$

$= 0.6\,\text{kgms}^{-1}$

(ii) Final momentum of the ball = Mass × Final velocity

$= mv = 0.01 \times 80$

$= 0.8\,\text{kgms}^{-1}$

(iii) Rate of the change of momentum

$$= \frac{\text{Final momentum} - \text{Initial momentum}}{\text{Time interval}}$$

$$= \frac{0.8 - 0.6}{2}$$

$= 0.1\,\text{kg ms}^{-2}$

(iv) Acceleration, $a = \frac{v - u}{t} = \frac{(80 - 60)}{2} = 10\,\text{ms}^{-2}$

(v) Force = Mass × Acceleration

$= ma = 0.01 \times 10 = 0.1\,\text{N}$

Q.21 Johnson takes 10 s to push a heavy box of mass 30 kg from rest to a constant speed of 1.5 ms^{-1} on a rough floor. The frictional force between the box and the floor is 30 N.

(i) What is the acceleration of the box during the 10 seconds? **[1]**

(ii) What is the net force acting on the box to achieve the motion? **[1]**

(iii) How much force did Johnson apply to push the box? **[1]**

Ans. (i) Given,

Initial velocity, $u = 0$ m/s

Final velocity, $v = 1.5$ m/s

Time, $t = 10$ s

Using the equation of motion,

$$v = u + at$$

Substitute the values,

$$1.5 = 0 + a \times 10$$

$$a = \frac{1.5}{10} = 0.15\,\text{m/s}^2$$

Acceleration = $0.15\,\text{m/s}^2$

(ii) From Newton's second law of Motion

$$F = ma$$

$$F = 30 \times 0.15 = 4.5 \text{ N}$$

$\therefore$ Net force = 4.5 N

(ii) The force applied by Johnson must overcome both the frictional force and the net force

$$\therefore \quad F_{applied} = F_{Friction} + F_{net}$$

Given, $F_{Friction} = 30$ N

$$F_{net} = 4.5 \text{ N}$$

$$\therefore \quad F_{applied} = 30 + 4.5 = 34.5 \text{ N}$$

$\therefore$ Applied force = 34.5 N

Q.22 **A bullet of mass 10 g travelling horizontally with a velocity of 150 m/s strikes a stationary wooden block and comes to rest in 0.03 s. Calculate the distance of penetration of the bullet into the block. Also, calculate the magnitude of the force exerted by the wooden block on the bullet.** **[3]**

Ans. Given, mass of bullet,

$$m = 10 \text{ g} = \frac{10}{1000} \text{ kg} = 0.01 \text{ kg}$$

Initial velocity, $u = 150$ m/s

Final velocity, $v = 0$ (since, bullet comes to rest)

Time, $t = 0.03$ s

From Newton's first law of motion, $v = u + at$

$$0 = 150 + a \times 0.03$$

$$\Rightarrow \quad a = \frac{-150}{0.03} = -5000 \text{ m/s}^2$$

Distance covered by the bullet before coming to rest is given by $v^2 = u^2 + 2as$

$$0 = (150)^2 + 2(-5000)\, s$$

$$\Rightarrow \quad s = \frac{(150)^2}{10000} = 2.25 \text{ m}$$

Magnitude of the force applied by the bullet on the block,

$$F = ma = 0.01 \times (-5000) = -50 \text{ N}$$

Q.23 **A bullet of mass 0.04 kg is moving with speed of 90ms^{-1} enters a heavy wooden block and stopped after a distance of 60 cm. What is the average resistance exerted by the block on bullet? How much time is taken by bullet to stop in block?** **[3]**

Ans. Given, mass of bullet, $m = 0.04$ kg

Initial velocity of bullet, $u = 90 \text{ ms}^{-1}$

Distance, $s = 60 \text{cm} = 0.6 \text{m}$, final velocity, $v = 0$,

$$t = ?, F = ?$$

From second equation of motion,

$$v^2 = u^2 + 2as$$

$$0 = 90 \times 90 + 2 \times a \times 0.6$$

$$0 = 8100 + 1.2a$$

$$\Rightarrow \quad a = -\frac{8100}{1.2} \text{ms}^{-2}$$

$$\therefore \quad \text{Retardation} = \frac{8100}{1.2} \text{ms}^{-2}$$

$$\therefore \text{Retarding force, } F = ma = 0.04 \times \frac{8100}{1.2} \text{N} = 270 \text{ N}$$

From first equation of motion, $v = u + at$

$$0 = 90 - \frac{8100}{1.2} \times t$$

$$t = \frac{90}{8100} \times 1.2 = \frac{1.2}{90} = \frac{1}{75} \text{ s}$$

$$t = 0.013 \text{ s}$$

Time taken by bullet to stop in block is 13 ms.

Q.24 **A bullet of mass 50 g moving with an initial velocity 100 ms^{-1}, strikes a wooden block and comes to rest after penetrating a distance of 2 cm in it. Calculate**

(i) initial momentum of bullet **[1]**

(ii) final momentum of bullet **[1]**

(iii) retardation caused by the block and **[1]**

(iv) resistance offered by the wooden block. **[1]**

Ans. Given, mass, $m = 50 \text{ g} = \frac{50}{1000} \text{kg} = 0.05$ kg

Initial velocity, $u = 100 \text{ ms}^{-1}$, final velocity, $v = 0$,

$$s = 2 \text{ cm} = 0.02 \text{ m}$$

(i) $\therefore$ Initial momentum of bullet, $p_i = mu$

$$= 0.05 \times 100 = 5 \text{ kg ms}^{-1}$$

(ii) Final velocity of bullet is zero, $v = 0$

So, final momentum, $p_f = mv = 0.05 \times 0$

$$= 0 \text{ kg ms}^{-1}$$

(iii) From second equation of motion, $v^2 = u^2 + 2as$

$$0 = (100)^2 + 2a \times 0.02$$

$$a = -\frac{100 \times 100}{2 \times 0.02}$$

$$= -2.5 \times 10^5 \text{ ms}^{-2}$$

Negative sign means there is retardation.

$\therefore$ Retardation $= 2.5 \times 10^5 \text{ ms}^{-2}$

(iv) Retarding or resistive force,

$$F = ma = 0.05 \times 2.5 \times 10^5$$

$\therefore$ Resistive force = 12500 N

GRAVITATION

Gravitation

- The force of **attraction** between any **two bodies** in the **universe** is called **force of gravitation.**
- The force with which the earth pulls the objects towards its centre is called the **gravitational force of the earth** or **gravity of the earth.**

Universal Law of Gravitation

- According to this law, the attractive force between any two bodies in the universe is **directly proportional** to the **product of their masses** and **inversely proportional to the square of distance** between their centres.

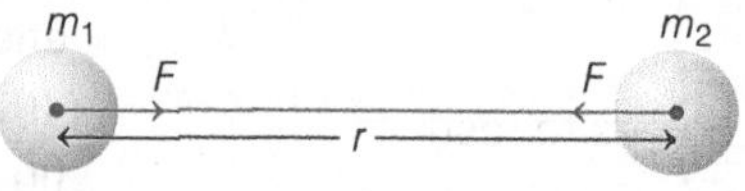

Gravitational force between two spherical bodies

Gravitational force, $\boxed{F = \frac{Gm_1m_2}{r^2}}$

where, F = force of attraction, m_1 and m_2 are the masses of the two bodies

r = distance between the bodies, G = universal gravitational constant = 6.674×10^{-11} Nm^2/kg^2

- If the **masses** of two bodies are **1 kg** each and the **distance** d between them is **1 m**, then

$\boxed{F = G}$ $[\because m_1 = m_2 = 1 \text{ kg and } d = 1 \text{m}]$

Hence, **the universal gravitational constant is defined as the gravitational force between two bodies of unit masses separated by a unit distance from each other and placed anywhere in space.**

- The SI unit of G is N - $m^2 kg^{-2}$.

Importance of Universal Law of Gravitation

- The universal law of gravitation successfully explained several phenomena given as below
  - (i) The force that binds us to the Earth.
  - (ii) The motion of the Moon around the Earth.
  - (iii) The motion of planets around the Sun.
  - (iv) The tides due to the Moon and the Sun.
  - (v) The flow of water in rivers is also due to gravitational force of the Earth on water.
  - (vi) This law is not significant between Ordinary bodies but significant for heavenly bodies.

Free Fall

- When objects **fall** towards the **earth** under the influence of earth's **gravitational force** alone, then these objects are called freely falling objects and such motion is called **free fall**.

Acceleration due to Gravity (*g*)

- Whenever an object **falls** towards the **earth**, an acceleration is involved. This acceleration is due to the **earth's gravitational pull** and is called **acceleration due to gravity**.

Or Acceleration due to gravity can be defined as the **acceleration** produced in the motion of a **freely falling object** due to **gravitational force** of Earth.

It is denoted by g and can be given as $\boxed{g = \frac{GM}{R^2}}$ M = mass of Earth, R = Radius of Earth

- The SI unit of g is the same as that of acceleration, i.e. m/s^2 or Nkg^{-1}.
- **Acceleration due to gravity** does not depend on the mass of a falling object. It depends only on the mass of the earth or **celestial bodies**.
- As **distance** of an object from the centre of the celestial body **increases**, the value of g **decreases**.
- Earth is **flattened at poles**, thus **radius** of the earth is **less at poles** than at **equator**. Hence, the value of ***g* is less at equator** than at **poles**.

Equations of Motion of Object under Gravity

The three general equations of motion can be applied for the motion of bodies under free fall as follows

General equations of motion	Equations of motion of a body under free fall $a = g$	Ascending motion (Upwards) $a = -g$	Descending motion (Downwards) $a = +g$
$v = u + at$	$v = u + gt$	$v = u - gt$	$v = u + gt$
$s = ut + \frac{1}{2}at^2$	$h = ut + \frac{1}{2}gt^2$	$h = ut - \frac{1}{2}gt^2$	$h = ut + \frac{1}{2}gt^2$
$v^2 = u^2 + 2as$	$v^2 = u^2 + 2gh$	$v^2 = u^2 - 2gh$	$v^2 = u^2 + 2gh$

where, u = initial velocity, v = final velocity, h = height traversed, t = time and g = acceleration due to gravity

- At highest point, maximum height, $h_{max} = \frac{u^2}{2g}$
- **Final velocity,** $v = 0$
- **Time to reach at maximum height,** $t = \frac{u}{g}$
- **Flight Time** The time an object remains in the air $t' = 2t\frac{2u}{g}$

Mass

Mass is the **quantity of matter** contained in a body. It is a **scalar quantity** and its SI unit is **kilogram**.

Weight

The weight of an object is the force with which it is attracted towards the earth. It is denoted by w.

Weight of an object, $\boxed{w = mg}$

Weight is a **vector quantity** and SI unit is **netwon**.

where, m = mass and g = acceleration due to gravity.

or $\boxed{w = \frac{GMm}{R^2}}$ $\left[\because g = \frac{GM}{R^2}\right]$

Here, M = mass of the earth and R = radius of the earth.

Important Points Regarding Weight

(i) Weight is a **vector quantity**, it acts in vertically downward direction and its SI unit is **newton** (N). Weight of 1 kg mass is 9.8 N (i.e. 1 kg-wt = 9.8 N).

(ii) Weight of an object is not constant, it changes from place to place.

(iii) In the space, where $g = 0$, weight of an object is zero.

(iv) At the centre of the earth, weight becomes zero. This is due to the fact that on going down to the earth value of g decreases and at the centre of the earth, $g = 0$.

(v) The value of g is constant at a given place. Therefore, at that place, the weight of an object is directly proportional to the mass.

(vi) Spring balance is used to measure the weight of a body and pan balance is used to measure the mass of a body.

(vii) Centre of gravity is a point in an object where the distribution of weight is equal in all directions.

(viii) The state when object does not weigh anything is called **weightlessness**.

(ix) The weight of an object on the moon is one-sixth of its weight on the earth.

Gravitational Units of Force

- The gravitational units of force are **kgf (kilogram force)** and gf **(gram force)** in **MKS system** and **CGS system**, respectively.
- **Kilogram force (kgf)** is the force exerted by one kilogram of mass in the gravitational field of Earth ($g = 9.8\ ms^{-2}$).

$$\begin{aligned} 1\text{kgf} &= \text{Mass} \times \text{Acceleration due to gravity} \\ &= 1\text{kg} \times 9.8\ \text{ms}^{-2} \\ &= 9.8\ \text{kgms}^{-2} \\ &= 9.8\ \text{N} \end{aligned}$$

- **Gram force (gf)** is the force exerted by a mass of 1g in the gravitational field of Earth.

$$\begin{aligned} 1\text{gf} &= 1\text{g} \times 980\ \text{cms}^{-2} \\ &= 980\ \text{g cms}^{-2} \\ &= 9.8\ \text{mN} \end{aligned}$$

$\therefore$ 1 gf = 980 dyne

and 1 kgf = 1000 gf

- kgf and gf are not accepted in SI system of units. It is used in the gravitational unit system, where length, mass and force are the base units.

EXAM ORIENTED QUESTIONS

TYPE - 1 01 Mark

Multiple Choice Questions

Q.1 The force of attraction between two unit point masses separated by a unit distance is called
(a) gravitational potential
(b) acceleration due to gravity
(c) gravitational field strength
(d) universal gravitational constant

Ans. (d) Force of attraction between two masses.

$$F = \frac{Gm_1m_2}{r^2}$$

If $m_1 = m_2 = 1\text{kg}$ and $r = 1\,\text{m}$

Then, $F = G$. Hence, universal gravitational constant is equal to the force of attraction between two unit point masses separated by a unit distance.

Q.2 Which pair of objects will have the strongest force of gravity between them?

(a)
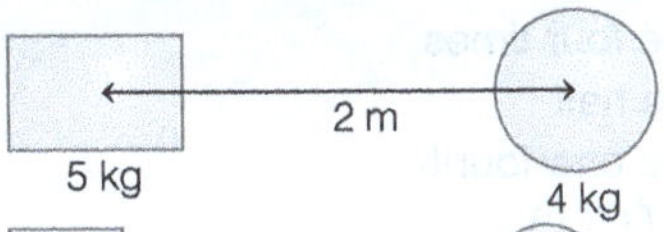

(b)
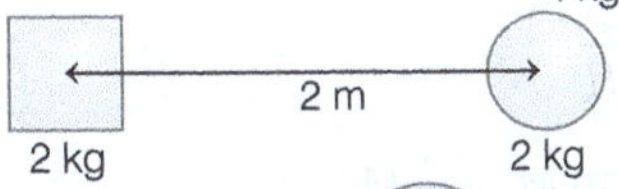

(c)
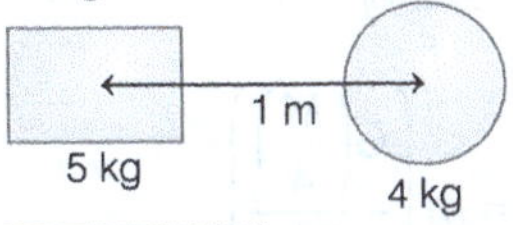

(d)
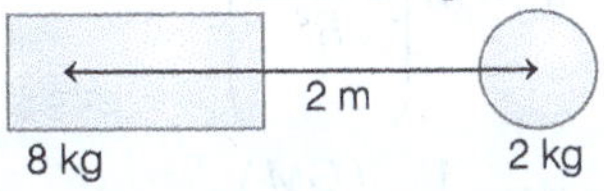

Ans. (c) $F = \frac{Gm_1m_2}{r^2} = \left(\frac{m_1m_2}{r^2}\right)G$

In option (a),

$$F = \left(\frac{5\times 4}{2^2}\right)G = 5G$$

In option (b),

$$F = \left(\frac{2\times 2}{2^2}\right)G = G$$

In option (c),

$$F = \left(\frac{5\times 4}{1^2}\right)G = 20G$$

In option (d),

$$F = \left(\frac{8\times 2}{2^2}\right)G = 4G$$

Therefore, c has the strongest force of gravity between them.

Q.3 Gravitational force between two objects is 10 N. If masses of both objects are doubled without changing distance between them, then the gravitational force would become
(a) 2.5 N (b) 20 N
(c) 40 N (d) 10 N

Ans. (c) Given, $F = 10\,\text{N}$

Now, mass of two objects are doubled, then force of attraction between them is

$$F' = \frac{G(2M)(2m)}{d^2}$$

$$F' = \frac{4GMm}{d^2} = 4\times 10 \qquad \left[\because F = \frac{GMm}{d^2}\right]$$

$$\Rightarrow \quad F' = 40\,\text{N}$$

Q.4 In the given figure, there are two protons.

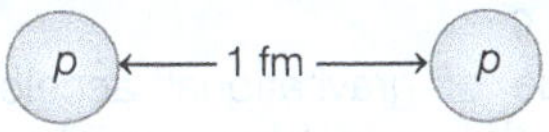

What will be the gravitational force between them? (Take, 1 fm = 10^{-15} m and mass of proton = 1.67×10^{-27} kg)
(a) 1.86×10^{-34} N (b) 5.86×10^{-34} N
(c) 2.8×10^{-34} N (d) 4.86×10^{-34} N

Ans. (a) The gravitational force between two protons is given by

$$F = \frac{GM_pM_p}{d^2}$$

where, $m_p = 1.67\times 10^{-27}$ kg, $d = 10^{-15}$ m

and $G = 6.67\times 10^{-11}\,\text{Nm}^2\,\text{kg}^{-2}$.

$$\therefore \quad F = \frac{6.67\times 10^{-11}\times 1.67\times 10^{-27}\times 1.67\times 10^{-27}}{10^{-15}\times 10^{-15}}$$

$$\Rightarrow \quad F = 1.86\times 10^{-34}\,\text{N}$$

Q.5 The value of acceleration due to gravity
(a) is same at equator and poles
(b) is least at poles
(c) is least at equator
(d) increases from pole to equator

Ans. (c) The value of g is less on equator than that of poles.

Q.6 A car falls off a ledge and drops to the ground in 0.9 s. If the value of g is 10 m/s^2, then speed of car on striking the ground is

(a) 6 m/s (b) 8 m/s
(c) 9 m/s (d) 18 m/s

Ans. (c) Initial velocity, $u = 0$

Acceleration due to gravity, $g = 10 \ m/s^2$

$\because v$ be the speed of car on striking the ground, then

$$v = u + gt = 0 + 10 \times 0.9 = 9 \ m/s$$

Q.7 An object is thrown vertically upwards and rises to a height of 20 m, then the velocity with which the object was thrown upward is [take, $g = 10 \ m/s^2$]

(a) 15 m/s (b) 25 m/s
(c) 10 m/s (d) 20 m/s

Ans. (d) Given, height, $h = 20$ m and $g = 10 \ m/s^2$

At highest point, final velocity, $v = 0$

$\therefore$ From equation, $v^2 = u^2 - 2gh$

$$0 = u^2 - 2 \times 10 \times 20$$

Initial velocity, $u = \sqrt{400} = 20 \ m/s$

Thus, object was thrown upward with velocity 20 m/s.

Q.8 The magnitude of weight of a body at the centre of Earth is

(a) zero
(b) equal to mass of the body
(c) greater than g
(d) less than g

Ans. (a) The value of gravitational acceleration (g) at the centre of Earth is zero, hence weight is

$$w = mg = m \times 0 = 0$$

Q.9 A brick is placed on a newton balance X and then on a beam balance Y.

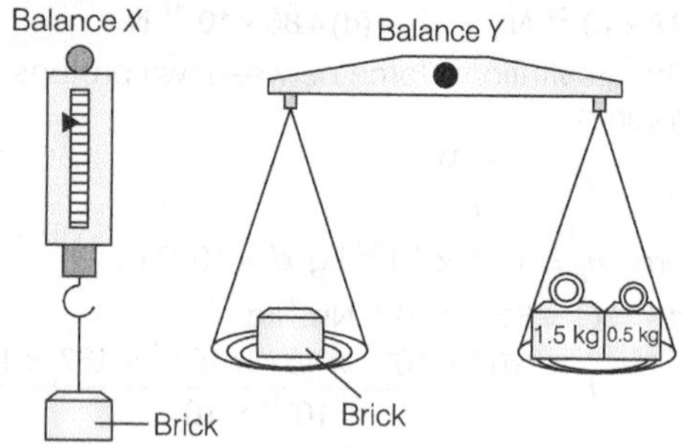

What is measured by each balance?

	Balance X	Balance Y
(a)	Mass	Mass
(b)	Mass	Weight
(c)	Weight	Mass
(d)	Weight	Weight

Ans. (c) X is a spring balance which is used to measure weight and forces whereas Y is a beam balance used for measuring or comparing mass.

Q.10 Four rocks on different planets have masses and weights as shown. Which planet has the greatest gravitational field strength?

	Mass/kg	Weight/N
(a)	2.0	14
(b)	2.5	20
(c)	3.0	21
(d)	3.5	19

Ans. (b) $w = mg \Rightarrow g = \frac{w}{m}$

In option a, $g = \frac{14}{2} = 7$

In option b, $g = \frac{20}{2.5} = 8$

In option c, $g = \frac{21}{3} = 7$

In option d, $g = \frac{19}{3.5} = 5.4$

Therefore, b has the greatest gravitational strength.

Q.11 If the mass of the Earth suddenly becomes $\frac{1}{4^{th}}$ of its original value, but its radius remains the same, how will the weight of an object on its surface change?

(a) It will remain the same
(b) It will become four times
(c) It will become half
(d) It will become one-fourth

Ans. (d) $w = mg = m\left(\frac{GM}{R^2}\right)$

Now, mass of Earth $M' = \frac{1}{4}M$

$$w' = m\left(\frac{G\left(\frac{M}{4}\right)}{R^2}\right)$$

$$w' = \frac{1}{4}m\left(\frac{GM}{R^2}\right)$$

$$w' = \frac{w}{4}$$

Q.12 The weight of any person on Moon is about 1/6th of that on Earth. He can lift a mass of 15 kg on the Earth. What will be the maximum weight which can be lifted by the same force applied by the person on the Moon?

(a) 15 kg (b) 30 kg
(c) 90 kg (d) 2.5 kg

Ans. (c) $\because$ Maximum weight which can be lifted $= mg$

$$= 15 \ kg \times 9.8 \ m/s^2 = 147 \ N$$

$\therefore$ Weight which can be lifted on Moon

$$= 147 \text{ N} \times \frac{1}{\frac{g_E}{6}}$$

($\because$ at Moon, acceleration due to gravity is 1/6th to that of Earth)

$$= \frac{147 \times 6}{9.8} = \frac{147}{1.63} = 90 \text{ kg}$$

TYPE - 2 01 Mark

Assertion-Reason Type Questions

Directions (Q. Nos. 1-6) In the following questions two statements are given as Assertion and Reason.

(a) Both A and R are true and R is the correct explanation of A.
(b) Both A and R are true but R is not the correct explanation of A.
(c) A is true but R is false.
(d) A is false but R is true.

Q.1 Assertion (A) When distance between two bodies is doubled and also mass of each body is doubled, then the gravitational force between them remains the same.

Reason (R) According to Newton's law of gravitation, product of force is directly proportional to the product of mass of bodies and inversely proportional to the square of the distance between them.

Ans. (a) According to Newton's law of gravitation,

$$F = \frac{Gm_1m_2}{r^2}$$

When m_1, m_2 and r are doubled,

$$F' = \frac{G(2m_1)(2m_2)}{(2r)^2}$$

$$= \frac{Gm_1m_2}{r^2}$$

Which is still equal to F.

i.e. Force remains the same.

Q.2 Assertion (R) The force of gravitation acts between any two objects in the universe.

Reason (R) Gravitational force depends on the masses of objects and the distance between them.

Ans. (a) Gravitational force, $F = \frac{Gm_1m_2}{r^2}$ act between any two masses, regardless of their size.

Q.3 Assertion (A) A body falling freely under gravity experiences no change in its acceleration.

Reason (R) The force acting on the body due to gravity is constant throughout its fall near the earth's surface.

Ans. (a) Near the earth's surface, the force due to gravity remains constant, so the acceleration g also remains constant.

Q.4 Assertion (A) Acceleration due to gravity decreases as we move to higher altitudes.

Reason (R) Acceleration due to gravity is inversely proportional to the square of the distance from the centre of the Earth.

Ans. (a) At higher altitudes, the distance from the Earth's centre increases, leading to a decrease in g.

According to $g = \frac{GM}{R^2}$, as the distance R increases, g decreases.

Q.5 Assertion (A) If we drop a stone and a sheet of paper from a balcony, then stone will reach the ground first.

Reason (R) The stone experiences less air resistance than sheet of paper.

Ans. (a) The air resistance not only depends on an object's velocity but also the shape, size and density of an object. Since, stone has higher density and small surface area compared to the sheet of paper. So, the stone will reach the ground first.

Q.6 Assertion (A) A body of mass 5 kg on earth has the same weight on the moon.

Reason (R) The gravitational force on the moon is one-sixth of that on the earth.

Ans. (d) Weight changes on the moon because g is $\frac{1}{6}$th of Earth's g. Mass remains the same but weight reduces.

TYPE - 3 01/02 Marks

Fill in the Blanks

Q.1 ...... [Kepler's second law/Newton's law of gravitation] states that the gravitational force between two objects are directly proportional to the product of their masses and inversely proportional to the square of the distance between their centres. **[1]**

Ans. Netwon's law of gravitation.

Q.2 During free fall, the initial velocity is ...... [zero/maximum] if the object starts from rest and the motion is considered to be uniformly .... [accelerated/decelerated] **[2]**

Ans. zero, accelerated.

Q.3 The motion of a freely falling object is independent of its .... [mass/weight] but depends on the value of .... [mass/g] at that location. **[2]**

Ans. mass, g

Q.4 The acceleration due to gravity on Earth's surface is approximately .... m/s^2. [9.8/10.2] **[1]**

Ans. 9.8

Q.5 The SI unit of force is ....[Newton/1 m/s^2] and it is defined as the force that produces an acceleration of .... [Newton/1 ms^2] in a body of mass 1 kg. **[2]**

Ans. Newton, 1 m/s^2

TYPE - 4   02 Marks

Very Short Answer Type Questions

Q.1 Amit buys few grams of gold at the poles as per the instruction of one of his friends. He hands over the same, when he meets him at equator. Will the friend agree with the weight of gold bought? If not, why?

Ans. No, his friend will not agree with the weight of gold bought because the acceleration due to gravity at poles is greater than that of at equator.

Thus, weight at pole > weight at equator.

Q.2 Why is true free fall not possible on Earth?

Ans. In a true free fall only gravitational force acts on an object. But in reality, the object also experiences air resistance in the direction opposite to its motion. Thus, true free fall is not possible on earth.

Q.3 Why at the centre of Earth, value of g is zero?

Ans. At the centre of Earth, g becomes zero because in all directions forces are equal in magnitude and opposite in direction which cancel each other.

Q.4 It is known to us that acceleration due to gravity on the Earth is six times greater than that of Moon. How does it affect the weight of an object on both the surfaces?

Ans. As, weight = mass × acceleration due to gravity

i.e. $w = mg$

$\therefore$ $w \propto g$ (because m is always constant)

So, weight of an object on Earth is six times greater than that on the Moon.

TYPE - 5   03 Marks

Short Answer Type Questions

Q.1 (i) Two particles are placed at some distance. If the mass of each particle is doubled, keeping the distance between them unchanged, what will be the value of gravitational force between them? **[2]**

(ii) An apple falls from a tree because of gravitational attraction between the Earth and apple. If F_1 is the magnitude of force exerted by the Earth on the apple and F_2 is the magnitude of force exerted by apple on Earth, then find the relation between F_1 and F_2. **[1]**

Ans. (i) Gravitational force, $F_1 = G\dfrac{Mm}{r^2}$

If mass of each particle is doubled, then

$$F_2 = G\frac{(2M)(2m)}{r^2}$$

or $$F_2 = 4G\frac{Mm}{r^2}$$

or $$F_2 = 4F_1 \quad \left(\because F_1 = G\frac{Mm}{r^2}\right)$$

(ii) From third law of motion, to every action, there is an equal and opposite reaction and they act on two different bodies but in opposite direction. So magnitudes of F_1 and F_2 are equal.

$\Rightarrow$ $$F_1 = -F_2$$

Q.2 (i) What are different gravitational units of force? **[2]**

(ii) Write equations of a body falling freely from rest with height h. **[1]**

Ans. (i) In MKS system, the gravitational unit of force is kilogram force (kgf).

One kilogram of force is the force due to gravity on a mass of 1 kg.

i.e. 1kgf = 9.8 N

In CGS system, the gravitational unit of force is gram force (gf).

One gram force is the force due to gravity on mass of 1 g.

1gf = 980 dyne.

(ii) Equations of a body falling freely from rest ($u = 0$) are

(i) $v = gt$

(ii) $h = \dfrac{1}{2}gt^2$

(iii) $v^2 = 2gh$

where, v = final velocity,

h = height,

g = acceleration due to gravity

and t = time

Q.3 How does the acceleration due to gravity differ from universal gravitational constant?

Ans. Acceleration due to gravity g can be defined as the acceleration produced in the motion of a freely falling object due to gravitational force of Earth.

Whereas, universal gravitational constant G is defined as the gravitational force between two objects of unit mass each separated by a unit distance from each other placed anywhere in space.

The universal gravitational constant and acceleration due to gravity are related as

$$g = \frac{GM}{R^2}$$

where, M is the mass of Earth and R is the radius of Earth.

Q.4 **(i) What is acceleration due to gravity? How is it related to the weight of an object? [1]**

(ii) Write the value and unit of acceleration due to gravity. [2]

Ans. (i) The rate at which the velocity of a freely falling body increases, is called the acceleration due to gravity. In other words, it is the acceleration produced in a freely falling body due to the gravitational force of attraction of the Earth.

It is related with weight as $w = mg$.

(ii) According to Newton's law of gravitation,

$$F = \frac{GMm}{r^2} \quad \ldots\text{(i)}$$

According to Newton's second law of motion,

$$F = ma \quad \ldots\text{(ii)}$$

From Eqs. (i) and (ii), we get

$$\frac{GMm}{r^2} = ma \Rightarrow a = \frac{GM}{r^2}$$

Here, $a = g = \frac{GM}{r^2}$

The value of acceleration due to gravity g is 9.8 and its unit is m/s^2.

Q.5 **Prove that, if a body is thrown vertically upwards, then the time of ascent is equal to the time of descent.**

Ans. For the upward motion, equation of motion will be (final velocity, $v = 0$)

$$v = u - gt_1 \Rightarrow 0 = u - gt$$

$$t_1 = \frac{u}{g} \quad \ldots\text{(i)}$$

and the downward motion,

$$v = u + gt_2$$

$$v = 0 + gt_2$$

The body falls back to the earth with the same speed as it was thrown vertically upwards.

$\because \quad v = u$

$\therefore \quad u = 0 + gt_2 \Rightarrow t_2 = \frac{u}{g} \quad \ldots\text{(ii)}$

From Eqs. (i) and (ii), we get

$$t_1 = t_2$$

$\Rightarrow$ Time of ascent = Time of descent

Q.6 **Differentiate between mass and weight.**

Ans.

Mass	Weight
It is a measure of the quantity of matter contained in the body at rest.	It is the force with which the Earth attracts to a body towards its centre.
It is a scalar quantity.	It is a vector quantity.
Its SI unit is kg.	Its SI unit is newton (N).
It is measured by a physical (or beam) balance.	It is measured by a spring balance which is calibrated to read in newton.
It is constant for a body and does not change with the change in place.	It is not constant for a body, but varies from place to place due to change in the value of g.

Q.7 **(i) According to universal law of gravitation, every object in this universe attracts every other object. Explain, why then a table and a chair lying in the same room do not collide with each other? [2]**

(ii) If the moon attracts the earth, then why does the earth not move towards the moon? [1]

Ans. (i) The magnitude of the gravitational force is significant only between massive bodies comparable to the Earth or other celestial bodies. Since, both the table and the chair have negligible mass compared to the Earth or celestial body, the gravitational force between the chair and the table is negligible and hence they don't collide.

(ii) The Earth and moon experience equal gravitational force towards each other. However, the mass of the Earth is much larger than that of the moon. Hence, the Earth's acceleration is less than that of the moon. Therefore, the Earth does not move towards the moon.

TYPE - 6 — 04 Marks

Long Answer Type Questions

Q.1 **(i) Will a sheet of paper fall slower than one that is crumpled into a ball in vacuum? Why? [1]**

(ii) Show mathematically that acceleration experienced by an object is independent of its mass. [2]

(iii) Show that value of $g = 9.8\ m/s^2$ (Take, $G = 6.7 \times 10^{-11} N\text{-}m^2/kg^2$, $M = 6 \times 10^{24}$ kg, $R = 6.4 \times 10^6$ m) [1]

Ans. (i) Both of them will fall at the same speed because acceleration produced in freely falling bodies is the same for all bodies, irrespective of their shapes or masses.

(ii) Consider a the body of mass m on the surface of the Earth, M be mass of the Earth, R be the distance between the body and centre of the Earth (radius of the Earth) and g is the acceleration due to gravity.

Let F be the force acting on the body.

According to Newton's second law of motion,

$$F = mg \quad ...(i)$$

According to Newton's law of gravitation,

$$F = G\frac{M \times m}{R^2} \quad ...(ii)$$

From Eqs. (i) and (ii), we get

$$mg = G\frac{M \times m}{R^2}$$

$\therefore g = \frac{GM}{R^2}$, thus g is independent of the mass of the body.

(iii) $\therefore g = \frac{GM}{R^2} = \frac{6.7 \times 10^{-11} \text{N - m}^2 \text{ kg}^{-2} \times 6 \times 10^{24} \text{kg}}{(6.4 \times 10^6 \text{m})^2}$

$$= \frac{6.7 \times 6}{6.4 \times 6.4} \times \frac{10^{-11+24}}{10^{12}} = 9.81 \times \text{N/kg or } 9.81 \text{ m/s}^2$$

$$= 9.81 \text{ m/s}^2 \approx 9.8 \text{ m/s}^2$$

Thus, the value of $g = 9.8 \text{ m/s}^2$.

Q.2 **A ball is thrown with a velocity *u* m/s. Show that under the free fall, it will fall on the ground with the same velocity.**

Ans. When the ball is thrown upwards, it will reach certain height h and starts falling. At maximum height h, the final velocity will be $v = 0$.

Maximum height reached by the ball, (acceleration $= -g$).

Using equation, $v^2 - u^2 = 2gh$

$$\Rightarrow \quad 0 - u^2 = -2gh$$

$$\Rightarrow \quad h = \frac{u^2}{2g} \quad ...(i)$$

In second case, when the ball starts to fall, the initial velocity $u = 0$. It will accelerate due to gravity i.e., $a = g$ and reach ground with velocity (say v_2).

Using, equation,

$$v_2^2 - u^2 = 2gh, \ v_2^2 - 0 = 2gh$$

$$\Rightarrow \quad v_2^2 = 2g\frac{u^2}{2g} \quad \left[\because h = \frac{u^2}{2g} \text{ from Eq. (i)}\right]$$

$$= u^2 \Rightarrow v_2 = u$$

$\therefore$ The ball reaches on the ground with the same velocity.

Q.3 The Earth and the Moon may be considered to be spheres that are solated in space with their masses concentrated at their centres. The masses of the Earth and the Moon are 6.00×10^{24} kg and 7.40×10^{22} kg respectively.

The radius of the Earth is R_E and the separation of the centres of the Earth and the Moon is $60R_E$ as illustrated in Figure.

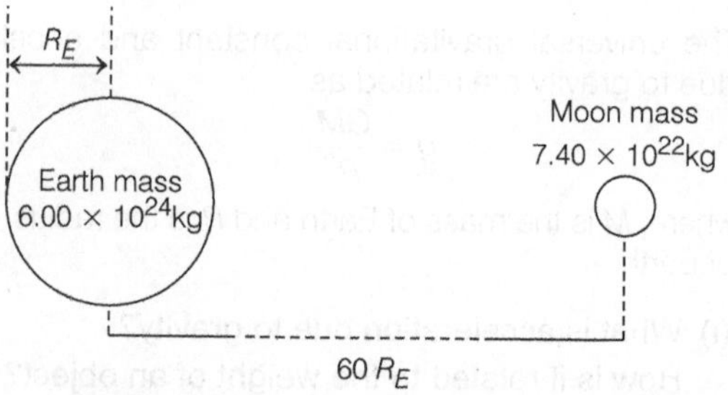

(i) Explain why there is a point between the Earth and the Moon at which the gravitational field strength is zero. **[2]**

(ii) Determine the distance, in terms of R_E, from the centre of the Earth at which the gravitational field strength is zero. **[2]**

Ans. (i) Since, gravitational fields of Earth and Moon are equal in magnitude and opposite in direction. So, resultant field is zero at a point in between them.

(ii) Let the distance from centre of Earth where the Gravitational field strength is zero be x.

$$g_E = g_M$$

$$\frac{GM_E}{x^2} = \frac{GM_M}{(60R_E - x)^2}$$

$$\left(\frac{x}{60R_E - x}\right)^2 = \frac{M_E}{M_M}$$

$$\frac{x}{60R_E - x} = \left(\frac{6.00 \times 10^{24}}{7.40 \times 10^{22}}\right)^{\frac{1}{2}}$$

$$\frac{x}{60R_E - x} = (81.0)^{\frac{1}{2}}$$

$$540R_E = 10x$$

$$\Rightarrow \quad x = 54$$

$\therefore$ Distance $= 54R_E$

TYPE - 7

03/04 Marks

Case Based Questions

Q.1 The gravitation is defined as the force of attraction between any two bodies in the universe. The earth attracts all objects lying on or near its surface towards its centre. The force with which the earth pulls the objects towards its centre is called gravitational force of the earth or gravity of the earth. Gravitation theory was first stated by Galileo Galilei in the late 16th and early 17th century and he gave the way to Issac Newton in 1687 to discover the Newton's theory of gravity, or the inverse-square law of gravitation. We can define gravitational force as a force that attracts any two objects with mass. We say it is attractive because it always tries to pull the masses together, it never push them apart.

(i) A body of mass 50 kg weighs 220 N on mars. **[1]** What is the acceleration due to gravity on mars?

(ii) Is value of g same at different places on earth? Give reason for your answer. **[1]**

(iii) Why G is called gravitation constant? **[1]**

(iv) How the gravitation is different from gravity of earth? **[1]**

Ans. (i) Given, Mass = 50 kg, weight = 220 N

So, acceleration due to gravity $= \frac{220}{50} = 4.4 \text{ m/s}^2$

(ii) No, the value of g is maximum at the poles and minimum at equator. The variation is occurs because of the oblong shape of the earth and rotation about its own axis.

(iii) The constant G is universal because it is independent of the nature and size of bodies.

(iv) Gravitation is the force of attraction between any two bodies, while gravity refers to the attraction between anybody and the earth.

Q.2 A scientist conducts an experiment by dropping a metallic ball from the top of a 100 m height cliff. In a second experiment, another ball is thrown downward with an initial velocity of 15 m/s. The acceleration due to gravity is $g = 10 \text{ m/s}^2$

(i) For the first experiment, how much time does it take for the ball to reach the ground? **[1]**

(ii) What is the velocity of the ball just before it hits the ground? **[1]**

(iii) At what height is the ball after 2s? **[1]**

Ans. (i) Given, initial velocity $u = 0$ m/s,

height, $s = 100$ m and acceleration (g) $= 10 \text{ m/s}^2$

Using the equation of motion, $s = \frac{1}{2}gt^2$

On substituting the values, we get

$$100 = \frac{1}{2} \times 10 \times t^2$$

$$t^2 = 20 \Rightarrow t = \sqrt{20} = 4.47 \text{ s}$$

(ii) Final velocity, $v = gt$

$$v = 10 \times 4.47 = 44.7 \text{ m/s}$$

(iii) Using equation of motion, $s = \frac{1}{2}gt^2$

$\therefore$ Substitutes the values,

$$s = \frac{1}{2} \times 10 \times (2)^2 \Rightarrow s = 5 \times 4$$

$$\therefore \quad s = 20 \text{ m}$$

Height from the ground,

$$h = 100 - 20 = 80$$

The ball is at a height of 80 m after 2s.

Q.3 A person throw a ball upwards from the top of a cliff. After reaching at a certain point, ball start falling downward towards the ground as shown in figure.

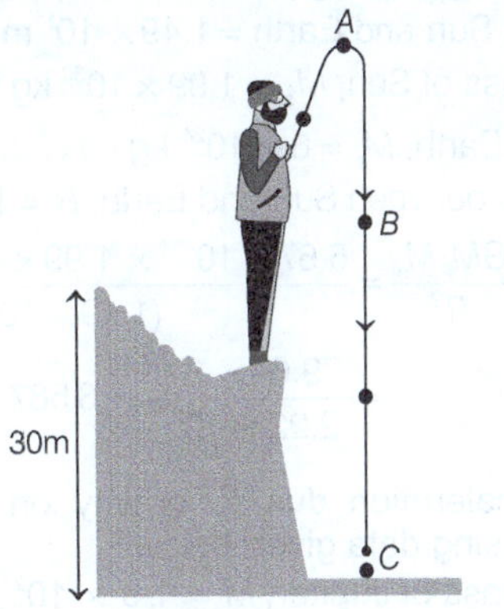

(i) Name the phenomenon involved in this ? **[1]**

(ii) At what point the velocity of the ball is zero. **[1]**

(iii) Calculate the time taken by the ball to reach the ground. **[1]**

(Given, distance $AB = 15$ m and $g = 10 \text{ m/s}^2$)

Ans. (i) Gravitation

(ii) At point A.

(iii) Using the equation of motion,

$$h = \frac{1}{2}gt^2$$

$$\text{or} \quad (BC + AB) = \frac{1}{2}gt^2$$

$$30 + 15 = \frac{1}{2} \times 10 \times t^2$$

$$t^2 = 9$$

$$\Rightarrow \quad t = 3 \text{ s}$$

TYPE - 8

Numerical Questions

Q.1 Find the gravitational force of attraction between Moon and a body of unit mass on the surface of Moon. **[2]**

(Take, mass of the Moon $= 7.4 \times 10^{22}$ kg,

radius of the Moon $= 1.74 \times 10^6$ m,

$G = 6.67 \times 10^{-11} \text{ N-m}^2/\text{kg}^2$)

Sol. Given, mass of the body, $m = 1$ kg

Mass of the Moon, $M = 7.4 \times 10^{22}$ kg

Radius of the Moon, $R = 1.74 \times 10^6$ m

$$\therefore \quad F = \frac{GMm}{R^2}$$

$$= \frac{6.67 \times 10^{-11} \times 7.4 \times 10^{22} \times 1}{(1.74 \times 10^6)^2} = 1.63 \text{ N}$$

Q.2 What is the gravitational force between Sun and Earth? (Take, mass of Sun = 1.99×10^{30} kg, mass of Earth = 6×10^{24} kg, $G = 6.67 \times 10^{-11}$ N-m^2/kg^2 and distance between Sun and Earth = 1.49×10^{11}m) **[2]**

Sol. Given, mass of Sun, $M_s = 1.99 \times 10^{30}$ kg

Mass of Earth, $M_e = 6 \times 10^{24}$ kg

Distance between Sun and Earth, $R = 1.49 \times 10^{11}$ m

$$\therefore \quad F = \frac{GM_s M_e}{R^2} = \frac{6.67 \times 10^{-11} \times 1.99 \times 10^{30} \times 6 \times 10^{24}}{(1.49 \times 10^{11})^2}$$

$$= \frac{79.64 \times 10^{43}}{2.22 \times 10^{22}} = 3.587 \times 10^{22} \text{ N}$$

Q.3 Find acceleration due to gravity on the surface of Jupiter using data given below.
(Take, mass of Jupiter, $M = 1.9 \times 10^{27}$ kg and radius of Jupiter, $R = 7.0 \times 10^7$m) **[2]**

Sol. Given, mass of Jupiter, $M = 1.9 \times 10^{27}$ kg

Radius of Jupiter, $R = 7.0 \times 10^7$m

Using formula of acceleration due to gravity,

$$g = \frac{GM}{R^2}$$

where, $G = 6.67 \times 10^{-11}$ N - m^2 kg^{-2}

$$= \frac{6.67 \times 10^{-11} \times 1.9 \times 10^{27}}{(7 \times 10^7)^2} = \frac{12.673 \times 10^{16}}{49 \times 10^{14}}$$

$$= 0.2586 \times 10^2 = 25.86 \text{ ms}^{-2}$$

Acceleration due to gravity on Jupiter is 25.86 ms^{-2}.

Q.4 A body weighs 25 kg on the surface of the Earth. If the mass of the Earth is 6×10^{24} kg, the radius of the Earth is 6.4×10^6 m and the gravitational constant is 6.7×10^{-11} N - m^{2}kg^{-2}. Calculate

(i) the acceleration produced in the body. **[1]**

(ii) the acceleration produced in the Earth. **[1]**

Sol. Given, $M_e = 6 \times 10^{24}$ kg, $m = 25$ kg

$R_e = 6.4 \times 10^6$ m and

$G = 6.7 \times 10^{-11}$N - m^2 / kg^2

$\therefore$ Gravitational force,

$$F = G \frac{M_e}{R_e^2} m$$

$$= \frac{6.7 \times 10^{-11} \times 6 \times 10^{24} \times 25}{(6.4 \times 10^6)^2}$$

$= 245.36$ N

(i) $\therefore$ Acceleration produced in the body,

$$a = \frac{F}{m} = \frac{245.36}{26}$$

$= 9.81$ m/s^2

(ii) $\therefore$ Acceleration produced in the Earth,

$$a = \frac{F}{M_e} = \frac{245.36}{6 \times 10^{24}}$$

$= 4.09 \times 10^{-23}$ m/s^2

Q.5 A ball is thrown up with a speed of 0.6 m/s.

(i) How high will it go before it begins to fall? **[1]**

(ii) How long will it take to reach that height? **[1]**

Sol. Initial speed, $u = 0.6$ m/s

Acceleration, $g = -9.8$ m/s^2

Final speed, $v = 0$

(i) We know, $v^2 - u^2 = 2gh$

$$0 - (0.6)^2 = 2 \times (-9.8) \times h$$

$$-0.36 = -19.6h$$

$$h = \frac{0.36}{19.6} = 0.0183 \text{ m}$$

(ii) Putting the values in the formula,

$$v = u + gt$$

$$0 = 0.6 - 9.8t \Rightarrow t = \frac{0.6}{9.8} = 0.06 \text{ s}$$

Q.6 An object is thrown vertically upwards to a height of 12 m. Calculate its

(i) velocity with which it was thrown upwards. **[1]**

(ii) time taken by the object to reach a height of 12m. **[1]**

Sol. Given, $h = 12$ m, $v = 0$, $g = -9.8 \text{m/s}^2$, $u = ?$, $t = ?$

(i) $\therefore \quad v^2 - u^2 = 2gh \Rightarrow 0 - u^2 = 2 \times (-9.8) \times 12$

$\Rightarrow \quad u = 15.33$ m/s

(ii) $\therefore \quad v = u + gt$

$$\Rightarrow \quad t = \frac{u}{g} = \frac{15.33}{9.8} = 1.56 \text{s}$$

Q.7 To find the height of a bridge over a river, when a stone is dropped freely in the river from the bridge. The stone takes 2 s to touch the water surface in the river. Calculate the height of the bridge from the water level. (Take, $g = 9.8$ m/s^2) **[2]**

Sol. Given, initial velocity of the stone, $u = 0$

Time taken, $t = 2$ s

Acceleration due to gravity, $g = 9.8$ m/s^2

Height of the bridge, $h = ?$

Using equation, $h = ut + \frac{1}{2}gt^2$

$$= 0 \times 2 + \frac{1}{2} 9.8 \, (2)^2 = \frac{1}{2} \times 9.8 \times 4 = 19.6 \text{ m}$$

Thus, the height of bridge above the water level is 19.6 m.

Q.8 A ball is thrown vertically upwards from the top of a building with an initial velocity of 20 m/s. The ball reaches the ground after 5 s. Calculate

(i) The height of the building. **[2]**

(ii) The velocity of the ball on reaching the ground. Take, $g = 10$ m/ s^2. **[1]**

Sol. Height of the building = H

Height covered from the top of the building upto the maximum height = h

Total height from the highest point to the ground

$= H + h$

Initial velocity, $u = 20$ m/s

Final velocity $v = 0$ (at highest point)

Applying third equation of motion,

$$v^2 = u^2 - 2gh$$

$$0 = 20^2 - 2 \times 10 \times h$$

$$h = 20 \text{ m}$$

Time taken by the ball to reach the highest point.

Applying the first equation of motion,

$$v = u - gt_1 \Rightarrow 0 = 20 - 10 \times t_1$$

$$t_1 = 2\text{s}$$

The entire motion is covered in 5 s.

So, the time taken to reach the ground from the highest point = 5 – 2 = 3 s

(i) Now, find the height of the building

Applying the second equation of motion

$$H + h = ut + \frac{1}{2}gt^2$$

$$H + 20 = 0 \times 3 + \frac{1}{2} \times 10 \times 3^2$$

$$H = 45 - 20$$

$$H = 25 \text{ m}$$

(ii) The velocity of ball on reaching the ground.

Applying the first equation of motion,

$$v = u + gt$$

$$v = 0 + 10 \times 3$$

$$v = 30 \text{ m/s}$$

Q.9 You are on the roof of the physics building, 46.0 m above the ground. Your physics professor, who is 1.80 m tall, is walking alongside the building at a constant speed of 1.20 m/s. If you wish to drop an egg on your professor's head, how far from the building should the professor be when you release the egg? Assume that the egg is in free fall. [2]

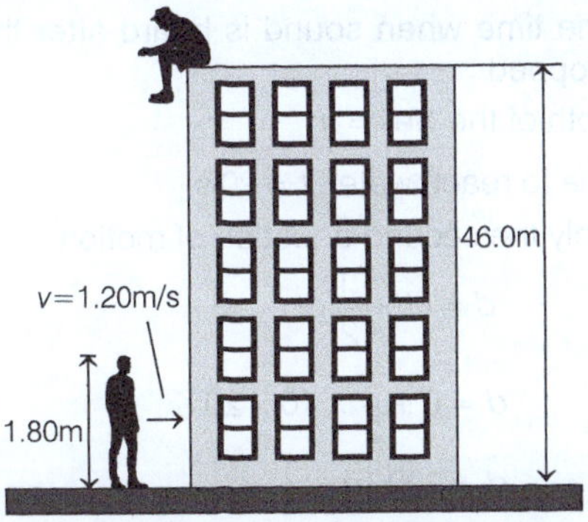

Sol. Height of the building, $H = 46$ m

Height of the physics professor, $h = 1.80$ m

So, egg has to cover a distance, $d = H - h$ by the time t to flush on his head.

Using the equation of motion,

$$d = ut + \frac{1}{2}gt^2$$

$$H - h = ut + \frac{1}{2}gt^2$$

$$46 - 1.80 = 0 + \frac{1}{2} \times 9.8 \times t^2$$

$$t^2 = 9$$

$$t = 3 \text{ s}$$

Since, professor is moving with

$$v = 1.20 \text{ m/s}$$

So, distance of professor from the building,

$$x = vt$$

$$x = 1.2 \times 3$$

$$x = 3.6 \text{ m}$$

Q.10 A stone is thrown vertically upward with an initial velocity of 40 m/s. Taking $g = 10$ m/s², find the maximum height reached by the stone. What is the net displacement and the total distance covered by the stone? [2]

Sol. Given, initial velocity, $u = 40$ m/s

Final velocity becomes zero, i.e. $v = 0$

(at maximum height)

From third equation of upward motion,

$$v^2 = u^2 - 2gh$$

$$(0)^2 = (40)^2 - 2 \times 10 \times h \Rightarrow 0 = 1600 - 20h$$

$$\Rightarrow \quad h = \frac{1600}{20} = 80 \text{ m}$$

∴ Maximum height reached by the stone = 80 m.

After reaching the maximum height, the stone will fall towards the Earth and will reach the Earth's surface covering the same distance.

So, distance covered by the stone = 80 + 80 = 160 m.

Because the stone starts from the Earth's surface and finally reaches the Earth's surface again, i.e. the initial and final positions of the stone are same.

So, displacement of the stone = 0.

Q.11 A firecracker is fired and it rises to a height of 1000 m. Find the

(i) velocity by which it was released. [1]

(ii) time taken by it to reach the highest point. (take, $g = 9.8$ m/s²) [1]

Sol. Given, height, $h = 1000$ m

Final velocity, $v = 0$

Acceleration due to gravity, $g = 9.8$ m/s²

(i) From the third equation of motion,

$$v^2 = u^2 + 2gh$$

$$\Rightarrow \quad 0 = u^2 - 2 \times 9.8 \times 1000$$

$$u = \sqrt{2 \times 9.8 \times 1000} = \sqrt{19600} = 140 \text{ m/s}$$

Velocity by which firecracker is released = 140 m/s

(ii) From the first equation of motion,

$$v = u + gt$$

$$\Rightarrow \quad 0 = 140 - 9.8t \Rightarrow t = \frac{140}{9.8} = 14.28 \text{ s}$$

Time taken, $t = 14.28$ s

Q.12 **A car falls off a ledge and drops to the ground in 0.5 s. Find**

(i) the speed on striking the ground, **[1]**

(ii) its average speed during 0.5 s and **[1]**

(iii) height of ledge from the ground.
(Take, $g = 10 \text{ m/s}^2$) **[1]**

Sol. Given, initial velocity, $u = 0$, time taken, $t = 0.5$ s, acceleration due to gravity, $g = 10 \text{ m/s}^2$

(i) $\because v = u + gt = 0 + 10 \times 0.5 = 5$ m/s

(ii) $\because v_{av} = \frac{u+v}{2} = \frac{0+5}{2} = 2.5$ m/s

(iii) $\because h = ut + \frac{1}{2}gt^2 = 0 + \frac{1}{2} \times 10 \times (0.5)^2 = 1.25$ m

Q.13 **A ball is thrown vertically upwards from the top of a building of height 25 m with an initial velocity 15 ms^{-1}. Taking $g = 9.8 \text{ ms}^{-2}$, calculate**

(a) the height to which it will rise before returning to the ground. **[1]**

(b) the velocity with which it will strike the ground. **[1]**

(c) the total time of journey. **[1]**

Sol. Given, $u = 15 \text{ ms}^{-1}$ (upwards)

Height of building, $h = 25$ m

(a) At the highest point, $v = 0$

For upward journey, from relation

$$v^2 = u^2 - 2gh \Rightarrow 0 = u^2 - 2gh$$

or $$h = \frac{u^2}{2g} = \frac{(15)^2}{2 \times 9.8} = \frac{225}{19.6} = 11.47 \text{ m}$$

(b) While returning from the highest point $u = 0$, total height travelled = 11.47 + 25 = 36.47 m

Let v be the velocity with which it strikes the ground. Then from relation,

$$v^2 = u^2 + 2gh \Rightarrow v^2 = 0 + 2 \times 9.8 \times 36.47$$

$$v^2 = 715 \Rightarrow v = 26.73 \text{ ms}^{-1}$$

(c) If the ball takes time t_1 to go to the highest point from the top of the building, then for upward journey, from relation

$$v = u - gt_1$$

$$0 = 11.47 - 9.8t_1 \Rightarrow t_1 = \frac{11.47}{9.8} = 1.17 \text{ s}$$

Now, for the downward journey from the highest point, if the ball takes time t_2 to reach the ground, then $u = 0$, $v = 26.73 \text{ ms}^{-1}$

From relation $v = u + gt_2$

$$\Rightarrow \quad t_2 = \frac{26.73}{9.8} = 2.72 \text{ s}$$

Hence, total time of journey, $t = t_1 + t_2$
$= 1.17 + 2.72 = 3.89$ s

Q.14 **From a cliff of 49 m high, a man drops a stone. One second later, he throws another stone. They both hit the ground at the same time. Find out the speed with which he threw the second stone.** **[3]**

Sol. For the first stone, $u = 0 \text{ ms}^{-1}$ and $h = 49$ m

As we know that, $h = ut + \frac{1}{2}gt^2$

$$\therefore \quad 49 = 0 \times t + \frac{1}{2} \times 9.8 \times t^2$$

$$\Rightarrow \quad t^2 = \frac{98}{9.8} = 10 \Rightarrow t^2 = \sqrt{10} = 3.16 \text{ s}$$

Thus, first stone would take 3.16 s to reach the ground. The time taken by second stone to reach the ground is one second less than that taken by the first stone as both the stones reach the ground at the same time.

i.e., for the second stone, $t = (3.16 - 1)\text{ s} = 2.16$ s

For the second stone,

$g = 9.8 \text{ ms}^{-2}$, $h = 49$ m, $t = 2.16$ s and $u = ?$

$$\therefore \quad s = ut + \frac{1}{2}gt^2$$

$$\Rightarrow \quad 49 = u \times 2.16 + \frac{1}{2} \times 9.8\,(2.16)^2$$

$$\Rightarrow \quad 49 - 22.86 = 2.16u \quad \text{or} \quad 26.14 = 2.16u$$

$$u = \frac{26.14}{2.16} = 12.1 \text{ ms}^{-1}$$

Thus, the second stone was thrown downward with a speed of 12.1 ms^{-1}.

Q.15 **A pebble is dropped freely in a well from its top. It takes 20 s for the pebble to reach the water surface in the well. Taking, $g = 10 \text{ m/s}^2$ and speed of sound = 330 ms^{-1}. Calculate**

(i) The depth of water surface and **[1]**

(ii) The time when sound is heard after the pebble is dropped **[1]**

Sol. (i) Depth of the well = d

Time to reach water, $t = 20$ s

Apply the second equation of motion,

$$d = ut + \frac{1}{2}gt^2$$

$$d = 0 + \frac{1}{2} \times 10 \times 20^2$$

$$d = 2000 \text{ m}$$

(ii) Time taken for the sound to be heard by the observer.

$$\text{Time } (t') = \frac{\text{Distance}}{\text{Speed}}$$

$$t' = \frac{2000}{330} = 6.06 \text{ s}$$

Total time after which sound will be heard,

$$T = t + t' = 20 + 6.06 = 26.06 \text{ s}$$

Q.16 **A stone is allowed to fall from the top of a tower 100 m high and at the same time, another stone is projected vertically upwards from the ground with a velocity of 25 m/s. Calculate when and where the two stones will meet.** **[4]**

Sol. Let after time t both stones meet and s be the distance travelled by the stone dropped from the top of a tower at which the stones will meet.

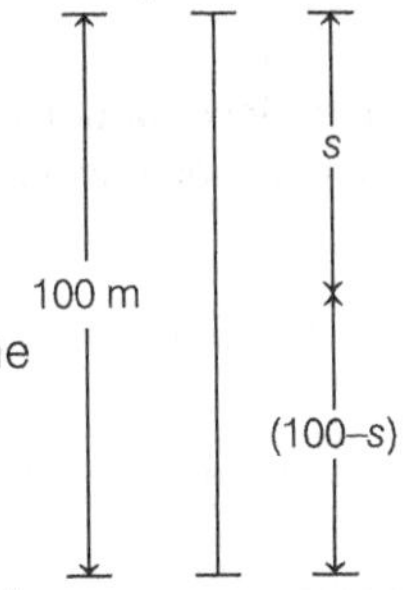

Distance travelled by the stone dropped = s

$\therefore$ Distance travelled by the stone projected upwards = $(100 - s)$ m

For the stone dropped from the tower,

$$s = ut + \frac{1}{2}gt^2 = 0 + \frac{1}{2}(10)t^2$$

[$u = 0$ because stone is dropped, i.e. it starts from rest]

$$s = 5t^2 \qquad \ldots \text{(i)}$$

For the stone projected upwards,

$$s' = ut - \frac{1}{2}gt^2$$

[due to upward motion, negative sign is taken]

$$(100 - s) = 25t - \frac{1}{2} \times 10t^2 \Rightarrow 100 - s = 25t - 5t^2$$

Substituting value of s from Eq. (i), we get

$$100 - 5t^2 = 25t - 5t^2$$

$$25t = 100 \Rightarrow t = 4 \text{ s}$$

So, the stones will meet after 4 s.

$$s = 5t^2 = 5 \times (4)^2 = 80 \text{ m}$$

So, the stones will be at a distance of 80 m from the top of tower or 20 m (100 m – 80 m) from the base of the tower.

Q.17 **How much would a 70 kg man weight on the Moon? What would be his mass on the Earth and on the Moon? (Take, acceleration due to gravity on the Moon = 1.63 m/s^2)** **[2]**

Sol. Let us calculate the weight of the man on the Moon.

Mass of the man on the Moon, $m = 70$ kg

Acceleration due to gravity, $g = 1.63$ m/s^2

We know that, weight is given by

$$W = m \times g = 70 \times 1.63 = 114.1 \text{ N}$$

Thus, the man weighs 114.1 N on the Moon. We know that the mass of a body is constant everywhere in universe. So, the mass of this man would be same on the Earth as well as on the Moon. Hence, the mass will be 70 kg on Earth as well as on Moon.

Q.18 **How does the weight of an object vary with respect to mass and radius of the Earth. In a hypothetical case, if the diameter of the Earth becomes half of its present value and its mass becomes four times of its present value, then how would the weight of any object on the surface of the Earth be affected?** **[2]**

Sol. Weight of the object, $w = mg = \dfrac{GMm}{R^2}$

If $\quad D' = \dfrac{D}{2}$

i.e., $\quad R' = \dfrac{R}{2}$

and $\quad M' = 4M$

Now, weight of the object,

$$w' = \frac{GM'm}{(R')^2}$$

$$\Rightarrow w' = \frac{G4Mm}{(R/2)^2} = \frac{16\,GMm}{R^2}$$

$$\Rightarrow w' = 16\,w$$

Thus, weight of the object will become 16 times of its original weight.

Q.19 **A particle weighs 120 N on the surface of the earth. At what height above the earth's surface will its weight be 30 N? (Radius of the earth = 6400 km)** **[2]**

Sol. Given, weight of particle on the surface of earth,

$$w = 120 \text{ N}$$

Weight of particle at height h above the earth's surface,

$$w_1 = 30 \text{ N}$$

The weight of a particle on the surface of the earth,

$$w = mg = \frac{GMm}{R^2} \qquad \left[\because g = \frac{GM}{R^2}\right]$$

Let w_1 be the weight of a particle at height h above the earth's surface.

$$\text{So, } \frac{w}{w_1} = \frac{G\dfrac{M}{R^2}}{G\dfrac{M}{(R+h)^2}} = \frac{(R+h)^2}{R^2}$$

Substituting given values, we get

$$\frac{120}{30} = \left(\frac{R+h}{R}\right)^2$$

$$\Rightarrow 4 = \left(\frac{R+h}{R}\right)^2$$

$$\Rightarrow 2 = \frac{R+h}{R}$$

$$\Rightarrow 2R = R + h$$

$$\Rightarrow R = h$$

$\therefore$ Height of the particle, h = Radius of the earth = 6400 km

FLUIDS

A substance which can flow is called fluid.

Liquids and gases are collectively known as **fluids**. Fluid flows under the action of an applied force and does not have a definite shape of its own. It takes the shape of that vessel in which it is placed.

Thrust and Pressure

- Thrust is the force acting on an object perpendicular to its surface. The effect of thrust depends on the area on which it acts.
- The unit of thrust is the same as that of force, i.e. the SI unit of thrust is **newton** (N) and CGS unit of thrust is dyne. It is a **vector quantity.**
- **Pressure** is the force acting on the unit area of an object.

$$\text{Pressure } (p) = \frac{\text{Force } (F)}{\text{Area } (A)} = \frac{\text{Thrust}}{\text{Area}}$$

- The SI unit of pressure is Nm^{-2}, which is also called **pascal** (Pa) named after the scientist **Blaise Pascal**. It is a **scalar quantity.**
- 1 **pascal** 1 pascal is the pressure exerted on a surface of area $1m^2$ by a force of 1N acting normally on it.

$$1 \text{ Pa} = 1 \text{Nm}^{-2}$$

- From the formula of pressure, it is clear that the same force can produce different pressures depending on the area over which it acts.
- **Pressure exerted on a surface depends upon the two factors**
  (i) area on which force is applied
  (ii) magnitude of applied force
- A force acting on a smaller area exerts a large pressure while the same force acting on a larger area exerts a small pressure.
- **Ways of Increasing Pressure** The pressure on a surface is increased by reducing the area of surface on which it is acting.
- **Ways of Decreasing Pressure** For the given thrust, the pressure on a surface is reduced by increasing the area of surface.

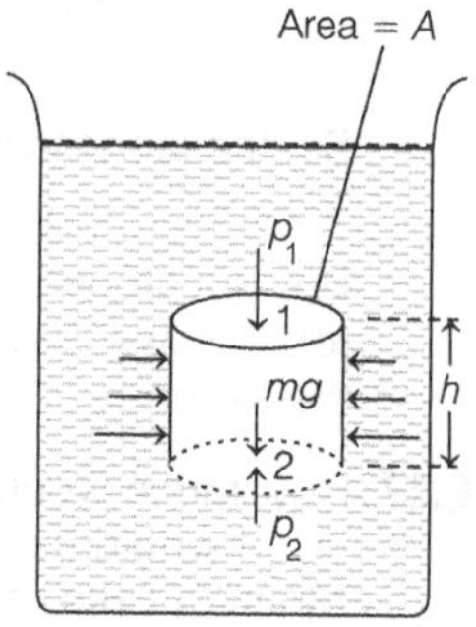

Pressure Exerted by a Liquid Column

- The pressure exerted by column of a liquid density ρ and height h is given as

$$p = h\rho g$$

where, g is the acceleration due to gravity.

- There is also atmospheric pressure (p_a) acting on the free surface of liquid.
  So total pressure, $p = p_a + h\rho g$
  Thus, the pressure p at a depth below the surface of a liquid open to the atmosphere is greater than atmospheric pressure by an amount ρgh.
- At a particular place on earth's surface, g is constant, therefore the liquid pressure at that point depends on height of the liquid column and density of the liquid.

- The excess pressure above the atmospheric pressure is usually called **gauge pressure** and the total pressure is called absolute pressure.

Laws of Liquid Pressure

(i) If a liquid is at rest, then the pressure exerted is same at all points on a horizontal plane.

(ii) Pressure at a given point inside the liquid is directly proportional to the density of the liquid.

(iii) Pressure for different liquids is different at the same depth.

(iv) Pressure is same in all directions and at all points in a horizontal plane at a given depth.

(v) A liquid seeks its own level.

Some Daily Life Consequences of Liquid Pressure

(i) **Broadness of base of a dam** Pressure of the water column increases with depth. Therefore, the wall of a dam is made thicker at the bottom because a thicker wall can withstand a greater pressure exerted by the water at a greater depth.

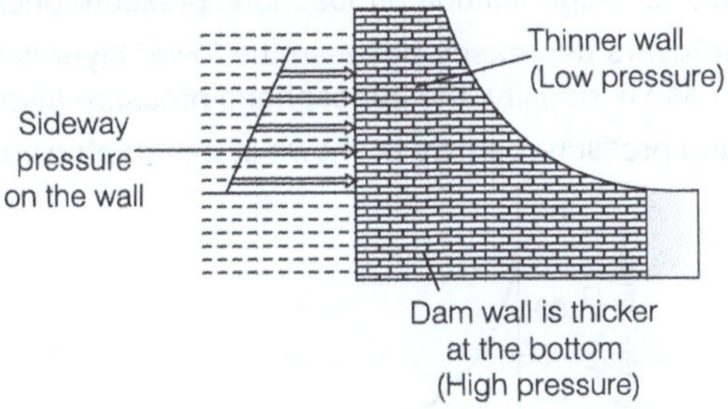

(ii) **Divers use special protective suit for diving in sea** When sea divers go deep inside the sea, pressure exerted by the liquid increases much more than that of divers blood pressure. To protect divers from this extreme pressure of liquid, they have to wear protective suits.

Transmission of Pressure in Liquids : Pascal's Law

- It states that, whenever an external pressure is applied on any part of a fluid contained in a vessel, it is transmitted undiminished and equally in all directions.
- Some applications of Pascal's law are

(i) **Hydraulic Brakes** This uses Pascal's law to increase the force of resistance in a vehicle's braking system.

(ii) **Hydraulic Lift (or Jack)** Pascal's law is used in this case to lift heavy objects.

(iii) **Hydraulic Press** It also works on the principle of Pascal's law for crushing of metallic materials and also for extracting juice from fruits and vegetables.

Atmospheric Pressure

- The gaseous envelope surrounding the earth is known as the earth's atmosphere and the pressure it exerts on the earth surface is known as the atmospheric pressure.
- Thus, the force exerted by air column on a unit area on the earth's surface is equal to its atmospheric pressure denoted by p_a.
- The value of atmospheric pressure on the surface of the earth at sea level is called 1 atmosphere (1 atm), it is nearly about 1.013×10^5 N/m^2.
- Atmospheric pressure at any place is measured by an instrument called **barometer.**

Common Manifestation and Consequences of the Atmospheric Pressure

(i) **Sucking soft drinks with a straw** When we suck soft drinks with a straw, air inside the straw goes into the lungs due to which air pressure inside the straw decreases. The atmospheric pressure at the surface of drinks becomes more than pressure inside straw. Thus, drinks move up into our mouth.

(ii) **Filling of syringe with a liquid** Similarly, when the syringe plunger is pulled up, air inside the barrel moves upwards. Due to excess atmospheric pressure at the surface of liquid, the liquid moves upward and fills the syringe.

Similar cases happen in

(a) action of rubber suckers and

(b) filling of ink into a fountain pen.

Variation of Atmospheric Pressure with Altitude

- As, we go to higher altitudes such as the top of a mountain, inside an aeroplane at high altitude, etc., the atmospheric pressure is found to decrease.
- Following are the reasons due to which atmospheric pressure decreases at higher altitudes
  (i) Density of air decreases at higher altitudes.
  (ii) Decrease in height of the air column above us.
- Our atmosphere consists of different parallel air layers. Each layer experiences a pressure on it due to the weight (or thrust) of above air column. Therefore, as the height of air column decreases and so thrust exerted by the air column also decreases. As a result, at a high altitude atmospheric pressure decreases.
- As we move up, the density of air layers decreases because the lower layer is more compressed as compared to the upper layers. Due to this decrease in density, the atmospheric pressure also decreases.
- A variation between the altitude and pressure/density is shown in the graph given below.

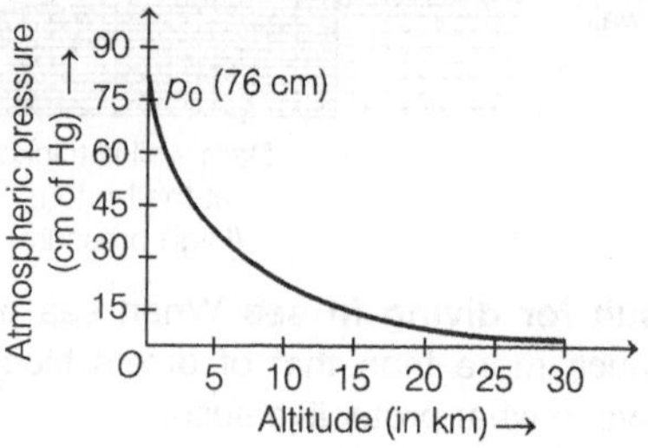

- The decrease in density of air with altitude is not linear. It is rapid at low altitude but slow at high altitude.

Applications of Atmospheric Variations

(i) **Weather Forecasting** Barometer can be used in determining the change in weather as follows

(a) If the barometric height at a place suddenly falls, it indicates coming of a storm or a cyclone.

(b) If barometric height gradually falls, it indicates possibility of rain.

(c) A sudden rise in barometric height indicates an extremely dry weather.

(d) A gradual increase in barometric height indicates dry weather.

(e) If there is no change in the barometric height, atmospheric pressure is normal and the weather will remain unchanged.

(ii) **Altimeter** A device which can be used to measure the altitude is known as altimeter. It is used in most aircraft and skydivers use wrist-mounted altimeter to know the exact altitude.

Buoyancy and Buoyant Force

- The tendency of a liquid to exert an upward force on an object immersed in it, is called **buoyancy**.
- An upward force which acts on an object when it is immersed in a liquid is called buoyant force. It is also called **upthrust**. It is denoted as F_B and its SI unit is **newton (N)**.
- When a body or a block is immersed in a liquid, the pressure exerted on the bottom surface is greater than the top surface because the bottom surface is at a greater depth. This pressure difference causes a net upward force which is called upthrust.
- **Upthrust is equal to the weight of the liquid displaced by the submerged part of the body.**

Mathematically,

Upthrust $F_B = V\rho g$

where, V is the volume of liquid displaced,

ρ is the density of liquid, g is the acceleration due to gravity

Unit of upthrust is N or kgf.

Characteristic Properties of Upthrust

(i) Larger the volume of the body submerged in the fluid, greater would be the upthrust.

(ii) The force acting vertically upward, i.e. upthrust acts at the centre of buoyancy, i.e. centre of gravity of displaced fluid.

(iii) For different fluids with the same volume of body inside the fluids, greater the density of fluid, greater the upthrust on it.

Factors Affecting Buoyant Force

(i) **Density of the fluid** The liquid having higher density exerts more upward buoyant force on an object than another liquid of lower density.

(ii) **Volume of object immersed in the liquid** As the volume of solid object immersed inside the liquid increases, the upward buoyant force also increases.
The magnitude of buoyant force acting on a solid object does not depend on the nature of the solid object. It only depends on its immersed volume.

Archimedes' Principle

- This principle states that when an object is fully or partially immersed in a liquid, it experiences a buoyant force or an upthrust, which is equal to the weight of liquid displaced by the object.
  i.e. Buoyant force or upthrust acting on an object = Weight of liquid displaced by the submerged part of the object

Density

- Density of a substance is defined as mass per unit volume.
- It is a **scalar quantity** and is represented by the Greek letter ρ,

$$\boxed{\rho = \frac{M}{V}}$$

- Its SI unit is kg m^{-3}, and its CGS unit is g cm^{-3}.
- Most substances expand on heating and contract on cooling.
- Thus, the density of a substance increases with decrease in temperature and *vice versa*.

Relative Density

- The relative density of a substance is the ratio of its density to density of water at 4°C.

$$\boxed{\text{Relative density} = \frac{\text{Density of substance}}{\text{Density of water}} = \frac{\rho_s}{\rho_w}}$$

- It is also given as the ratio of the mass of the substance to the mass of equal volume of water at 4°C.

$$\boxed{\text{Relative density} = \frac{\text{Mass of certain volume of substance}}{\text{Mass of same volume of water}} = \frac{m_s}{m_w}}$$

- It has **no units** because it is a ratio of similar quantities.
- In the SI system, the density of water is 1000 kg m^{-3}. Thus, we have

$$\boxed{\text{Relative Density} = \frac{\text{Density of a substance}}{1000\,\text{kg}\,\text{m}^{-3}}}$$

$$\boxed{\therefore\ \text{Density of a substance in kg m}^{-3} = 1000 \times \text{Relative density}}$$

- Now, the density of water in the CGS system is 1 g cm^{-3}. Thus, we have

$$\text{Relative density} = \frac{\text{Density of a substance}}{1\,\text{g}\,\text{cm}^{-3}}$$

$$\therefore\ \text{Density of a substance in g cm}^{-3} = \text{Relative density}$$

Measurement of the Relative Density of a Solid by Archimedes' Principle

$$\text{Relative density} = \frac{\text{Mass of certain volume of subtance}}{\text{Mass of same volume of water}}$$

- According to the Archimedes' principle, the mass of water of volume equal to that of the body is obtained by finding the mass of water displaced by the body when it is completely immersed in water. Thus, we have

$$\text{Relative density} = \frac{\text{Weight of body in air}}{\text{Weight of body in air} - \text{Weight of body in water}}$$

- If W_1 is the weight of the body in air and W_2 is the weight of the body in water, then

$$\text{Relative density} = \frac{W_1}{W_1 - W_2}$$

Measurement of the Relative Density of a Liquid by Archimedes' Principle

- $\text{Relative density} = \dfrac{\text{Weight of a given volume of liquid}}{\text{Weight of the same volume of water}}$
- According to the Archimedes' principle, a solid immersed in water displaces the liquid or water equal to its own volume.

$$\text{Relative density} = \frac{\text{Weight of the body in air} - \text{weight of the body in liquid}}{\text{Weight of body in air} - \text{Weight of the body in water}}$$

- If W_1 is the weight of the body in air, W_2 is the weight of the body in liquid and W_3 is the weight of the body in water, then relative density is a pure ratio. It has no unit.

$$\text{Relative density} = \frac{W_1 - W_2}{W_1 - W_3}$$

Relation between the Density of Liquid, Density of Floating Body and Submerged Volume of floating Body

$$\frac{\text{Volume of immersed part of body}}{\text{Volume of body}} = \frac{\text{Density of body}}{\text{Density of liquid}}$$

$$\frac{V_1}{V_2} = \frac{\rho_l}{\rho_s}$$

where, V_1 = volume of the body, V_2 = volume of the liquid displaced

ρ_l = density of liquid, ρ_s = density of the body

Apparent Weight of a Floating Body

If a body is completely immersed in a liquid, its effective weight gets decreased. The decrease in its weight is equal to the upthrust on the body.

Hence, the apparent weight of the body is given as

$$w_{\text{app}} = w_{\text{actual}} - \text{upthrust} \Rightarrow \boxed{w_{\text{app}} = w_{\text{actual}}\left(1 - \frac{\rho_l}{\rho_s}\right)}$$

where, ρ_s = density of body and ρ_l = density of liquid.

Special Cases

Three possibilities may now arise

(i) If $\rho_s < \rho_l$, then in this condition, the upthrust applied by the fluid will be greater than the weight of the body. This means, the released body gradually moves up towards the fluid surface till the upthrust becomes equal to the weight of the body. At this point, the body floats and is partially immersed in the fluid.

(ii) If $\rho_s = \rho_l$, then the upthrust of the liquid balances the weight of the body.

Hence, the body will float which is completely submerged just below the surface of the fluid.

(iii) If $\rho_s > \rho_l$, then the upthrust of the liquid is less than the weight of the liquid, i.e. it is not sufficient to balance the weight of the body, so the body sinks.

Floatation

- **Principle of floatation** The weight of a floating body is equal to the weight of the liquid displaced by its submerged part.
- A body immersed in liquid experiences two forces
  (i) Its weight in the downward direction through its centre of gravity *G*.
  (ii) The upthrust due to the liquid in the upward direction through the centre of gravity of the displaced liquid. This centre is called the centre of buoyancy *B*.

Laws of Floatation

When a body of density ρ is placed in a liquid of density ρ_2.

- **Case I** When $w > F_B$ or $\rho > \rho_2$, i.e. the weight of the body is greater than the weight of the displaced liquid, the body will sink.

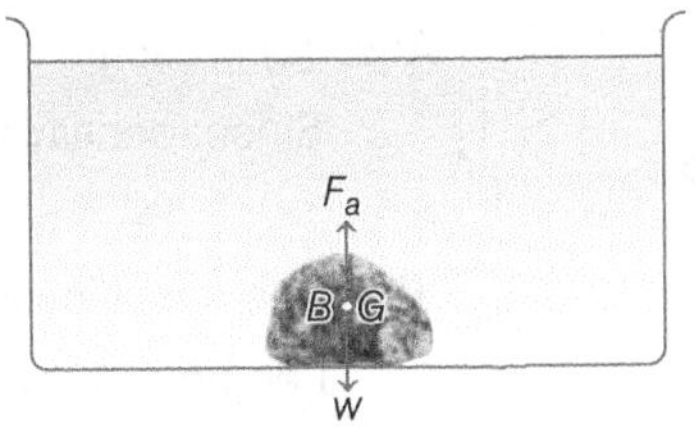

- **Case II** When $w = F_B$ or $\rho = \rho_2$, i.e. the weight of the body is equal to the weight of the displaced liquid, the body will float with its body submerged just below the surface of the liquid.

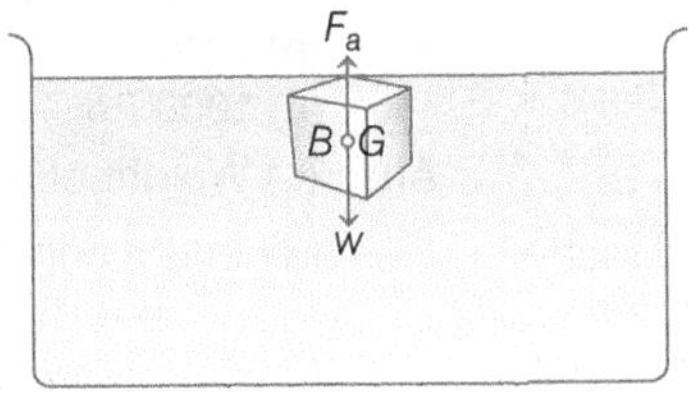

- **Case III** When $w < F_B$ or $\rho < \rho_2$, i.e. the weight of the body is less than the weight of the liquid displaced, the body will float partially above the surface of the liquid.

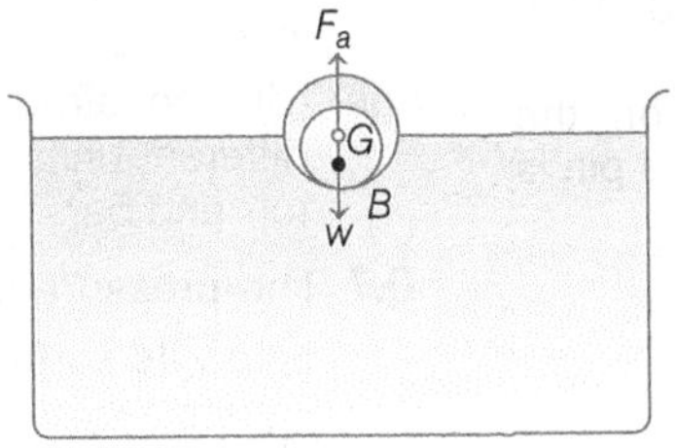

Some Applications of Principle of Floatation

Some applications of principle of floatation are

(i) **Submarines** are made to sink or float in water in accordance with the law of floatation.
(ii) **Ships** also float on water, even though they are made of metals, in accordance with the law of floatation.
(iii) **Balloons** filled with hydrogen rises up in the air which is also an application of the law of floatation.
(iv) **Icebergs** also float in the sea, based on the principle of floatation.

EXAM ORIENTED QUESTIONS

TYPE - 1 01 Mark

Multiple Choice Questions

Q.1 A girl stands on a box having 60 cm length, 40 cm breadth and 20 cm height in three ways. In which of the following cases, pressure exerted by the girl will be

(a) maximum when length and breadth form the base
(b) maximum when breadth and height form the base
(c) maximum when height and length form the base
(d) the same in all the above three cases

Ans. (b) Now, according to question, when base is formed by breadth and height, area will be minimum and so pressure will be maximum.

Q.2 At which point of vessel, pressure is minimum?

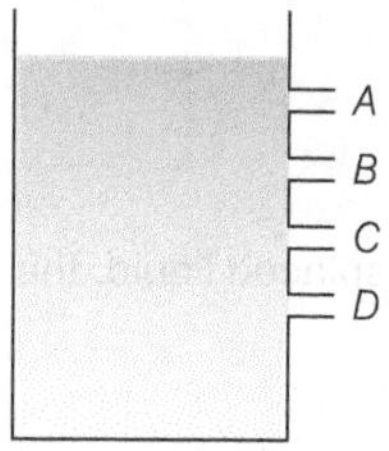

(a) A (b) B
(c) C (d) D

Ans. (a) As we know, pressure exerted by liquid is directly proportional to the height of the vertical column. Therefore, pressure at point A is minimum and at point D, pressure is maximum.

Q.3 A man tries to press a drawing pin into a wooden block. He exerts a force of 10N on the flat head of the pin which has an area of 5 mm^2.
What is the pressure exerted by the pin on the wooden block if the area of the sharp end of the pin is 0.2 mm^2?

(a) 2 Nm^{-2} (b) 2×10^6 Nm^{-2}
(c) 50 N m^{-2} (d) 5×10^7 Nm^{-2}

Ans. (d) Given, Force = 10 N

$$\text{Area} = 0.2\ mm^2 = 0.2\times10^{-6}\ m^2$$

$$p = \frac{\text{Force}}{\text{Area}} = \frac{10}{0.2\times10^{-6}} = 5\times10^7\ N\ m^{-2}$$

Q.4 The pressure produced by the block standing on one side shown in the diagram is P.

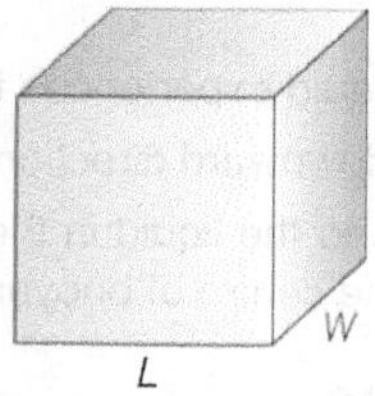

What is the pressure if we double the size of its length (L), width (W) and height (H)?

(a) $\frac{P}{2}$ (b) $4P$ (c) $2P$ (d) $8P$

Ans. (c) Pressure of original block, $\rho gH = P$

Since, density is same for same object, new pressure

$$\rho g\times2H = 2\times\rho gH = 2P$$

Q.5 The specification of a textbook is given as follow

Length = 30 cm, Width = 16 cm

Thickness = 5 cm, Mass = 0.8 kg

Find the maximum pressure exerted on the table by this book. (Take, $g = 10\ m/s^2$)

(a) 8 Pa (b) 100 Pa
(c) 1000 Pa (d) 1500 Pa

Ans. (c) Weight of the book $w = mg = 0.8\times10 = 8$ N

Minimum contact area, A = width $\times$ thickness $= 0.16\times0.05 = 0.008\ m^2$

Maximum pressure $= F/A = 8/0.008 = 1000$ Pa

Q.6 The unit of atmospheric pressure is

(a) torr (b) pascal
(c) bar (d) All of these

Ans. (d) The atmospheric pressure can be measured in different units other than N/m^2, which are pascal (Pa), torr and bar.

Q.7 The pressure inside a liquid of density ρ at a depth h below its surface is

(a) $\frac{h}{\rho g}$ (b) $h\rho g$
(c) $\frac{\rho}{hg}$ (d) $\frac{hg}{\rho}$

Ans. (b) The pressure exerted by a liquid of density ρ at depth h is $p = \rho hg$

where, g is the acceleration due to gravity.

Q.8 Four different liquids are poured into identical measuring cylinders. The diagrams shows the depths of the liquids and their densities.
Which liquid causes the largest pressure on the base of its measuring cylinder ?

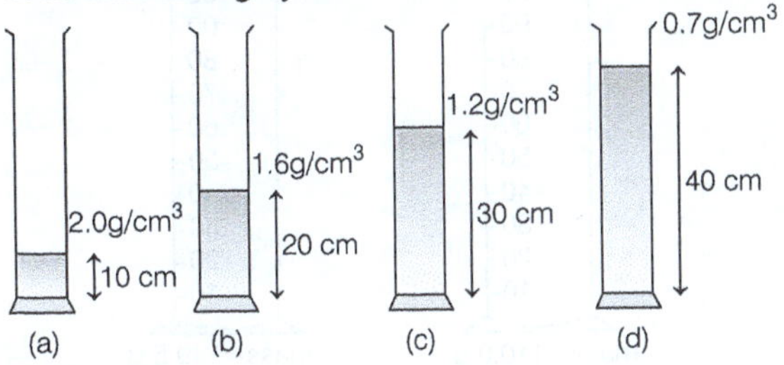

Ans. (c) Pressure $= \rho gh$

Pressure by liquid in

(a) $= 2.0 \times 980 \times 10 = 19600 \text{ g cm}^{-1}\text{s}^{-2}$

(b) $= 1.6 \times 980 \times 20 = 31360 \text{ g cm}^{-1}\text{s}^{-2}$

(c) $= 1.2 \times 980 \times 30 = 35280 \text{ g cm}^{-1}\text{s}^{-2}$

(d) $= 0.7 \times 980 \times 40 = 27440 \text{ g cm}^{-1}\text{s}^{-2}$

The largest pressure is exerted by the liquid (c).

Q.9 Why the dam of water reservoir is thick at the bottom?
(a) Quantity of water increases with depth
(b) Density of water increases with depth
(c) Pressure of water increases with depth
(d) Temperature of water increases with depth

Ans. (c) The water reservoir in a dam is thick at the bottom because at maximum depth, the pressure of water is maximum and to bear this maximum pressure, dam should be thick at the bottom.

Q.10 The diagram shows a mercury manometer connected to a gas container.

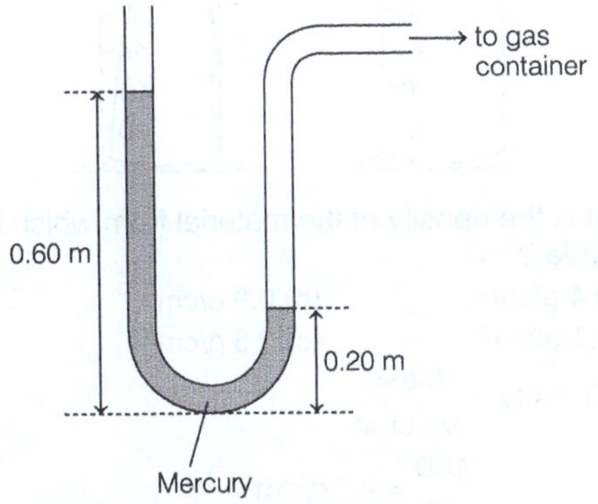

The density of mercury is 14,000 kg/m³.
The gravitational field strength g is 10 N/kg.
What is the pressure difference between the gas in the container and the atmosphere?
(a) 28000 Pa (b) 42000 Pa
(c) 56000 Pa (d) 84000 Pa

Ans. (c) Here, $h = (0.60 - 0.20) = 0.40$ m

Pressure difference $= \rho gh$

$= 14000 \times 10 \times 0.40$

$= 56000$ Pa

Q.11 Suppose the narrow piston's area is 5 cm² and wide piston's area is 50 cm², if the weight of block is 1800 N. The magnitude of force to lift the block in hydraulic machine would be
(a) 1800 N (b) 18000 N (c) 18 N (d) 180 N

Ans. (d) We know that, $\dfrac{F_2}{F_1} = \dfrac{A_2}{A_1}$

Here, $F_2 = 1800$ N, $A_2 = 50 \text{ cm}^2$ and $A_1 = 5 \text{ cm}^2$

$\therefore \quad F_1 = F_2\left(\dfrac{A_1}{A_2}\right) = 1800 \times \dfrac{5}{50}$

$F_1 = 180$ N

Hence, the force required to lift the block is 180 N.

Q.12 What is the name of the device which transmits pressure in order to do work?
(a) Hydrostatic paradox (b) Altimeter
(c) Pascal vessel (d) Hydraulic machine

Ans. (d) Hydraulic machine is used to transmit pressure in order to do work.

Q.13 The diagram as shown in the figure is a device which makes use of the principle of transmission of pressure.

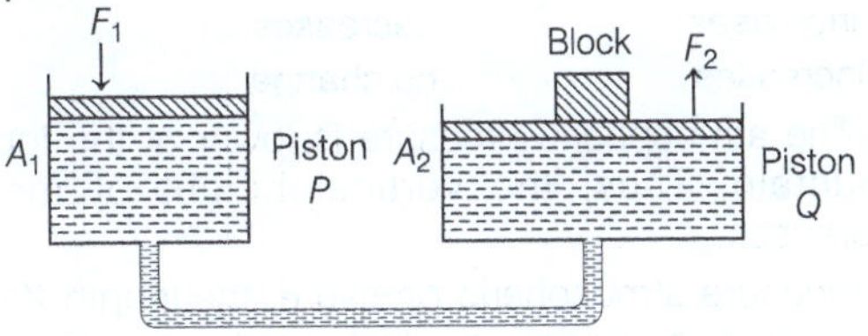

Which of the following is correct about the forces F_1 and F_2?
(a) $F_1 = F_2$ (b) $F_1 > F_2$
(c) $F_2 > F_1$ (d) $F_1F_2 = 1$

Ans. (c) As shown in the figure, $A_2 > A_1$

$\Rightarrow \quad F_2 > F_1 \quad (\because \text{ pressure is constant})$

Q.14 The device used to measure atmospheric pressure is
(a) Mercury barometer
(b) Aneroid barometer
(c) Fortin barometer
(d) All of the above

Ans. (d) The device used to measure atmospheric pressure is called barometer. The commonly used barometers are simple (mercury barometer), Aneroid barometer and Fortin barometer.

Q.15 Why does a person experience nosebleeds at high altitudes?
(a) Due to high oxygen concentration
(b) Due to decreased atmospheric pressure
(c) Due to increased humidity
(d) Due to lower body temperature

Ans. (b) At higth attitude, the atmospheric pressure becomes lower than the blood pressure inside the body. This pressure difference causes the blood in the blood vessels exerts an excess pressure on the blood vessels which might rupture them causing nose bleeds.

Q.16 A simple mercury barometer is carried to the top of a mountain, where the atmospheric pressure is less than from its base.

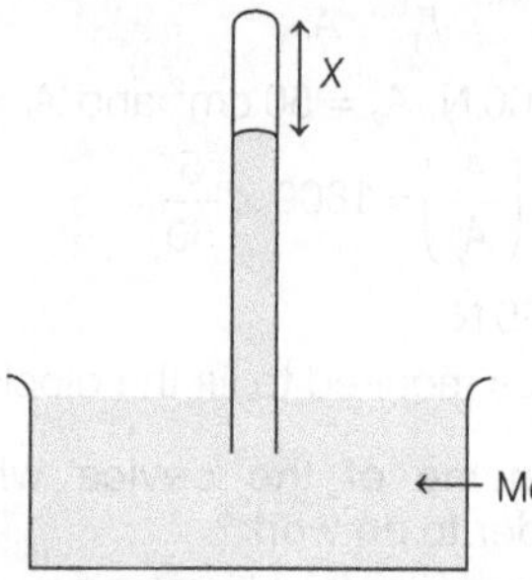

How does the length X of the space above the mercury and the pressure in this space, change as the barometer is taken from the base to the top of the mountain?

	Length of X	Pressure
(a)	decreases	decreases
(b)	decreases	no change
(c)	increases	decreases
(d)	increases	no change

Ans. (d) The atmospheric pressure is lower at the top of a mountain. Thus, the vertical height of mercury decreases.

To measure atmospheric pressure, the length X of the space must be a vacuum which exerts no pressure.

Q.17 When a ball is fully immersed in a liquid, its weight get decreased. It happens due to

(a) gravitational force (b) magnetic force
(c) buoyant force (d) friction force

Ans. (c) When a ball is fully immersed in a liquid, its weight decreases due to buoyant force.

Q.18 Which of the following is correct about the fact that bodies like stones and metals sink in water?

(a) They have higher density compared to water.
(b) They have lesser density compared to water.
(c) They have the same density as that of water.
(d) None of the above

Ans. (a) Bodies like stones and metals sink in water because they have higher density as compared to water.

Q.19 A body of weight w is floating in a liquid. Its apparent weight will be

(a) equal to w (b) less than w
(c) zero (d) greater than w

Ans. (c) When a body is floating in a liquid, then its apparent weight becomes zero.

Q.20 The mass of a measuring cylinder is measured before and after pouring a liquid into it.

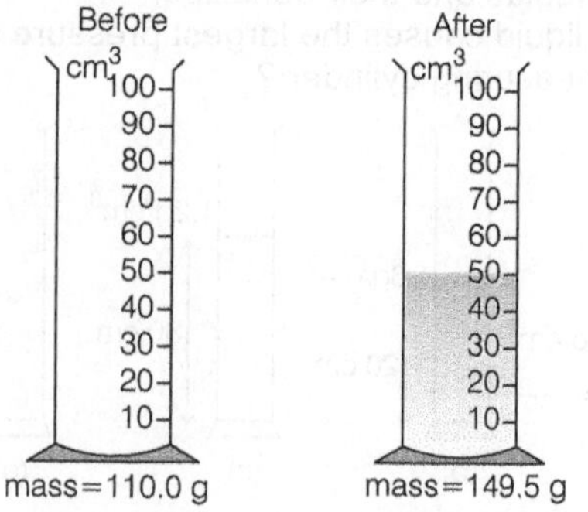

What is the density of the liquid ?

(a) 0.79 g/cm³ (b) 1.3 g/cm³
(c) 1.4 g/cm³ (d) 2.2 g/cm³

Ans. (a) Mass of liquid = mass of cylinder with liquid – mass of empty cylinder

$= 149.5 - 110.0 = 39.5$ g

$$\text{Density} = \frac{\text{Mass of the liquid}}{\text{Volume of the liquid}}$$

$$= \frac{39.5}{50} = 0.79 \text{ g/cm}^3$$

Q.21 An object of mass 100 g immersed in water as shown in the diagram.

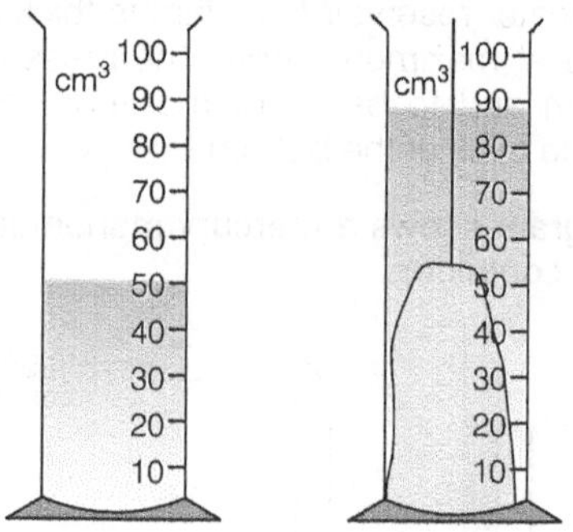

What is the density of the material from which the object is made ?

(a) 0.4 g/cm³ (b) 0.9 g/cm³
(c) 1.1 g/cm³ (d) 2.5 g/cm³

Ans. (d) $\text{Density} = \dfrac{\text{Mass}}{\text{Volume}}$

$$= \frac{100}{40} = 2.5 \text{ g/cm}^3$$

Q.22 When a fish needs to rise in water, it diffuses oxygen gas from its blood into the bladders. This causes its volume to...... and its average density to ....

(a) decreases, decreases
(b) increases, increases
(c) increases, decreases
(d) decreases, increases

Ans. (c) When the fish wants to rise in water it transfers oxygen from its blood into the bladder. This increases its volume since the mass remain same, so the average density decreses. Now, the fish displaces more water and so the upthrust on fish increases due to which it rises up.

TYPE - 2 01 Mark

Assertion-Reason Type Questions

Directions (Q. Nos. 1- 5) In the following questions two statements are given as Assertion and Reason.

(a) Both A and R are true and R is the correct explanation of A.

(b) Both A and R are true but R is not the correct explanation of A.

(c) A is true but R is false.

(d) A is false but R is true.

Q.1 Assertion (A) Cyclones are associated with low-pressure areas.

Reason (R) Low pressure systems cause air to converge, leading to the formation of cyclones.

Ans. (a) In low pressure areas, the air becomes lighter and starts to rise. This upward movement creates a vacuum-like effect at the surface, causing surrounding air to flow inward. As this air converges and rises, it cools and condenses, releasing latent heat, which further lowers the pressure and intensifies the cyclone activity.

Q.2 Assertion (A) Mountain climbers use oxygen cylinders at very high altitudes.

Reason (R) Oxygen level in the atmosphere decreases at high altitudes.

Ans. (a) The percentage of oxygen remains constant, but the reduced atmospheric pressure lowers the oxygen's partial pressure, making it harder to breath.

Q.3 Assertion (A) A ship floats in water despite being made of materials denser than water.

Reason (R) The overall relative density of the ship, including air-filled spaces, is less than 1.

Ans. (a) The ship's hollow structure decreases its overall density, making it less dense than water, so it floats.

Q.4 Assertion (A) A floating body displaces a weight of liquid equal to its own weight.

Reason (R) The volume of liquid displaced by the floating body is always equal to the volume of the body.

Ans. (c) A floating body displaces a weight of liquid equal to its shown weight, but the volume of liquid displaced depends on the shape and density of the body, not necessarily equal to the body's volume.

Q.5 Assertion (A) When a ship moves from a river into the sea, it rises slightly.

Reason (R) Sea water is denser than river water.

Ans. (a) A ship floats based on the principle of buoyancy, which states that the buoyant force is equal to the weight of the displaced fluid. Since sea water is denser than river water, the ship needs to displace less volume of sea water to balance its weight, causing it to rise slightly when moving from a river into the sea.

TYPE - 3 01/02 Marks

Fill in the Blanks

Q.1 When the same force acts on a smaller area, the pressure .... [remains constant/increases] **[1]**

Ans. increases

Q.2 The pressure exerted by a liquid at a point depends on the .... [height/mass] of the liquid column above that point. **[1]**

Ans. height

Q.3 Pascal's law states that the pressure applied to a .... [solid/liquid] fluid is transmitted equally in all directions. **[1]**

Ans. liquid

Q.4 Pascal's law helps in the operation of ...... [mechanical/ hydraulic] brakes in vehicles. **[1]**

Ans. hydraulic

Q.5 The .... [Volume/surface area] of the body submerged in the fluid determines the magnitude of the buoyant force. **[1]**

Ans. volume

Q.6 The buoyant force is independent of the .... [shape/ fluid type] of the submerged object. **[1]**

Ans. shape

Q.7 According to Archimede's principle, a body immersed in a fluid experiences an upward .... [force/volume] equal to the weight of the fluid displaced. **[1]**

Ans. force

Q.8 The volume of the fluid displaced by an object is equal to the .... [volume/weight] of the object submerged in the fluid. **[1]**

Ans. volume

Q.9 Relative density is a ...... [dimensionless/dimensional] quantity because it has no unit. **[1]**

Ans. dimensionless

Q.10 The pressure in a liquid increases with an increase in the .... [height/volume] of the liquid, at greater depths the pressure is .... [less/greater] **[2]**

Ans. height, greater

Q.11 In a hydraulic system, a small force applied to a small .... [volume/area] is transmitted to a .... [smaller/larger] area. **[2]**

Ans. area, larger

Q.12 A submarine dives deeper by increasing its ...[weight/density] and rises to the surface by decreasing its .... [volume/density] **[2]**

Ans. weight, density

Q.13 A substance will float in a liquid if its .... [volume/density] is less than the .... [volume/density] of the liquid. **[2]**

Ans. density, density

TYPE - 4 — 02 Marks

Very Short Answer Type Questions

Q.1 Why is it difficult to hold a school bag having a strap made of thin and strong string?

Ans. It is difficult to hold a school bag having a strap made of a thin and strong string because the area under the strap is small. Hence, a large pressure is exerted by the straps on the fingers or shoulders. Due to the large pressure, the straps tend to cut the skin and hence pain is caused.

Q.2 Why do solids exert pressure only in downward direction but fluids in all directions?

Ans. As we know, solids exert thrust or force only due to its weight by earth, but fluid exerts force due to its random motion in all directions. So, fluid exerts pressure in all directions but solid does not.

Q.3 What do you mean by the term fluid pressure?

Ans. The pressure exerted by fluids (both liquids and gases) due to its weight in all the directions is called fluid pressure.

Q.4 The blood pressure in human is greater at the feet than at the brain. Give reason.

Ans. As we know, pressure p is directly proportional to the depth h. Since, the height of blood column in the human body is more at feet than at brain so the blood exerts more pressure at the feet than at the brain.

Q.5 Why multi-storeyed building has water tanks placed at a greater height?

Ans. This is because, the greater the height of the water tanks, more will be the pressure of the water in taps of the houses. Therefore, for good supply of water, the tanks are placed at good height, from where the supply of water has to be made.

Q.6 Why does the pressure exerted by water on a diver at a depth inside the sea is different than inside the river?

Ans. At a certain depth inside the sea, the pressure acting on the body of divers will be more than inside the river at same depth as the density of seawater is higher than river water.

Q.7 What are the laws of liquid pressure?

Ans. The laws of liquid pressure are as follows

(i) In a liquid at rest, pressure is same at all points on a horizontal plane.

(ii) Pressure inside liquid is directly proportional to density of liquid.

Q.8 Why are the cabins of aeroplanes flying at high altitudes pressurised?

Ans. When an aeroplane takes OFF, it suddenly gains height, due to which the pressure outside it decreases rapidly as compared to the pressure of the oxygen dissolved in the blood of human bodies. Due to this pressure difference, the fine capillaries of nose may burst and bleeding may start. Therefore, in order to protect the passengers from this, the pressure needs to be maintained to be the same as that of the ground level. Hence, the cabins of the aeroplanes are pressurised.

Q.9 What is the principle involved in the hydraulic lift?

Ans. The principle involved in the hydraulic lift is the Pascal's law which states that the pressure applied in any part of a liquid column is transmitted undiminished and equally in all directions.

Q.10 Name the given instrument and why it is used?

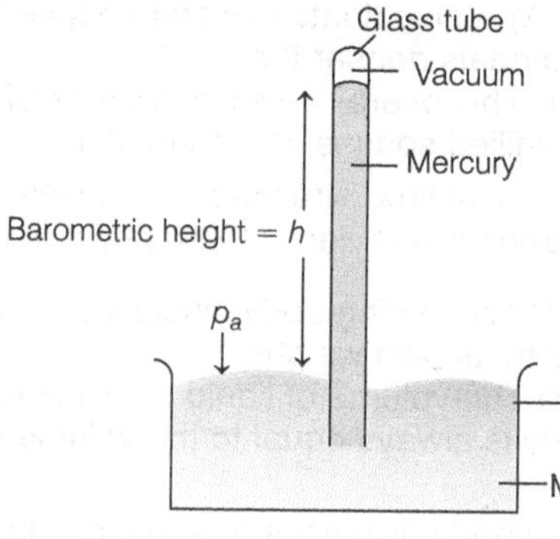

Ans. The given instrument is a simple barometer or mercury barometer. It is used to measure the atmospheric pressure with the help of vertical height of mercury column above the mercury level in the trough to the level in tube.

Q.11 **Give two consequences of atmospheric pressure.**

Ans. The two consequences of atmospheric pressure are as follows

(i) Sucking a drink with a straw.

(ii) Filling of syringe with a liquid.

Q.12 **Why are straws used to drink soft drinks?**

Ans. When we suck a drink through a straw, air inside the straw goes into the lungs due to which air pressure inside the straw decreases. The atmospheric pressure at the surface of drinks becomes greater than the pressure inside the straw. Thus, drinks move up into our mouth.

Q.13 **Explain why liquid does not come out from dropper till its bulb is not pressed?**

Ans. As, the air pressure at the outlet and the pressure inside the bulb are equal, the liquid does not come out. However when bulb is pressed, its pressure increases and liquid starts coming out of the dropper.

Q.14 **What is an altimeter? State its principle.**

Ans. An altimeter is a device used in an aircraft to measure its altitude.

The principle of altimeter is that, with an increase in the height above the sea level, the atmospheric pressure decreases. Thus, a barometer that measures the atmospheric pressure can be utilised in order to measure the altitude of a place above the sea level.

Q.15 **Why does a block of plastic released under water, come up to the surface of the water?**

Ans. The upthrust or buoyant force acting on the block of plastic by the water is greater than the weight of the plastic block. So, plastic block comes up to the surface of water.

Q.16 **A small block is held under water in a tall jar as shown in figure.**

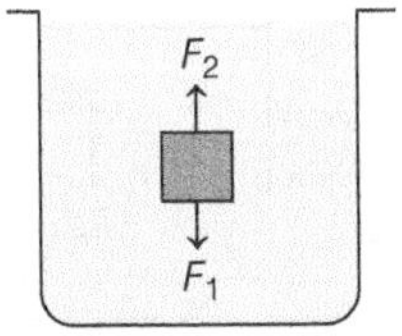

The two forces F_1 and F_2 are acting on the block. Name these forces.

Ans. The force F_1 represents the weight of the block in downward direction and force F_2 represents the upthrust on the block due to water.

Q.17 **Give two characteristic properties of upthrust.**

Ans. The upthrust has the following characteristic properties

(i) The larger the volume of the body submerged in a fluid, the greater is the upthrust.

(ii) For the same volume inside the fluid, the greater the density of fluid, the greater is the upthrust.

Q.18 **Define relative density. Give its mathematical form.**

Ans. The relative density of a substance is the ratio of its density to that of water at 4°C.

Relative density of a substance

$$= \frac{\text{Density of the substance}}{\text{Density of water at } 4^\circ \text{C}}$$

In other words,

Relative density of a substance

$$= \frac{\text{Mass of the substance}}{\text{Volume of the substance}} \times \frac{\text{Volume of water}}{\text{Mass of water}}$$

$$\left[\because \text{Density} = \frac{\text{Mass}}{\text{Volume}}\right]$$

Q.19 **Give the relation among volume of submerged part of a floating body, the densities of liquid and the body. Explain the meaning of symbols used.**

Ans. The relation between volume of submerged part of a floating body, the densities of liquid and the body is given as

$$\frac{V'}{V} = \frac{\rho_s}{\rho_l}$$

where, V' = volume of immersed part of body,

V = total volume of body,

ρ_s = density of body

and ρ_l = density of liquid.

Q.20 **Why an unloaded ship is filled with sand at its bottom?**

Ans. An unloaded ship floats with its very small volume inside water. As a result, its equilibrium is unstable.

So, it may get blown over on its side by strong winds. Therefore, sand or stones are loaded at its bottom so that centre of gravity of the ship shifts downward and the equilibrium of the ship becomes stable.

TYPE - 5 — 03 Marks

Short Answer Type Questions

Q.1 (i) **State the SI units of thrust and pressure.** **[1]**

(ii) **In which situation we exert more pressure on ground, when we stand on one foot or on the both feet? Justify your answer.** **[2]**

Ans. (i) The SI unit of thrust is newton (N). The SI unit of pressure is N/m^2 or pascal (Pa).

(ii) We exert more pressure on ground when we stand on one foot than the both feet, as the area of one foot is half than that of two feet and $p \propto \frac{1}{A}$.

Q.2 A jar contains a fluid of density *d* upto a height *h*. The acceleration due to gravity is *g* and the atmospheric pressure is p_0.

(i) Give the expression for the total pressure at the base of jar. **[1]**

(ii) What will be the pressure at the free surface? **[1]**

(iii) Give the lateral pressure at this depth on the inner side of jar. **[1]**

Ans. (i) Total pressure at the base of jar = Atmospheric pressure + Pressure due to liquid column

$$p = p_0 + hdg$$

(ii) Pressure at free surface is equal to atmospheric pressure.

(iii) Lateral pressure at this depth on the inner side of jar = hdg.

Q.3 A piece of glass is being lifted by a suction cup as shown.

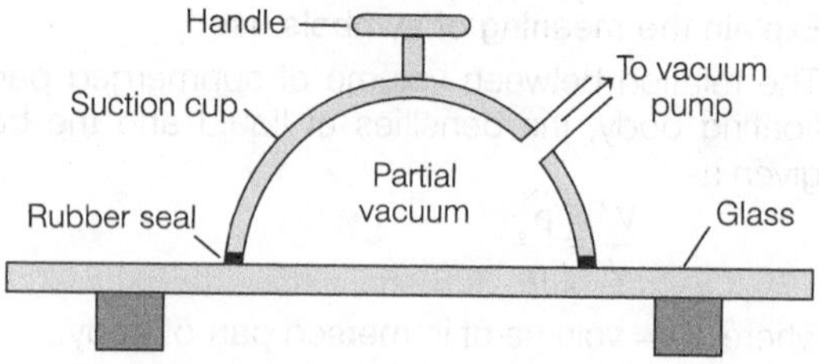

Air can be removed from the cup by a vacuum pump to create a partial vacuum inside the cup. The suction effect will take place when the air pressure inside the cup is lesser than the atmospheric pressure outside, which is 100,000 Pa. The area of the glass covered by the rubber seal of the suction cup is 0.0025 m^2.

(i) If the pressure inside the cup is reduced to 20,000 Pa, then calculate the heaviest weight of glass that can be lifted with this cup. **[1]**

(ii) Given that the glass weighs 14 kg, calculate the smallest amount of pressure to be reduced inside the suction cup to lift the glass. **[1]**

(iii) Explain why a suction cup with a larger diameter can lift a heavier object than one with a smaller diameter when both are given the same pressure difference to work with? **[1]**

Ans. (i) Let the heaviest weight of glass be *W*.

$$p_{atm} - p_{cup} = \frac{W}{A}$$

$$100{,}000 - 20{,}000 = \frac{W}{0.0025} \Rightarrow W = 200\text{ N}$$

(ii) Let the smallest amount of pressure to be reduced be p_s.

$$p_{atm} - p_{cup} = \frac{140}{0.0025}$$

$$100{,}000 - p_s = 56000$$

$$p_s = 44000\text{ Pa}$$

(iii) A suction cup with a larger diameter has more contact area with object and thus greater lifting force.

Q.4 Explain the following

(i) A dam has broader walls at the bottom than at the top. **[1]**

(ii) A sharp tip is provided at the end of a pin. **[1]**

(iii) It is easier to cut with a sharp knife than with a blunt one. **[1]**

Ans. (i) Since, water pressure increases with depth, therefore the walls of a dam is made thicker at the bottom because a thicker wall can withstand a greater pressure exerted by the water at greater depth.

(ii) Pins, needles and nails are provided with a sharp tip, so that the area of contact between the pin and the given surface would be least. Thereby, on applying minimal effort, it would be able to exert high pressure on the surface and hence will easily penetrate through it.

(iii) Because sharp knife has lesser area of cross-section. Hence, with lesser force, more pressure is exerted and thus it becomes easy to cut through sharp knife.

Q.5 State Pascal's law and give its two applications.

Ans. Pascal's law states that, whenever an external pressure is applied on any part of a fluid contained in a vessel, it is transmitted undiminished and equally in all directions.

Two applications of Pascal's law are

(i) Hydraulic Jack (ii) Hydraulic Press

Q.6 Explain how Pascal's law applied in a hydraulic lift with suitable diagram?

Ans.

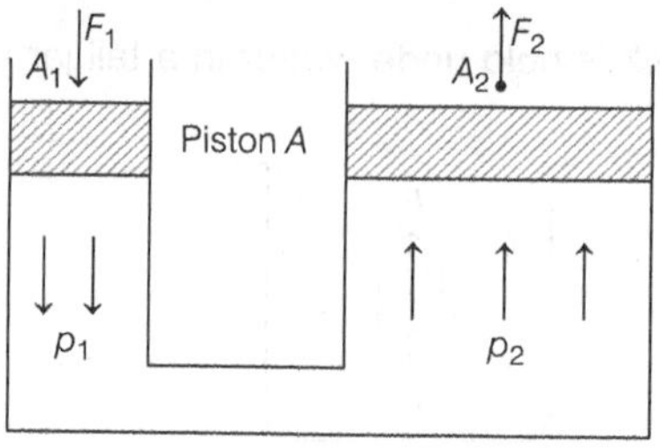

The principle of hydraulic machine states that a small force applied on a smaller piston produces a large force on a bigger piston.

Hydraulic machines work on Pascal's law i.e. pressure exerted in a confined liquid is transmitted equally in all directions throughout the liquid.

Hence,

According to Pascal's law, $p_1 = p_2$

Pressure applied on the piston *A*,

$$p_1 = \frac{F_1}{A_1}$$

Pressure applied on the piston B,

$$p_2 = \frac{F_2}{A_2}$$

$\because$ $p_1 = p_2$

$\therefore$ $\frac{F_1}{A_1} = \frac{F_2}{A_2}$

or, $\frac{F_2}{F_1} = \frac{A_2}{A_1}$

Since, $A_2 > A_1$ so $F_2 > F_1$.

Thus, a small force applied at piston A can produce a large force on piston B.

This is the principle of a hydraulic machine which acts as a force multiplier.

Q.7 (i) Which system is shown in given diagram? **[1]**

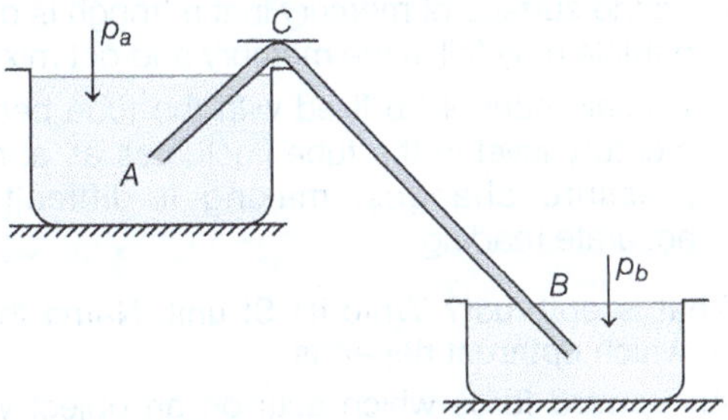

(ii) Explain the working of above system. **[2]**

Ans. (i) The given figure shows the siphon system.

(ii) Water is supplied from a higher level to a lower level using a siphon system. To transfer water from higher level vessel to lower level vessel, first air is sucked out from the lower end B of the rubber tube. As a result, the pressure inside the tube decreases and becomes less than the atmospheric pressure. Due to excess pressure at A, water rises in the tube through the end A and reach level C, then water flows down to the lower level B.

Q.8 What does the weather forecast states, if

(i) air is humid and Hg falls suddenly? **[1]**

(ii) air pressure rises steeply? **[1]**

(iii) air pressure falls gradually? **[1]**

Ans. (i) It indicates storm or cyclone.

(ii) It indicates weather is dry.

(iii) It indicates the possibility of rain.

Q.9 How volume of the object immersed affects the buoyant force?

Ans. As, the volume of solid object immersed inside the liquid increases, the upward buoyant force also increases. The magnitude of buoyant force acting on a solid object does not depend on the nature of the solid object. It only depends on its volume.

Q.10 When you immerse an empty plastic bottle in a bucket of water, it comes above the surface of it. Why does this happen? How can it remains immersed in water and why?

Ans. When we immerse an empty plastic bottle in a bucket of water, the upward force (upthrust or buoyant force) exerted by water on the bottle is greater than the plastic bottle weight. Therefore, plastic bottle comes above the surface of it. To keep the bottle completely immersed, an external force which is equal to the difference between the upward force and the weight of the bottle must be applied on the bottle in downward direction. This is because the upthrust on the bottle due to water must be balanced.

Q.11 When a fresh egg is put into a beaker filled with water, it sinks in water. But when a lot of salt is dissolved in the water, the egg begins to rise and then floats. Why?

Ans. The density of salt solution is greater than that of pure water. Due to its much higher density, the salt solution exerts much more upward buoyant force on the egg, making the egg rise and then float.

Q.12 Why does a nail sink in water while a piece of cork floats on it?

Ans. The weight of water displaced by a nail is less than its own weight, so it sinks in water. Whereas, a piece of cork displaces water more than its own weight, so it floats on water. Also, the density of cork is less than the density of iron.

Q.13 There are four balls A, B, C and D which displace10 mL, 24 mL, 15 mL and 12 mL of a liquid respectively, when immersed completely. Which ball will undergo the maximum apparent loss in weight?

Ans. As the volume of a solid object is immersed in a liquid, a buoyant force acts on the object in the upward direction. The magnitude of the force depends on the volume displaced by the object. As the ball B displaces maximum volume of 24 mL, therefore ball B will undergo maximum apparent loss in weight.

Q.14 If the density of a body is 800 kg/m^3. Will it sink or float when dipped in a bucket of water? (Take, density of water = 1000 kg/m^3)

Ans. Since, its density is less than that of water, according to the Archimedes' principle, if the density of body is less than the density of liquid, then the upthrust applied by the fluid will be greater than the weight of the body. Hence, it will float.

Q.15 (i) When a golf ball is lowered into a measuring cylinder containing water, the water level rises such that volume marker indicates 40 cm^3, when the ball is completely submerged. If the mass of ball in air is 44 g, calculate its density. **[1]**

(ii) A 0.5 kg sheet of tin sinks in water but if the same sheet is converted into a boat or a box, it floats. Give reason. **[2]**

Ans. (i) Mass of ball, $m = 44$ g

Volume, $V = 40$ cm^3

Density, $\rho = \frac{m}{V} = \frac{44}{40} = 1.1 \text{ g/cm}^3$

(ii) The density of tin is higher than that of water, so the sheet of tin sinks in water. But when the same sheet of tin is converted into a boat or box, a lot of air is trapped in the boat or box. Then, the average density of boat or box made of tin sheet becomes lower than that of water. Therefore, it floats in water.

TYPE - 6 — 04 Marks

Long Answer Type Questions

Q.1 Find experimentally the relation between pressure and depth of a liquid from the surface.

Ans. Take a cylindrical thin vessel, make some holes at different heights in the vessel. Mark the holes P, Q, R, S. Fill up the vessel with a liquid (say water).

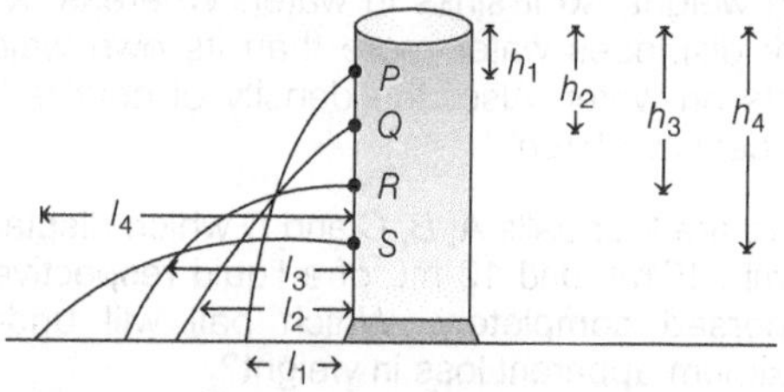

It is observed that the horizontal range of water coming out is minimum for water coming out of hole P. Similarly, the horizontal range of water coming out from hole S is maximum as its depth is maximum from surface. This gives the relation that, pressure is directly proportional to the depth of liquid from surface.

Q.2 Two holes are made in a sealed oil can. Explain why?

Ans. When one hole is made at one side of a completely filled oil can, the pressure due to the column of the oil is much less than the atmospheric pressure of the air outside. So, it becomes difficult for the oil to come out from the hole. Now, if another hole is made of the opposite side of the top cover of the can then air can enter into the can through the hole which exerts an excess pressure on the oil column inside the can and hence it becomes easier for the oil to flow out of the can.

Q.3 Why mercury is used as a barometric liquid?

Ans. Advantages of using mercury as barometric liquid are as follows

(i) Mercury neither wets nor sticks to the glass tube, due to which it gives accurate reading.

(ii) As it is shiny and opaque in nature, it can be easily seen while taking observations.

(iii) As, the vapour pressure of mercury is negligible, therefore the vapours in the torricellian vacuum does not affect the barometric height.

(iv) Its density is very high having low vapour pressure. Thus, it stays in the column without affecting the barometric height.

Q.4 Write four disadvantages of a simple barometer?

Ans. (i) There is no protection to the glass tube of barometer.

(ii) It is inconvenient to move the barometer from one place to another.

(iii) As the surface of mercury in the trough is open, dust particle may fall in the mercury and get mixed with it.

(iv) A scale cannot be fixed with the tube because the mercury level in the tube fluctuates as atmospheric pressure changes, making it difficult to take accurate reading.

Q.5 What is upthrust? Write its SI unit. Name the factors on which upthrust depends.

Ans. An upward force which acts on an object when it is immersed in a liquid is called buoyant force or upthrust. Its SI unit is newton (N).

Upthrust depends upon the

(i) volume of the body submerged in the fluid.

(ii) density of the liquid.

Q.6 (i) A cube of side 5 cm is immersed in water and then in saturated salt solution. In which case, will it experience a greater buoyant force ? If each side of the cube is reduced to 4 cm and then immersed in water, what will be the effect on the buoyant force experienced by the cube as compared to the first case for water ? Give reason for each case. [2]

(ii) A ball weighing 4 kg and of density 4000 kg/m^3 is completely immersed in water of density 10^3 kg/m^3. Find the force of buoyancy on it. (Take, $g = 10$ ms^{-2}) [2]

Ans. (i) Buoyant force, $F = V\rho g$

Buoyant force depends upon volume and density, Since saturated salt solution have higher density than the water, so in saturated solution, cube will experience a greater buoyant force.

If each side of the cube is reduced to 4 cm, the volume of cube will decrease less. So, buoyant force will be less than as compared to the first case for water.

(ii) The magnitude of the buoyant force depends on the density of the fluid.

Volume of solid

$$= \frac{\text{Mass}}{\text{Density}} = \frac{4}{4000} = \frac{1}{1000} \text{ m}^3$$

Buoyancy, $F = V\rho g$

$$= \frac{1}{1000} \times 1000 \times 10$$

$$= 10 \text{ N}$$

TYPE - 7 — 03/04 Marks

Case Based Questions

Q.1 A diver dives into the ocean and observes that the pressure increases as he goes deeper. He also notices that a leak in his diving suit at a deeper level allows water to enter at high speed.

(i) Why does the pressure increase as the diver goes deeper? **[1]**

(ii) State the relationship between depth and liquid pressure. **[1]**

(iii) Why does water enter the leak at high speed at greater depths? **[1]**

Ans. (i) Pressure increases with depth because the weight of the water column above exerts force on the diver.

(ii) Liquid pressure is directly proportional to the depth,

$$p = h\rho g$$

(iii) At greater depths, the pressure difference between the water outside and the air inside the suit increases, forcing water to enter at high speed.

Q.2 A mountaineer climbs a high mountain and notices that as he ascends, he feels difficulty in breathing. He also observes that a sealed packet of chips expands at a higher altitude. Additionally, while descending, he notices that his water bottle, which was empty at the top, is crushed inward.

(i) Why does the mountaineer feel difficulty in breathing at high altitudes? **[1]**

(ii) Explain why the sealed packet of chips expands as the mountaineer ascends. **[1]**

(iii) How does atmospheric pressure vary with altitude? **[1]**

Ans. (i) The mountaineer feels difficulty in breathing because the atmospheric pressure decreases at higher altitudes, reducing the oxygen availability in the air.

(ii) The external atmospheric pressure decreases with altitude, causing the packet to expand so as to balance the pressure inside and outside of the packet.

(iii) Atmospheric pressure decreases with increasing altitude due to the decrease in density of air.

Q.3 In 1643, Torricelli designed a simple barometer using mercury as the barometric liquid as shown in figure. **[3]**

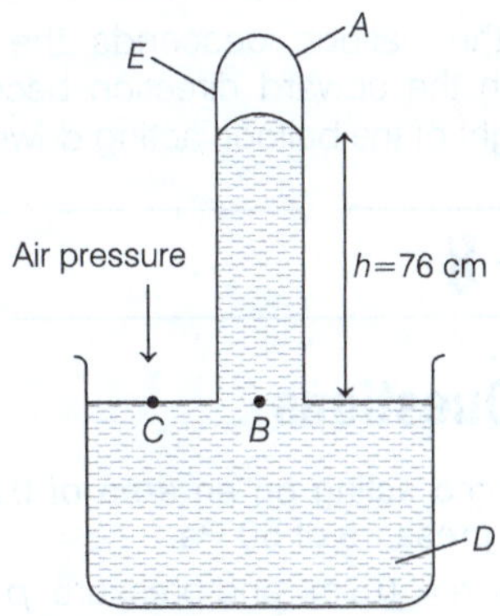

S.No.	Description	Label
a.	Sea level pressure	*E*
b.	Torricellian vacuum	
c.	Mercury reservoir	
d.	Pressure at this point is equal to atmospheric pressure	

Ans.

S.No.	Description	Label
a.	Sea level pressure	*E*
b.	Torricellian vacuum	*A*
c.	Mercury reservoir	*D*
d.	Pressure at this point is equal to atmospheric pressure	*C* & *B*

Q.4 A weather scientist conducts an experiment using a hot-air balloon. The balloon is partially inflated and attached to a basket. As the balloon rises, the scientist observes that the balloon expands, the weight of the basket decreases, and the balloon eventually stabilizes at a certain height. The scientist also places a container of water in the basket and observes the water level inside a tube attached to the container.

(i) Why does the hot-air balloon expand as it rises? **[1]**

(ii) How does the concept of buoyancy help the balloon stabilizes at a certain height? **[1]**

(iii) If the balloon descends, what changes would occur in the buoyant force acting on it? **[1]**

Ans. (i) The balloon expands because atmospheric pressure decreases with altitude, allowing the trapped air to exert more pressure outward.

(ii) The balloon stabilizes when the upward buoyant force equals the downward gravitational force (weight).

(iii) When the balloon descends the buoyant force acting in the upward direction becomes less than the weight of the balloon acting downwards.

TYPE - 8

Numerical Questions

Q.1 Find the force acting on an area of 0.5 m^2 which will produce a pressure of 50 Pa. **[2]**

Sol. Here, area, $A = 0.5\ m^2$ and pressure, $p = 50$ Pa

We know that, $p = \frac{F}{A}$

Force, $F = p \times A$

$= 50 \times 0.5 = 25$ N

Q.2 A cube each of side 10 cm is placed inside a liquid. Calculate the thrust exerted by the liquid on any face, if the pressure at the face of cube is 5 Pa. **[2]**

Sol. Given, $p = 5$ Pa

Area of the cube, $A = 10\ cm \times 10\ cm$

$= 100\ cm^2 = 100 \times 10^{-4}\ m^2$

$\therefore$ Thrust exerted by the liquid on the face of the cube,

$F = p \times A$

$= 5 \times 100 \times 10^{-4}$

$= 5 \times 10^{-2}$ N

Q.3 The two thigh bones (femurs), each of cross-sectional area 10 cm^2 support the upper part of a human body of mass 40 kg. Estimate the average pressure sustained by the femurs. **[2]**

Sol. Given, $A = 20 \times 10^{-4} m^2$ ($\because$ 2 thigh bones)

$F = 40$ kg - wt $= 400$ N ($\therefore g = 10\ m/s^2$)

$$p_{av} = \frac{F}{A} = \frac{400}{20 \times 10^{-4}}$$

$= 2 \times 10^5\ N/m^2$

Q.4 Which of the two will exert more pressure, 80 kg mass on 10 m^2 or 40 kg mass on 4 m^2? **[2]**

Sol. Pressure exerted by 80 kg mass on 10 m^2

$$= \frac{80 \times 9.8}{10} = 78.4\ Nm^{-2} \quad \left(\text{As, } p = \frac{F}{A} = \frac{mg}{A}\right)$$

Pressure exerted by 40 kg mass on 4 m^2

$$= \frac{40 \times 9.8}{4} = 98\ Nm^{-2}$$

So, the second body (40 kg) will exert more pressure.

Q.5 A 50 kg girl wearing high heels shoes balances on a single heel. The heel is circular with a diameter 1.0 cm. What is the pressure exerted on the horizontal floor? **[2]**

Sol. Given, mass of girl, $m = 50$ kg

Diameter of circular heel $(2r) = 1.0$ cm

$\therefore$ Radius, $r = 0.5\ cm = 5 \times 10^{-3}$ m

Area of circular heel, $A = \pi r^2$

$= 3.14 \times (5 \times 10^{-3})^2\ m^2$

$= 78.50 \times 10^{-6} m^2$

$\therefore$ Pressure exerted on the horizontal floor,

$$p = \frac{F}{A} = \frac{mg}{A}$$

$$= \frac{50 \times 9.8}{78.50 \times 10^{-6}}$$

$= 6.24 \times 10^6$ Pa

Q.6 A hydraulic automobile lift is designed to lift cars with a maximum mass of 3000 kg. The area of cross-section of the piston carrying the load is 425 cm^2. What will be maximum pressure would the smaller piston have to bear? **[2]**

Sol. Given, maximum mass that can be lifted, $m = 3000$ kg

Area of cross-section, $A = 425\ cm^2 = 4.25 \times 10^{-2} m^2$

$\therefore$ Maximum pressure on the bigger piston,

$$p = \frac{F}{A} = \frac{mg}{A}$$

$$= \frac{3000 \times 9.8}{4.25 \times 10^{-2}} = 6.92 \times 10^5 \text{ Pa}$$

According to Pascal's law, the pressure applied on an enclosed liquid is transmitted equally in all directions.

$\therefore$ Maximum pressure on smaller piston

= Maximum pressure on bigger piston

$p' = p = 6.92 \times 10^5$ Pa

Q.7 A boy weighing 40 kgf is wearing shoes with heel of area of cross-section 10 cm^2, while a girl weighing 25 kgf is wearing sandals with heel of area of cross-section 0.5 cm^2. Compare the pressure exerted on ground by their heels when they stand on heel of one foot. **[3]**

Sol. Given, $F_1 = 40$ kgf,

$A_1 = 10 cm^2 = 10 \times 10^{-4} m^2$

$\therefore$ Pressure exerted by the boy, $p_1 = \frac{F_1}{A_1}$

$$= \frac{40}{10 \times 10^{-4}} = 4 \times 10^4 \text{ kgf m}^{-2} \quad \text{...(i)}$$

Also, $F_2 = 25$ kgf, $A_2 = 0.5\ cm^2 = 0.5 \times 10^{-4}\ m^2$

$\therefore$ Pressure exerted by the girl, $p_2 = \frac{F_2}{A_2}$

$$= \frac{25}{0.5 \times 10^{-4}} = 50 \times 10^4 \text{ kgf m}^{-2} \quad \text{...(ii)}$$

Hence, from Eqs. (i) and (ii), we get

$$\frac{p_2}{p_1} = \frac{50 \times 10^4}{4 \times 10^4} = \frac{25}{2} = 25:2$$

Q.8 If two forces in the ratio 5 : 9 act on two areas in the ratio 10 : 3, then find the ratio of pressure exerted. **[2]**

Sol. Ratio of areas = 10 : 3, i.e. $A_1/A_2 = 10/3$

Ratio of forces = 5 : 9, i.e. $F_1/F_2 = 5/9$

Ratio of pressures = $\frac{p_1}{p_2}$

$$= \frac{F_1}{A_1} \times \frac{A_2}{F_2}$$

$$= \frac{F_1}{F_2} \times \frac{A_2}{A_1} = \frac{5}{9} \times \frac{3}{10} = \frac{1}{6}$$

Therefore, the ratio of pressures is 1:6.

Q.9 The density of the atmosphere at sea level is $1.29\ kg/m^3$. Assume that it does not change with altitude, then how high would the atmosphere extend? **[2]**

Sol. Given, $\rho = 1.29\ kg/m^3$,

$g = 9.8\ m/s^2$, $h = ?$

As, $p = \rho g h$

$1.01 \times 10^5 = 1.29 \times 9.8 \times h$

$$h = \frac{1.01 \times 10^5}{1.29 \times 9.8}$$

$= 7989.24$ m $\approx$ 8 km = 8 km (Approx)

Q.10 A U-tube is initially partially filled with mercury. Then water is poured into one arm and oil is added to the other arm. Determine the ratio of the height of the columns so that the mercury levels remain the same in both arms. (Given, density of water = $10^3\ kgm^{-3}$, density of oil = $800\ kg\ m^{-3}$).

Ans. Since, the mercury level remain the same in both the arms of the U-tube, therefore pressure of water column on the mercury is equal to the pressure of oil column on the mercury.

$h_1 \rho_1 g = h_2 \rho_2 g$

where, h_1 = height of water column

ρ_1 = density of water

h_2 = height of oil column

ρ_2 = density of oil

$$\therefore \quad \frac{h_1}{h_2} = \frac{\rho_2}{\rho_1} = \frac{800}{10^3} = \frac{8}{10}$$

Hence, $h_1 : h_2 = 8 : 10$

Q.11 The relative density of silver is 10.8. The density of water is $10^3\ kg/m^3$. What is the density of silver in SI unit? **[2]**

Sol. Relative density of silver = 10.8

$$\text{Relative density of silver} = \frac{\text{Density of silver}}{\text{Density of water}}$$

$$10.8 = \frac{d_s}{10^3\ kg/m^3}$$

$$d_s = 10.8 \times 10^3\ kg/m^3$$

Q.12 A uniform mercury column is supported by a card as shown in the figure. The height of the mercury column is 760 mm. The density of mercury is $13600\ kg\text{-}m^{-3}$.

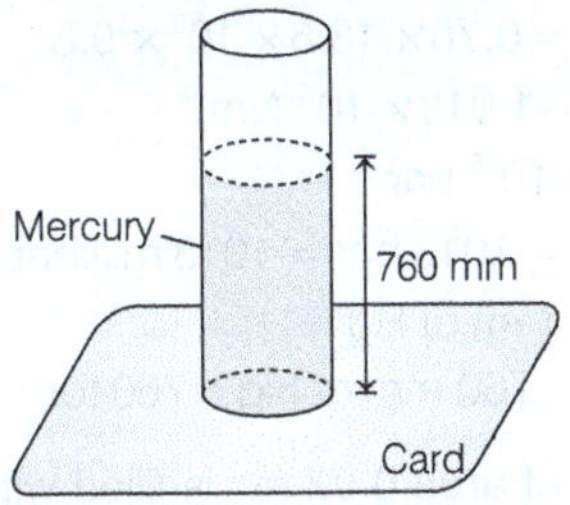

(i) Find the pressure exerted on the card by the mercury column. **[1]**

(ii) If the cross-sectional area of the column is $5\ cm^2$ and the height remains unchanged, prove without using $p = \rho g h$, the pressure exerted on the card by the mercury column is the same as in (i). **[1]**

Sol. (i) Pressure = $\rho g h$

$= 13600 \times 10 \times 0.76 = 103.360$ kPa

(ii) Volume of mercury column

$= 5 \times 76 = 380\ cm^3 = 380 \times 10^{-6}\ m^3$

Mass of mercury column

$= \rho V = 13600 \times 380 \times 10^{-6} = 5.168$ kg

$$\text{Pressure} = \frac{F}{A} = \frac{51.68}{5 \times 10^{-4}} = 103.360\ \text{kPa}$$

Q.13 A cylindrical vessel having a diameter of 40 cm has water filled upto a height of 21 cm. Ignoring the atmospheric pressure, find

(i) the thrust at the bottom of the vessel. **[2]**

(ii) pressure at a depth of 10 cm from the free surface. **[1]**

[Take, density of water = $10^3\ kg\ m^{-3}$, $g = 10\ m/s^2$]

Sol. Radius of the vessel = 20 cm = 0.2 m

$$\text{Volume of the vessel} = \pi(0.2)^2 \times \frac{21}{100}\ m^3$$

$$= \frac{22}{7} \times 0.04 \times \frac{21}{100}\ m^3 = 2.64 \times 10^{-2}\ m^3$$

(i) The thrust at the bottom of the vessel = weight of the liquid contained in the vessel

= Volume × density × g

$= 2.64 \times 10^{-2} \times 10^3 \times 10\ N = 2.64 \times 10^2 = 264\ N$

(ii) Pressure of water column at a height of 10 cm from the free surface = $h \rho g$

$$\text{where, } h = \frac{10}{100} = 0.1\ m$$

$$\therefore \quad p = 0.1 \times 10^3 \times 10 = 10^3\ Pa$$

Q.14 Express standard atmospheric pressure in **[1×3]**

(i) Nm^{-2} (ii) bar (iii) torr

Sol. As we know,

(i) Standard atmospheric pressure = 76 cm of Hg

Also, pressure $(p) = \rho hg$

where, $h = 76$ cm $= 0.76$ m

$\rho(\text{Hg}) = 13.6 \times 10^3 \text{ kgm}^{-3}$, $g = 9.8 \text{ ms}^{-2}$

$\Rightarrow 1 \text{ atm} = 0.76 \times 13.6 \times 10^3 \times 9.8$

$= 1.013 \times 10^5 \text{ Nm}^{-2}$

(ii) $1 \text{ Nm}^{-2} = 10^{-5}$ bar

$\Rightarrow 1 \text{ atm} = 1.013 \text{ bar} = 1013$ millibar

(iii) 1 torr = 1 mm of Hg

$\Rightarrow$ 1 atm = 760 mm of Hg = 760 torr

Q.15 A container of area 0.02 m^2 is filled with water. Find the pressure at the bottom of the container, if a weight is placed on the piston (as shown in the figure). **[2]**

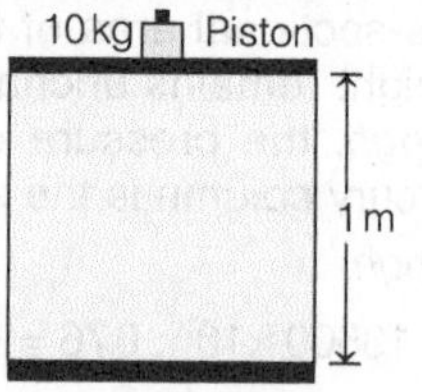

Sol. The pressure at the bottom is given by

$$p = \frac{mg}{A} + \rho gh = \frac{10 \times 9.8}{0.02} + 10^3 \times 9.8 \times 1 = 14.7 \text{ kPa}$$

Q.16 The figure shows two vertical tubes P and Q each closed at the upper end. The pressure in the space above the mercury meniscus in tube P is negligibly small. There is a small amount of air in this space in the tube Q.

The density of mercury is $13.6 \times 10^3 \text{ kg/m}^3$. The gravitational force on a mass of 1 kg is 10 N.

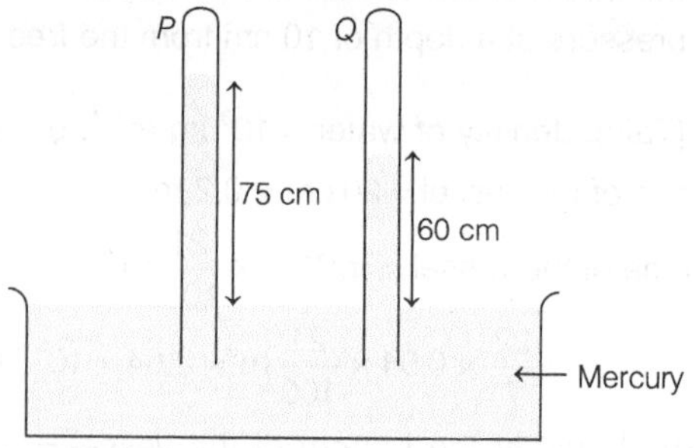

Using the data given in the figure, determine.

(i) The atmospheric pressure in Pa, at the time. **[1]**

(ii) The pressure in Pa, exerted by the air in the space at the top of tube Q. **[2]**

Sol. (i) Atmospheric pressure = ρgh of tube P

$= 13.6 \times 10^3 \times 10 \times 0.75 = 102000$ Pa

(ii) Air pressure at top of tube Q

= Atmospheric pressure – Liquid pressure due to 60 cm of mercury

$= (102000) - 13.6 \times 10^3 \times 0.6 \times 10 = 20400$ Pa

Q.17 The figure below shows a vessel containing water of density 10^3 kg m^{-3}. Its top surface is 30 cm wide. A cube of 10 cm is immersed inside the vessel as shown.

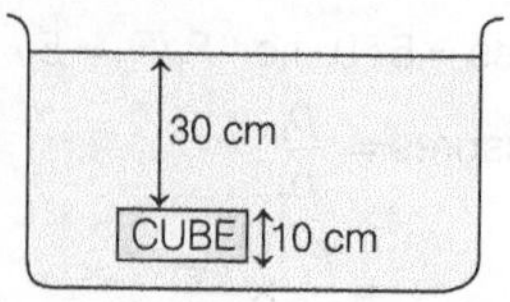

Find

(i) the pressure at the top of the cube. **[1]**

(ii) the pressure at the bottom of the cube. **[1]**

(iii) the resultant pressure on the cube. **[1]**

(vi) the resultant thrust on the cube. **[1]**

[Atm pressure $= 10^5$ Pa, $g = 9.8 \text{ m/s}^2$]

Sol. (i) Atmospheric pressure, $p_a = 10^5$ Pa.

Depth at the top of the cube from free surface of water $(h_1) = 30$ cm

$= 0.3$ m

$\therefore$ Pressure at the top of the cube,

$p_t = p_a + h_1 \rho g$

$\Rightarrow p_t = 10^5 + 0.3 \times 10^3 \times 9.8$

$= 10^5 + 2.94 \times 10^3 \text{ Pa} = 1.03 \times 10^5$ Pa

(ii) Depth at the bottom of the cube from free surface of water = (10 + 30) cm = 40 cm = 0.4 m

$\therefore$ Pressure at the bottom of the cube

$p_b = p_a + h\rho g$

$= 10^5 + 0.4 \times 10^3 \times 9.8$ Pa

$= 10^5 + 3.92 \times 10^3 \text{ Pa} = 1.04 \times 10^5$ Pa

(iii) The resultant pressure on the cube is

$p_R = p_b - p_t = (1.04 - 1.03) \times 10^5 \text{ Pa} = 10^3$ Pa

(iv) The area of the base of the cube is $= (10 \times 10) \text{ cm}^2$

$= 100 \text{ cm}^2 = 0.01 \text{ m}^2$

$\therefore$ Resultant thrust (F) = Resultant pressure × Area of base of cube

$\Rightarrow F = 10^3 \times 0.01 \text{ N} = 10$ N

Q.18 A tube of length ($L = 100$ cm) filled with a liquid of density $12 \times 10^3 \text{ kg m}^{-3}$ is placed inclined with the vertical such that level A of liquid is at a height 70 cm from the horizontal is shown in figure.

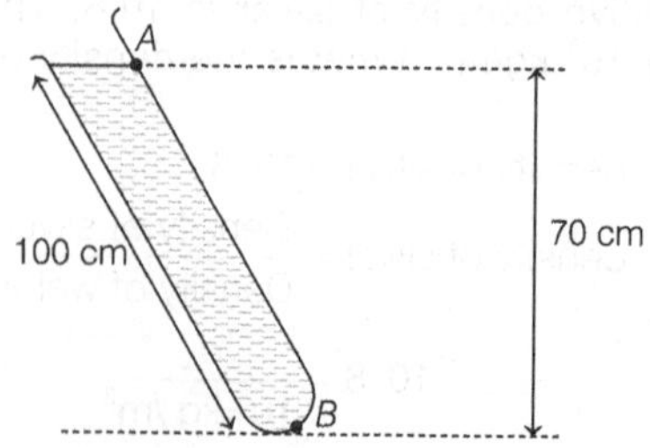

(i) Calculate the pressure at point A. **[1]**

(ii) Calculate the pressure at point B. **[1]**

(iii) Calculate the pressure at point B when the tube is made vertical. **[1]**

Take atmospheric pressure $p_a = 1.013 \times 10^5$ Pa

Ans. Given, $\rho = 1.2 \times 10^3$ kg m^{-3},

$g = 9.8$ ms^{-2}

(i) Pressure at point A = Atmospheric pressure p_a

$= 1.013 \times 10^5$ Pa

(ii) Pressure at point B = Atmospheric pressure + pressure due to liquid column of vertical height 70 cm

$= p_a + \rho gh = 1.013 \times 10^5 + 1.2 \times 10^3 \times 9.8 \times 0.70$

$= 1.09 \times 10^5$ Pa

(iii) Now, the tube is vertical. So, the pressure at point B is

Pressure = Atmospheric pressure + Pressure due to liquid column of height 100 cm

$= p_a + \rho gL$

$= 1.013 \times 10^5 + 1.2 \times 10^3 \times 9.8 \times 1 = 1.13 \times 10^5$ Pa

Q.19 The figure shows a simple hydraulic press.

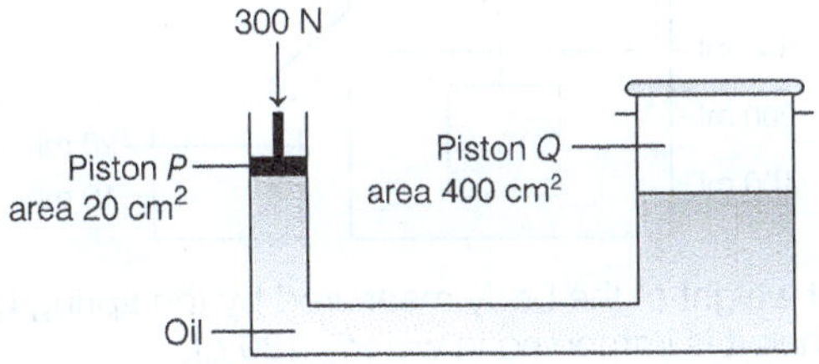

The area of piston P is 20 cm^2 and the area of piston Q is 400 cm^2. Piston P exerts a downward force of 300 N on the oil.

(i) Calculate the pressure, in N/cm^3, exerted by pistion P on the oil. **[1]**

(ii) Calculate the force exerted by the oil on piston Q. **[1]**

(iii) Piston P moves down 5 cm. **[1]**

(a) Calculate the volume of oil that moves over to pistion Q.

(b) Calculate the height that piston Q rises.

(iv) State why oil and not air is used in the hydraulic press? **[1]**

Sol. (i) Pressure $= \frac{F}{A} = \frac{300}{20} = 15$ N/cm^2

(ii) Let the force be F_Q.

$$\frac{F_Q}{A_Q} = 15 \Rightarrow F_Q = 15 \times 400 = 6000 \text{ N}$$

($\because$ Pressure is constant)

(iii) (a) Volume $= 20 \times 5 = 100$ cm^3

(b) Height $= \frac{100}{400} = 0.25$ cm

(iv) Oil is incompressible whereas air is compressible.

Q.20 A solid floats in water with (2/3)rd of its volume below the surface of water. Calculate the density of solid. **[3]**

Sol. Let the density and volume of solid be ρ and V, respectively.

$\therefore$ Weight of solid $= V\rho g$

Volume of solid in water $= \frac{2}{3}V$

= Volume of water displaced

Weight of the water displaced $= V'\rho' g = \frac{2}{3}V \times 10^3 \times g$

$\because$ Weight of body = Weight of water displaced

or $\quad V\rho g = \frac{2}{3}V \times 10^3 g$

$\Rightarrow \quad \rho = \frac{2}{3} \times 10^3 = 666.67$ kg m^{-3}

Q.21 A ball filled with air has a volume of 500 cm^3. Calculate the minimum force applied by a child to put it completely inside the water. (Take, $g = 10$ m s^{-2}) **[3]**

Sol. Given that,

Volume, $V = 500$ cm$^3 = 500 \times 10^{-6}$ m^3,

$g = 10$ ms^{-2}, $F = ?$

Force required to put the ball inside the water

= Buoyant force

= Weight of water displaced $= mg$ ...(i)

Now, we know that,

Mass of water = Density of water × Volume

$m = \rho V$

On substituting this value in Eq. (i) , we get

Force $= \rho Vg$

$= (1000 \text{ kg m}^{-3}) \times (500 \times 10^{-6} \text{ m}^3) \times (10 \text{ ms}^{-2})$

$= 1000 \times 500 \times 10^{-6} \times 10 = 5$ N

$\therefore$ Minimum force applied by a child to put the ball completely inside the water is 5 N.

Q.22 A body weighs 450 gf in air and 310 gf when completely immersed in water. Find

(i) the volume of the body. **[1]**

(ii) the loss in weight of the body. **[1]**

(iii) the upthrust on the body. **[1]**

Sol. Given, weight of the body in air = 450 kgf

Weight of the body in water = 310 kgf

Density of water = 1 g cm^{-3}

(i) Volume of the body $= \frac{\text{Loss in weight}}{\text{Density of water}}$

$= \frac{(450 - 310)}{1} = 140$ cm^3

(ii) Loss in weight = Weight of the body in air − Weight of the body in water

$= 450 - 310 = 140$ gf

(iii) Upthrust on the body = Loss in weight = 140 gf

Q.23 When an object is suspended form a spring balance the reading is 10 N. When the object is completely submerged in water, the reading is 4 N.

(i) Calculate the buoyant force. **[1]**

(ii) Calculate the volume of the object. **[1]**

(iii) Calculate the density of the object. **[1]**

(Take, density of water $\rho_w = 1000\ kg/m^3$ and $g = 10 m/s^2$)

Ans. (i) Given, actual weight, $W = 10$ N

Apparent weight $W_A = 4$ N

$\therefore$ Buoyant force, $W - W_A$

$F_B = 10 - 4$

$F_B = 6$ N

(ii) Let the volume of water displaced by the object be V.

Hence, Buoyant force $= V\rho_w g$

or $6 = V \times 1000 \times 10$

$\therefore\ V = 6 \times 10^{-4}\ m^3$

$\because$ Volume of object = Volume of water displaced

$\therefore$ Volume of object $= 6 \times 10^{-4}\ m^3$

(iii) Actual weight $W = 10$ N or kg m/s^2

or $mg = 10$

$\therefore\ V\rho_s g = 10$

where, ρ_s is the density of the object.

$6 \times 10^{-4} \times \rho_s \times 10 = 10$

$\rho_s = 1666.67\ kg/m^3$

Q.24 A vessel of area of cross-section 80 cm × 30 cm and height 150 cm is filled with a liquid of density $1.25 \times 10^3\ kg\ m^{-3}$.

Note Ignore the atmospheric pressure

(i) Calculate the thrust at the bottom of the vessel. **[1]**

(ii) Calculate the pressure at the bottom of the vessel. **[1]**

(iii) Calculate the net force experienced by a metal foil of cross-section 5 cm^2 placed at a depth of 6 cm from the free surface of liquid.

(Take, $g = 9.8\ m/s^2$)

Ans. Area of cross-section

$$A = 80\ cm \times 30\ cm = \frac{80}{100} m \times \frac{30}{100} m = 0.24\ m^2$$

Height $h = 150$ cm $= 1.5$ m

Volume = 80 cm × 30 cm × 150 cm

$$= \frac{80}{100} \times \frac{30}{100} \times \frac{150}{100} = 0.36\ m^3$$

(i) Thrust at the bottom of the vessel $= mg$

or $V\rho g$

$= 0.36 \times 1.25 \times 10^3 \times 9.8 = 4.4 \times 10^3$ N

(ii) Pressure at the bottom of the vessel $= \dfrac{\text{Thrust}}{\text{Area}}$

$$= \frac{4.4 \times 10^3}{0.24} = 1.83 \times 10^4\ N.m^{-2} \text{ or Pa}$$

(iii) Net force on the metal foil will be zero because the force exerted on each of two faces (top and bottom) of a foil, by the liquid will be equal and opposite.

Q.25 An object suspended from a spring balance is immersed in water filled inside an overflow jar. The water displaced by the object is collected in an empty beaker placed below the spout of the overflow jar. If the reading on the spring balance is 180 gf, then calculate the pressure exerted due to the immersion of object at the bottom of the container. Will there be any change in pressure at the bottom of the container if the object is dropped into water?

The height of the overflow jar up to the spout is 10 cm and the area of the lower face of the block is 4 cm^2. **[2]**

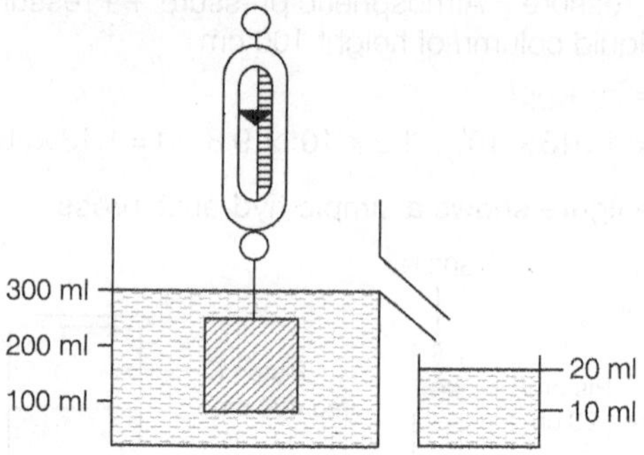

Ans. Net weight of the body measured by the spring balance when it is immersed in water = 180 gf

$= 1800 \times 0.001 = 1.8$ N

$$\text{Pressure} = \frac{\text{Force}}{\text{Area of the block}} = \frac{1.8\ N}{4 \times 10^{-4}\ m^2} = 4500\ Pa$$

When an object is dropped, the pressure at the bottom increases due to an increase in the height of the water column.

Q.26 A body of weight 4 N weighs 3 N when submerged in water. Find

(i) the volume and the relative density of the solid. **[2]**

(ii) the weight of the solid when it is immersed in a liquid of density 0.7 g cm^{-3}. **[2]**

[Take, density of water $= 1 g\ cm^{-3}$, $g = 10\ m/s^2$]

Sol. (i) Weight of the body in air = 4 N

Weight of the body in water = 3 N

$\therefore$ Weight of displaced liquid = (4 − 3) N = 1N

$$\therefore \text{Mass of the liquid} = \frac{1}{10} = 0.1 kg = 100\ g$$

$$\therefore \quad \text{Volume} = \frac{\text{Mass}}{\text{Density}} = \frac{100}{1} = 100\ cm^3$$

$$\text{Mass of the solid} = \frac{4}{10} kg = 400\ g$$

$$\text{Density of the solid} = \frac{400}{100} = 4\ gcm^{-3}$$

Relative density of the solid $= \frac{4}{1} = 4$

(ii) Volume of the liquid displaced $= 100\ cm^3$

Density of the given liquid $= 0.7\ g\ cm^{-3}$

$\therefore$ Mass of the displaced liquid $= 100 \times 0.7 = 70\ g$

$\therefore$ Weight of the displaced liquid $= \frac{70}{1000} \times 10\ N$

$= 0.7\ N$

$\therefore$ Weight of the solid in the liquid $= (4 - 0.7)\ N$

$= 3.3\ N$

Q.27 **The volume of 50 g of a substance is 20 cm^3. If the density of water is 1 g cm^{-3}, will the substance float or sink?** **[2]**

Sol. Given, mass of substance, $m = 50\ g$

Volume of substance, $V = 20\ cm^3$

$\therefore$ Density of substance,

$$\rho = \frac{\text{Mass}}{\text{Volume}} = \frac{50}{20} = 2.5\ g\ cm^{-3}$$

i.e. the density of the substance is greater than the density of water, so it will sink in the water.

Q.28 **A body weighs 65 g in air, 60.5 g in water and 56 g in a liquid. Calculate the relative density of the liquid.** **[2]**

Sol. Loss in weight of the body in water

$= 65 - 60.5 = 4.5\ g$

Loss in weight of the body in liquid

$= 65 - 56 = 9\ g$

$\therefore$ Relative density of the liquid

$$= \frac{\text{Loss of weight in liquid}}{\text{Loss of weight in water}} = \frac{9}{4.5} = 2$$

Q.29 **A cubical object of side 4 cm has fallen in a well. If mass of the cube is 2 kg, then state whether this object will float or sink in water. (Take, density of water = 1000 kg m^{-3})** **[3]**

Sol. Given that,

Mass of the object, $m = 2\ kg$

Side of cube $= 4\ cm = 0.04\ m$ $[\because 1\ m = 100\ cm]$

Since, volume of cube $= (\text{side})^3$

$\therefore$ Volume of the object, $V = (0.04\ m)^3$

$= 0.000064\ m^3$

As we know that,

$$\text{Density} = \frac{\text{Mass of the object}}{\text{Volume of the object}}$$

$$\Rightarrow \quad \text{Density} = \frac{2}{0.000064}\ kgm^{-3}$$

$$= \frac{2000000}{64}\ kgm^{-3} = 31250\ kg\ m^{-3}$$

Here, density of the object (i.e. 31250 kgm^{-3}) is greater than the density of water (i.e. 1000 kgm^{-3}).

Therefore, the object will sink in water.

Q.30 **A body weighs 85.2 gf in air, 78.5 gf in water and 74.8 gf in a liquid.**

(i) Find the relative density of the liquid. **[2]**

(ii) How much will it weigh if immersed in a liquid of relative density 0.79? **[2]**

Ans. (i) Weight of the body in air $= w$gf

$= 85.2\ g\ f$

Weight of the body in liquid $= w_1$ gf

$= 74.8\ g\ f$

Weight of the body in water $= w_2$ gf

$= 78.5\ g\ f$

$$\text{Relative density} = \frac{w - w_1}{w - w_2} = \frac{85.2 - 74.8}{85.2 - 78.5} = \frac{10.4}{6.7} = 1.55$$

(ii) Relative density of liquid $= 0.79$

$$\text{Relative density} = \frac{w - w_1}{w - w_2}$$

$$\Rightarrow \quad 0.79 = \frac{(852 - w_1)}{(85.2 - 78.5)}$$

$$852 - w_1 = 6.7 \times 0.79$$

$$w_1 = 79.9\ gf$$

Therefore, the weight of the body in the given liquid is 79.9 gf.

Q.31 **Ishita noted down the following observations in her notebook.** **[2]**

(i) Weight of the stone in air = 280 g-wt

(ii) Weight of the stone in pure water = 240 g-wt

(iii) Weight of the stone in salty water = 190 g-wt

Find the relative density of salty water.

Sol. Relative density of salty water

$$= \frac{\text{Loss in weight in salty water}}{\text{Loss in weight in pure water}}$$

$$= \frac{280 - 190}{280 - 240} = \frac{90}{40} = \frac{9}{4} = 2.25$$

Q.32 **A piece of wood of volume 300 cm^3 and density 0.66 g cm^{-3} floats in a liquid of density 1.05 g cm^{-3}.**

(i) Calculate the volume of wood which remain above the surface of liquid. **[2]**

(ii) Calculate the required force to submerge the wood under water. (Take, $g = 9.8\ m/s^2$) **[2]**

Ans. Given, $V = 300\ cm^3$,

$\rho_s = 0.66\ g\ cm^{-3}$, $\rho_2 = 1.05\ g\ cm^{-3}$

(i) Let $V'\ cm^3$ be the volume of wood which remain above the surface of liquid.

$\therefore$ Submerged volume of wood

$= V - V' = (300 - V')$

By the principle of floatation,

Weight of wood piece = Weight of the liquid displaced by the submerged part of the wood

$300 \times 0.66 \times 9.8 = (300 - V') \times 1.05 \times 9.8$

$$V' = \frac{300 \times (1.05 - 0.66)}{1.05}$$

$V' = 111.4 \text{ cm}^3$

(ii) When piece of wood is totally submerged

upthrust $= V \times \rho_2 \times g$

$= 300 \times 1.05 \times g = 315\text{gf}$ (upwards)

Weight of wood $= V \times \rho_s \times g = 300 \times 0.66 \times g$

$= 198\text{gf}$ (downward)

$\therefore$ Force required to keep the wood inside water

= Upthrust – Weight of wood piece

$= (315 - 198)$ gf $= 117$ gf

Q.33 **A weather forecasting plastic balloon has volume of 12m^3 and it is filled with hydrogen, which has a density of 0.09 kg/m^3. The equipment carried by the balloon has a negligible volume compared to its own volume. The mass of the empty balloon is 6 kg. The balloon is floating in air, which has a density of 1.2 kg/m^3.**

Calculate

(i) The mass of hydrogen inside the balloon. **[1]**

(ii) The combine mass of hydrogen and the balloon. **[1]**

(iii) The total mass of hydrogen gas, balloon and equipment. **[1]**

(iv) The mass of air displaced by the balloon and the mass of the equipment using the law of floatation. **[1]**

Ans. Given, volume of plastic balloon

$$V_{\text{balloon}} = 12 \text{ m}^3$$

Mass of empty balloon, $m_{\text{balloon}} = 6$ kg

Density of hydrogen,

$$\rho_{\text{Hydrogen}} = 0.09 \text{ kg/m}^3$$

Density of air, $\rho_{\text{Air}} = 1.2 \text{ kg/m}^3$

Mass of hydrogen in ballon (m_{hydrogen})

$m_{\text{hydrogen}} = V_{\text{balloon}} \times \rho_{\text{hydrogen}}$

$= 12 \times 0.09$

$= 1.08$ kg

(ii) Mass of hydrogen and balloon (M),

$= m_{\text{balloon}} + m_{\text{hydrogen}}$

$= (6 + 1.08)$ kg

$= 7.08$ kg

(iii) Let the mass of equipment be x. Therefore,

Total mass

$(M_{\text{Total}}) = m_{\text{balloon}} + m_{\text{hydrogen}} + x$

$= 6 + 1.08 + x$

$= (7.08 + x)$ kg

(iv) Weight of displaced air = Upthrust

$W = V_{\text{balloon}} \times \rho_{\text{air}} \times g$

$\Rightarrow \quad mg = V_{\text{balloon}} \times \rho_{\text{air}} \times g$

$\Rightarrow \quad m = V_{\text{balloon}} \times \rho_{\text{air}}$

$\therefore \quad m = 12 \times 1.2$

or $\quad m = 14.4$ kg

According to the law of floatation,

Mass of air displaced (m_{air})

= Total mass (M_{Total}) of the balloon system

$14.4 = 7.08 + x$

$x = 7.32$ kg

Therefore, the mass of the equipment is 7.32 kg.

Q.34 **Two identical blocks X and Y of different materials float on water such that 80% of X and 20% of Y remain submerged inside water. Compare**

(i) The density of X and Y. **[2]**

(ii) The buoyant force on A and B. **[1]**

Ans. Let ρ_X and ρ_Y be the densitities of blocks X and Y.

The fraction of a floating object's volume submerged in a fluid is given by

$$\frac{\text{Volume submerged}}{\text{Total Volume}} = \frac{\text{Density of object}}{\text{Density of fluid}}$$

For block X,

$$\frac{80}{100} = \frac{\rho_X}{\rho_{\text{water}}}$$

$$\rho_X = 0.8 \rho_{\text{water}} \quad \ldots\text{(i)}$$

For block Y,

$$\frac{20}{100} = \frac{\rho_Y}{\rho_{\text{water}}}$$

$$\rho_Y = 0.2 \rho_{\text{water}} \quad \ldots\text{(ii)}$$

From Eqs. (i) and (ii),

$$\frac{\rho_X}{\rho_Y} = \frac{0.8}{02} = \frac{4}{1}$$

$\therefore$ The density of block X is 4 times the density of block Y.

(ii) If V is the volume of each block.

Then, $\dfrac{\text{Buoyant force on } X}{\text{Buoyant force on } Y} = \dfrac{V\rho_X g}{V\rho_Y g}$

$$= \frac{\rho_X}{\rho_Y} = 4:1$$

Q.35 **A piece of copper floats in mercury. Given that the density of copper is 4.2×10^3 kg m^{-3} and that of mercury is 13.6×10^3 kg m^{-3}. Calculate the fraction of volume of a copper piece that remains outside the mercury.** **[2]**

Sol. Fraction of copper piece that remains inside mercury,

$$\frac{V'}{V} = \frac{\rho}{\rho'} = \frac{4.2 \times 10^3}{13.6 \times 10^3} = 0.31$$

Fraction of copper piece that remains outside mercury

$= 1 - 0.31 = 0.69$

06

HEAT

Heat

- Heat possessed by the body is the total internal energy of the molecules of the body. Total internal energy is equal to **sum of kinetic and potential energies** of all individual molecules.
- Heat is the form of energy which flows from **hotter body** to **colder body** by virtue of temperature difference, when bodies are kept in contact.
- The process of transfer of heat is a **non-mechanical process**, i.e. there is no mechanical work involved in the process of heat transfer.
- The amount of heat is measured in **joule** (SI unit).
- Another widely used unit for the heat is **calorie**, where 1 cal = 4.186 J (or nearly 4.2 J). or 1 J = 0.24 cal

  Similarly, 1 kcal = 1000 cal

  The CGS unit of heat is **erg**, where 1 erg $= 10^{-7}$ J.

Temperature

- The degree of hotness or coldness is called temperature. It is a fundamental physical quantity.
- Its SI unit is **kelvin** (K). Another units of temperature are **Celsius** (°C) and **Fahrenheit** (°F).
- Temperature of a body is measured by a device called **thermometer**.
- The temperature on celsius and fahrenheit scales are related as

$$\boxed{\frac{C}{5} = \frac{F-32}{9} \quad \text{or} \quad F = 32 + \frac{9}{5}C}$$

- The temperature on celsius and kelvin scales are related as $K = 273 + C$
- The relationship between these different scales of temperature is given below as

$$\boxed{\frac{C-0}{100} = \frac{F-32}{180} = \frac{K-273}{100}}$$

where, C = temperature on celsius scale, F = temperature on fahrenheit scale,

and K = temperature on kelvin scale.

Thermal Expansion

- When heat is supplied to the material, its dimensions (length, breadth and height) change due to change in its temperature.
- The phenomenon of changing in dimensions of an object due to heat supply, is known as thermal expansion.
- There are three types of thermal expansion, linear expansion, areal expansion and volume expansion.

(i) Linear Expansion

Expansion in **length** of a body due to **increase in its temperature** is called linear expansion.

(ii) Areal (or superficial) Expansion

Expansion in **area** of a body due to **increase in temperature** is called areal or superficial expansion.

(iii) Volumetric expansion

Expansion in the **volume** of the body due to **increase in temperature** is called volumetric expansion.

Anomalous Expansion of Water

- In the case of fluids, with the rise of temperature, the **volume increases**. Therefore, the **density decreases**.
- But water shows an **anomalous behaviour**, as it contracts on heating between the temperature 0°C to 4°C.
- When water is **cooled** below the room temperature (i.e. normal temperature), the **volume** of given amount of water **decreases**. Until its temperature reaches to 4°C, and hence **density increases**.
- The graph shows the variation of volume of 1 kg of water with temperature from 0°C to 10°C.

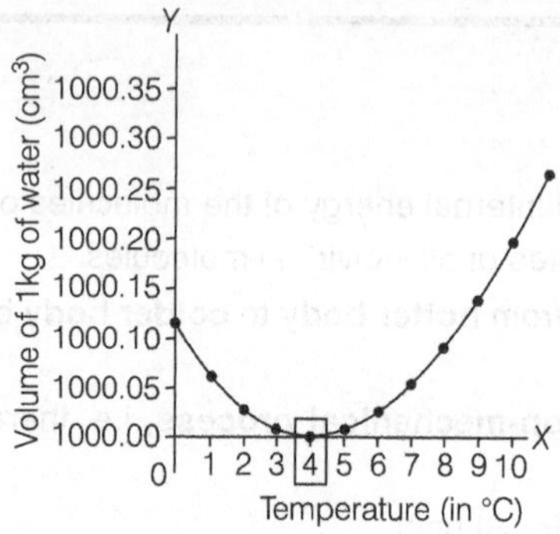

- The graph shows the variation of density of water with respect to temperature from 0°C to 10°C.

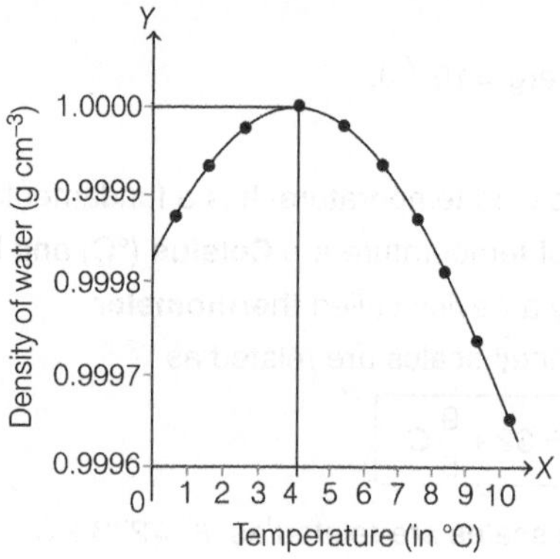

- Other substances that to show the anomalous behaviour are silver iodide from 80°C to 141°C and silica below – 80°C.

Consequences of Anomalous Expansion of Water

Preservation of Aquatic Life

As the temperature starts to drop **below 4°C**, the density of water **increases**, causing the colder water to **sink** while relatively warmer water **rises** to the surface. This process continues until the entire water **reaches 4°C**. When the temperature **falls** further, the upper layer begins to **freeze**, forming an ice layer. This **ice layer** acts as an insulating blanket, preventing further **heat loss** and keeping the water below at 4°C in liquid form, providing a livable environment for fish and other aquatic organisms.

Bursting of Pipes

In winter, as the atmospheric temperature starts falling below 4°C, water in pipelines expands and exerts a very large pressure on the pipes which causes bursting of pipes.

Destroying of Crops During Very Cold Nights

In cold nights, water inside the plant cells expands due to fall in temperature. It causes rupturing of plant cells resulting in plant's death. In order to save plants against it, crop fields are filled with water because water releases heat as it freezes, keeping the plants temperature above the freezing point.

EXAM ORIENTED QUESTIONS

TYPE - 1 — 01 Mark

Multiple Choice Questions

Q.1 Which of the following is not the unit of heat?
(a) Calorie (b) Erg (c) Torr (d) Joule

Ans. (c) Torr is not the unit of heat, it is the unit of pressure.

Q.2 Temperature in kelvin is obtained by
(a) subtracting 273 from the temperature in degree celsius.
(b) adding 273 with the temperature in degree celsius.
(c) adding 32 with the temperature in degree celsius.
(d) subtracting 32 from the temperature in degree celsius.

Ans. (b) $T_K = 273 + T_C$

Q.3 The length between the –10°C and 120°C markings of a mercury-in-glass thermometer is 20 cm.

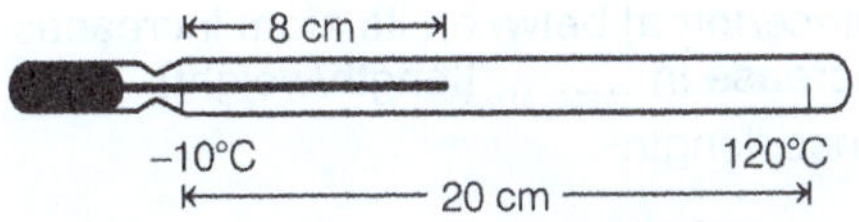

What is the temperature reading taken directly from the thermometer when the mercury thread is 8 cm from the –10°C mark ?
(a) 34° C (b) 42° C
(c) 44° C (d) 52° C

Ans. (b) The reference points for this thermometer are –10°C and 120°C. The span is 130°C for the length of 20 cm.

Unknown temperature calculated $= \frac{8}{20} \times 130°\text{C} = 52°\text{C}$

However, temperature reading from thermometer

$$= 52\ °\text{C} - 10\ °\text{C} = 42\ °\text{C}$$

Q.4 On heating a liquid of cubical expansion γ in a container having coefficient of linear expansion $\frac{\gamma}{3}$, the level of liquid in the container will
(a) rise (b) fall
(c) remain stationary (d) firstly rise then fall

Ans. (c) remain stationary

If linear expansion is α, then

$$\gamma = 3\alpha$$

Here, $\alpha = \frac{\gamma}{3}$. So, $\gamma' = 3 \times \frac{\gamma}{3}$

Thus, $\gamma' = \gamma$

Hence, volume expansion remains unchanged.

Q.5 What happens to a liquid with a high coefficient of expansion when heated?
(a) Its density increases
(b) Its volume decreases
(c) It evaporates faster
(d) It expands significantly

Ans. (d) It expands significantly

A high coefficient of expansion means the liquid's volume increases greatly with temperature.

Q.6 Water shows an anomalous behaviour
(a) at 0°C (b) at 4°C
(c) above 4°C (d) between 4°C and 0°C

Ans. (d) Water shows an anomalous behaviour between 4°C and 0°C, as it expands with decreasing temperature.

Q.7 Water is cooled from 4°C to 0°C. It
(a) expands (b) first expands, then contracts
(c) contracts (d) Both (a) and (b)

Ans. (a) Due to anomalous expansion of water, the volume of water increases as the temperature falls from 4°C to 0°C.

Q.8 The density of water is maximum at
(a) 0°C (b) 100°C (c) 4°C (d) 273°C

Ans. (c) Water has maximum density at 4°C.

Q.9 Which one of the following graphs correctly represents the variation of volume of 1kg of water with temperature?

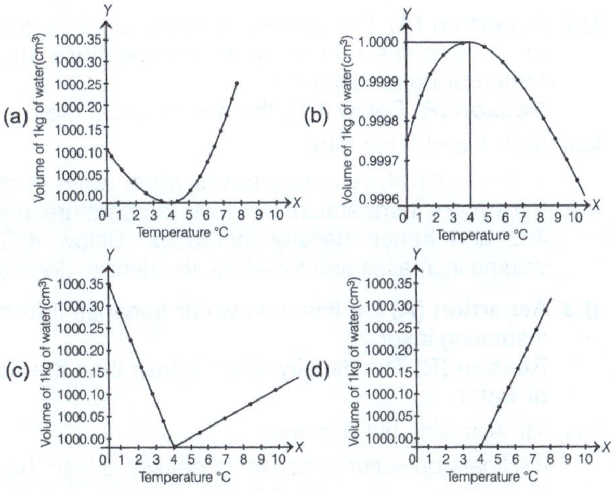

Ans. (a) As the temperature decreases, the volume of water decreases. Volume of water becomes minimum at 4°C. As temperature goes below 4°C, its volume starts increasing.

Q.10 The volume of 1g of water at 4°C is

(a) 0.995 cm^3 (b) 1.008 cm^3

(c) 1.000 cm^3 (d) 1.006 cm^3

Ans. (c) At 4°C, the density of water is exactly 1g/cm^3. So, at that temperature if mass is 1g, the volume will be 1.000 cm^3.

Q.11 Surface of the lake is at 2°C. Find the temperature of the bottom of the lake.

(a) 2°C (b) 3°C

(c) 4°C (d) 1°C

Ans. (c) The dense layer of water will be at the bottom of the lake. The density of water is maximum at 4°C. So, the temperature of bottom of the lake will be 4°C.

TYPE - 2 01 Mark

Assertion-Reason Type Questions

Direction (Q. Nos. 1-5) In the Following questions statement are given Assertion and Reason.

(a) Both A and R are true and R is the correct explanation of A.

(b) Both A and R are true but R is not the correct explanation of A.

(c) A is true but R is false.

(d) A is false but R is true.

Q.1 Assertion (A) Thermal expansion occurs in all states of matter.

Reason (R) Expansion occurs because particles vibrate more vigorously when heated.

Ans. (a) Heat increases particle's movement, causing expansion in solids, liquids and gases.

Q.2 Assertion (A) The density of water remains constant as it is cooled from room temperature until its temperature reaches 4°C.

Reason (R) Below 4°C, the density increases.

Ans. Both A and R are false.

The volume of water decreases when water is cooled from room temperature until its temperature reaches 4°C and hence density increases. Below 4°C, the volume increases and therefore, the density decreases.

Q.3 Assertion (A) Ice floats on water because it forms an insulating layer.

Reason (R) The density of ice is less than the density of water.

Ans. (d) A is false but R is true.

Ice floats on water because its density is less than that of water, forming an insulating layer that prevents water bodies from freezing completely.

Q.4 Asserton (A) Hope's experiment demonstrates the anomalous expansion of water.

Reason (R) Water contracts when cooled from 10°C to 4°C and expands below 4°C.

Ans. (a) Hope's experiment proves water's unique property of contracting until 4°C and then expanding as it cools further, causing the bottom layer to remain at 4°C while the top freezes.

Q.5 Assertion (A) Pipes burst during extreme winters in cold regions.

Reason (R) Water expands on freezing due to its anomalous behavior.

Ans. (a) Both A and R are true and R is the correct explanation of A.

The expansion of water upon freezing, exerts pressure on pipes, causing them to burst in cold regions.

TYPE - 3 01/02 Marks

Fill in the Blanks

Q.1 If heat energy is given to a substance and its temperature remains constant, then the substance undergoes a change in ....[state/volume] **[1]**

Ans. state

Q.2 A metal rod expands when heated as the .... [distance/force] between its atom increases causing an increase in .... [length/weight] **[2]**

Ans. distance, length

Q.3 Fishes survive in ponds even when the atmospheric temperature is well below.........°C. [0/4] **[1]**

Ans. 0°C

Q.4 On heating from 0°C to 4°C, the volume of water ....[increases/deceases] and the density of water ....[increses/decreases]. **[2]**

Ans. decreases, increases

Q.5 The temperature at which density of water is maximum, is .... °C. (0/4) **[1]**

Ans. 4

TYPE - 4 02 Marks

Very Short Answer Type Questions

Q.1 Two bodies *P* and *Q* have quantity of heat 1000 J and 100 J and their respective temperatures are 90°C and 24°C. Both of them are kept in contact. How does the heat flow between them?

Ans. Flow of heat does not depend on heat contained by the body. Flow of heat is due to temperature difference only.

So, heat will flow from body *P* to *Q*, as the temperature of body *P* is more than that of body *Q*.

Q.2 Why does a piece of ice when touched with hand appear cool? Explain.

Ans. On touching ice, heat is transferred from our hand to the ice.

Q.3 When does heat stop flowing from one object to another?

Ans. The flow of heat from one object to another object depends on the temperature difference between them. Heat will continue to flow until the temperatures of both objects become equal.

Q.4 How can we say that one body is hotter than other? Give a term to find out the degree of hotness. Write its units of measurement also.

Ans. If on touching a body, heat from that body flows towards our hand, then we can conclude that the body is hot.

Temperature determines the degree of hotness or coldness of a substance. It is a fundamental quantity. Its units of measurement are

(i) Kelvin (K) (ii) Celsius (°C)

(iii) Fahrenheit (°F)

Q.5 Why do cooling rooms have hollow walls filled with air?

Ans. Air is a poor conductor of heat. So, it act as insulation for cold storage rooms. The air trapped inside the hollow bricks reduces heat transfer. In this way, air helps to maintain low temperature inside the storage room.

Q.6 What do you mean by thermal expansion, write its types?

Ans. Thermal expansion of a substance is the increase in its size with the increase in temperature.

It is of three types

(i) Linear expansion (ii) Areal expansion

(iii) Volumetric expansion

Q.7 Write any two substances other than water that also show anomalous behaviour.

Ans. The substances other than water that show the anomalous behaviour are

(i) silver iodide from 80°C to 141°C,

(ii) silica below –80°C.

Q.8 Draw a diagram showing the temperature of various layers of water in an ice covered pond.

Ans.

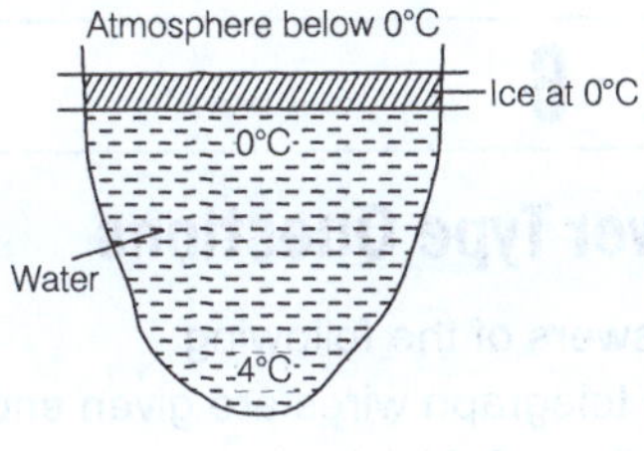

Q.9 How crops are destroyed due to the anomalous behaviour of water?

Ans. When temperature of the water within plant tissue decreases below 4°C, water expands in the capillary tubes and exerts pressure on it, causing them to burst. For this reason, crops are destroyed due to the anomalous behaviour of water.

TYPE - 5   03 Marks

Short Answer Type Questions

Q.1 How can you say that heat is a form of energy?

Ans. From the kinetic theory of matter, it is clear that the molecules of water have greater energy than those of ice and the molecules of steam have greater energy than those of water.

When we supply heat to a block of ice to convert it into water, we increase the energy of its molecules. As, it is clear that the supplying heat to a substance increases the energy of that substance. Hence, we can say that heat is a form of energy.

Q.2 Is 'touching' a proper method to measure the hotness of an object? Explain with example.

Ans. No, touching is not a proper method to measure the hotness of an object.

Illustration Take three vessels *A*, *B* and *C* and fill tap water in them. Heat vessel *A* slightly and put some ice cubes in vessel *C*. Now, put the three vessels side by side. Put your right hand in vessel *A* and left hand in vessel *C* for about two minutes.

Now, put both the hands in vessel *B*. Your right hand feels that the water in vessel *B* is cold, while your left hand feels that it is warm. This example explains that the feeling on touching depends on our condition. Same object may feel warm or cold depending on the temperature of our hand.

Q.3 Write two difference between heat and temperature.

Ans. Differences between heat and temperature

Heat	Temperature
It is a form of energy that is transferred from one body to another as the result of difference in temperature.	It is the measure of degree of hotness or coldness of a body, expressed in terms of any of several arbitrary scales, like celsius, fahrenheit and kelvin.
SI unit of heat is joule (J).	SI unit of temperature is kelvin (K).
It is not a fundamental quantity.	It is a fundamental quantity.

Heat	Temperature
Heat has ability to do work.	Temperature can only be used to measure the degree of heat.
The amount of heat lost by any hotter body is equal to the heat gained by colder body.	The fall in temperature of hotter body may not be equal to temperature rise in colder body.
Heat is measured by the principle of calorimetry.	Temperature is measured by a thermometer.

Q.4 Thermal expansion can be a problem.

Small gaps are left in railway lines and in bridges, as shown in figure.

(a) Explain in detail why the gaps are needed. **[2]**

(b) State one other problem caused by thermal expansion and explain how it can be solved **[1]**

Ans. (a) When railway tracks are laid, gaps are left between two successive lengths of the railway lines. Similarly, the roads on bridges are made in small sections with a small gap between the two sections. During summer, the metal railway lines and bridges expand due to the rise in temperature. The gaps allow this expansion and prevent the buckling or deformation of the track.

(b) When hot water is poured into a glass tumbler, cracks are developed in the glass due to the un-even expansion of the inner and outer surfaces of the glass. To prevent it, the tumblers are made of thin glass.

Q.5 Most substances expand when they are heated.

(a) (i) State one example where expansion is useful.

(ii) State one example where expansion causes a problem. **[1]**

(b) Explain using ideas about molecules, why solids expand when heated. **[1]**

(d) When equal volumes are heated through the same temperature rise, the expansions of solids, liquids and gases are different.

Complete each of the two sentences using one of these expressions. **[1]**

Ans. (a) (i) Expansion is useful in bimetallic strips, which are used in electric thermostats.

(ii) Expansion of railway lines and concrete bridges on hot days.

(b) When heated, molecules of a solid have more potential and kinetic energies. Therefore, they vibrate faster than before and with larger amplitude. The distance between the molecules increases and the solid expands.

(c) 1. The expansion of a solid is **slightly smaller** than the expansion of a liquid.

2. The expansion of a gas is **much larger** than the expansion of a liquid.

Q.6 If a given mass of water is heated from 0°C to 10°C, sketch the volume-temperature graph to show the behaviour of water.

Ans. The volume-temperature graph is shown below

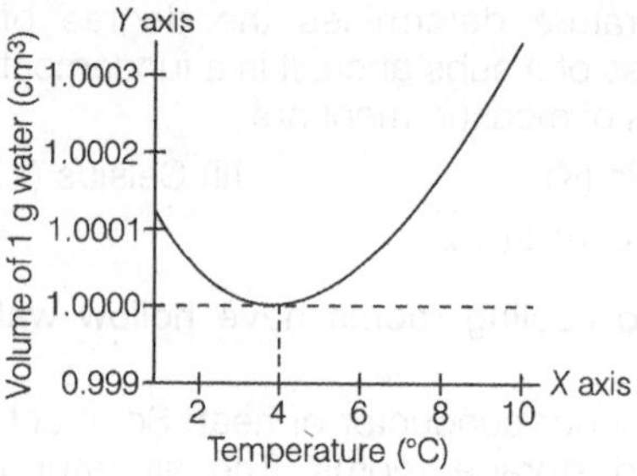

The above graph shows that the volume of water first decreases on heating it from 0°C to 4°C and then increases on further heating it from 4°C to 10°C. Thus, water has minimum volume at 4°C.

Q.7 Draw a graph showing the variation of density of water with temperature.

Ans. The density-temperature graph is shown below

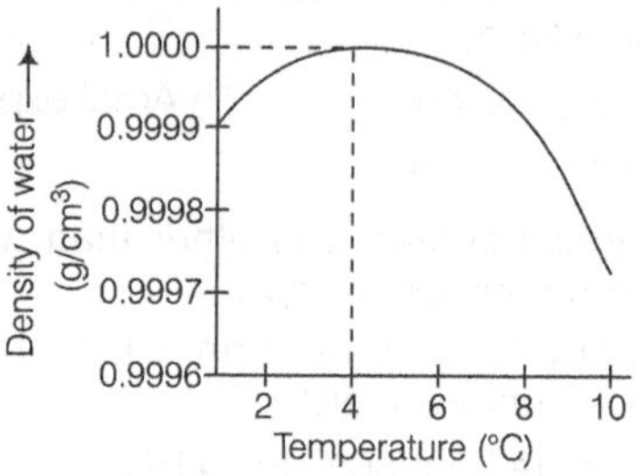

The above graph shows that when water is heated from 0°C, the density of water first increases from 0°C to 4°C and then decreases above 4°C. Thus, the water has maximum density at 4°C.

TYPE - 6 — 04 Marks

Long Answer Type Questions

Q.1 Give answers of the following

(i) Why telegraph wires are given enough sag? **[2]**

(ii) Why the soft drink bottles are made of thick glass? **[2]**

Ans. (i) Since, wires are made up of metal and metal contracts when temperature falls, Therefore telegraph wires are kept loose, so that they may not break on contraction in winters.

(ii) In soda water/soft drink bottles, some gases remain in it, when it is packed. During summers, the temperature of the gas increases due to which gas expands (volume expansion of gas) and exerts a large pressure on the wall and cap of the bottle. If the glass of the bottle is not sufficiently thick and strong, it may crack down to expansion force.

Q.2 Draw a graph showing the variation of density of water with temperature.
Answer the following questions based on the drawn graph.

(i) At what temperature, density of water is maximum? [1]

(ii) What happens to the density of water as it is cooled from 10°C to 4°C? [1]

(iii) What happens to the density of water as it is cooled from 4°C to 0°C? [2]

Ans.

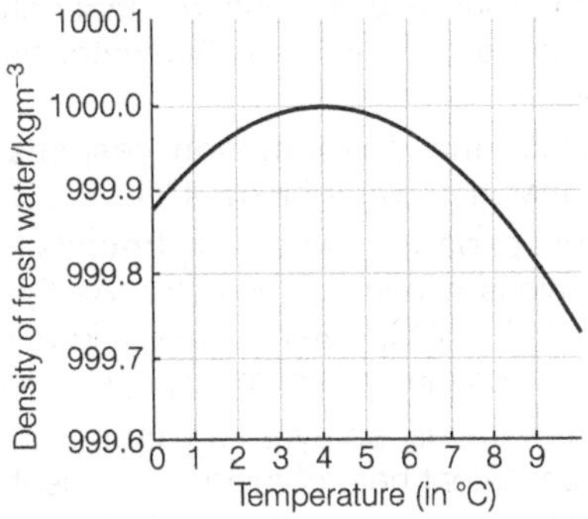

(i) The density of water is maximum at 4°C.

(ii) The density of water increases as it is cooled from 10°C to 4°C.

(iii) The density of water decreases as it is cooled from 4°C to 0°C.

Q.3 How does the anomalous expansion of water help in preserving the aquatic life during every cold weather?

Or **How do fish survive in frozen lakes?**

Or **How are aquatic animals able to survive inside a frozen pond?**

Ans. In cold weather, when the atmospheric temperature starts falling below 0°C, the temperature of the water at the surface of a pond starts falling as it radiates heat to the atmosphere. As the temperature of water on the surface falls upto 4°C, its density increases and hence it sinks to the bottom and this continues till the temperature of the entire water reaches to 4°C. Now, when the water on the surface cools further below 4°C, it starts expanding and hence the density of the surface layer of water decreases. So, it remains on the surface of the lake and gradually freezes into ice. So, it prevents the heat from the water in the layer below to flow into the atmosphere. This is the reason why aquatic life is preserved during very cold weather.

Q.4 Describe Hope's experiment with its construction and observation.

Ans. Scientist TC Hope in year 1805 devised an arrangement, known as Hope's apparatus to demonstrate the anomalous behaviour of water.

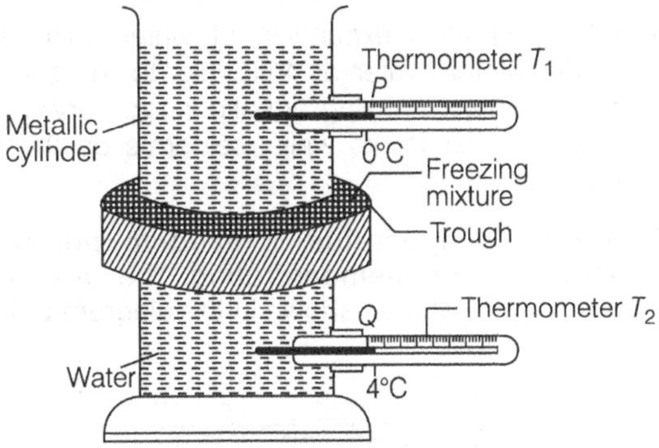

Construction

- It consists of a long cylindrical jar with two opening side, one near the top and the other near the bottom to fit thermometers.
- Two thermometers T_1 and T_2 are fitted air tight on the two openings of the cylindrical jar as shown in figure.
- The cylindrical jar is filled with water. The cylindrical trough at the central portion of the jar is filled with a freezing mixture of ice and common salt.

Observations

- Initially, both thermometers T_1 and T_2 display the same temperature, which corresponds to room temperature.
- The temperature recorded by the lower thermometer T_2 begins to decrease and eventually stabilizes at 4°C, while the temperature recorded by the upper thermometer T_1 remains almost unchanged during this period.
- Once the temperature of the lower thermometer T_2 stays constant at 4°C, the upper thermometer T_1 shows a gradual decrease, reaching 0°C after which it also stabilizes.

TYPE - 7 — 03/04 Marks

Case Based Questions

Q.1 A scientist conducts an experiment by gradually cooling a sample of water from 10°C to 0°C in a laboratory. The water is kept in a glass container. He observes that the water level first decreases and then increases.

(i) Explain why the water level first decreases and then increases during cooling. [2]

(ii) At what temperature is the density of water the highest? **[1]**

(iii) Why is the anomalous expansion of water significant for aquatic life in cold regions? **[1]**

Ans. (i) The water level decreases as the water cools from 10°C to 4°C because the density of water increases. Below 4°C, water expands instead of contracting, causing the water level to increase. This behaviour is due to the anomalous expansion of water.

(ii) The density of water is highest at 4°C.

(iii) The anomalous expansion of water ensures that during winter, water at 4°C sinks to the bottom of water bodies, allowing aquatic life to survive in the warmer lower layers while ice forms on the upper surface.

Q.2 The Hope's apparatus is used to perform an experiment for demonstrating the anomalous expansion of water as shown in the diagram below. **[3]**

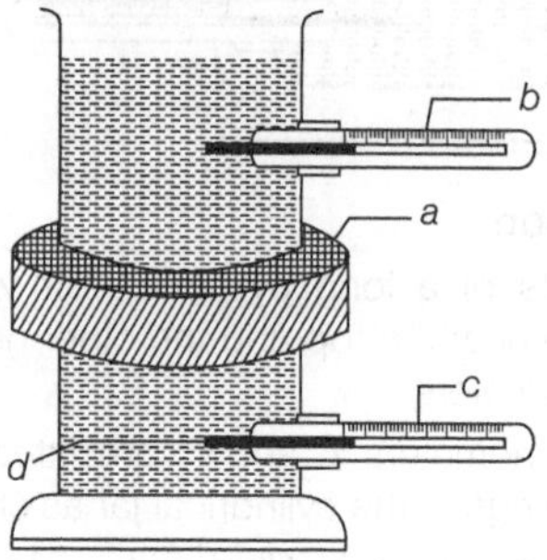

Complete the table, using the labels from the figure. The first label is done for you.

S.No.	Description	Label
a.	The pure water is filled in the cylinder	d
b.	The freezing mixture is filled in the cylinder.	
c.	Thermometer attains steady state after 0°C	
d.	Thermometer remains constant at 4°C	

Ans.

S.No.	Description	Label
a.	The pure water is filled in the cylinder	d
b.	The freezing mixture is filled in the cylinder.	a
c.	Thermometer attains steady state after 0°C	b
d.	Thermometer remains constant at 4°C	c

Q.3 During a harsh winter, a farmer notices that water pipes in his field burst, and his crops begin to wither. To protect the crops, he sprays water over the plants at night. By morning, the plants are covered in thin layer of ice but they remain unharmed.

(i) Why do water pipes burst during extremely cold nights? **[1]**

(ii) How does spraying water on crops help protect them from frost damage? **[1]**

(iii) What property of ice ensures that only the surface of a pond freezes while the water below remains liquid ? **[1]**

(iv) Explain the phenomenon responsible for the expansion of water below 4°C. **[1]**

Ans. (i) Water expands when it freezes due to the anomalous expansion of water. As the temperature drops below 4°C, water increases in volume, exerting pressure on the walls of the pipe, causing it to burst.

(ii) When water is sprayed on crops, it freezes and releases latent heat of fusion. This heat prevents the temperature of the plant cells from falling below freezing, protecting the crops from frost damage.

(iii) Ice is less dense than liquid water, so it floats. This creates an insulating layer on the surface, preventing the water below from losing heat and freezing completely.

(iv) Below 4°C, water molecules arrange themselves into a crystalline structure, which occupies more space than liquid water, causing it to expand.

ENERGY FLOW AND SOURCES OF ENERGY

Ecosystem

An ecosystem is a system where biotic components (producers, consumers and decomposers interact with abiotic components (like water, air, and soil) to maintain the flow of energy and nutrients in nature.

Producers (Plants) make their own food using sunlight.

Consumers (Humans and animals) depend on plants or other animals for food.

- **Primary consumers** These are herbivores that obtain their food directly from plants (producers). **Example** Deer, rabbit, etc.
- **Secondary Consumers** These are carnivores or omnivores that obtain their food by eating primary consumers. **Example** Frog, fox.
- **Tertiary consumers** These are top predators that obtain their food by eating secondary consumers. **Example** Lion, eagle.

Decomposers (bacteria, fungi) break down dead matter, recycling nutrients back into the environment.

Energy flow in an Ecosystem

- Sun is the ultimate source of energy for all the living organisms or the plants.
- Nearly 60% energy from the sun is absorbed by the atmosphere, 10% of it is used in reaching land and water and as 8% of it is absorbed by the plants.
- The planets which are also called the **producers**, synthesize organic substances by the process of photosynthesis. Out of total energy absorbed by the plants only 0.02% is used in **photosynthesis**.
- The chemical energy stored in plants, called the **grass primary production**, is used for respiration of the plants and some process of oxidation of organic substances.
- The rest of the energy, called the **not primary production**, is stored for growth and development of the plants.
- The **primary consumers** (herbivores) use a **small part of energy** from the producers to obtain their food and the rest is wasted in decay of producers.
- The **secondary consumers** (carnivores) use a **small part of energy** stored as food in the primary consumers and some part for respiration and the rest is stored in them as food.
- The **tertiary consumers** (also carnivores) obtain energy as food from the secondary consumers and utilise a small part of it for respiration and the rest is wasted in their decay and decompostion.
- From the above discussion, it is clear that energy flow in an ecosystem is occur only in **one direction** i.e. energy flow in an ecosystem is linear.

Application of Laws of Thermodynamics in Energy Flow

- According to the first law of thermodynamics, energy can neither be created nor can be destroyed, but can only be transformed from one form to another.
- When a certain amount of one form of energy is destroyed in the ecosystem, it get converted into another form of energy. **For example** solar energy is converted into chemical energy by plants during photosynthesis.

- According to the second law of thermodynamics, when energy is put to work, some part of the energy is always converted into some unuseful forms.
- When a certain amount of energy is used in the ecosystem to produce useful work, some of the energy is wasted in some other form. For example energy used in respiration and decay is converted into some unuseful form of energy such as heat.

So, we can say that flow of energy in an ecosystem takes place according to the laws of thermodynamics.

Sources of Energy

- Any source which is capable of providing energy in a convenient form at a steady rate over a long period of time is called a source of energy.
- A good source of energy can be characterised by the following factors
  - (i) It should do a large amount of work per unit volume or mass.
  - (ii) It should be easily accessible.
  - (iii) It should be easy to store and transport from the place of their production to consumers.
  - (iv) It should be economical, i.e. should give more amount of energy at a lesser cost.

Renewable or Non-Conventional Sources of Energy

Non-conventional sources of energy are those sources of energy which are being produced continuously in nature and are inexhaustible. These are also called **renewable** or **alternative source of energy.** e.g. Solar energy, wind energy, hydro energy, bio fuels (such as wood, bio-gas and alcohol), hydro energy from ocean (tidal energy, sea waves energy and ocean thermal energy).

Solar Energy

- Sun is the most powerful source of radiation energy.
- The average energy that reaches the surface of the upper atmosphere of the earth per second per unit area in metres is known as the **solar constant** and its value is near about 1.34 kWm^{-2}.

Production of Electricity from Solar Energy

- Electricity from solar energy can be obtained from two devices which are **solar cells** and **solar power plants.**

Solar Cells

- They can directly convert solar energy into electricity.
- They are usually made from **semiconductor material** like silicon and gallium.
- If sunlight is incident on an impurity added semiconductor, a potential difference is produced in its surface which helps in the flow of current through the circuit connected with the semiconductor.
- To increase the production, a large number of solar cells are arranged over a large area and this arrangement is known as a **solar panel**.
- To effectively use the solar panel at night, a strong battery (secondary coil) is charged by the solar panel during the day time.

Solar Power Plant

- In solar power plants, large concave reflectors are used which helps in focusing the sun's rays at one point.
- At the focus of the reflectors, black painted water pipes are present which gets heated which in turn heats up the water flowing through the pipes.

- The water starts boiling which produces steam that is used to rotate a steam turbine which drives a generator for the production of electricity.

Wind Energy

- The kinetic energy produced by the large mass of moving air is known as the **wind energy**.

Production of Electricity from Wind Energy

- Wind energy is used by wind turbines to drive a wind generator to produce electricity.
- The kinetic energy of the wind helps in rotating the blades of the wind mill (or turbine) which turn helps in the rotation of the generator attached with the windmill which helps in producing electricity.
- To produce sufficient amount of electricity large number of wind generators are arranged over a big area which is known as a **wind form**.

Biomass as source of energy

- The wastes and dead parts of living beings like plants, trees and animals is called **biomass**. They contain carbon compounds. The chemical energy stored in the bio mass is called **bio energy**.
- Bio gas is a mixture of gases produced during the decomposition of bio mass in the absence of oxygen. The main constituent of bio gas is **methane** (65%) and rest is a mixture of **carbon dioxide, hydrogen and hydrogen sulphide**.
- The set-up used to produce bio-gas is called **bio-gas plant**.

Tidal Energy

- Due to the gravitational attraction between moon and earth sea, water level rises and falls. Thus the tides are produced.
- Energy possessed by rising and falling water in tides is known as **tidal energy.**
- The rise of sea water is called **high tide**, whereas the fall of sea water is called **low tide**.
- The tidal waves in the sea build up and recede (rise and fall) twice a day.
- Tidal energy can be harnessed by building dams across the narrow openings to the sea, however this is not a very effective source for producing large amount of energy.

Nuclear Energy

- Energy contained in the nucleus of atom is called **nuclear energy.** It is released during a **nuclear reaction.**
- Nuclear reaction can be of two types, nuclear fission and nuclear fussion.
- The phenomenon of splitting of a heavy nucleus into two lighter nuclei along with a release of a amount of energy when it is bombarded with slow moving neutrons, is known as **nuclear fission**.

- The phenomenon of the combination of two lighter nuclei into a heavier nucleus along with a release of a tremendous amount of energy is known as **nuclear fusion.**

Production of Electricity from Nuclear Energy

- Electricity can be produced from nuclear energy by **controlled chain reaction** of nuclear fission of a radioactive substance like uranium -235.
- This set up is called **nuclear power plant.**
- The heat energy released in the process of fission is absorbed by the water present in the power plant.
- This heat produces steam which is used to rotate a turbine which helps in rotating a generator which is turn produces electricity.

Energy from Falling Water

- The kinetic energy possessed by the flowing water is known as **hydro energy.**
- Water from water falls at a certain height possesses potential energy which gets converted into kinetic energy as it reaches the bottom of the water falls.

Production of electricity from hydro energy.

- Water from flowing rivers are collected in dams which are constructed at a high altitude.
- The potential energy of the water stored in the dams, when allowed to fall, gets converted to kinetic energy which helps in rotating the turbines present at the bottom of the dams.
- The rotating turbines in turn helps in rotating the generator present at the base of the dams which is used in generating electricity.

Non-Renewable or Conventional Sources of Energy

- The sources of energy which have accumulated in nature over a very long period of time and cannot be quickly replaced when exhausted are called non-renewable or conventional sources of energy.

Coal

- It is a naturally occurring material which is a mixture of carbon and compounds of carbon containing hydrogen, nitrogen, oxygen and sulphur. It is mainly found in deep mines under the surface of the earth. It is used for heating purposes in home and industries.

Petroleum

- It is **dark coloured viscous liquid**, also known as **crude oil**. It is found under the earth's crust trapped in between rocks. It is a mixture of many hydrocarbons along with water, salt, earth particles and some compounds of carbon, oxygen, nitrogen and sulphur.
- The crude petroleum after it is purified can be used as good fuel since it produces a lot of heat.

Natural Gas

- It mainly consists of **methane** (CH_4) (about 97%) and small quantities of **ethane** (C_2H_6) and **propane** (C_3H_8).
- When natural gas in liquid form is subjected to high pressure, we get **Compressed Natural Gas (CNG)** which is used as fuel in vehicles like cars, buses and trucks.

Energy Degradation

- It is observed that in the process of transformation of energy, the entire energy isn't converted into something useful.
- As this part of energy is not available for productive use, hence it is known as **degraded form of energy.**

- Some examples of energy degradation are
  (i) When electrical appliances are running with the help of electricity, some part of energy gets converted into heat energy, sound energy, etc.
  (ii) When food is cooked over fire, major part of heat energy is radiated in the atmosphere which is of no use to us.
  (iii) No machine can give full efficiency. It means that only a fraction of input energy is used for doing work and the rest gets wasted.

Greenhouse Effect

- The process of **warming of the earth's surface** and its lower atmosphere by the absorption of infrared radiation of long wavelength emitted out from the surface of the earth is known as the greenhouse effect.
- The gases such as carbon dioxide, methane, nitrous oxide, ozone chlorofluorocarbons (CFCs), etc which are good absorbers of long wavelength infrared radiation are known as **greenhouse gases**.

Sources of Greenhouse Gases

- **Water vapour** The main sources of water vapour are industrial exhaust, vehicular exhaust, burning of fuels and volcanic eruptions
- **Carbon dioxide** (CO_2) Respiration, burning of fossil fuels for energy, decomposition of limestone, volcanic eruptions, etc., all processes proceed with the liberation of carbon dioxide into the atmosphere.
- **Hydrocarbons (Methane,** CH_4) These are obtained by the incomplete combustion of fossil fuels in automobile engines and by anaerobic decomposition of organic matter or vegetation.
- **Oxides of nitrogen** Combustion of fossil fuels such as coal, oil, gasoline, etc., in automobile engines and power plants at high temperature produces oxides of nitrogen

Advantages of Greenhouse Effect

- It helps in maintaining the optimum temperature necessary for survival.
- It is necessary for evaporation of water and formation of clouds, leading to rain,

Global Warming

- The increase in the average temperature of the earth above its normal temperature is called global warming. It occurs due to increase in concentration of greenhouse gases.
- If concentration of the greenhouse gases increase above a certain level, they prevent the outflow of heat from the surface of the earth leading to an increase in the over all average temperature of the earth's surface which causes global warming.

Cause of Global Warming

1. The concentration of chlorfluorocarbons is increasing at a rate of 5% per year.
2. The concentration of carbon dioxide has increased up to 25% due the industrial growth, combustion of fossil fuels, clearing of forests and leakage in natural gas pipelines.
3. The concentration of methane has doubled due to agriculatural sources such as rice cultivation and animal husbandary, natural gas exploration, burning of biomass, etc.

Impact of Global Warming on Life on the Earth

Present Consequences

(i) The change in regional climate has an immediate effect on simple organism and plants.
(ii) The variable changes in the climate in different parts of the world has created difficulties and forced people and animal to migrate from one place to the other.
(iii) The change in blooming season of different plants.
(iv) The change in the world's ecology.
(v) The increase in the heat stroke deaths.

Future Consequences

With the present rate of increase in the temperature, it is predicted that the average temperature of Earth's surface will become 64°C by the end of the year 2100.

Such a rise in the temperature of the earth might result in

(i) Dislocation and disappearance of plant and animal species.

(ii) Warming of ocean.

(iii) Melting of glaciers and increase in the water level of the oceans.

(iv) Shifting in farming region.

(v) Increase in new diseases and health related deaths.

(vi) Change in regional climate.

(vii) Variable change in the climate.

(viii) Increase in cost of air conditioning.

Ways to Minimise the Impact of Global Warming

To minimise the impact of global warming the following three main measures must be taken.

(i) **Technological Measures** The economic growth and population growth increase the consumption of fuel and hence both are responsible for the release of greenhouse gases.

Following are the technological measures

(a) Use of renewable sources of energy.

(b) Using battery operated transportation vehicles.

(c) Use of bio-char stoves for cooking.

(ii) **Economic Measures** These arise because of growing industries and deforestation which increases the greenhouse effect.

Following economic measures are needed

(a) Reforestation and sustainable use of land.

(b) Industries to pay carbon tax.

(iii) **Policy Measures** To check global warming, following are the policy measures taken by the government.

(a) Educating children to live a sustainable life.

(b) Controlling population.

EXAM ORIENTED QUESTIONS

TYPE - 1 01 Mark

Multiple Choice Questions

Q.1 Which of the following is a non-renewable source of energy?
(a) Wood (b) Sun (c) Fossil fuels (d) Wind

Ans. (c) Non-renewable sources of energy are those which are exhaustible and cannot be replaced, once they have been used. Non-renewable sources of energy are also known as conventional sources of energy.
Fossil fuels are non-renewable sources of energy, whereas wood, the sun and wind are renewable sources of energy.

Q.2 Which environmental hazard is not contributed by the combustion of fossil fuels?
(a) Acid rain
(b) Greenhouse effect
(c) Destruction of wildlife habitat
(d) Air pollution

Ans. (c) Combustion of fossil fuels does not lead to the destruction of wildlife habitat. However, hydroelectric power projects, acid rain, air pollution and the greenhouse effect lead to the devastation of wildlife habitats, soil erosion, man-made floods, etc.

Q.3 Acid rain happens because
(a) Sun leads to heating of upper layer of atmosphere
(b) burning of fossil fuels results in the release the oxides of carbon, nitrogen and sulphur in the atmosphere
(c) electrical charges are produced due to friction amongst clouds
(d) the Earth's atmosphere contains acids

Ans. (b) Acid rain happens because of several human activities of polluting the atmosphere. The emission of oxides of carbon, sulphur and nitrogen from the industries, burning of fossil fuels, etc., and also by the natural phenomena such as emission from volcanoes make the water vapour in the cloud more acidic thereby causing acid rain.

Q.4 Fuel used in thermal power plants is
(a) water (b) uranium
(c) biomass (d) fossil fuel

Ans. (d) The thermal power plant generates electric power from heat produced by burning fossil fuels i.e. coal and petroleum. Everyday we burn a large amount of fossil fuels to generate electricity.

Q.5 In a hydro power plant,
(a) potential energy possessed by stored water is converted into electricity
(b) kinetic energy possessed by stored water is converted into potential energy
(c) electricity is extracted from water
(d) water is converted into steam to produce electricity

Ans. (a) In a hydro power plant, water from the top of the dam is allowed to fall through pipelines over the blades of a turbine at the bottom of the dam. In this process, the potential energy of water changes into its kinetic energy which is transferred to the turbine.
The moving turbine rotates the armature of a generator to produce electricity, and turbine changes the kinetic energy into electricity. Thus, potential energy possessed by stored water is converted into electricity.

Q.6 Which of the following is employed for harnessing the potential energy of surface water stored in a reservoir?
(a) Thermal power plant
(b) Nuclear power plant
(c) Tidal power plant
(d) Hydroelectric power plant

Ans. (d) In a hydroelectric power plant, the kinetic energy of flowing river water is first converted into potential energy. A huge amount of water is stored in a reservoir (dam) and finally, when the stored dam water flows downhill, the stored potential energy of water is harnessed in the form of electrical energy with the help of turbine.

Q.7 Which one of the following forms of energy leads to least environmental pollution in the process of its harnessing and utilisation?
(a) Nuclear energy
(b) Thermal energy
(c) Solar energy
(d) Geothermal energy

Ans. (c) Solar energy leads to the least environmental pollution in the process of its harnessing and utilisation. In nuclear energy, the emission of radiation is a high risk for environmental contamination.
In thermal energy, heat produced by burning fossil fuels causes huge environmental pollution. In geothermal energy, noise pollution is created by drilling operations at geothermal sites.

Q.8 Solar energy is the universal source of energy. It is converted into chemical energy by

(a) photovoltaic cells (b) solar cooker

(c) solar concentrators (d) green plants

Ans. (d) Solar energy is the universal source of energy that is used by all living organisms for their survival on the Earth. The green plants convert solar energy into chemical energy - food or biomass of plants, by the process of photosynthesis.

Q.9 Ocean thermal energy is due to

(a) energy stored by waves in the ocean

(b) temperature difference at different levels in the ocean

(c) pressure difference at different levels in the ocean

(d) tides arising out in the ocean

Ans. (b) The water at the surface of the sea or ocean is heated by the sun while the water in deeper sections is relatively cold. This difference in temperature between these layers, ranging from 10°C to 30°C is exploited to obtain energy. Thus, ocean thermal energy is due to temperature differences at different levels in the ocean.

Q.10 The major problem in harnessing nuclear energy is how to

(a) split nuclei

(b) sustain the reaction

(c) dispose of spent fuel safely

(d) convert nuclear energy into electrical energy

Ans. (c) The major hazard of nuclear power generation is the storage and disposal of spent or used fuels. Improper nuclear waste storage and disposal result in environmental contamination as well as the risk of accidental leakage of nuclear radiation.
It happened in the Chernobyl disaster 1986 and Fukushima nuclear disaster in 2011 which caused great damage to the living beings and habitates.

Q.11 Name the radiation which are absorbed by the green house gases.

(a) X-rays (b) Visible

(c) Infrared (d) Ultraviolet

Ans. (c) The short wavelength (high frequency) infrared radiations come from sun to earth's surface and after reflection from surface, turn into long wavelength infrared radiations, these long wavelength radiations are absorbed by greenhouse gases.

Q.12 The increase of carbon dioxide gas in atmosphere will cause

(a) Increase in temperature

(b) No change in temperature

(c) Decrease in temperature

(d) Increase in humidity

Ans. (a) Increase in the carbon dioxide cause an increase in temperature because they will absorb more heat from sun rays and radiate less.

Q.13 Without greenhouse effect, the average temperature of earth's surface would have been

(a) 0°C (b) – 18°C (c) 33°C (d) 15°C

Ans. (b) The greenhouse effect traps heat in Earth's atmosphere, making the planet, warm enough to support life. Without it, the earth's average temperature would be very cold, around – 18°C.

Q.14 Which of the following is the effect of global warming?

(a) The greenhouse effect

(b) Climate changing effect human to

(c) The effect on agriculture

(d) All of the above

Ans. (d) Global warming leads to increased greenhouse effect, climate changes affecting humans and disruptions in agriculture.

TYPE - 2

01 Mark

Assertion-Reason Type Questions

Directions (Q. Nos. 1-3) In the following questions two statements are given as Assertion and Reason.

(a) Both A and R are true and R is the correct explanation of A.

(b) Both A and R are true but R is not the correct explanation of A.

(c) A is true but R is false.

(d) A is false but R is true.

Q.1 Assertion (A) Biogas is considered a renewable source of energy.

Reason (R) Biogas is produced by the decomposition of organic matter by anaerobic bacteria.

Ans. (a) Biogas is renewable because plant and animal waste is continuously produced and decomposes to release energy.

Q.2 Assertion (A) Nuclear energy is a reliable source of electricity generation.

Reason (R) Nuclear energy generation emits large amounts of carbon dioxide.

Ans. (c) Nuclear energy is reliable because it can produce electricity continuously, but it does not emit carbon dioxide, instead it produces radioactive waste.

Q.3 Assertion (A) Water vapour is most abundant greenhouse gas in the atmosphere.

Reason (R) Water vapour forms clouds, which reflect sunlight back into space, cooling the earth.

Ans. (c) Water vapour is indeed the most abundant greenhouse gas but it doesn't directly cool the Earth by reflecting sunlight. Instead, it contributes to warming by trapping heat, amplifying the greenhouse effect.

TYPE - 3 01/02 Marks

Fill in the Blanks

Q.1 The .... (potential/kinetic) energy of wind is called wind energy. **[1]**

Ans. kinetic

Q.2 The process used for refining of petroleum is known as .... (evaporation/fractional distillation) **[1]**

Ans. fractional distillation

Q.3 Biogas is produced by the .... (digestion/combustion) of organic waste and is a .... (renewable/non-renewable) source of energy. **[1]**

Ans. digestion, renewable

Q.4 Global warming means .... (increase/decrease) in average effective temperature near the Earth's surface due to .... (decrease/increase) in the amount of greenhouse gases in its atmosphere. **[1]**

Ans. increase, increase

TYPE - 4 02 Marks

Very Short Answer Type Questions

Q.1 State the law which governs the energy flow in an ecosystem.

Ans. According to the first law of thermodynamics, the energy can be transformed from one form to the other form, but it can neither be created nor destroyed.

According to the second law of thermodynamics, when energy is put to work, a part of it is always converted in un-useful form, such as heat, mainly due to friction and radiation.

Q.2 Give the names of two energy sources that you would consider to be exhaustible. Give reason for your choice.

Ans. Fossil fuels like coal and petroleum are exhaustible. The conditions that existed on the earth and led to their formation, no longer exist today. Thus, the rate at which they are used up today, will lead to their depletion soon.

Q.3 Explain, why fossil fuels are considered as non-renewable sources of energy?

Ans. Fossil fuels are considered as non-renewable sources of energy because they are exhaustible and cannot be replaced quickly.

Q.4 Explain, how does burning of fossil fuels cause water pollution?

Ans. Burning of fossil fuels releases acidic oxides which leads to acid rain and causes water pollution by affecting the water resources.

Q.5 Name any two energy sources that you would consider to be renewable. Give reasons for your choice.

Ans. Hydro power, as water is replenished by water cycle. Wind power, as wind keeps blowing due to uneven heating of the earth by the sun.

Q.6 Can any source of energy be pollution free? Why or why not?

Ans. No, source of energy can not be pollution free. If any source of energy is exploited or used, it causes environmental pollution. For example, CNG produces greenhouse gases such as carbon dioxide. Hydro power plants disturb the vegetation of that region and destroy the habitat of many plants and animals. The windmills disturb the rainfall pattern of the region.

The manufacturing of solar cells also has environmental hazards associated with it.

Q.7 Give any two disadvantages of fossil fuels.

Ans. (i) The fossil fuels are non-renewable sources of energy and once used cannot be renewed.

(ii) Fossil fuels are not burnt completely. They leave ashes after burning.

Q.8 Why are we looking at alternative sources of energy?

Ans. We are looking at alternative sources of energy because the fossil fuels cannot be replenished and the rate, at which we are using them, will exhaust them soon.

To meet the rising demand, we have to develop alternative sources of energy.

Q.9 Name any two important hydroelectric power projects in India.

Ans. Two important hydroelectric power projects in India are

(i) Bhakra-Nangal Project (Satluj river)

(ii) Hirakund Project (Mahanadi river)

Q.10 Give the uses of inlet chamber in the biogas plant.

Ans. It connects the mixing tank and the digester tank. It has a slope to ensure smooth flow of slurry into the digester tank.

Q.11 List two practical uses of biogas in rural areas.

Ans. The two practical uses of biogas in rural areas are as follows

(i) It is used for lighting.

(ii) It is an excellent cooking fuel which burns without smoke.

Q.12 Bio-gas is considered to be a boon to the farmers. Give reasons.

Ans. Bio-gas is considered to be a boon to the farmers, because

(i) It is a source of excellent manure, rich in nitrogen and phosphorus.

(ii) Farmers can produce clean fuel from bio-waste.

Q.13 **What are the limitations of harnessing wind energy?**

Ans. Following are the limitations of harnessing wind energy

(i) It can be established only at those places, where wind blows for most of the part of the year.

(ii) The set up of wind farm is very expensive.

Q.14 **Expand OTEC. On which principle is it based?**

Ans. The full form of OTEC is Ocean Thermal Energy Conversion.

It is based on the exploitation of the temperature difference between upper and lower layers of the ocean to harness energy.

Q.15 **What is a nuclear waste? What are the hazards of nuclear waste to living things?**

Ans. The byproducts obtained in a nuclear reaction are called nuclear wastes. These are radioactive wastes and can emit radiations (α, β and γ) which may cause skin cancer and severe genetic disorders.

Q.16 **List the causes of increasing energy requirement.**

Ans. The causes of increasing energy requirement are

(i) Due to the increase in population, the number of users are increasing rapidly. Thus, the energy requirement is increased.

(ii) Improved technology which is more energy dependent.

(iii) Increasing wastage of energy forces to exploit more and more sources of energy.

Q.17 **How does construction of dams across the river get linked with the production of greenhouse gases?**

Ans. The vegetation which is submerged, rots in anaerobic condition and releases large amount of methane (CH_4) in nature which is a greenhouse gas.

TYPE - 5 — 03 Marks

Short Answer Type Questions

Q.1 **Increasing demand of fossil fuels has caused harm to our environments. List its three side effects. Suggest three measures to reduce the consumption of fossil fuels.**

Ans. The three side effects of burning fossil fuels are as given below

(i) Air pollution

(ii) Global warming

(iii) Acid rain

The three measures to reduce the consumption of fossil fuels are as below

(i) controlling population.

(ii) using public transport instead of private vehicles.

(iii) using renewable sources of energy.

Q.2 **Why is there so much emphasis on changing over from petrol or diesel driven automobiles to CNG driven vehicles?**

Ans. There is so much emphasis on changing over from petrol or diesel driven automobiles to CNG (Compressed Natural Gas) driven vehicles because of the following reasons.

(i) It does not produce smoke.

(ii) On burning CNG it produces CO_2 and water.

(iii) It does not leave unburnt hydrocarbons, lead particulates, etc., which pollute the environment.

Q.3 **If energy in the universe is constant, why is the world yelling out for energy crisis? What does judicious use of energy imply?**

Ans. The energy in the universe is constant. However, when it is converted into non-usable forms, it cannot be converted back into usable forms and hence, it gets wasted. If all the energy is converted into some non-usable form, we will suffer the crisis for usable form of energy.

Judicious use of energy implies minimisation of wastage of energy by controlled use of the sources and enabling reuse of energy wherever possible e.g., banning the cutting of trees, etc.

Q.4 **Plastic production is increasing day-by-day despite of the fact that plastic is harmful for the environment. Based on the above statement, answer the following.**

(i) What are the harmful effects of plastic usage?

(ii) In our day-to-day situation, what are the alternative that we can use instead of plastics?

(iii) What can we learn as a good citizen concerning this issue?

Ans. (i) Burning of plastics cause pollution. Plastics cause harm to the cattle/animals, if it enters inside their alimentary canal.

(ii) Paper bags/jute bags can be used instead of plastic bag.

(iii) Every citizen should be discouraged to use plastics as a source of packaging and storing as it is non-biodegradable.

Q.5 **Give three traditional uses of solar energy.**

Ans. The three traditional uses of solar energy are as follows

(i) For drying clothes.

(ii) For obtaining salt from sea water.

(iii) For reducing moisture content in food grains after harvesting.

Q.6 What are the limitations of solar energy?

Ans. The limitations of solar energy are as follows

(i) Energy reaching on the surface of the earth is very much diffused.

(ii) It is not available uniformly all the time and at all the places.

(iii) It is not available at night and in cloudy days.

Q.7 What prevents us in making use of solar cell panels to meet all our domestic needs of electricity?

Ans. The following factors prevent the use of solar cell panels to meet all our domestic needs of electricity.

(i) High cost of installation.

(ii) Limited availability of special grade silicon to make solar cells.

(iii) Technology to obtain pure silicon is too expensive.

(iv) Cost of material used (silver) to connect the solar cell in a solar panel is high.

(v) Unavailability of afficient systems to store electrical energy generated by solar panels.

Q.8 What human activities are responsible for the increase of the carbon dioxide?

Ans. Human activities responsible for the increase of the carbon dioxide are as follows

(i) The burning of fuels, deforestation, transportation and industrial production.

(ii) Increase in population.

(iii) Construction of hydro power plant, which is disturbing ecological balance.

Q.9 Describe the three limitations to harness energy from wind?

Ans. The limitations of harnessing wind energy are as follows

(i) It can be established only at those places, where wind blows for most of the time of a year.

(ii) Wind speed should be greater than 15 km/h.

(iii) Wind energy farm requires quite large area of land i.e. nearly 2 hectares of land is needed for 1 MW generation of electricity.

TYPE - 6

04 Marks

Long Answer Type Questions

Q.1 (a) What are the constituents of biogas? **[2]**

(b) **It is advantageous to convert biomass into a biogas rather than burning biomass directly. Explain, why?** **[2]**

Ans. (a) The main constituent of biogas are

(i) Methane (CH_4) $\rightarrow$ 65-75% (combustible)

(ii) Carbon dioxide (CO_2) $\rightarrow$ 20-30% (non-combustible)

(iii) Hydrogen sulphide (H_2S) $\rightarrow$ traces (combustible)

(iv) Hydrogen (H_2) $\rightarrow$ 5-10% (combustible)

(v) Nitrogen (N_2) $\rightarrow$ 2-6% (non-combustible)

(b) It is advantageous to convert biomass into a biogas rather than burning biomass directly because of the following reasons

(i) Direct burning creates air pollution to a very large extent.

(ii) It releases greenhouse gas such as CO_2.

(iii) Direct burning results in low calorific value.

Q.2 Write a note on solar energy. Explain the process by which solar energy can be harnessed directly.

Ans. It is the energy obtained from the Sun. It provides us heat and light. The nuclear fusion reaction taking place inside the Sun keeps on liberating enormous amounts of heat and light energy.

A little less than half (47%) of solar energy which falls on the top of the atmosphere reaches the Earth's surface, the rest is refracted back to the space.

The various devices which are commonly used for harnessing solar energy are called solar energy devices.

e.g., Solar cooker, solar panel and solar cell.

Solar cell is a device which converts solar energy into electrical energy. These cells are made from semiconductors like silicon and germanium. It has the advantage that it is environment-friendly and is also available in abundance but availability of special grade silicon for making solar cell is limited. These cells are also known as photovoltaic cells.

Solar cells have no moving parts, require little maintenance and work without the use of any focussing device. This is the chief advantage of solar cells. These can be set up in remote and inaccessible places easily, where power transmission is expensive and not commercially viable.

Q.3 Explain tidal energy, its harnessing and limitations.

Ans. Due to the gravitational attraction of moon, water surface rises and falls, so that the waves are formed. These waves are called tidal waves and energy possessed by the rising and falling water tides is known as tidal energy.

The rise of sea water due to gravitational pull of the Moon is called high tide, whereas the fall of sea water is called low tide. The tidal waves in the sea build up and recede (rise and fall) twice a day.

The enormous movement of water between the high tides and low tides provides a very large source of energy in the coastal areas of the world.

The tidal energy can be harnessed by constructing a tidal dam across a narrow opening to the sea.

Limitations of Tidal Energy

Tidal energy is not considered as major source of energy due to the following reasons

(i) Less availability of suitable sites for building tidal dams.

(ii) The rise and fall of sea water during tides is not enough to generate electricity on a large scale.

Q.4 How to minimise the impact of global warming?

Ans. To minimise the impact of global warming the following three main measures must be taken

(i) **Technological Measures** The economic growth and population growth increase the consumption of fuel and hence both are responsible for the release of greenhouse gases. Following are the technological measures

(a) Use of renewable sources of energy.

(b) Using battery operated transportation vehicles.

(c) Use of bio-char stoves for cooking.

(ii) **Economic Measures** These arise because of growing industries and deforestation which increase the greenhouse effect. Following economic measures are needed

(a) Reforestation and sustainable use of land.

(b) Industries to pay carbon tax.

(iii) **Policy Measures** To check global warming, following are the policy measures must be taken by the government

(a) Educating children to live sustainable life style.

(b) Controlling population.

TYPE - 7 03/04 Marks

Case Based Questions

Q.1 **The kinetic energy of flowing water or the potential energy of water at height is a traditional source of energy. The power plants which convert the potential energy of flowing water into electricity are called hydro power plants. Electricity being produced by these power plants is called hydroelectricity.**

Flowing water possesses kinetic energy, which can be used to rotate the blades of a turbine. The turbine rotates the shaft of a generator to which it is connected and this generates the electricity.

As, there are very few water falls which could be used as source of potential energy, so hydro power plants are mostly associated with dams. A quarter of the total energy requirement in India is met by hydro power plants.

(a) What is the principle of generating hydroelectricity? [1]

(b) What is the primary reason, dams are used for hydro power plants instead of natural waterfalls? [1]

(c) Write any three disadvantages of hydroelectricity. [1]

Ans. (a) The water flowing in a river is collected in a high rise dam, constructed on the river to obstruct the flow of water.

Since, water is collected at a significant height above the ground level, the kinetic energy of flowing water is converted into potential energy. This potential energy of stored water in a dam is then converted into kinetic energy of flowing water. The water from the high level is carried through the pipes to turbine located near the bottom of the dam, which is connected to the electric generator. When the water turbine rotates, then the armature of the generator also rotates rapidly and generates electricity.

(b) There are very few natural waterfalls that can be used as a source of potential energy. Dams are constructed to store water at a height, which possesses a large amount of potential energy which allows for consistent electricity generation.

(c) The disadvantages of hydroelectricity are as follows

(i) A large variety of plants, animals and their habitats get submerged in water.

(ii) It decreases the fertility of the soil in the downstream area and affects crops.

(iii) It creates the problem of satisfactory rehabilitation of displaced people.

Q.2 **A huge amount of energy is generated in the form of heat or electricity from wastes. Each month millions of tonne of waste is produced. Either they become a part of landfill or are exported to the third world countries causing huge environmental impact in terms of wild life, ecosystem and to human health.**

To cope up with this various technologies aiming, to compress and dispose waste, while attempting the generation of energy from them are being used.

(a) What do you mean by waste to energy? [1]

(b) How does waste in landfills impact wildlife, ecosystems and human health? [1]

(c) What are the potential benefits of generating energy from waste? [1]

Ans. (a) Energy can be generated in the form of heat or electricity from waste, this is called waste to energy. Many methods like, gasification, pyrolysis, depolymerisation etc. are used in this process.

(b) Waste in landfills releases harmful substances that contaminate the environment, disrupt ecosystems harm wildlife, and pose health risks to human.

(c) Generating energy from waste reduces landfill usage, mitigates environmental damage, and provides a sustainable source of heat and electricity.

08

LIGHT

Light

- Light is a form of energy that helps us to see. It is an electromagnetic wave, which does not require any medium for its propagation.

Reflection of Light

- The phenomenon of **bouncing back** of light rays in the same medium on striking a smooth surface is called reflection of light.

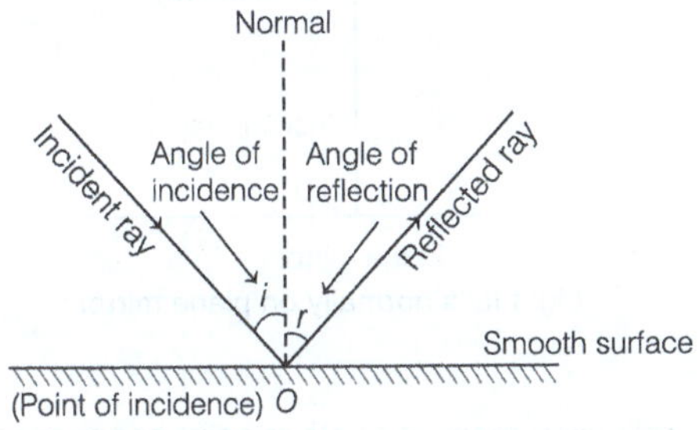

Reflection of light from a smooth surface

Terms Related to Reflection of Light

The terms used in understanding of reflection of light are as follows

(i) **Reflecting surface** It is a highly polished surface which reflects most of the light rays falling on it.

(ii) **Incident ray** It is that light ray which falls on the reflecting surface.

(iii) **Reflected ray** It is that light ray which bounces back in the same medium by the smooth surface after reflection.

(iv) **Point of incidence** It is the point at which incident ray strikes on the smooth surface.

(v) **Normal** It is a line drawn perpendicular to the reflecting surface and passing through the point of incidence.

(vi) **Angle of incidence** ($\angle i$) It is the angle made by incident ray with the normal.

(vii) **Angle of reflection** ($\angle r$) It is the angle made by reflected ray with the normal.

(viii) **Plane of incidence** It is the plane that contains the incident ray and the normal.

(ix) **Plane of reflection** It is the plane that contains the reflected ray and the normal.

Types of Reflection

(i) **Regular Reflection** The reflection in which parallel light rays are reflected in only **one direction** and the reflected rays are also **parallel** to each other is called regular reflection. Regular reflection takes place from **smooth surfaces**.

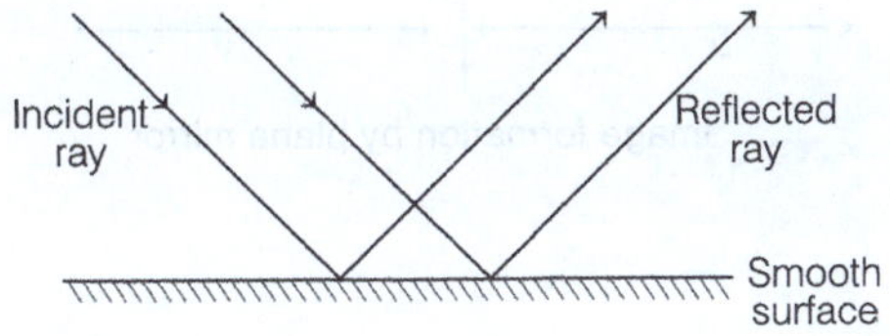

(ii) **Irregular (Diffused) Reflection** The reflection in which parallel light rays reflect in **different directions** and the reflected rays are **not parallel** to each other is called irregular reflection. Irregular reflection takes place from **rough or uneven surfaces**.

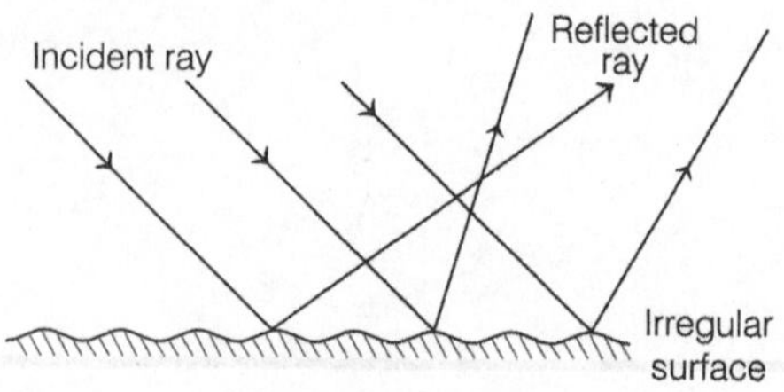

Laws of Reflection

- **Angle of incidence** ($\angle i$) is always equal to the **angle of reflection** ($\angle r$).

  i.e. $\boxed{\angle i = \angle r}$

- The **incident ray**, the **reflected** ray and the **normal** at the point of incidence, all lie in the same plane.

Note *A ray of light which is incident normally on a mirror is reflected back along its own path.*

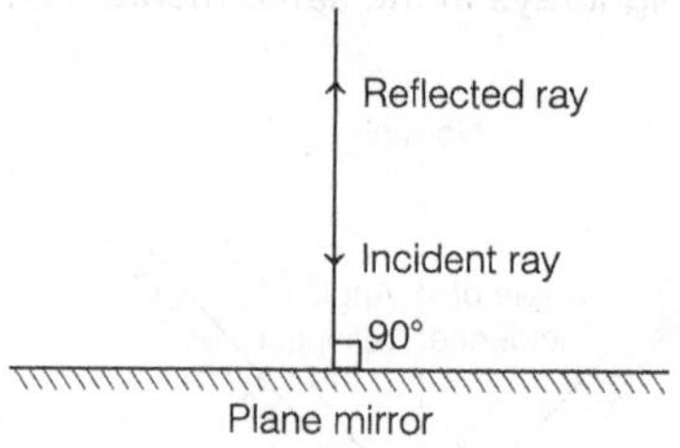

Light falls normally on plane mirror

Image

- If light rays coming from a point after reflection meet at another point or appear to come from another point, then the **second point** is called the **image of the first point**.
- Images are of two types
  - (i) **Real image** If the light rays coming from a point **actually meet after reflection**, then the image formed is called a real image.
  - (ii) **Virtual image** If the light rays coming from a point do not actually meet but appears to meet at a point after reflection, then the image formed is called a virtual image.

Plane Mirror

- **Mirror** is a polished surface which reflects almost all the light incident on it. If the reflecting surface of a mirror is plane, then the mirror is called a plane mirror. Image formed by plane mirror is always **virtual**.
- **Formation of image by a plane mirror** is given below

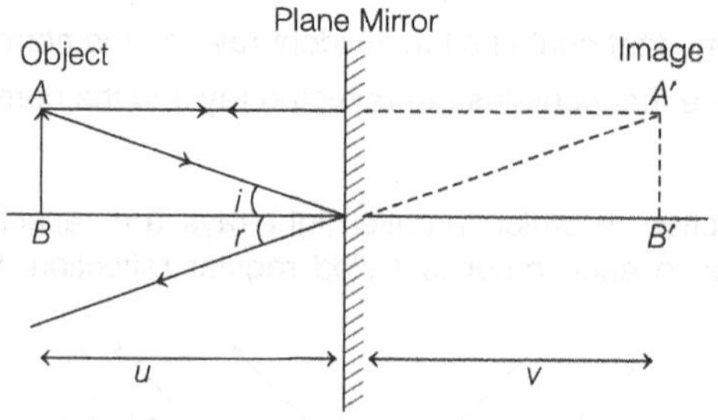

Image formation by plane mirror

REVISION NOTES

- **Properties of Image formed by a plane mirror**
  (i) It is always **virtual** and **erect**. i.e. formed behind the mirror.
  (ii) The **size of image** is equal to the **size of the object**.
  i.e. $AB = A'B'$
  (iii) The distance between the image and the mirror is equal to the distance between the object and the mirror.
  i.e. $u = v$
  (iv) The image is **laterally inverted**, i.e. left seems to be right and *vice-versa*.

Number of Images by a Pair of Inclined Plane Mirror

- When two mirrors are inclined at a certain angle, then the number of images formed by them is given by $n = \frac{360°}{\theta}$
- If $\frac{360°}{\theta}$ is **even**, then the actual number of images are

$$\boxed{n = \frac{360°}{\theta} - 1}$$

- If $\frac{360°}{\theta}$ is **odd**, then the actual number of images are

$$\boxed{n = \frac{360°}{\theta}}$$

  (i) For **symmetrical** position of object, the number of images is $\frac{360°}{\theta} - 1$ or $(n - 1)$.
  (ii) For asymmetrical position of object, the number of images is $\frac{360°}{\theta}$ or (n).
- If $n = \frac{360°}{\theta}$ is fraction, then the number of images would be equal to its integral part.

Images Formed by Two Parallel and Perpendicular Plane Mirrors

- If two plane mirrors are placed **parallel to** each other, (angle θ between them is zero) as shown in figure. Then number of images $= \frac{360°}{\theta} = \infty$ (infinite).
  i.e. Two parallel mirrrors form **infinite number** of images of an object placed between them.
  Here, I_1, I_2, I_3 ..... are the images of the object O.

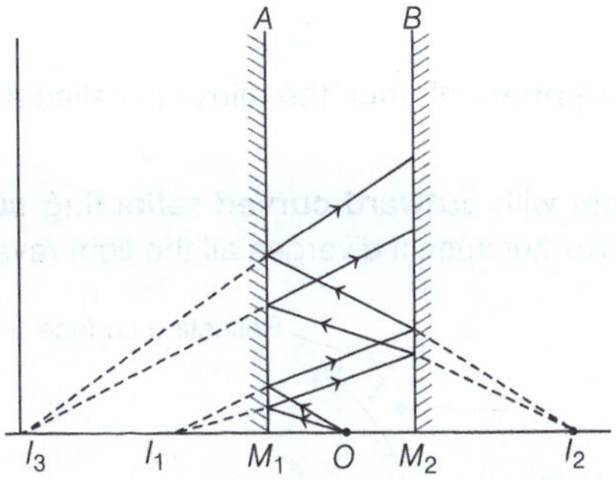

REVISION NOTES

- If two plane mirrors inclined at an angle of 90° i.e. **perpendicular** to each other as shown in figure, then number of images $= \frac{360^\circ}{90^\circ} - 1 \Rightarrow 4 - 1 = 3$

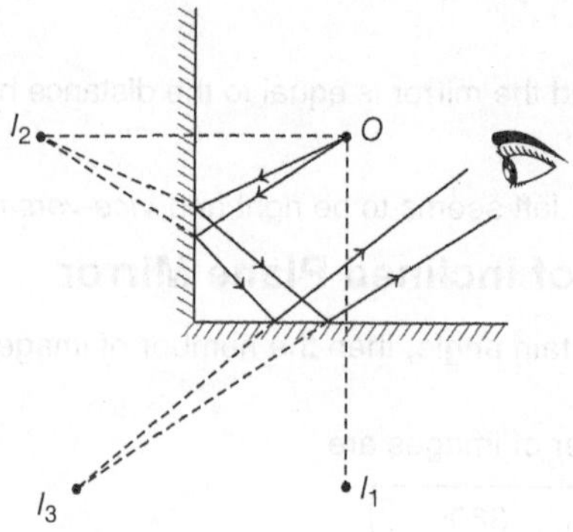

Here, I_1, I_2 and I_3 are the three images of the object O.

Uses of Plane Mirror

- Plane mirrors are commonly used as looking mirror in dressing room, in making periscopes, kaleidoscopes, etc.

Lateral Inversion

- The phenomenon of interchange of left and right sides in the image of an object formed by plane mirror is called lateral inversion.
- When you stand in front of plane mirror, left seems to be right and right **seems to be left**.

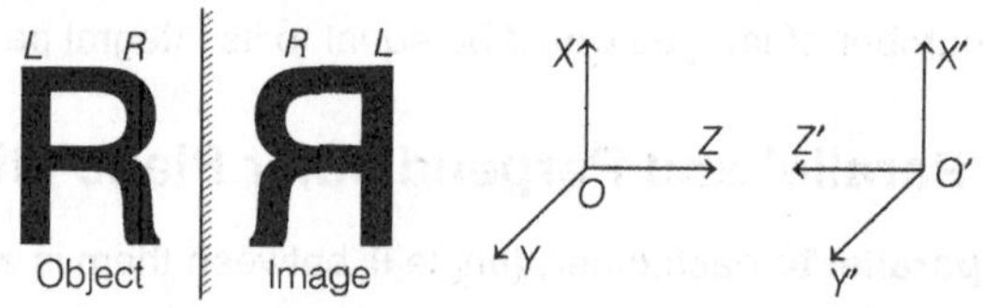

- The uppercase letters A, H, I, M, O, T, U, V, W, X and Y do not show noticeable lateral inversion when viewed in the plane mirror.

Spherical Mirrors

- If the **reflecting surface** of a mirror is **spherical**, then the mirror is called a spherical mirror.
- Spherical mirrors are of two types
  (i) **Convex mirror** The spherical mirror with **outward curved reflecting surface** is called convex mirror. Convex mirror is also called **diverging mirror** because it diverges all the light rays falling on its surface.

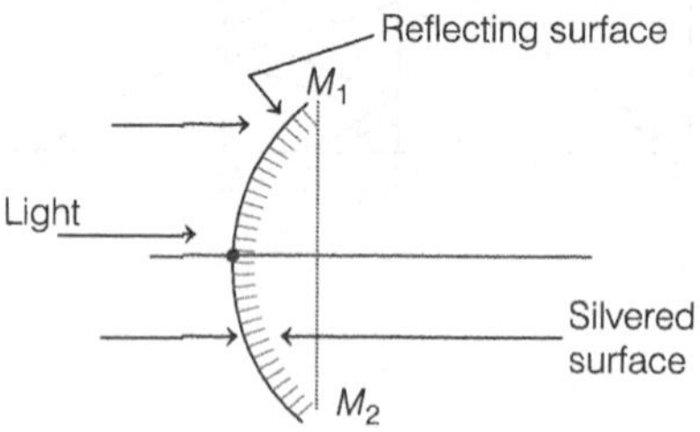

Convex mirror

(ii) **Concave mirror** The spherical mirror with **inward curved reflecting surface** is called concave mirror.

Concave mirror is also called **converging mirror** because it converges all the rays falling on its surface.

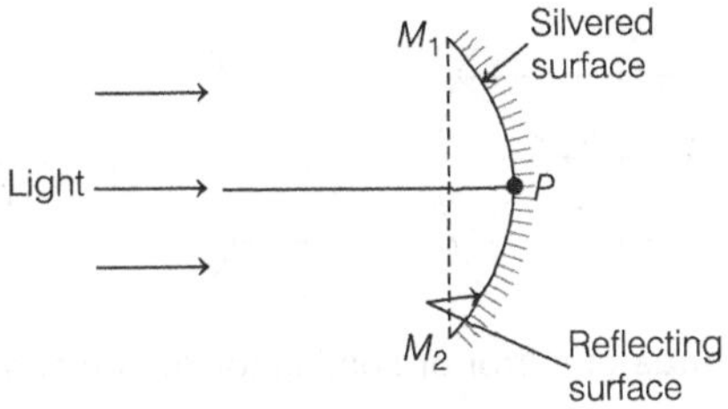

Concave mirror

Some Definitions Related to Spherical Mirrors

- **Centre of Curvature** It is the centre of the sphere of which the mirror is a part. In the figures given below, it is marked by *C*.
  In case of concave mirror, the centre of curvature lies in front of it, while in case of convex mirror, the centre of curvature lies behind it.
- **Radius of Curvature** It is the radius of sphere of which mirror is a part. In the figure, it is shown by *R*.
- **Pole** It is the mid-point of the reflecting surface of the spherical mirror. In the figure, it is shown by *P*.
- **Principal Axis** It is the line joining the pole and centre of curvature. In the figure, line passing through *PC* is the principal axis.
- **Principal Focus of a Spherical Mirror** It is a point on the principal axis of the mirror at which the light rays coming parallel to principal axis after reflection actually meet or appear to be coming from it.
- It is represented by *F*. For a **concave mirror**, the **focus is in front of the mirror**, while for a **convex mirror**, the **focus is behind the mirror**.

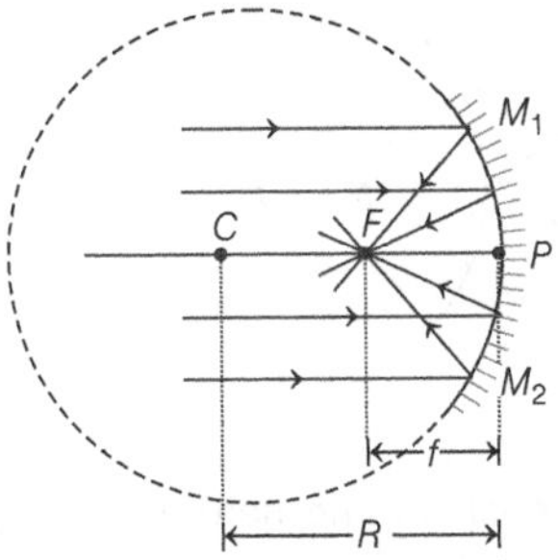

Principal focus for concave mirror

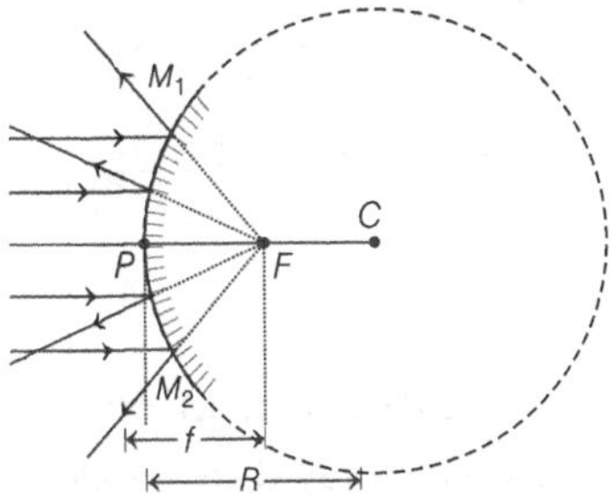

Principal focus for convex mirror

- The **focus of a concave mirror is real**, while the **focus of a convex mirror is virtual**.
- **Focal Length** The distance between pole and principal focus of a spherical mirror is called its focal length.
  It is represented by *f*.
  Focal length (*f*) of spherical mirrors is related to radius of curvature (*R*) as $\boxed{f = \frac{R}{2}}$
- **Focal Plane** A plane perpendicular to the principal axis and passing through focus is called focal plane.

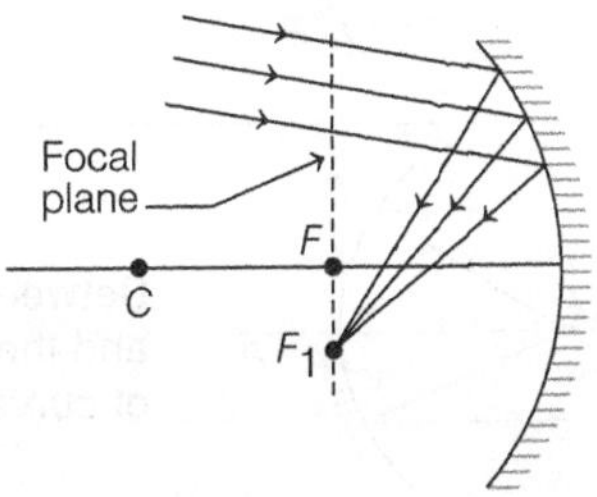

REVISION NOTES

- Reflection on light rays from spherical mirror in different conditions is discussed below
  (i) The **rays** coming **parallel** to the **principal axis** pass through the **focus** after reflection or appear to come from focus as shown in figure.

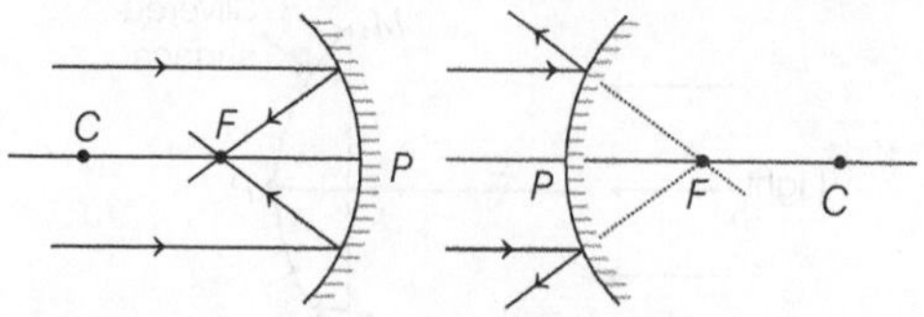

  (ii) The **rays coming through the focus** of mirror or coming towards focus, becomes **parallel to principal axis** as shown in figure.

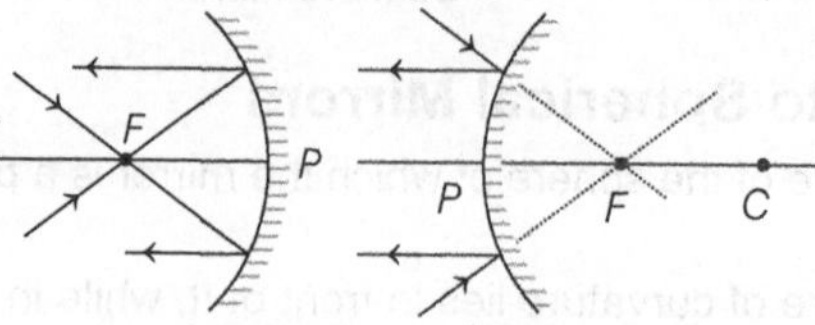

  (iii) The light **rays coming through centre of curvature** or towards centre of curvature, **reflect on the same path.**

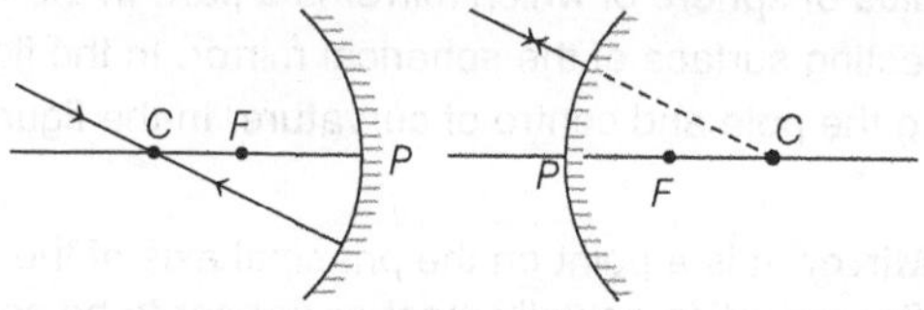

  (iv) A ray incident **obliquely to principal axis**, towards a point *P* on the concave or convex mirror is **reflected obliquely**, the following laws of reflection are shown in figure.

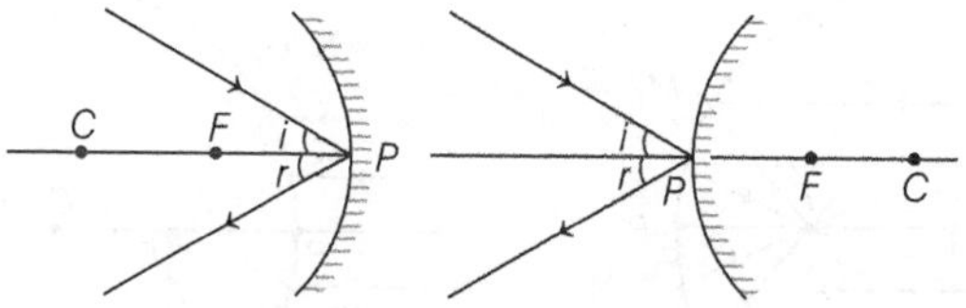

Image Formation by a Concave Mirror

The table given below illustrates the ray diagram along with the position and nature of image formed by concave mirror for various positions of the object.

S. No.	Position of Object	Ray Diagram	Position of Image	Nature and Size of Image
(i)	At infinity	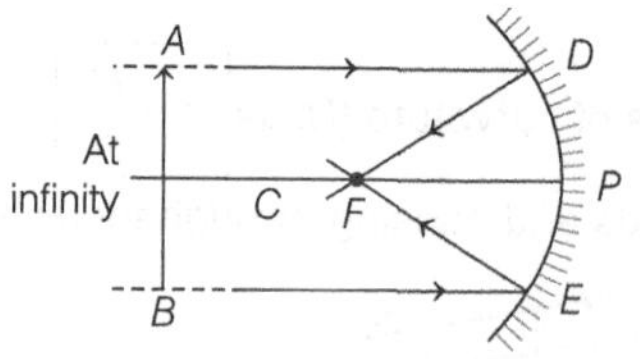	At focus	Real, inverted and extremely diminished in size
(ii)	Beyond the centre of curvature but at finite distance from the mirror	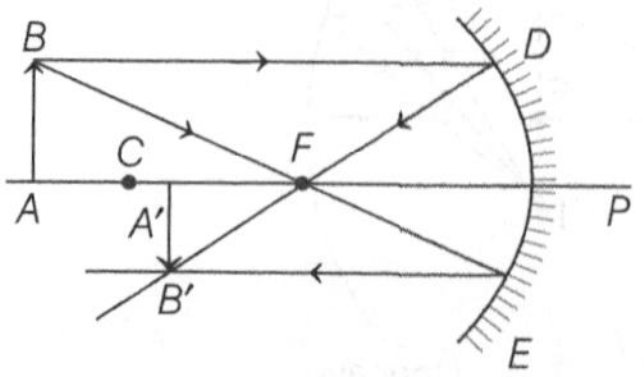	Between focus and the centre of curvature	Real, inverted and diminished

(iii)	At the centre of curvature from the mirror	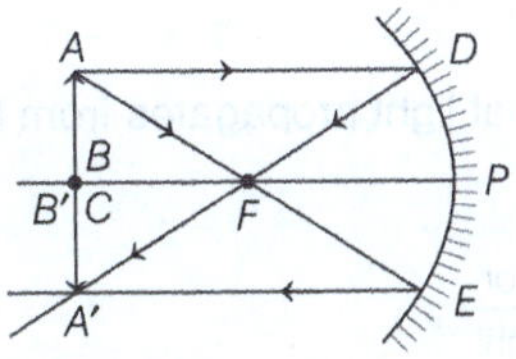	At the centre of curvature	Real, inverted and same size as that of object
(iv)	Between focus and centre of curvature	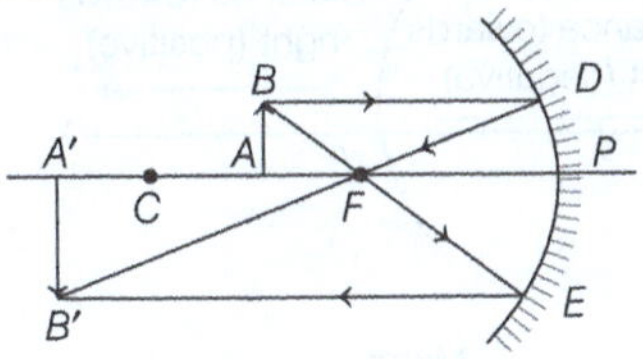	Beyond the centre of curvature	Real, inverted and magnified
(v)	At the focus	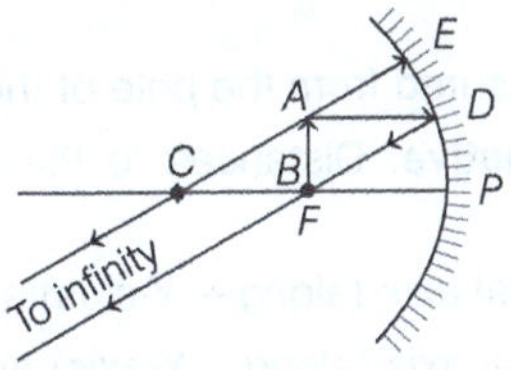	At infinity	Real, inverted and extremely magnified
(vi)	Between the pole and focus	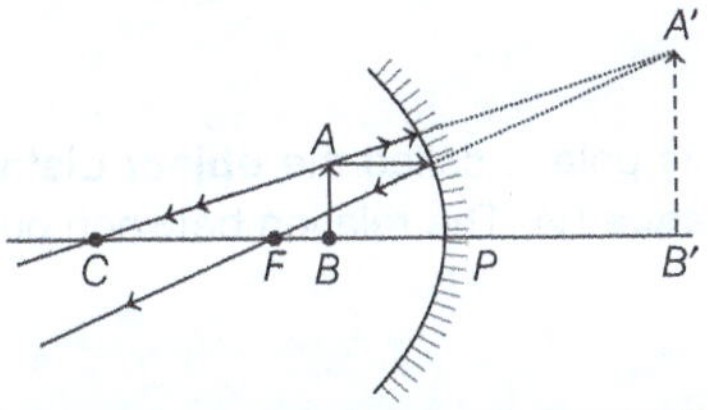	Behind the mirror	Virtual, erect and magnified

Image Formation by a Convex Mirror

For studying the image formed by convex mirror, there are only two positions of the object that are considered. Firstly, when the object is at infinity and the second position is when the object is at a finite distance from the mirror.

S. No.	Position of Object	Ray Diagram	Position of Image	Nature and Size of Image
(i)	At infinity	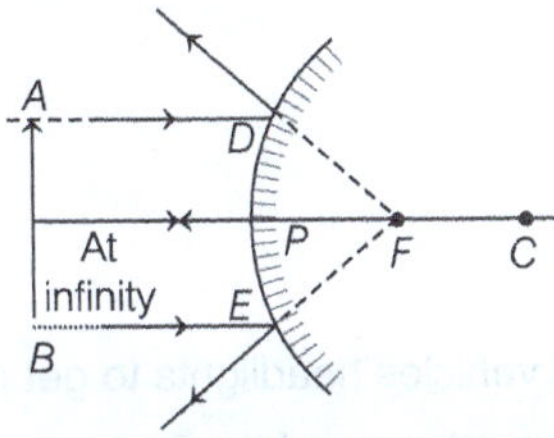	At the principal focus, behind the mirror	Virtual, erect and extremely diminished
(ii)	Between infinity and the pole (i.e., at finite distance)	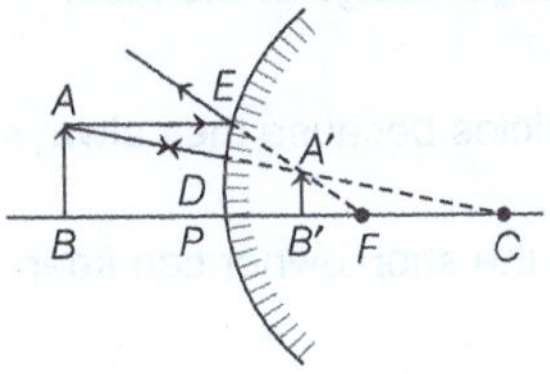	Between the principal focus and the pole, behind the mirror	Virtual, erect and diminished

Sign Convention for Spherical Mirror

(i) The object is always placed to left of the mirror such that light propagates from left to right.

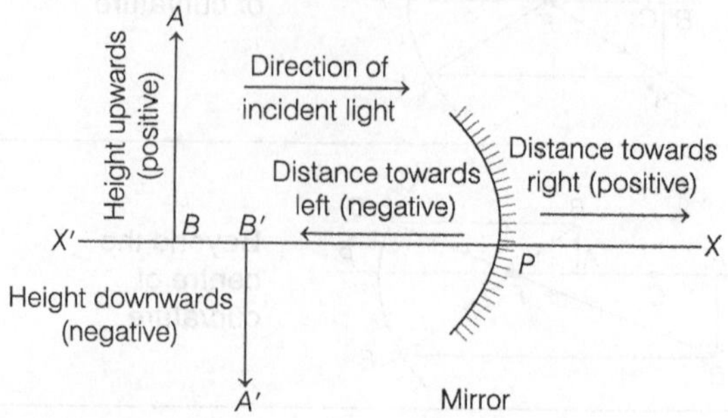

(ii) All distances parallel to principal axis (X-axis) are measured from the pole of the mirror.

(iii) Distances to the left of pole (along $-X$-axis) are **negative**. Distances to the right of pole (along $+X$-axis) are **positive**.

(iv) Distances measured perpendicularly above the principal axis (along $+Y$-axis) are taken as **positive.**

(v) Distances measured perpendicularly below the principal axis (along $-Y$-axis) are taken as **negative**.

Mirror Formula

In a spherical mirror, the distance of the object from its pole is called the **object distance** (u). The distance of the image from pole of the mirror is called the **image distance** (v). The relation between quantities (u, v and f) is called mirror formula. It is expressed as $\frac{1}{v}+\frac{1}{u}=\frac{1}{f}$

Linear Magnification

The ratio of the height of image to the height of object is called linear magnification. If is represented by m.

i.e., Magnification, $m=\frac{\text{Height of image } (h_i)}{\text{Height of object } (h_0)}$

Or Magnification, $m=\frac{\text{Image distance}}{\text{Object distance}}=\frac{-v}{u}$

Uses of Spherical Mirrors

Some uses of the spherical mirrors are given below

(i) For concave mirrors

- These are commonly used in torches, search-lights and vehicles headlights to get powerful parallel beams of light.
- Concave mirrors are used as shaving mirrors to see larger image of the face.

(ii) For convex mirrors

- These are commonly used as rear view mirrors in vehicles because they always give an erect image and have wider field of view as they are curved outwards.
- Big convex mirrors are used as shop security mirrors, the shop owner can keep an eye on the customers to look for thieves and shoplifters among them.

EXAM ORIENTED QUESTIONS

TYPE - 1 01 Mark

Multiple Choice Questions

Q.1 Which of the following is correct about law of reflection?

(a) $\frac{i}{r}$ = constant (b) $\frac{\sin i}{\sin r}$ = constant

(c) $i + r$ = constant (d) $i = r$

Ans. (d) According to the law of reflection, angle of incidence is always equal to the angle of reflection.

Q.2 The image formed by plane mirror is always

(a) real

(b) virtual

(c) virtual and laterally inverted

(d) real and laterally inverted

Ans. (c) Plane mirror always forms a virtual, erect and laterally inverted image.

Q.3 Which diagram shows reflection by a plane mirror?

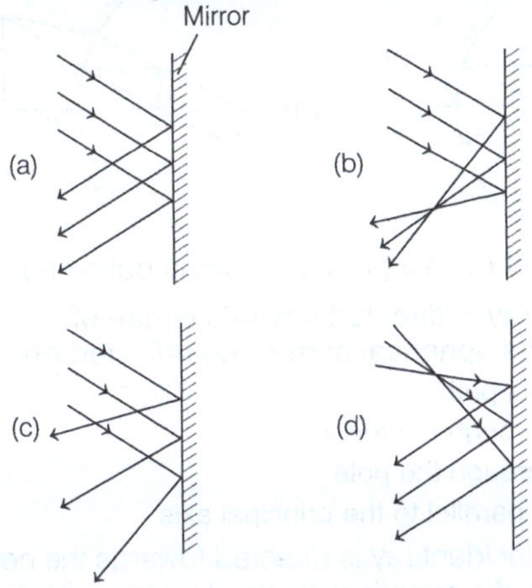

Ans. (a) Parallel light rays incident on a mirror surface are reflected in one direction only i.e. reflected rays are also parallel.

Q.4 The diagram shows a ray of light directed at a plane mirror.

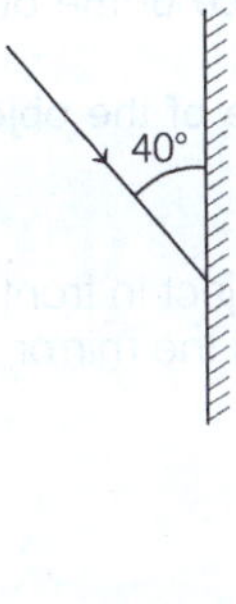

What are the angle of incidence and the angle of reflection?

	Angle of incidence	Angle of reflection
(a)	40°	40°
(b)	40°	50°
(c)	50°	40°
(d)	50°	50°

Ans. (d) The angle of incidence is the angle between the incident ray and the normal to the mirror surface. Similarly the angle of reflection is the angle between the reflected ray and the normal to the mirror surface.

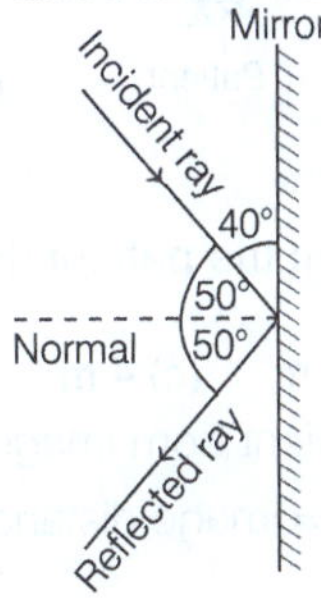

Q.5 Two plane mirrors are placed parallel to each other as shown in figure.

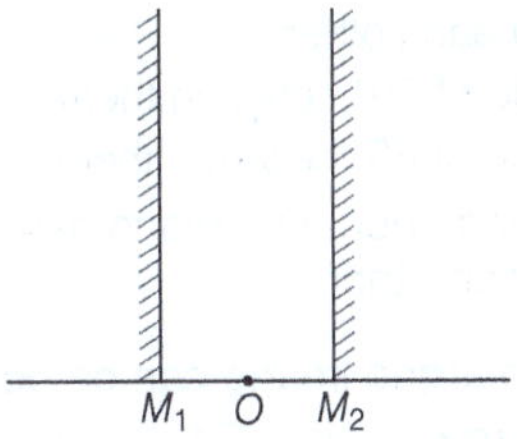

How many images are formed in this mirror arrangement?

(a) Infinite (b) 0

(c) 1 (d) 2

Ans. (a) When two plane mirrors are placed parallel to each other, then infinite number of images are formed.

Q.6

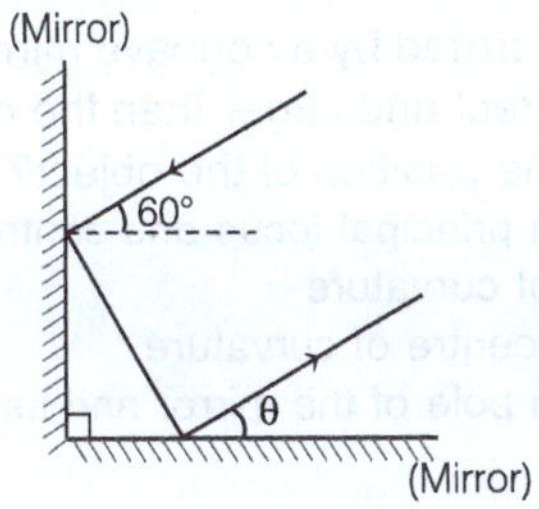

The value of θ in the above figure is

(a) 45° (b) 60° (c) 90° (d) 30°

Ans. (b) According to question,

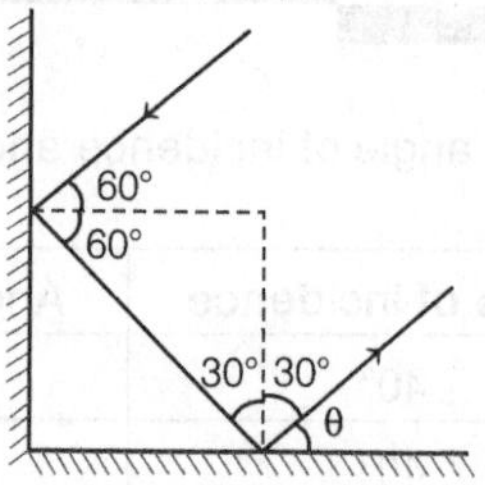

The value of θ is 60°.

Q.7 The diagram shows a patient having her eyes tested. A chart with letters on it is placed behind her and she sees the chart reflected in a plane mirror.

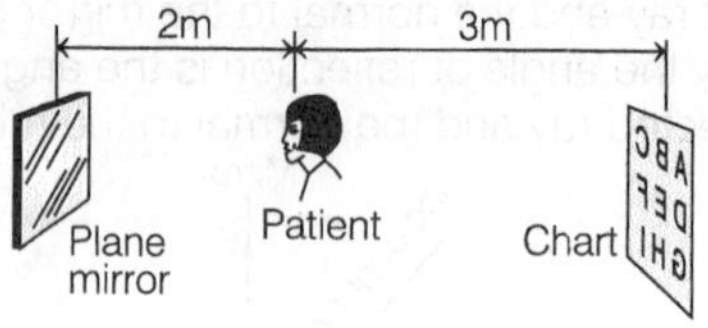

How far away from the patient does the chart seem to be?

(a) 2 m (b) 5 m (c) 4 m (d) 7 m

Ans. (d) Distance of patient from image = 5 + 2 = 7 m

∵ object distance = image distance for plane mirror image.

Q.8 In a barber's shop, two plane mirrors are placed

(a) perpendicular to each other

(b) parallel to each other

(c) at an angle of 60° between them

(d) at an angle of 45° between them

Ans. (b) In a barber's shop, two plane mirrors are placed parallel to each other.

Q.9 A real and enlarged image can be obtained by using a

(a) convex mirror

(b) plane mirror

(c) concave mirror

(d) either plane or convex mirror

Ans. (c) Concave mirror gives an enlarged and real image, when the object is placed between centre of curvature and focus.

Q.10 The image formed by a concave mirror is observed to be virtual, erect and larger than the object, where should be the position of the object?

(a) Between principal focus and centre of curvature.

(b) Centre of curvature

(c) Beyond centre of curvature

(d) Between pole of the mirror and its principal focus

Ans. (d) If the object is placed between the pole of the mirror and its principal focus, then virtual, erect and magnified image will be formed.

Q.11 The image of an object formed by the given mirror is real, inverted and is of magnification.

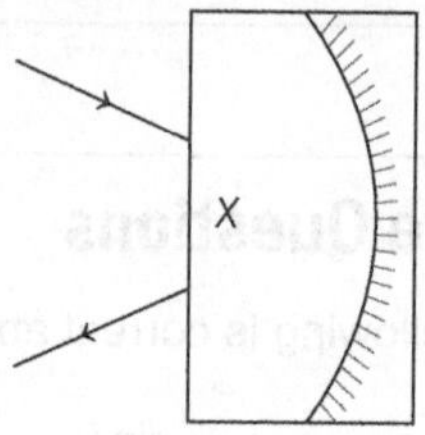

Which mirror is inside the box *X*?

(a) Plane mirror (b) Concave mirror

(c) Convex mirror (d) Diverging mirror

Ans. (b) As the image formed is real, so the concave mirror is inside the box *X*.

Q.12 Which of the following is the correct ray diagram for image formation?

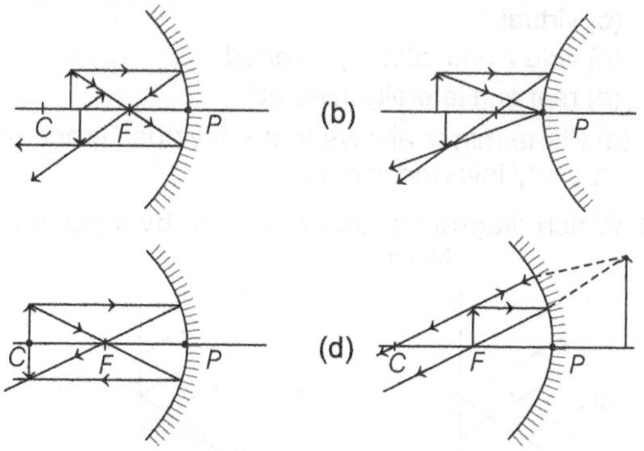

Ans. (c) The correct ray diagram is shown in option (c).

Q.13 An incident ray is directed towards centre of curvature of a spherical mirror, the reflected ray

(a) retraces its path

(b) passes through the focus

(c) passes through the pole

(d) becomes parallel to the principal axis

Ans. (a) When an incident ray is directed towards the centre of curvature of a spherical mirror, then the reflected ray will retrace the path of incident ray.

Q.14 The image of an object in front of a convex mirror is formed

(a) at the object itself

(b) at twice the distance of the object in front of the mirror

(c) at half the distance of the object in front of the mirror

(d) behind the mirror

Ans. (d) The image of an object in front of a convex mirror is always formed behind the mirror

Q.15 If the image is at the distance of 30 cm from the mirror and magnification is −1, where is the object placed?

(a) − 30 cm (b) − 60 cm

(c) 60 cm (d) 30 cm

Ans. (a) Given, $m = -1, v = -30$ cm

We have, $m = -\frac{v}{u}$

$\Rightarrow \quad -1 = -\frac{-30}{u}$

$\therefore \quad u = -30$ cm

TYPE - 2 01 Mark

Assertion-Reason Type Questions

Directions (Q. Nos. 1-5) In the following questions two statements are given as Assertion and Reason.

(a) Both A and R are true and R is the correct explanation of A.
(b) Both A and R are true but R is not the correct explanation of A.
(c) A is true but R is false.
(d) A is false but R is true.

Q.1 Assertion (A) When a concave mirror is held under water, its focal length will increase.

Reason (R) The focal length of a concave mirror is independent of the medium which is placed.

Ans. (d) The focal length of mirror is independent of the medium. So, it remains same for water or air.

Q.2 Assertion (A) When a light ray passing through the centre of curvature incident on the reflecting surface of concave mirror, it reflects back along the same path.

Reason (R) Incident ray falling normally upon the reflecting surface of concave mirror reflects back along the same path.

Ans. (a) It follows law of reflection, $\angle i = \angle r$.

Angle of incidence = Angle of reflection = 0°

The ray of light retraces its path.

Q.3 Assertion (A) Large concave mirrors are used to concentrate sunlight to produce heat in solar cookers.

Reason (R) Concave mirror converges the light rays falling on it to a point.

Ans. (a) Concave mirror converges the light rays falling on it to a point known as focus. So, large concave mirrors are used to concentrate sunlight to produce more heat in solar cookers.

Q.4 Assertion (A) A convex mirror always forms a virtual, erect and diminished image.

Reason (R) Convex mirrors diverge the incident rays such that they appear to originate from a virtual focus.

Ans. (a) Convex mirror always produce virtual images because the reflected rays never meet but appear to diverge from a point behind the mirror. This is why convex mirrors are used as rear view mirrors.

Q.5 Assertion (A) Linear magnification produced by a convex mirror is always less than 1.

Reason (R) The size of the image formed by a convex mirror is always smaller than the size of the object.

Ans. (a) For a convex mirror, the image is always virtual, erect and smaller than the object. The magnification $m = \frac{-v}{u}$, where $v < u$, resulting in $|m| < 1$. Hence, the size of the image is always smaller than the object, leading to magnification less than 1.

TYPE - 3 01/02 Marks

Fill in the Blanks

Q.1 The image formed by a concave mirror is real, if the object is placed ....[beyond the focus/at the pole] **[1]**

Ans. beyond the focus

Q.2 The virtual image is always formed on the .... side of the mirror. [opposite/same] **[1]**

Ans. opposite

Q.3 According to the new cartesian sign convention, distances measured in the direction of the incident light are taken as ...... [negative/positive] **[1]**

Ans. positive

Q.4 Focal length of a ...... (concave/negative) mirror is always ...... (convex/negative) in the cartesian sign convention. **[2]**

Ans. concave, negative

Q.5 A ray of light parallel to the principle axis of a concave mirror passes through the ......(focus/pole) while for a convex mirror, it appears to diverge from the .... (focus/centre of curvature) **[2]**

Ans. focus, focus

TYPE - 4 02 Marks

Very Short Answer Type Questions

Q.1 Give the difference between angle of incidence and angle of reflection.

Ans. **Angle of incidence** It is the angle made by incident ray with normal.

Angle of reflection It is the angle made by reflected ray with normal.

Q.2 Draw a labelled diagram to show the laws of reflection of light. **[2]**

Ans.

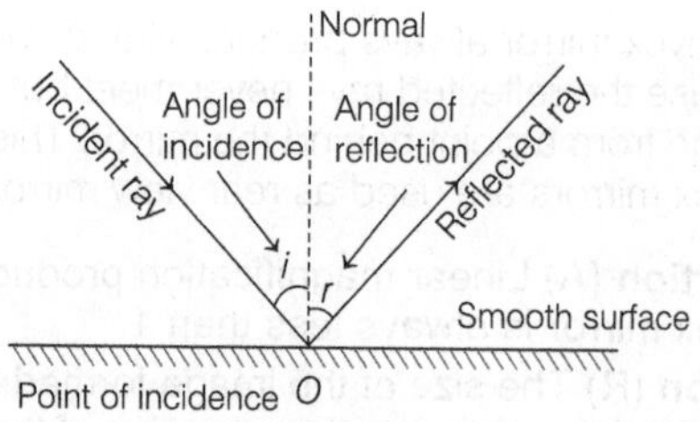

Q.3 The diagram shows an incident ray and normal on a plane mirror. Draw the reflected ray and find the angle between the incident ray and reflected ray.

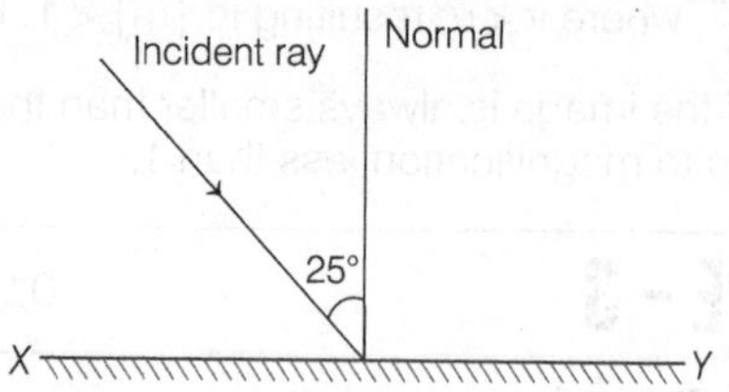

Ans. Angle between the incident ray and reflected ray is 50°.

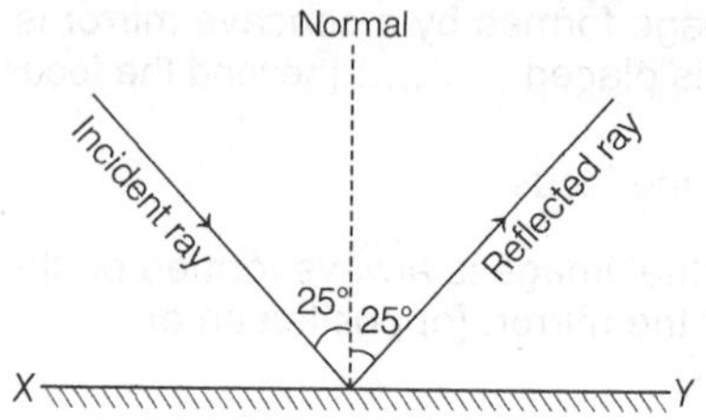

Q.4 When a plane mirror is placed horizontally on levelled ground at a distance of 40 m from the foot of a tower, the top of the tower and its image in the mirror subtend an angle of 90° at the eye. What is the height of the tower?

Ans.

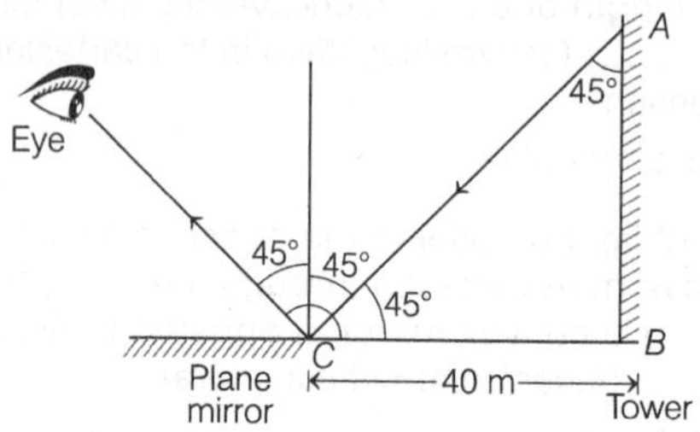

From geometry of figure, height of tower *AB* is 40 m.
As, in right angle ΔABC,

$$\angle CAB = \angle BCA = 45^\circ$$

$$\therefore \quad CB = AB = 40 \text{ m}$$

Q.5 Give one use of each of the following.
(i) Regular reflection **[1]**
(ii) Irregular reflection **[1]**

Ans. (i) Regular reflection helps in the formation of virtual images as in case of plane mirror.
(ii) Irregular reflection helps in illuminating the areas, where light is not falling directly.

Q.6 Give the convenient condition to locate the image formation in case of plane mirror.

Ans. To form an image in case of plane mirror there must be two rays meeting virtually. So that, a virtual image of same size is obtained behind the mirror.

Q.7 An object *AB* is placed in front of a plane mirror. Draw a labelled diagram to show the formation of image of *AB*.

Ans.

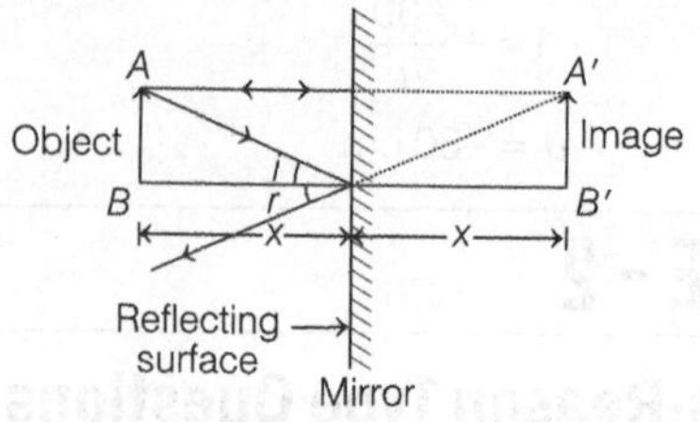

Image $A'B'$ is virtual, erect and equal in size of the object.

Q.8 Under what condition in an arrangement of two plane mirrors, incident ray and reflected ray will always be parallel to each other, whatever may be angle of incidence? Show the same with the help of diagram?

Ans. When plane mirrors are placed at 90° to each other, then the incident and reflected rays will always be parallel to each other, whatever may be the angle of incidence.
The rays are shown below

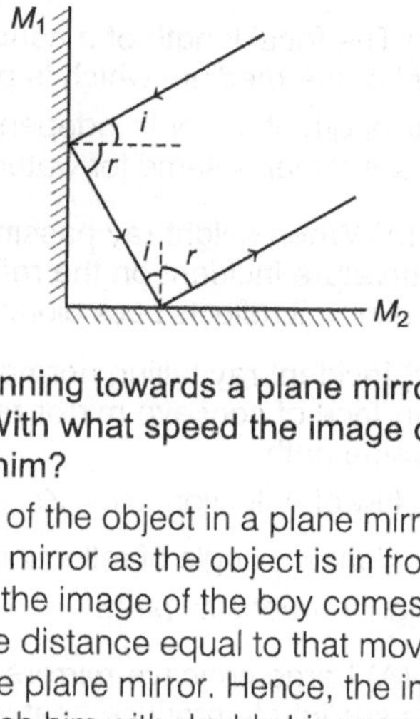

Q.9 A boy is running towards a plane mirror with a speed of 2 m/s. With what speed the image of the boy approach him?

Ans. The image of the object in a plane mirror is as far behind the mirror as the object is in front of it. Therefore, the image of the boy comes near the mirror through the distance equal to that moved by the boy towards the plane mirror. Hence, the image of the boy will approach him with double his speed i.e., with 4 m/s.

Q.10 A student is standing in the centre of a room. He wants to fix a plane mirror in front of him on a wall. What should be the smallest length of the mirror taken by him, so as to enable him to see full image of the back wall?

Ans. In order to see the full image of the back wall, the student should take the smallest length of the mirror to be one-third of the height of the wall.

Q.11 No matter how far you stand from a mirror your image appears to be erect and same distance from the mirror as that of you. What will be the type of mirror?

Ans. The mirror will be plane mirror, because it always forms erect and virtual image (where object distance and image distance are equal).

Q.12 What do you mean by lateral inversion? Write the letters of English alphabet which in front of plane mirror do not show lateral inversion.

Ans. When we look through the plane mirror, the left part of the object appears as the right part of the image and *vice-versa*. This is called lateral inversion. The following letters do not show lateral inversion,

A, H, I, M, O, T, U, V, W, X, Y

Q.13 Draw a ray diagram showing image formation, when object is in between principal focus and pole in case of concave mirror and give nature of image.

Ans. Image formation when object is in between principal focus and the pole.

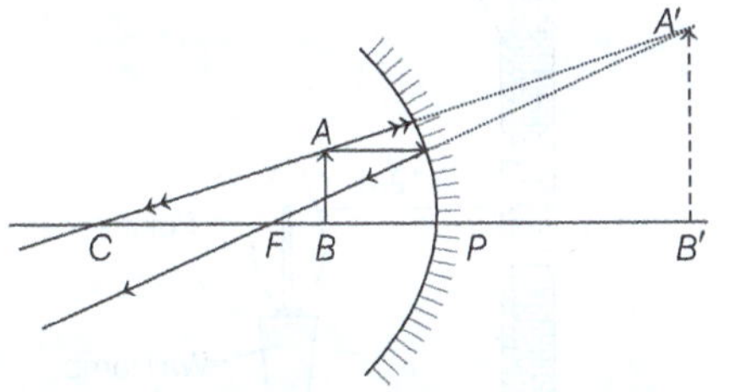

Nature Virtual, erect, magnified and behind the mirror.

Q.14 We wish to obtain an erect image of an object, using a concave mirror of focal length 15 cm. What should be the range of distance of the object from the mirror? What is the nature of image? Is the image larger or smaller than the object? Draw a ray diagram to show the image formation in this case. **[2]**

Ans. The object should be kept at a distance less than 15 cm from the mirror. The image is virtual and erect. The image is larger than the object.

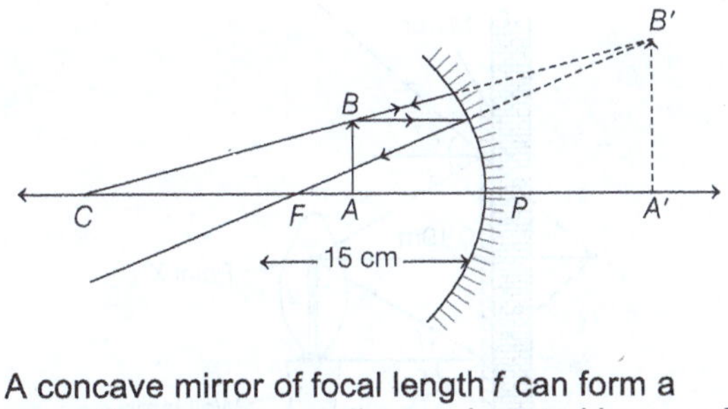

Q.15 A concave mirror of focal length *f* can form a magnified, erect as well as an inverted image of an object placed in front of it. Justify this statement stating the position of object with respect to the mirror in each case for obtaining these images.

Ans. When an object is placed between focus and pole of concave mirror, the image formed is virtual, magnified and erect.

However, when an object is placed between centre of curvature and focus of concave mirror, the image formed is real, magnified and inverted.

Q.16 Rays from the sun converge at a point 15 cm in front of a concave mirror. Where should an object be placed, so that its image formed is equal to the size of the object?

Ans. As we know that for concave mirror, if object is placed at infinity, its image will be formed at focus. Thus, from the question, focal length of given mirror will be 15 cm and for same size of image. In case of concave mirror, object must be placed at centre of curvature. So, when we place the object ($15 \times 2 = 30$ cm) in front of concave mirror we get same size of image.

Q.17 The plane mirror and convex mirror form virtual images of objects. Can they produce real images under same circumstances? Explain.

Ans. Yes, a plane mirror and a convex mirror form real images of object, if object is virtual as shown in Figs. (a) and (b).

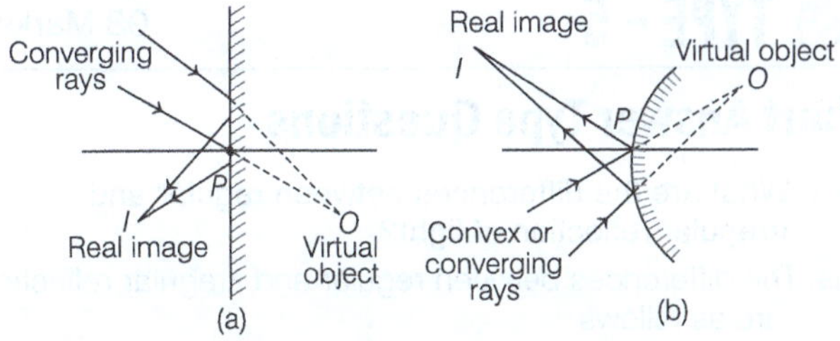

Q.18 What is the nature of the image formed by a concave mirror, when object is placed at centre of curvature?

Ans. The following are the nature of images

(i) The image is also formed at centre of curvature.

(ii) The image is real, inverted and of same size as that of object.

Q.19 **(i) What will be the type of mirror, when image formed is diminished for all positions?** **[1]**

(ii) Inner curved surface of large shining spoon acts as what type of mirror? **[1]**

Ans. (i) If image formed is diminished for all positions, the mirror should be convex mirror.

(ii) Inner curved surface of large shining spoon acts as concave mirror.

Q.20 Why do we prefer a convex mirror as a rear view mirror in vehicles?

Ans. As, we know that the field of view of a convex mirror is wider than that of concave mirror, so we prefer convex mirror as a rear view mirror for vehicles.

Q.21 Name the mirror used in the following cases.

(i) Headlight of car (ii) Solar furnace

Ans. (i) Concave mirror is used to get powerful parallel beam of light.

(ii) Concave mirror as it can converge light of the sun in a small area.

Q.22 Can we change focal length of a given spherical mirror by changing the object distance from the mirror?

Ans. No, we cannot change focal length of a spherical mirror by changing the object distance (*u*). By changing *u*, *v* will change but *f* will remain the same.

Q.23 A concave mirror is used as a head mirror by ENT specialists. The same mirror can also be used as a shaving mirror. Why?

Ans. A concave mirror converges the ray of light falling on it in a direction parallel to the principal axis, on to its focus. This is the reason that ENT specialists use it as a head mirror.

The concave mirror is used as a shaving mirror because when an object is held between the pole and principal focus of a concave mirror which forms a virtual, erect and magnified image of an object.

TYPE - 5 — 03 Marks

Short Answer Type Questions

Q.1 What are the differences between regular and irregular reflection of light?

Ans. The differences between regular and irregular reflection are as follows

Regular reflection	Irregular reflection
It takes place on a smooth polished surface.	It takes place on rough surface.
The reflected rays are parallel to each other after reflection.	Reflected rays are not parallel to each other after reflection.
Reflected rays move only in a fixed direction.	Reflected rays can move in any direction.

Q.2 Shows an old coin displayed in a museum.

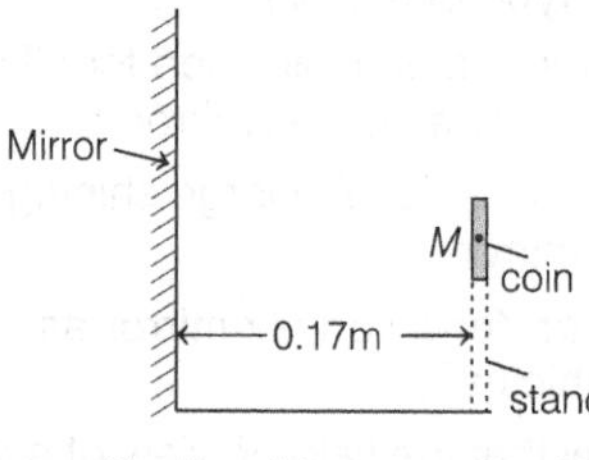

The coin is vertical and is supported by a transparent stand. A vertical mirror 0.17 m behind the coin ensures that the back of the coin can be seen by a visitor looking from the line *P*.

***M* is a point on the back of the coin.**

(i) On figure,

(a) draw two rays of light from *M* to show how its image is produced **[1]**

(b) label the image *I*. **[1]**

(ii) State the distance from point *M* on the coin to its image. **[1]**

Ans. (i) (a) and (b)

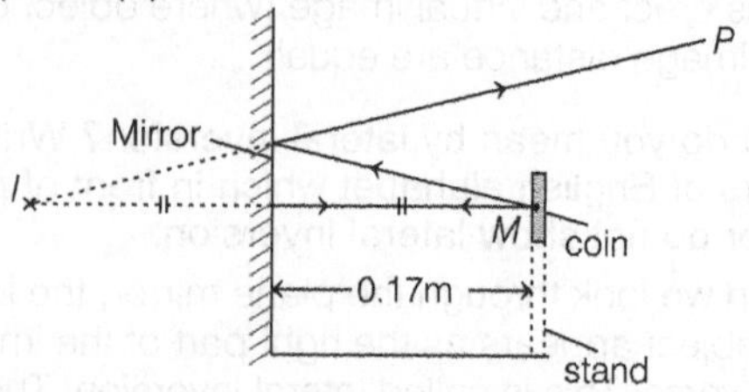

(iii) The distance from *M* to the mirror is 0.17 m.

The image distance behind the mirror is also 0.17 m.

The total distance from *M* to its image is

Distance = 0.17 + 0.17 = 0.34 m

Q.3 A room is illuminated by wall lamps. Figure shows a mirror on the wall behind one of the lamps.

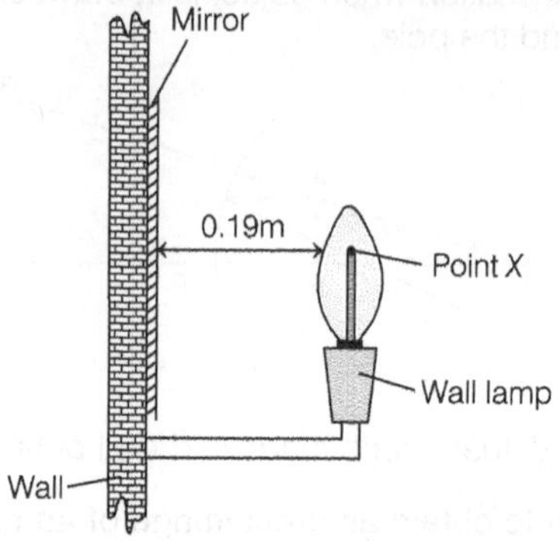

***X* is a point on the filament of the lamp. It is 0.19 m in front of the mirror.**

(i) On figure, draw rays from *X* and locate the image of *X*. Lable the image *I*. **[1]**

(ii) State the distance between *I* and the mirror. **[1]**

(iii) Suggest one advantage of placing a mirror behind the lamp in the room. **[1]**

Ans. (i)

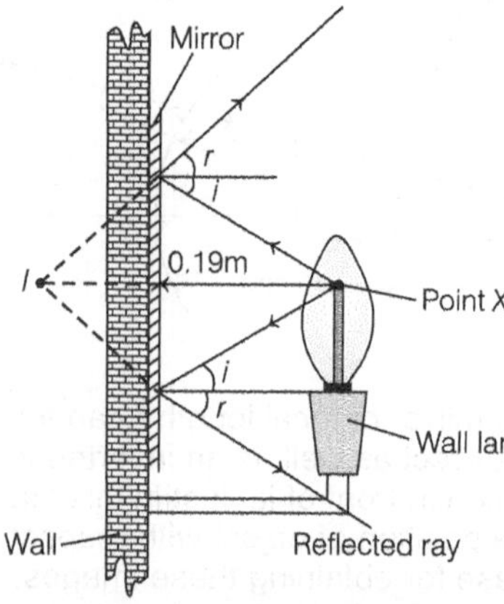

(ii) Since point *X* is at a distance of 0.19 m in front of the mirror, the image *I* will also be at a distance of 0.19 m behind the mirror.

∴ distance between I and the mirror is 0.19 m.

(iii) The light travelling towards the wall is reflected back into the room by the mirror. This makes the room brighter and no light is wasted.

Q.4 Give three uses of a plane mirror.

Ans. The three uses of a plane mirror are

(i) The most common use of plane mirror is that it is used as looking mirror in dressing room.

(ii) It is used at the corners of a blind curve on highways to enable drivers to see the approaching traffic.

(iii) It is used in instruments such as periscope solar cooker, etc.

Q.5 How can you identify the three types of mirrors without touching?

Ans. Placing an object in front of a mirror and observing the image of the object for different positions.

(a) The image by plane mirror is formed of same size.

(b) An erect and smaller image is formed by convex mirror.

(c) An inverted image of different size beyond focal point and within this point enlarged and erect image is formed by concave mirror.

Q.6 (i) **How can you distinguish between plane mirror, convex mirror and concave mirror by merely looking at the image formed in each case?** **[2]**

(ii) **Name a mirror that can give an erect and enlarged image of an object.** **[1]**

Ans. (i) By looking into mirror and going close to it, the mirrors can be identified. If image is of same size and erect it is a plane mirror.

If image is of bigger size and erect it is a concave mirror. If image is of smaller size and erect it is a convex mirror.

(ii) Concave mirror gives erect and enlarged image of an object.

Q.7 A concave mirror of small aperture forms a sharper image, why?

Ans. The rays of light travelling parallel to the principal axis after reflection from a concave mirror meet at a single point, only if the beam of light is narrow or if the mirror is of small aperture.

In case, a wide beam of light falls on a concave mirror of large aperture, the rays after reflection from the mirror do not come to focus at a single point. Therefore, it follows that, if the aperture of the concave mirror is small, the image formed will be sharper.

Q.8 **If the image formed by a mirror for all positions of the object placed in front of it is always erect and diminished, what type of mirror is it? Draw a ray diagram to justify your answer. Where and why do we generally use this type of mirror?**

Ans. The mirror is convex mirror.

Ray diagram for formation of images by a convex mirror

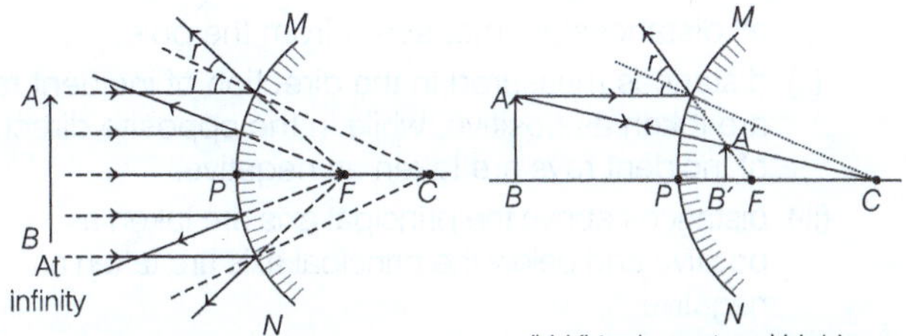

(a) Virtual, erect and highly diminished image at F

(b) Virtual, erect and highly diminished image between P and F

We generally use convex mirrors as rear view mirrors in vehicles to have a wider field of view.

Q.9 **Draw a ray diagram showing the image formation by a convex mirror when an object is placed**

(i) **at infinity** **[2]**

(ii) **at finite distance from the mirror.** **[1]**

Ans. (i) The virtual, erect and highly diminished image of the object forms at focus F behind the mirror.

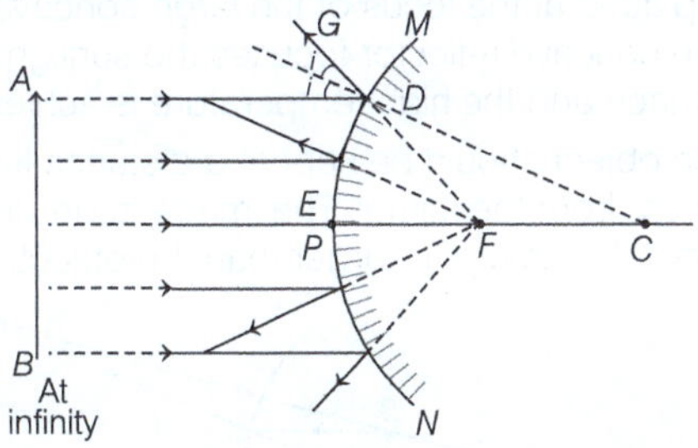

(ii) The virtual, erect and diminished image of the object forms between focus F and pole P behind the mirror.

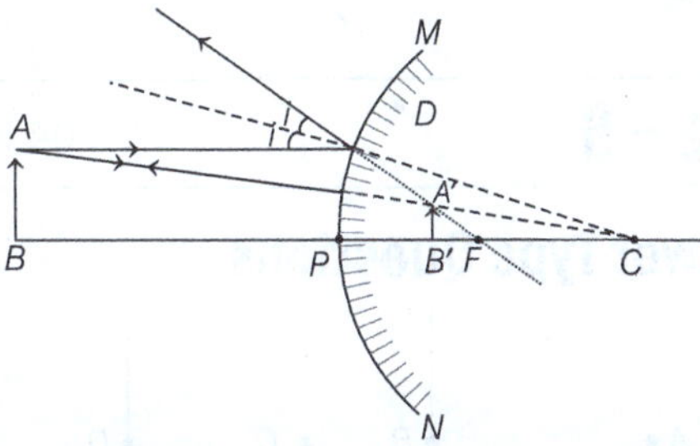

Q.10 Discuss the sign convention used in reflection of light.

Ans. Sign conventions,

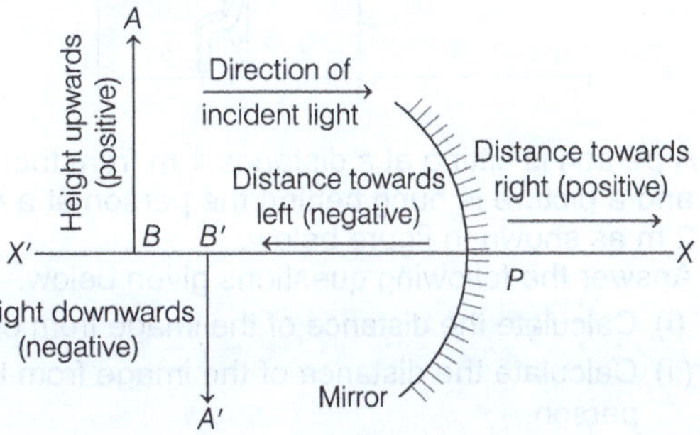

The following are conclusions that

(i) all distances are measured from the pole.

(ii) distances measured in the direction of incident rays are taken as positive, while in the opposite direction of incident rays are taken as negative.

(iii) distances above the principal axis are taken as positive and below the principal axis are taken as negative.

Q.11 **(i) Name the type of mirror used in a solar furnace. How is high temperature achieved by this device?** **[1]**

(ii) We wish to obtain an erect image of an object, using a concave mirror of focal length 15 cm. What should be the range of distance of the object from the mirror? What is the nature of image? Is the image larger or smaller than the object? Draw a ray diagram to show the image formation in this case. **[2]**

Ans. (i) Concave mirror is used in solar furnace. The furnace is placed at the focus of the large concave reflector. The concave reflector focuses the sunlight on the furnace and the high temperature is achieved.

(ii) The object should be kept at a distance less than 15 cm from the mirror. The image is virtual and erect. The image is larger than the object.

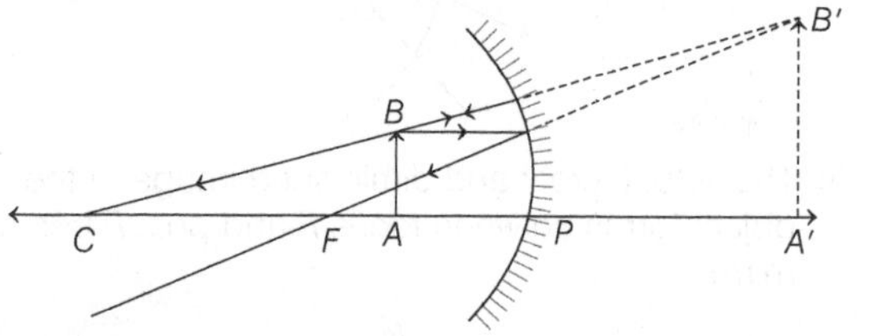

TYPE - 6

04 Marks

Long Answer Type Questions

Q.1

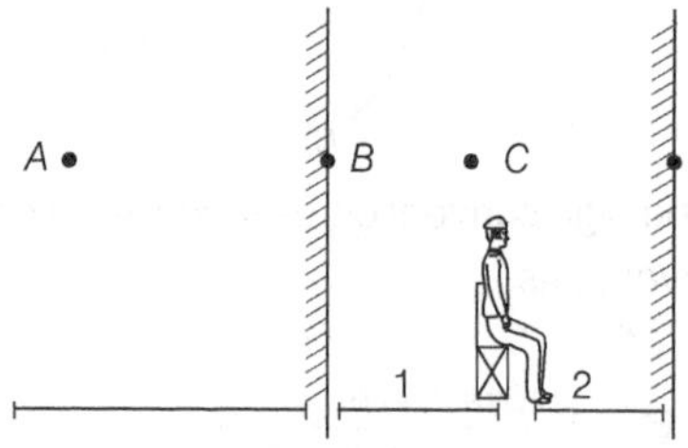

A person is sitting at a distance 1 m from the mirror and a picture is hung behind the person at a distance 2 m as shown in figure below.

Answer the following questions given below.

(i) Calculate the distance of the image from object. **[1]**

(ii) Calculate the distance of the image from the person. **[1]**

(iii) Name the phenomenon used to form the image of the painting. **[1]**

(iv) At what point the image will be formed? Also write the nature of the image. **[1]**

Ans. (i) Distance of object from the mirror

$= (1+2) = 3$ m

Distance of image $= 2 \times 3 = 6$ m.

(ii) Image formed behind the mirror = 3 m

Person is sitting at a distance = 1 m

Distance between image and the person $= 3 + 1 = 4$ m

(iii) Laws of reflection

(iv) The image will be formed at point *A* and the nature of image will be virtual and same size of as object.

Q.2 **Write the differences between concave and convex mirrorrs.**

Ans. **Differences between a concave and convex mirror**

Concave Mirror	Convex Mirror
The spherical mirror with inward curved reflecting surface is called a concave mirror.	The spherical mirror with outward curved reflecting surface is called a convex mirror.
The light rays incident on it converge after reflection.	The light rays incident on it diverge after reflection.
The image formed by it is real as well as virtual depending on the position of object.	The image formed by it is always virtual for all positions of the object in front of it.
For an object away from the centre of curvature, the image is diminished, for an object at centre of curvature, the image is of same size and for an object within the centre of curvature, the image is magnified.	The image is always diminished for all positions of the object in front of it.

Q.3 **A student has three concave mirrors *A*, *B* and *C* of focal lengths 20 cm, 15 cm and 10 cm, respectively. For each concave mirror, he performs the experiment of image formation for three values of object distance of 30 cm, 10 cm and 20 cm.**

Give reasons for the following.

(i) For the three object distances, identify the mirror which will form an image equal in size to that of object. Find atleast one value of object distance. **[1]**

(ii) Out of the three mirrors, identify the mirror which would be preferred to be used for shaving purpose. **[1]**

(iii) For the mirror *B*, draw a ray diagram for image formation for any two given values of object distance. **[2]**

Ans. (i) When an object is placed at the centre of curvature (i.e., double the distance of focal length) of concave mirror, the image formed is equal in size to that of object. So, for object distance 20 cm, the mirror C with focal length 10 cm is used as

$$u = R = 2f = 2 \times 10 \text{ cm} = 20 \text{ cm}.$$

(ii) For shaving purpose, mirror B ($f = 15$ cm) would be preferred to form an enlarged and erect image of the face at distance 10 cm.

(iii) (a) For $u = 30$ cm

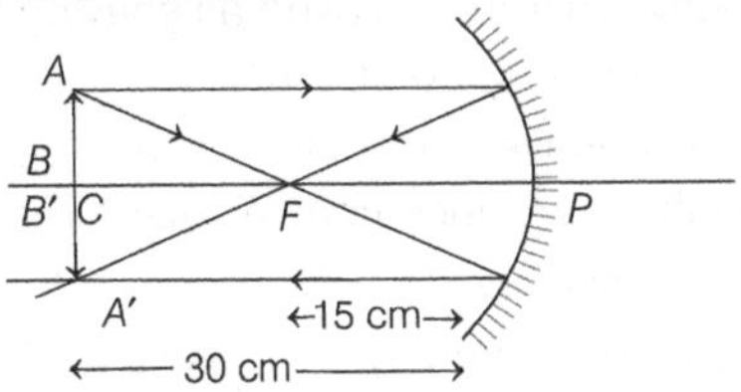

(b) For $u = 10$ cm,

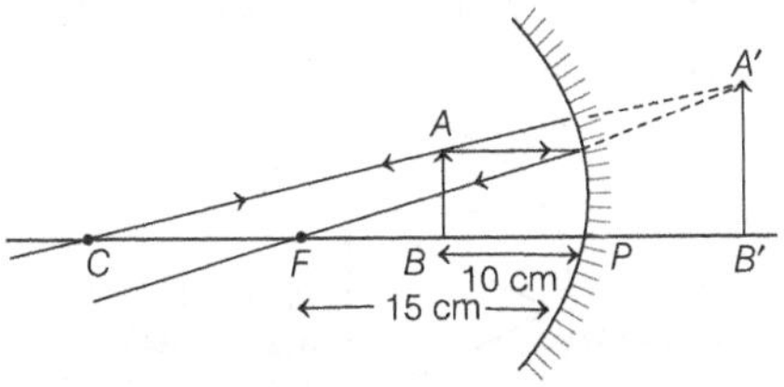

Q.4 For a spherical mirror, we have $\frac{1}{v} + \frac{1}{u} = \frac{1}{f} = \frac{2}{R}$

where, u = distance of an object from pole of mirror,

v = distance of an image from pole of mirror,

f = focal length of mirror

and R = radius of curvature.

We called this formula as mirror formula and is applicable to concave mirror as well as convex mirror.
Using the above formula, answer the following questions.

(a) If we change the value of u by moving an object, then how is focal length f affected? **[1]**

(b) If the radius of curvature of a spherical mirror is 30 cm. What is its focal length? **[1]**

(c) Focal length of a mirror depends neither on u nor on v but it depends only on radius of curvature of the mirror. Explain. **[2]**

Ans. (a) If we change the value of u by moving an object, the distance of an image v changes. But focal length of mirror is not affected.

(b) If $R = 30$ cm, then $f = \frac{R}{2} = \frac{30}{2} = 15$ cm

(c) Focal length of the mirror is the point where rays actually meet or appears to meet after the reflection. It is half of the radius of curvature. Thus, it does not depend on the distance of object or image.

Q.5 A student wants to project the image of a candle flame on the walls of the school laboratory by using a mirror.

(a) Which type of mirror should he use and why? **[1]**

(b) At what distance, in terms of focal length f of the mirror, should he place the candle flame to get the magnified image on the wall? **[1]**

(c) Draw a ray diagram to show the formation of the image in this case. **[1]**

(d) Can he use this mirror to project a diminished image of the candle flame on the same wall? State how, if your answer is yes and why not, if your answer is no. **[1]**

Ans. (a) He should use a concave mirror because it can produce a real inverted and magnified image.

(b) He should place the candle flame between focus and centre of curvature of the mirror to get the magnified image on the wall.

(c)

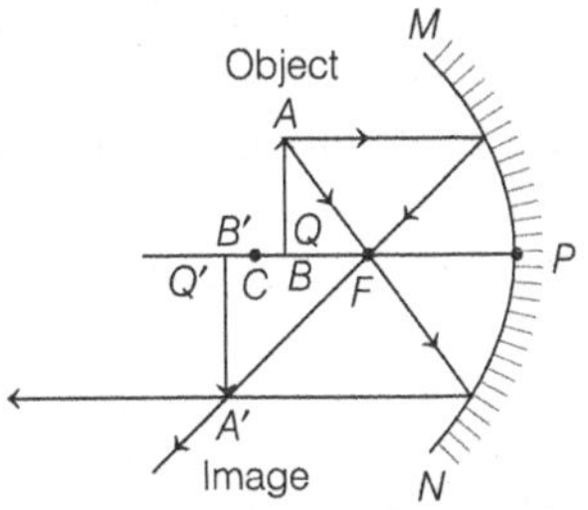

(d) Yes, when object is located at infinity the diminished image is obtained.

Q.6 (i) Give the name of the mirror that

(a) can give real as well as virtual image of an object.

(b) will always give virtual and diminished image of an object.

(c) will always give virtual image of same size of an object.

(d) is used by a doctor to examine teeth. **[2]**

(ii) With the help of a ray diagram, explain the use of concave mirror as solar concentrators. **[2]**

Ans. (i) (a) The given mirror is concave mirror.

(b) The given mirror is convex mirror.

(c) The given mirror is plane mirror.

(d) The given mirror is concave mirror.

(ii) Ray diagram

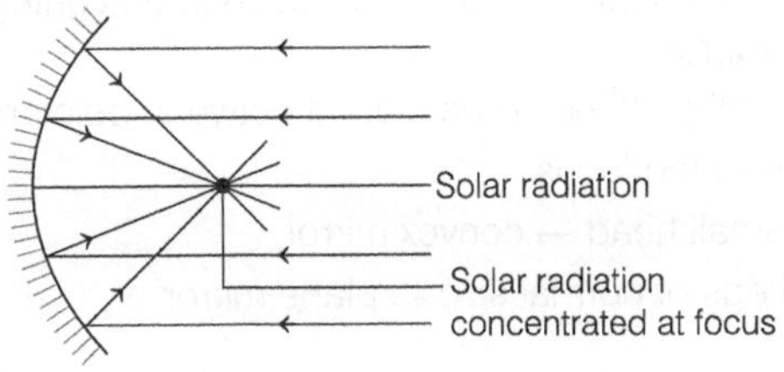

The solar radiation is concentrated at the focus of a concave reflector.

Q.7 (a) From the given table, showing object distance and focal length of three concave mirrors, answer the following questions.

S. No.	Object distance (cm)	Focal length (cm)
(i)	30	20
(ii)	10	15
(iii)	20	10

I. Out of three, in which part the mirror will form the image having same size as the object? **[1]**

II. Which mirror is used as a make-up mirror? **[1]**

III. (a) Draw the ray diagrams for part I and II.

(b) No matter how far you stand from a mirror, your image appears erect and diminished. Identify the type of mirror. **[1]**

Ans. (a) I. The mirror will form an image of same size as that of object in part (iii).

II. In part (ii), concave mirror is being used as a make-up mirror.

III. (a) The ray diagrams are as given below

Part I.

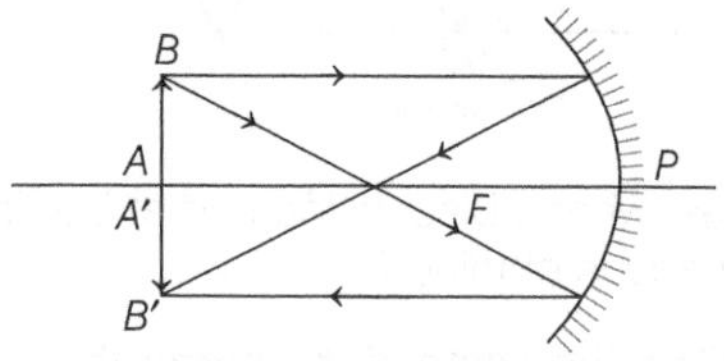

Part II.

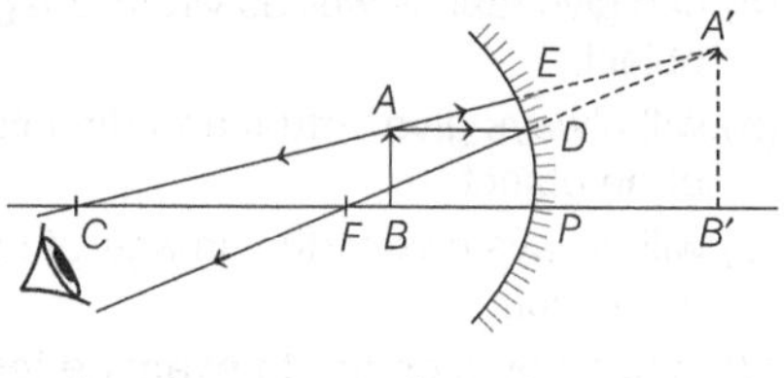

(b) The mirror is convex mirror.

Q.8 (i) What should be the position of the object when a concave mirror is to be used

(a) as a shaving mirror and **[1]**

(b) in torches producing parallel beam of light? **[1]**

(ii) A man standing in front of a mirror, find his image having a very small head and legs of normal size. What types of mirror are used in designing such a mirror? **[2]**

Ans. (i) (a) Object should be placed between pole and focus.

(b) At the focus.

(ii) Small head → convex mirror.

Legs of normal size → plane mirror.

Q.9 Write the uses of concave mirror and convex mirror.

Ans. Some uses of the spherical mirrors are given below

(i) **For concave mirrors**

- These are commonly used in torches, search-lights and vehicles headlights to get powerful parallel beams of light.
- Concave mirrors are used as shaving mirrors to see larger image of the face.
- Large concave mirrors are used to concentrate sunlight to produce heat in solar furnaces.

(ii) **For convex mirrors**

- These are commonly used as rear view mirrors in vehicles because they always give an erect image and have wider field of view as they are curved outwards.

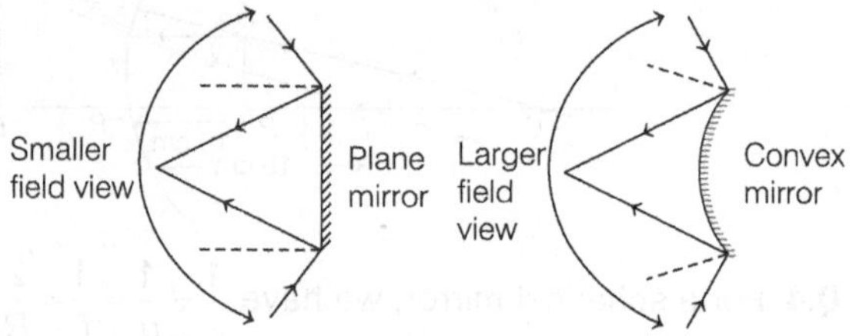

- Big convex mirrors are used as shop security mirrors, the shop owner can keep an eye on the customers to look for thieves and shoplifters among them.

TYPE – 7 03/04 Marks

Case Based Questions

Q.1 A plane mirror is mounted on a wall. A person stands in front of the mirror and looks at their image. The person is standing 3 metres away from the mirror. The image formed appears to be the same size as the person and is behind the mirror.

(a) What is the nature of the image formed by the plane mirror ? **[1]**

(b) If the person moves 1 m closer to the mirror, how will the image distance change ? **[1]**

(c) How would the image change, if a concave mirror were used instead ? **[1]**

Ans. (a) The image formed by a plane mirror is virtual, erect and of the same size as the object.

(b) If the person move 1 m closer to the mirror, the new object distance will be 3 – 2 = 2 m. The image will appear at the same distance on the other side, so the total distance between the object and image will be 2+2 = 4 m.

(c) Concave mirror would form a real and inverted image, that could either be diminished or magnified depending on the objects distance from the mirror.

Q.2 **The angles which the lines makes on both sides of the *B* will be equal as shown in the figure given below.**

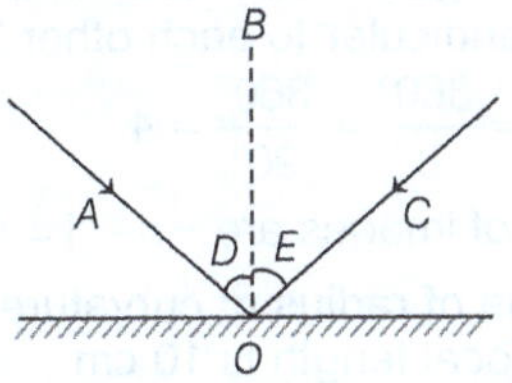

Complete the table using the lables from the figure. The first lable is done for you.

S.No.	Description	Lable
(a)	Normal	B
(b)	Angle of incidence	[1]
(c)	Angle of reflection	[1]
(d)	Incident ray	[1]
(e)	Reflected ray	[1]

Ans.

S.No.	Description	Lable
(a)	Normal	B
(b)	Angle of incidence	D
(c)	Angle of reflection	E
(d)	Incident ray	A
(e)	Reflected ray	C

Q.3 **Shows a very large plane mirror, inclined at 45° to the horizontal, beneath a pattern on the high ceiling of a hall.**

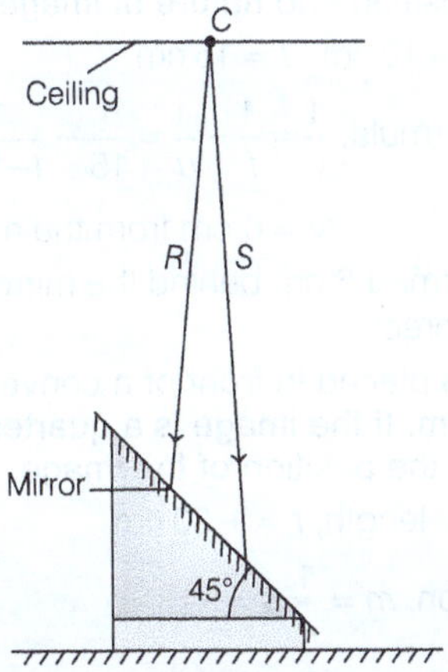

The mirror is set on a stand at head-height immediately below the centre *C* of the pattern. *R* and *S* are two rays of light from *C* that strike the mirror.

(i) On figure, continue the rays *R* and *S* after they strike the mirror. **[1]**

(ii) On figure, show how these rays are used to locate the image of *C* and mark and lable the position of this image with the letter *I*. **[1]**

(iii) State two characteristics of this image. **[1]**

(iv) Suggest how the mirror helps visitors to the hall to see the pattern on the ceiling. **[1]**

Ans. (a) (i) & (ii)

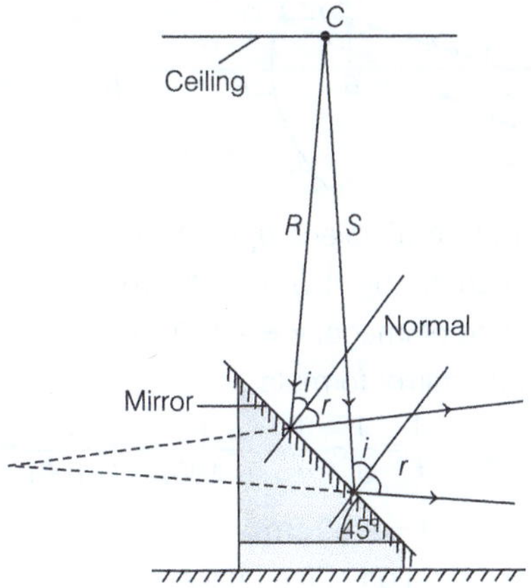

(iii) I. Virtual

II. Same

(iv) It is more comfortable for a visitor to see the ceiling's pattern in the mirror at his eyes level instead of looking up and straining his neck.

Q.4 **Hold a concave mirror in your hand and direct its reflecting surface towards the sun. Direct the light reflected by the mirror on to a white card-board held close to the mirror. Move the card-board back and forth gradually until you find a bright, sharp spot of light on the board. This spot of light is the image of the sun on the sheet of paper, which is also termed as "Principal Focus" of the concave mirror.**

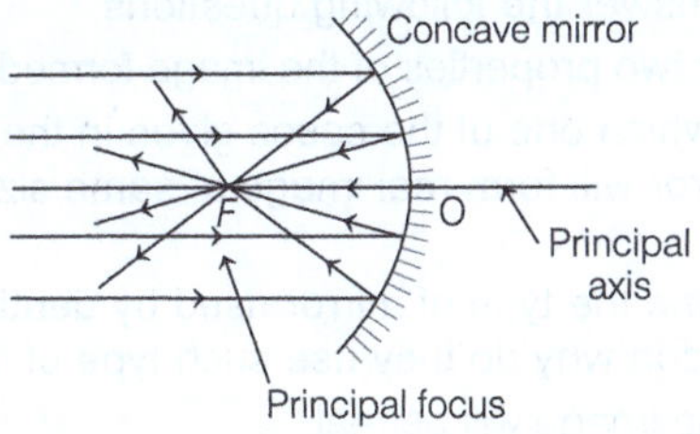

(i) If the distance between the mirror and the principal focus is 15 cm, find the radius of curvature of the mirror. **[1]**

(ii) Draw a ray diagram to show the type of image formed when an object is placed between pole and focus of a concave mirror. **[1]**

(iii) An object 10 cm in size is placed at 100 cm in front of a concave mirror. If its image is formed at the same point where the object is located, find

(a) focal length of the mirror, and

(b) magnification of the image formed with sign as per New Cartesian sign convention. **[1]**

Ans. (i) Given, focal length, $f = 15$ cm

Radius of curvature, $R = 2f = 2 \times 15 = 30$ cm

(ii)

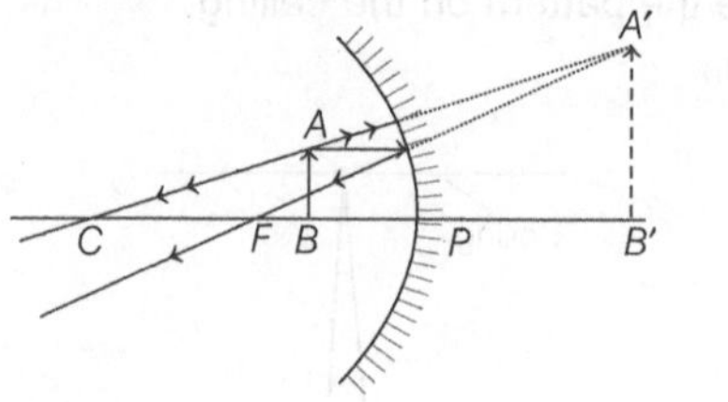

(iii) Given, size of object, $h_o = 10$ cm

Distance of object, $u = -100$ cm

Distance of image, $v = -100$ cm

(a) Using mirror formula,

$$\frac{1}{f} = \frac{1}{u} + \frac{1}{v} = \frac{1}{(-100)} + \frac{1}{(-100)} = \frac{-2}{100}$$

$f = -50$ cm

(b) Magnification of the image,

$$m = \frac{-v}{u} = \frac{-(-100)}{-100} = -1$$

Q.5 **A student took concave mirrors of different focal lengths and performed the experiment to see the image formation by placing an object at different distances with these mirrors as shown in the following table.**

Case No.	Object distance	Focal length
I	45 cm	20 cm
II	30 cm	15 cm
III	20 cm	30 cm

Now, answer the following questions

(i) List two properties of the image formed in case I. [1]

(ii) In which one of the cases given in the table, the mirror will form real image of same size and why? [1]

(iii) Name the type of mirror used by dentists. Give reason why do they use such type of mirrors. [1]

Ans. (i)(a) The image will be real.

(b) The image will be inverted and diminished.

(ii) In Case II, the mirror will form real image of same size because the position of object is at centre of curvature.

(iii) Dentists use concave mirrors to see magnified image of the teeth of patients.

TYPE - 8

Numerical Questions

Q.1 **How many images will be formed, if two mirrors placed perpendicular to each other ? [2]**

Ans. $\theta = 90^\circ \Rightarrow n = \frac{360^\circ}{\theta} = \frac{360^\circ}{90^\circ} = 4$

The number of images are $= n - 1 = 4 - 1 = 3$ **[2]**

Q.2 **Find the value of radius of curvature of a concave mirror, if its focal length is 10 cm. [2]**

Ans. Given, $f = 10$ cm, $R = ?$

$\because \quad f = \frac{R}{2} \Rightarrow R = 2f \Rightarrow R = 2 \times 10 = 20$ cm

Q.3 **A concave mirror is made by cutting a portion of hollow glass sphere of radius 30 cm. Find the focal length of the mirror. [2]**

Ans. Given, radius $(R) = 30$ cm.

As, $f = \frac{R}{2}$ (where, f = focal length of the mirror)

$= \frac{30}{2} = 15$ cm

Q.4 **What is the name given to linear distance between the pole and principal focus of a spherical mirror? If this distance is 25 cm, how far is the centre of curvature from the pole of the spherical mirror? [2]**

Ans. The linear distance between the pole and principal focus of a spherical mirror is called focal length.

If the focal length of the spherical mirror is 25 cm, then its radius of curvature is

$$R = 2f = 2 \times 25 = 50 \text{ cm}$$

Thus, centre of curvature of a spherical mirror should be at a distance of 50 cm from the pole.

Q.5 **An object is placed at a distance of 10 cm from a convex mirror of focal length 15 cm. Find the position and nature of image. [2]**

Ans. Given, $u = -10$ cm, $f = 15$ cm

By mirror formula, $\frac{1}{v} = \frac{1}{f} - \frac{1}{u} = \frac{1}{15} - \frac{1}{(-10)} = \frac{5}{30}$

$v = 6$ cm from the mirror

Image is formed 6 cm behind the mirror, so image is virtual and erect.

Q.6 **An object is placed in front of a convex mirror of focal length 30 cm. If the image is a quarter of the size of object, find the position of the image. [2]**

Ans. Given, focal length, $f = +30$ cm

Magnification, $m = \frac{1}{4}$, $v = ?$

We know that, $m = \frac{f - v}{f}$ $\left(\because \text{Mirror formula, } \frac{1}{v} + \frac{1}{u} = \frac{1}{f}\right)$

$$\Rightarrow \quad \frac{1}{4} = \frac{30 - v}{30} \Rightarrow 30 = 120 - 4v$$

$$v = \frac{90}{4} = 22.5 \text{ cm}$$

As, v is positive, therefore a virtual and erect image will be formed on the side of the object.

Q.7 **A concave shaving mirror is of focal length 50 cm. How far should the mirror be held from the face to produce an image of two fold magnification?** **[2]**

Ans. $\because\ m = -\frac{v}{u} = 2$ and $f = -50$ cm

$$\Rightarrow \quad v = -2u$$

Using the mirror formula, $\frac{1}{u} + \frac{1}{v} = \frac{1}{f}$

$$\Rightarrow \quad \frac{1}{u} + \frac{1}{(-2u)} = \frac{1}{f} \Rightarrow \frac{2-1}{2u} = \frac{1}{f} \Rightarrow f = 2u$$

$$\therefore \quad u = \frac{f}{2} = -\frac{50}{2} = -25 \text{ cm}$$

Q.8 **An object is held 6 cm from a concave mirror of focal length 12 cm. Find the position, nature and magnification of the image.** **[3]**

Ans. Given, $u = -6$ cm and $f = -12$ cm

Using the mirror formula, $\frac{1}{u} + \frac{1}{v} = \frac{1}{f}$

$$\Rightarrow \quad \frac{1}{v} = \frac{1}{f} - \frac{1}{u} \Rightarrow \frac{1}{v} = \frac{1}{-12} - \left(\frac{1}{-6}\right)$$

$$\Rightarrow \quad \frac{1}{v} = -\frac{1}{12} + \frac{1}{6} \Rightarrow \frac{1}{v} = \frac{-1+2}{12} = \frac{1}{12} \Rightarrow v = 12 \text{ cm}$$

As, $m = -\frac{v}{u} = \frac{-12}{-6} = 2$

The image formed is virtual, erect and magnified.

Q.9 **A convex mirror used for rear view on an automobile has a radius of curvature of 3 m. If a bus is located at 5 m from this mirror. Find the position, nature and magnification of the image.** **[3]**

Ans. Given, radius of curvature, $R = 3$ m

Distance of the bus, $u = -5$ m

Image of the bus, $v = ?$

Magnification of the image, $m = ?$

We know that, $f = \frac{R}{2} = \frac{3}{2}$ m

Using mirror formula, $\frac{1}{f} = \frac{1}{v} + \frac{1}{u}$

$$\Rightarrow \quad \frac{1}{v} = \frac{1}{f} - \frac{1}{u} = \frac{2}{3} - \frac{1}{(-5)} = \frac{10+3}{15} = \frac{13}{15}$$

$$v = \frac{15}{13} = 1.15 \text{ m}$$

$$\therefore \quad m = -\frac{v}{u} = -\frac{15/13}{-5} = \frac{3}{13} = 0.23$$

The image is virtual, erect and 1.15 m behind the mirror.

Q.10 **A candle flame is held 3 cm away from a concave mirror of radius of curvature 24 cm. Where is the image formed? What is the nature of the image?** **[3]**

Ans. Given, object distance, $u = -3$ cm

Radius of curvature, $R = -24$ cm

$$\because \quad f = \frac{R}{2} = \frac{-24}{2} = -12 \text{ cm}, v = ?$$

Apply mirror formula to calculate the value of v.

$$\frac{1}{f} = \frac{1}{u} + \frac{1}{v} \text{ or } \frac{1}{v} = \frac{1}{f} - \frac{1}{u}$$

$$= \frac{1}{-12} - \frac{1}{(-3)} = \frac{1}{-12} + \frac{1}{3} = \frac{-1+4}{12}$$

$$\Rightarrow \quad \frac{1}{v} = \frac{3}{12} = \frac{1}{4}$$

$$\therefore \quad v = 4 \text{ cm}$$

We, know, $m = \frac{-v}{u} = -\frac{4}{(-3)} = +1.33$

$\therefore$ The image formed is virtual, erect and magnified.

Q.11 **An object 5 cm tall was placed in front of a spherical mirror at 20 cm distance from the mirror. If a virtual image of 10 cm tall was formed behind the mirror, find the focal length of the mirror and the position of the image. Name the type of mirror used.** **[3]**

Ans. Given, $u = -20$ cm, $h_i = 10$ cm and $h_o = 5$ cm

As we know, $m = \frac{h_i}{h_o} = \frac{10}{5} = 2$

where, h_i = size of image, h_o = size of object, and m = magnification.

Also, $m = -\frac{v}{u} \Rightarrow 2 = \left(\frac{-v}{-20}\right) \Rightarrow v = 40$ cm

From mirror formula, $\frac{1}{f} = \frac{1}{v} + \frac{1}{u}$

where, u = object distance, v = image distance and f = focal length.

$$\frac{1}{f} = \frac{1}{40} + \frac{1}{(-20)} = \frac{1-2}{40} = \frac{-1}{40} \Rightarrow f = -40 \text{ cm}$$

So, mirror is concave.

Q.12 **A concave mirror produces three times magnified (enlarged) real image of object placed at 10 cm in front of it. Where is the image located?** **[3]**

Ans. Real image is inverted. So, magnification is negative.

Thus, $m = -3 = \frac{\text{Image size}}{\text{Object size}} = \frac{h_i}{h_o}$

$$\Rightarrow \quad \frac{\text{Image size}}{\text{Object size}} = -\frac{v}{u} \quad \begin{pmatrix}\text{where, } v = \text{image distance} \\ \text{and } u = \text{object distance}\end{pmatrix}$$

$$\Rightarrow \quad -3 = \frac{-(v)}{(-10)} \quad (\because \text{object is placed in front of mirror})$$

$$\Rightarrow \quad -3 = \frac{v}{10}$$

∴ Image distance = –30 cm

Negative sign shows that image is real, so it will be formed in front of the mirror.

Q.13 **A real image one-fifth the size of an object is formed at a distance of 18 cm from a mirror. What is the nature of mirror? Calculate its focal length.** **[3]**

Ans. Given, magnification, $m = \frac{-1}{5}$

$v = -18$ cm

$\therefore \quad m = \frac{-v}{u} \Rightarrow \frac{-1}{5} = -\frac{(-18)}{u}$

$\Rightarrow \quad u = (-5) \times 18 = -90$ cm

Using mirror formula,

$$\frac{1}{f} = \frac{1}{v} + \frac{1}{u} = \frac{-1}{18} + \frac{1}{(-90)} = \frac{-5-1}{90} = \frac{-6}{90}$$

$f = -15$ cm

Thus, real, inverted and smaller image is formed in the concave mirror.

Q.14 **A spherical mirror produces an image of magnification – 1 on a screen placed at a distance of 50 cm from the mirror.**

(a) Find the distance of the image from the object.

(b) What is the focal length of the mirror?

(c) Draw the ray diagram to show the image formation in this case. **[4]**

Ans. (a) Given, $m = -1$, $v = -50$ cm

$\therefore$ Magnification, $m = \frac{-v}{u} \Rightarrow -1 = \frac{50}{u} \Rightarrow u = -50$ cm

Therefore, the image is real and inverted and of same size as that of the object.

∴ Distance of image from the object = 0

(b) $\frac{1}{f} = \frac{1}{u} + \frac{1}{v}$

Substituting $u = -50$ cm and $v = -50$ cm

$$\frac{1}{f} = \frac{1}{(-50)} + \frac{1}{(-50)} \Rightarrow \frac{1}{f} = \frac{-2}{50}$$

$f = -25$ cm

The focal length of the mirror is –25 cm, indicating it is a concave mirror.

As, object distance = image distance = 50 cm

(c)

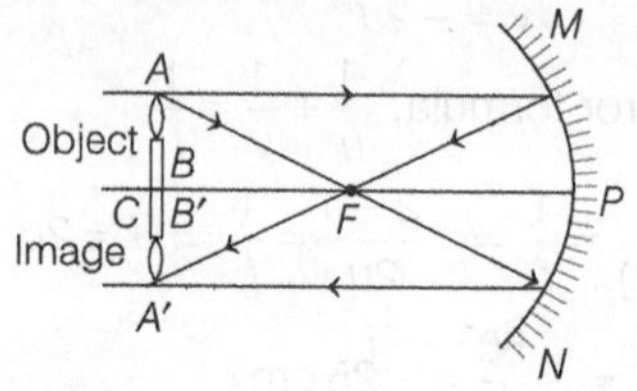

Q.15 **In a converging mirror of focal length 16 cm, where would an image be formed. If the distance of the object is 32 cm in front of it. Also, find the nature and the size the image formed.** **[2]**

Ans. Given, $u = -32$ cm, $f = -16$ cm

$$\frac{1}{f} = \frac{1}{u} + \frac{1}{v} \Rightarrow \frac{1}{v} = \frac{1}{(-16)} - \left(\frac{1}{-32}\right)$$

$$\frac{1}{v} = -\frac{1}{16} + \frac{1}{32}$$

$v = -16$ cm

$$M = \frac{-v}{u} = \frac{16}{(-16)} = -1$$

09

SOUND

Sound is a form of energy produced by vibrating objects and propagates in the form of **mechanical waves**.

Propagation of Sound in a Medium

Sound propagates through a medium by creating disturbances, not by moving particles forward. The vibrating source displaces a **particle**, which exerts a force on the adjacent particles, causing it to move. This process repeats as each particle returns to its original position, transferring the disturbance through the medium until it reaches the ear.

Longitudinal Waves

- The waves in which particles of the medium vibrate parallel to the direction of wave propagation is called longitudinal wave.
- Sound waves are the **longitudinal waves**, they move in the air in the form of **compression** and **rarefaction**.
- **Compression** When a vibrating object moves forward, it pushes air particles closer, creating a region of **high pressure** and **density** called compression. It is denoted by *C*.
- **Rarefaction** When the vibrating object moves backward, it pulls air particles apart, forming a region of **low pressure** and **density** called rarefaction. It is denoted by *R*.

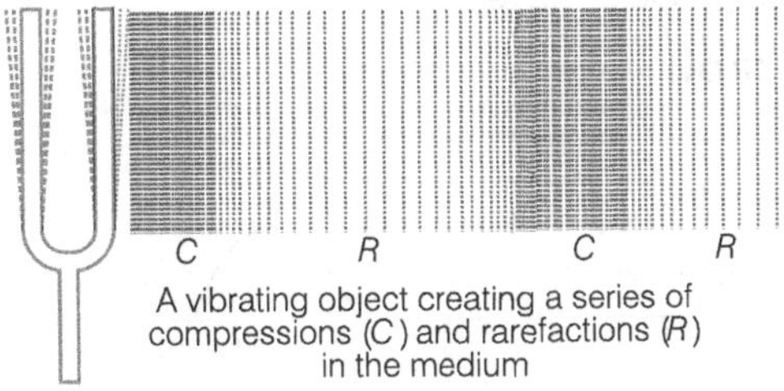

A vibrating object creating a series of compressions (*C*) and rarefactions (*R*) in the medium

Transverse Waves

- The waves in which particles of the medium vibrate perpendicular to the direction of wave propagation are called transverse waves.
- The light is an electromagnetic wave and is transverse in nature.
- Transverse wave is composed of crest and trough.
- **Crest** The position of maximum upward displacement is called crest.
- **Trough** The position of maximum downward displacement is called trough.
- Transverse waves can only travel through solids and on the surface of liquid.

Sound Propagation Requires a Material Medium

- The substance through which sound travels is called a medium. The medium can be a **solid, liquid** or **gas**. A material medium is necessary for the propagation of sound from one place to another.
- For propagation of sound, medium should have following properties

  (i) The medium must be **elastic** so that its particles can come back to their initial positions after displacement on either side.

(ii) The medium must have **inertia** so that particles can store mechanical energy.

(iii) The medium should be **frictionless**, so that there is no loss of energy in propagation of sound through it.

Some Terms Related to Sound Waves

1. **Wavelength** The distance between the two **consecutive compressions** C or two **consecutive rarefactions** R is called the wavelength of the sound wave. It is represented by λ. Its SI unit is **metre** (m).
2. **Frequency** The number of vibrations made by a particle of a medium in one second is called the frequency of the wave. It is denoted by ν. Its SI unit is **hertz** (Hz).

   1 hertz = 1 vibration per second
3. **Time Period** Time taken by two consecutive **compressions** or **rarefactions** to cross a fixed point is called the time period of the wave. It is denoted by T. Its SI unit is **second** (s).

$$\boxed{\text{Time period } (T) = \frac{1}{\text{Frequency } (\nu)}}$$

4. **Amplitude** When a wave passes through a medium, the maximum displacement of the particle of the medium on either side of its mean position, is called amplitude of the wave. It is denoted by A. Its SI unit is **metre** (m).
5. **Wave velocity** The **distance** travelled by the sound wave in one second is called velocity of the wave or speed of the wave. It is represented by v. Its SI unit is **metre per second** (m/s or ms^{-1}).

Displacement-Time Graph

A displacement-time graph shows how the displacement of one point on the wave varies over time.

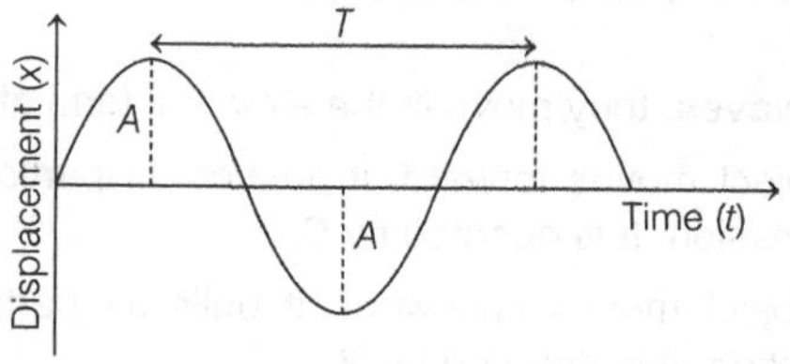

Here, A is amplitude and T is the time period of wave.

Displacement-Distance Graph

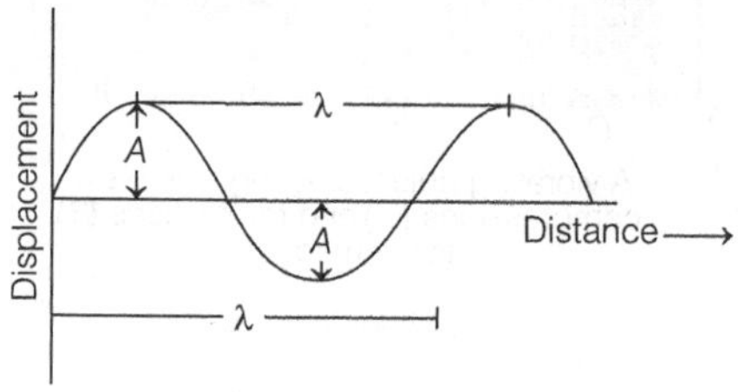

Relationship between Wavelength, Wave Velocity and Frequency

Wave velocity, $$v = \frac{\text{Distance travelled} (\lambda)}{\text{Time taken} (T)}$$

We know that, Frequency, f or $\nu = \frac{1}{T}$

$\therefore$ $$v = \lambda \times \nu \text{ or } v = \nu\lambda$$

or $$\boxed{\text{Velocity (Speed)} = \text{Frequency} \times \text{Wavelength}}$$

Speed of Sound in Different Media

Speed of sound is different in different media. The speed of sound **depends** on the **properties of medium** through which it travels. It **decreases**, when we go from **solid** to **gaseous state**. i.e. The speed of sound is more in solids, less in liquids and least in gases (since solids are much more elastic than liquids and gases).
The speed of sound is 5100 m/s in steel 1450 m/s in water and 330 m/s in air at 0°C.
Speed of sound in any medium depends on the following two factors
(i) The elasticity E of the medium and the density ρ of the medium as given below.

$$v = \sqrt{\frac{E}{\rho}}$$

Factors Affecting Speed of Sound in Gas

(i) **Effect of Density** Speed of sound is **inversely proportional** to the **density** of the gas. Therefore, speed of sound decreases with the increase in the density of gas.

(ii) **Effect of Temperature** The speed of sound **increases** with the **increase** in the **temperature of the gas**. This is because as the temperature increases, density of the gas decreases, thereby increasing the speed of sound. The speed of sound in air V_t at a certain temperature t (° C) is given as

$$\boxed{V_t = V_0 + 0.61t}$$

Where V_0 is the speed of sound in air at 0°C.

(iii) **Effect of Humidity** The density of the moist air is less than the density of dry air. Therefore, the speed of sound in moist air is slightly greater than in dry air. So, speed of sound **increases** with the **increase in humidity**.

(iv) **Effect of Direction of Wind** If the direction of wind is in the direction of propagation of sound, then speed of sound **increases**. Otherwise, the speed of sound **decreases**.

Factors not Affecting Speed of Sound

Speed of sound in gas is not affected by the change in

(i) pressure (ii) amplitude of wave (iii) wavelength or frequency of wave

Comparison of Speed of Sound with Speed of Light

The sound needs a medium to propagate, whereas light does not. The speed of sound in air is about 344 ms^{-1} at 22°C and 331 ms^{-1} at 0°C, whereas speed of light in air is $3 \times 10^8 ms^{-1}$. Thus, **speed of light is much greater than the speed of sound**. Due to this consequence, we see the lightning much sooner than we hear the thunder.

Range of Hearing

The average frequency range over which the human ear is **sensitive** is called **audible range**. It typically ranges from 20 Hz to 20000 Hz (20 kHz). A human ear it not sensitive in the range of 200 Hz to 3000 Hz. Children under the age of 5 and some animals, such as dogs can hear up to 25000 Hz.

Infrasonic Sound

The sound of frequencies lower than 20 Hz (infrasonic frequency) are known as **infrasonic sounds** or **infrasound**, which cannot be heard by human beings. Earthquakes and some animals like whales, elephants and rhinoceroses produce infrasonic sound of frequency as low as 5 Hz.

Ultrasonic Sound

The sounds of frequencies higher than 20000 Hz or 20 kHz are called as ultrasonic sounds or **ultrasound** which cannot be heard by human beings. Dogs can hear ultrasonic sounds of frequency upto 50000 Hz. Bats can hear ultrasonic sounds having frequencies up to 120000 Hz.

Properties of Ultrasounds

- Ultrasounds are high frequency waves.
- They travel in a straight line without bending around corners.
- They can penetrate into matter to a larger extent.

Applications of Ultrasound

Some of the important applications of ultrasound are given below

- **In Cleaning Minute Parts of Machines** Ultrasound is used to clean parts located in hard-to-reach-places, such as spiral tubes, odd-shaped machines and electronic components, etc.
- **In Internal Investigation of Human Body** Ultrasound is used to investigate the internal organs of human body such as liver, uterus and heart, etc.
- **In Industries** Ultrasound is used in industries for detecting flaws (cracks, etc.) in metal blocks without damaging them. It is also used for drilling holes or making cuts of desired shapes in materials like glass.

Use of Ultrasonic Waves by Bats

Bats search for prey and fly in dark night by **emitting** and **detecting** reflections of **ultrasonic waves**. This method used by some animals like bats, tortoises and dolphins to locate the objects by hearing the echoes of their ultrasonic squeaks is known as **echolocation**.

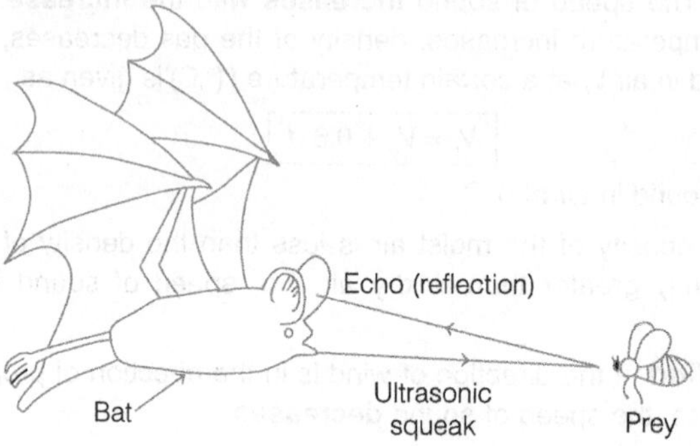

Bats can search their prey in the darkness of night by the method of echolocation

Differences between Ultrasonic Waves and Supersonic Waves

Ultrasonic Wave	Supersonic Wave
The sound waves of frequencies greater than 20000 Hz are called ultrasonic waves.	It refers to the movement of an object with a speed greater than the speed of sound.
The speed of ultrasonic waves is equal to the speed of sound.	A supersonic object moves faster than the sound waves.
It is widely used in medical imaging, cleaning, industrial applications etc.	It is widely used in aircraft, missiles and supersonic transport (e.g., jets)

EXAM ORIENTED QUESTIONS

TYPE - 1 01 Mark

Multiple Choice Questions

Q.1 What happens to the particles of the medium during the propagation of sound?

(a) They move along with the wave.

(b) They oscillate about their mean position.

(c) They do not move at all.

(d) They accelerate continuously.

Ans. (b) During the propagation of sound, particles of the medium do not travel with the wave. Instead, they oscillate about their mean position in the direction of the wave propagation.

Q.2 In a sound wave, where are the density and pressure of the medium maximum and where are they minimum?

(a) At compressions, both are minimum and at rarefactions, both are minimum.

(b) At compressions, both are maximum and at rarefaction, both are maximum.

(c) At compression, both are minimum and at rarefaction, both are maximum.

(d) At compressions, both are maximum and at rarefactions, both are minimum.

Ans. (d) In a sound wave compression refers to the regions where the particles are pushed closer together, resulting in higher particle density and pressure (density and pressure are maximum). Rarefaction refers to regions where the particles are spread apart, leading to lower density and pressure (density and pressure are minimum).

Q.3 Which diagram shows an example of a longitudinal wave?

(a) Light travelling from a lamp to a screen

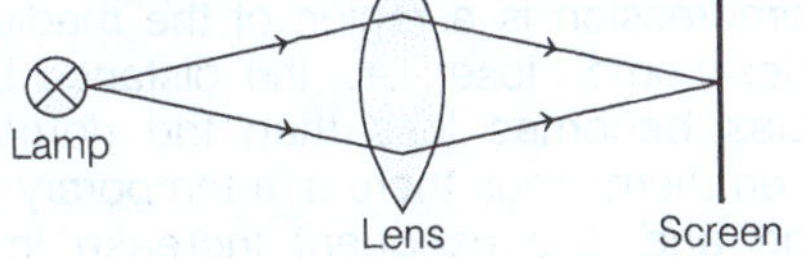

(b) A spring pushed backwards and forwards

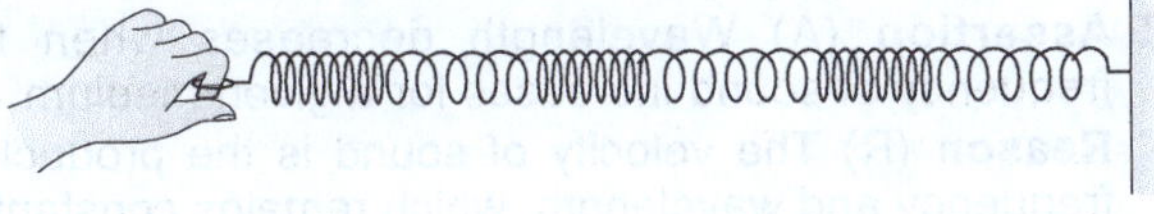

(c) A spring pushed up and down

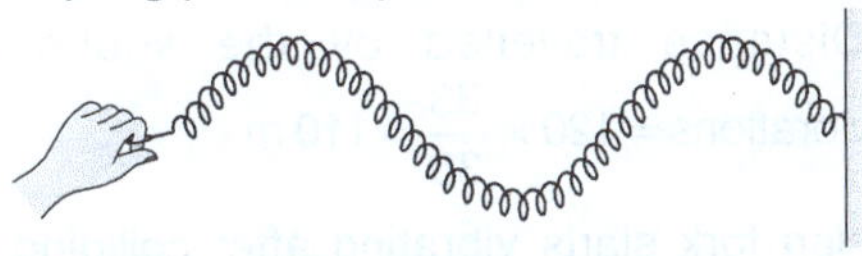

(d) A water ripple caused by a dipper moving up and down

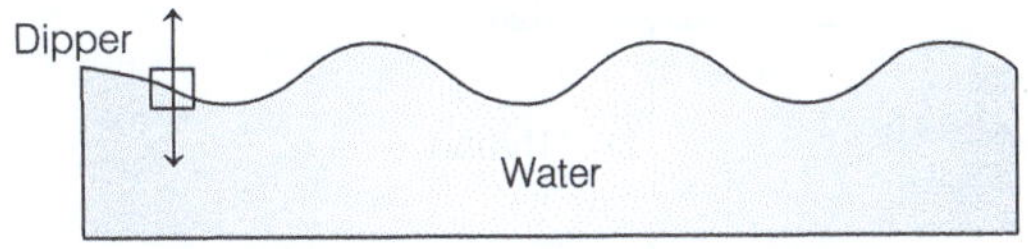

Ans. (b) A longitudinal wave comprises compressions and rarefactions.

When it passes through a medium, the particles of a medium vibrate forward and backward, parallel to the directions of the motion of the wave.

Q.4 A person is listening to a tone of 400 Hz sitting at a distance of 500 m from the source of the sound, then the time interval between the successive

(a) compressions from the source is 2.5 ms

(b) rarefactions from the source is 3.5 ms

(c) Both (a) and (b)

(d) Neither (a) nor (b)

Ans. (a) The time interval between the successive compressions or rarefactions will be given as

$$\text{Time interval} = \frac{1}{\text{Frequency}} = \frac{1}{400} = 0.0025 \text{ s} = 2.5 \text{ ms}$$

Q.5 In a displacement-distance graph of a wave, the wavelength is the

(a) distance between a crest and a trough

(b) distance between two consecutive troughs

(c) distance between two consecutive crests

(d) Both (b) and (c)

Ans. (d) In waves, wavelength is the distance between two consecutive crests (or troughs).

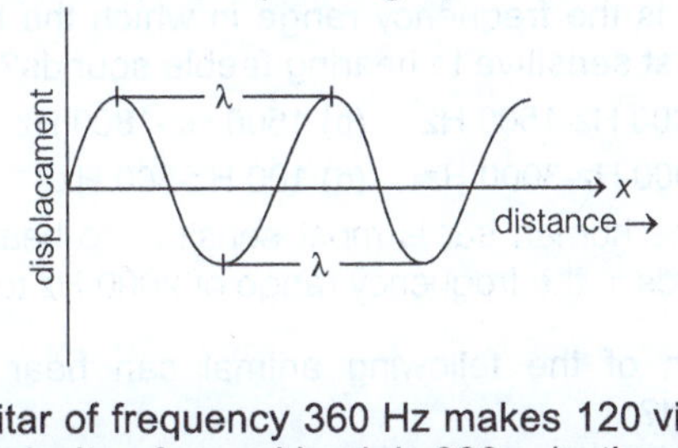

Q.6 A guitar of frequency 360 Hz makes 120 vibrations. If the velocity of sound in air is 330 m/s, then how much distance is travelled by the sound in air?

(a) 90 m (b) 100 m (c) 110 m (d) 140 m

Ans. (c) Given, frequency, $\nu = 360$ Hz

Velocity, $v = 330$ m/s

Wavelength, $\lambda = ?$

As, $\lambda = \frac{v}{\nu} = \frac{330}{360} = \frac{33}{36}$ m

$\therefore$ Distance travelled by the sound wave of 120 vibrations $= 120 \times \frac{33}{36} = 110$ m.

Q.7 **A tuning fork starts vibrating after colliding a ball as shown below. The tuning fork produces sound of frequency 500 Hz due to its vibration.**

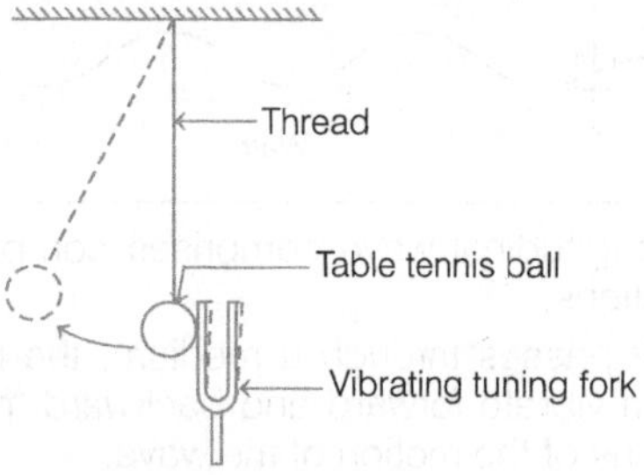

If the wavelength of sound produced by tuning fork due to its vibration is 90 cm, then speed of sound will be

(a) 332 m/s (b) 350 m/s (c) 450 m/s (d) 380 m/s

Ans. (c) Given, wavelength, $\lambda = 90$ cm $= 0.9$ m

Frequency, $f = 500$ Hz

$\therefore$ Speed of sound wave produced by tuning fork,

$v = f\lambda = 500 \times 0.9 = 450$ m/s

Q.8 **When a sound wave of wavelength 2 m in air enters medium *Z*, its wavelength changes to 3 m. Find the speed of sound in medium *Z* given that the speed of sound in air is 340 ms^{-1}.**

(a) 340 ms^{-1} (b) 510 ms^{-1}

(c) 680 ms^{-1} (d) 1020 ms^{-1}

Ans. (b) In air, $f = \frac{340}{2} = 170$ Hz

In medium *Z*, *f* remains unchanged.

$v = 170 \times 3.0 = 510\ ms^{-1}$

Q.9 **What is the frequency range in which the human ear is most sensitive to hearing feeble sounds?**

(a) 1000 Hz-1500 Hz (b) 1500 Hz-1800 Hz

(c) 2000 Hz-3000 Hz (d) 100 Hz-500 Hz

Ans. (c) The human ear is most sensitive to hearing feeble sounds in the frequency range of 2000 Hz to 3000 Hz.

Q.10 **Which of the following animal can hear infrasonic sound?**

(a) Elephant (b) Human

(c) Whales (d) Both (a) and (c)

Ans. (d) Whales and elephants can produce and hear infrasonic sound.

Q.11 **What is the term for sounds with frequencies above 20,000 Hz?**

(a) Audible sound (b) Ultrasonic sound

(c) Infrasonic sound (d) Supersonic sound

Ans. (b) Sound waves with frequencies higher than the upper limit of human hearing which is around 20kHz are called ultrasonic sound.

Q.12 **The properties of ultrasound that make it useful are**

(a) high power and high speed

(b) high power and good directivity.

(c) high frequency and high speed.

(d) high frequencies and bending around the object

Ans. (b) high power and good directivity.

The ultrasound can travel along a well defined straight path. It does not bend appreciably at the edges of an obstacle because of its small wavelength (i.e. it has high directivity.

Q.13 **Sonar make use of**

(a) Infrasonic sound (b) Ultrasound

(c) Supersonic sound (d) light

Ans. (b) Ultrasound is used in sonar because of its high frequency and small wavelength allow it to travel large distance without bending around obstacles.

TYPE - 2

01 Mark

Assertion-Reason Type Questions

Directions (Q. Nos. 1- 5) In the following questions two statements are given as Assertion and Reason.

(a) Both A and R are true and R is the correct explanation of A.

(b) Both A and R are true but R is not the correct explanation of A.

(c) A is true but R is false.

(d) A is false but R is true.

Q.1 **Assertion** (A) Compression and rarefaction involve changes in density and pressure.

Reason (R) When particles are compressed, density of medium increases and when they are rarefied, density of medium decreases.

Ans. (a) Compression is a region of the medium in which particles come closer i.e., the distance between the particles becomes less than the normal distance between them. Thus there is a temporary decrease in volume and a consequent increase in density of medium. Similarly, in rarefaction, particles get farther apart and have a consequent decrease in density.

Q.2 **Assertion** (A) Wavelength decreases when the frequency of sound increases for a given medium.

Reason (R) The velocity of sound is the product of frequency and wavelength, which remains constant in a given medium.

Ans. (a) The speed of sound in a given medium is constant under the same conditions (temperature, pressure, etc.).

According to the formula,

$$v = f \times \lambda$$

where, v = velocity, f = frequency, λ = wavelength

If v is constant and f increases, λ (wavelength) must decrease to satisfy the equation.

Q.3 Assertion (A) The velocity of sound in hydrogen gas is less than the velocity of sound in oxygen gas.

Reason (R) The density of oxygen is greater than the density of hydrogen.

Ans. (d) The velocity of sound in a gas is inversely proportional to the square root of its density. Oxygen is 16 times denser than hydrogen, so the velocity of sound in hydrogen is four times the velocity of sound in oxygen.

Q.4 Assertion (A) The speed of sound is greater in solids than in gases.

Reason (R) Solids have closely packed particles, allowing faster transmission of sound wave.

Ans. (a) Sound waves travel through a medium by vibrating its particles. The speed of sound is directly proportional to the elasticity and inversely proportional to the density of the medium. In solids, particles are closely packed, making the medium more elastic compared to gases. This enables faster transmission of sound in solids than in gases.

Q.5 Assertion (A) Ultrasound waves can be used to clean delicate instruments.

Reason (R) Ultrasound waves create tiny vibrations that extract dirt and impurities.

Ans. (a) Ultrasound waves produce high-frequency vibrations that extract dirt and impurities from delicate surfaces without causing damage, making them ideal for cleaning sensitive instruments.

TYPE - 3 — 01/02 Marks

Fill in the Blanks

Q.1 Sound waves are .... (longitudinal/transverse) because the particle displacement is .... [perpendicular/parallel] to the direction of wave propagation. **[2]**

Ans. longitudinal, parallel

Q.2 Wave velocity is defined as the .... [speed/velocity] at which .... [particle/energy] is transferred from one place to another by wave motion. **[2]**

Ans. speed, energy

Q.3 When the frequency of the sound is increased, the wavelength .... (increases/decreases) **[1]**

Ans. decreases

Q.4 The speed of sound in a solid is .... [greater/smaller] than the speed of sound in air. **[1]**

Ans. greater

Q.5 The formula for the speed of sound is given by .... $\left(v = f\lambda \,/\, v = \dfrac{\lambda}{f}\right)$ **[1]**

Ans. $v = f\lambda$

Q.6 Whales and elephants can produce and hear sound of frequencies below .... Hz. (20 Hz/50 Hz) **[1]**

Ans. 20 Hz

TYPE - 4 — 02 Marks

Very Short Answer Questions

Q.1 (i) Who would hear the sound of the explosion first a man on the boat in a lake 100 m away from the explosion or the diver 100 m under the lake below the explosion. **[1]**

(ii) Provide a reason for your answer in part (a) considering the propagation of sound in air and water. **[1]**

Ans. (i) The diver will hear the sound of the explosion on the surface of the lake first because sound travels faster in water than in air.

(ii) The speed of sound in water is approximately 4 times faster than in air. This is because water has a higher density than air. Which facilitates quicker transmission of sound waves.

Q.2 Suppose you and your friend are on the Moon. Will you be able to hear any sound produced by your friend?

Ans. No, I will not be able to hear any sound produced by my friend because the sound waves require some material medium, such as air to propagate. Since, there is no atmosphere or air on the Moon, so the sound produced by my friend will not reach me. Hence, I will not be able to hear.

Q.3 How does the sound produced by a vibrating object in a medium reach your ear?

Ans. A vibrating object produces sound waves by disturbing the particles in the medium. This disturbance, caused by vibration, propagates through medium and finally reach our ears. The ear drums in our ears, vibrates due to the sound wave and therefore, we hear the sound produced by an object.

Q.4 If you place your ear close to an iron railing which is tapped a distance away, you hear the sound twice. Explain why?

Ans. Sound travels much faster through solids than through air. So, the vibration from the tapping travel through iron quicker and reaches our ears first. Then we hear the sound which travels through the air.

Q.5 **A tuning fork is producing sound, prove with an activity that sound is produced by it during vibrations.**

Ans. Take a tuning fork and vibrate it with a rubber pad. Now, touch the suspended ball gently with the prong of the vibrating tuning fork.

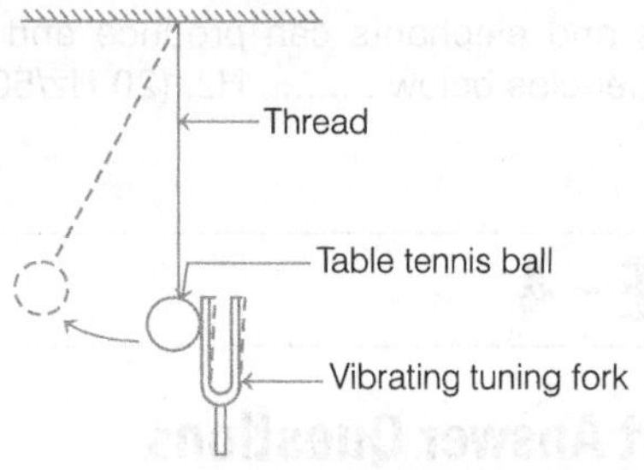

When we touch the ball with tuning fork, a sound will be produced due to vibration of fork and ball also starts vibrating and comes into motion. So, it proves that sound is produced due to vibrations.

Q.6 **Why is the speed of sound independent of pressure?**

Ans. We know that,

The speed of sound in gas,

$v = \sqrt{\frac{\gamma p}{\rho}}$ where p is pressure, ρ is density and γ is ratio of specific heat. When pressure increases, volume decreases, but mass remains same. So, density unchanged.

Hence, there is no change in sound with change in pressure.

Q.7 **What is the range of frequencies associated with**

(i) infrasound and **[1]**

(ii) ultrasound? **[1]**

Ans. (i) Sound waves having frequencies less than 20 Hz and greater than zero are called infrasound.

(ii) Sound waves having frequencies more than 20000 Hz are called ultrasound.

Q.8 **Why do we hear the sound produced by the humming bees while the sound of vibrations of pendulum is not heard?**

Ans. The frequency of vibrations of pendulum is below of 20 Hz (infrasound). We cannot hear infrasound but humming bees produce audible sound which can be heard by human beings.

Q.9 **How are ultrasonic waves different from ordinary sound waves? State two applications of ultrasound.**

Ans. Ultrasonic waves have greater frequency than 20000 Hz, thereby having high energy while ordinary sound waves have not that much energy.

Applications of ultrasound are given below

(i) In the treatment of muscular pains.

(ii) In the diagnosis of diseases.

TYPE - 5 03 Marks

Short Answer Type Questions

Q.1 **(i) By what type of medium, can longitudinal waves be transmitted? Explain it in brief.** **[1]**

(ii) Name the types of waves and two examples associated with compressions and rarefactions. **[2]**

Ans. (i) Since, longitudinal waves travel in the form of compressions and rarefactions, so they involve changes in the volume and density of medium.

As all media, i.e., solids, liquids and gases have volume elasticity. Hence, these waves (longitudinal waves) can be transmitted through all the three types of media.

(ii) There are two types of waves

(a) Longitudinal waves (b) Transverse waves

e.g. The waves which are formed by consecutive compressions and rarefactions travel along a slinky, when it is pushed and pulled at one end, are the longitudinal waves.

The following figure shows longitudinal waves.

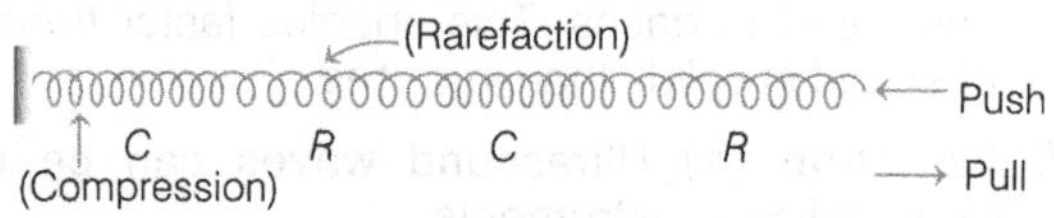

Q.2 **What are the essential properties of a medium that enable the propagation of sound waves?**

Ans. The essential properties of a medium that enables the propagation of sound waves are

(a) The medium must be elastic i.e., the particles are capable of vibrating about their mean position.

(b) The medium must have inertia, so that its particles may store mechanical energy.

(c) The medium should be frictionless, so that there is no loss of energy in propagation of sound through it.

Q.3 **Draw displacement-time graph of a wave and show on it the amplitude and time period of wave.**

Ans. The figure below shows the variation of displacement with time for a particle of the medium at a given position, when a wave propagates through the medium.

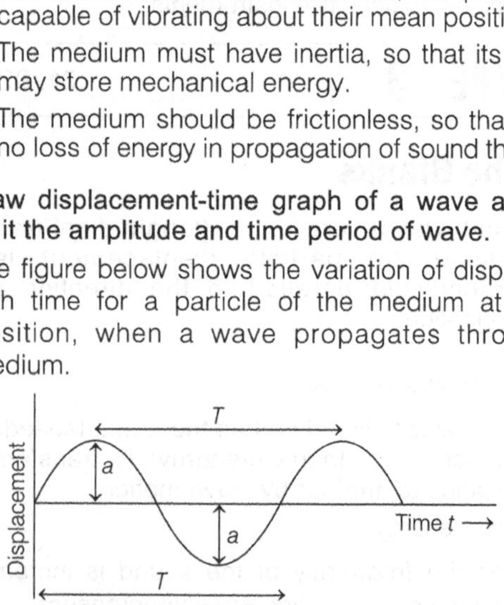

Q.4 (i) Sound waves *A* and *B* are travelling in two different media. Find which wave will be travelling faster when

(a) *A* is travelling in water and *B* is travelling in CO_2. **[1]**

(b) *A* is travelling in CO_2 and *B* is travelling in hydrogen. **[1]**

(ii) Lightning and thunder are produced simultaneously. But thunder is heard a few seconds after the flash is seen, why? **[1]**

Ans. (i) (a) *A* is travelling faster since, sound travels faster in liquids than in gases.

(b) We know that,

$$\text{Speed of wave} \propto \frac{1}{\sqrt{\text{Density}}}$$

Since, the density of hydrogen (i.e., 0.083 kg/m³) is less than that of oxygen (i.e., 1.43 kg/m³). Therefore, the speed of wave will be greater in hydrogen gas. From the above discussion, it is cleared that *B* is moving faster.

(ii) Thunder and lightning both happens at the same time but we see the flash of light much sooner. Than we heard the thunder. The reason is that the speed of light (i.e. 3×10^8 m/s) is much greater compared to the speed of sound (i.e., ≈ 343 m/s).

Q.5 (i) Which has shorter wavelength infrasonic or ultrasonic? **[1]**

(ii) Can dolphin detect ultrasonic waves? **[1]**

(iii) Name any one living organism which can detect infrasonic waves. **[1]**

Ans. (i) Ultrasonic wave has shorter wavelength.

(ii) Yes, dolphin can detect ultrasonic waves.

(iii) Rhinoceros can detect infrasonic waves.

Q.6 (i) Write two main properties of ultrasound. **[1]**

(ii) Mention one application of ultrasound in **[2]**

(a) industries (b) medical field.

Ans. (i) (a) Ultrasound can travel in a straight line without bending around the corners.

(b) It can penetrate into matter to a large extent.

(ii) (a) In industries, ultrasound is used to detect cracks and flaws in metal blocks.

(b) In medical field, ultrasound is used to break stones in gall bladder and kidney.

Q.7 How do bats use echolocation to detect obstacles and locate prey.

Ans. Bats emit high-frequency sound waves that bounces off objects. The returning echoes provide information of distance, shape, size and movement. Bats use this data to navigate around obstacles and locate prey accurately.

TYPE - 6 04 Marks

Long Answer Type Questions

Q.1 Define an experiment to show that sound needs a material medium for its propagation.

Ans. Experiment to show that sound needs a material medium for its propagation is given below.

Take an electric bell and an airtight glass bell jar. The electric bell is suspended inside the airtight bell jar. The bell jar is connected to a vacuum pump, as shown in the given figure. If you press the switch, you will be able to hear the bell.

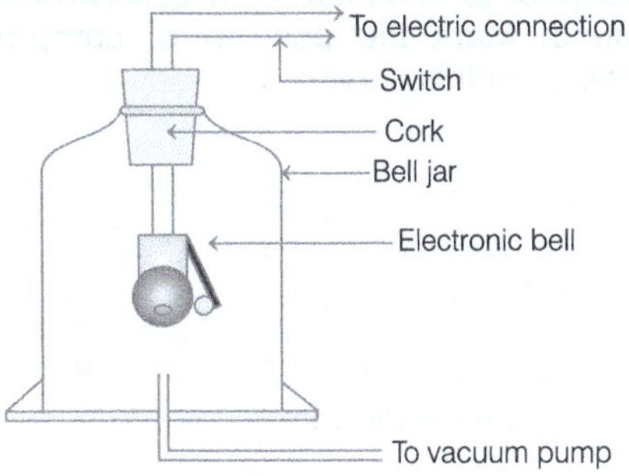

Bell jar experiment showing sound cannot travel in vacuum

Now, start the vacuum pump.

When the air in the jar is gradually pumped out the sound becomes fainter, although the same current is passing through the bell.

After sometime, when less air is left inside the bell jar, you will hear a very feeble sound. On removal of complete air, no sound is heard.

This confirms that sound needs a material medium for its propagation.

Q.2 Write the difference between the propagation of sound and light waves.

Ans.

	Sound Waves	Light Waves
1. Medium Requirement	Sound waves require a medium (solid, liquid or gas) to propagate. They cannot travel through a vacuum.	Light waves can travel through a vacuum as well as through various media.
2. Speed of Propagation	The speed of sound in air is approximately 343 m/s, which is significantly slower compared to light.	The speed of light in a vacuum is approximately 3×10^8 ms^{-1}, which is about a million times faster than sound.

	Sound Waves	Light Waves
3. Behaviour in Mediums	The speed of sound increases in denser media (like solids) compared to gases.	The speed of light decreases, when it travels through optically denser media.
4. Wave Types	Sound waves are longitudinal waves, meaning the particle displacement is parallel to the direction of wave propagation.	Light waves are transverse electromagnetic waves, meaning the oscillations are perpendicular to the direction of wave propagation.

Q.3 Draw a curve showing density or pressure variation with respect to distance for a disturbance produced by sound. Mark the position of compression and rarefaction on this curve.

Ans.

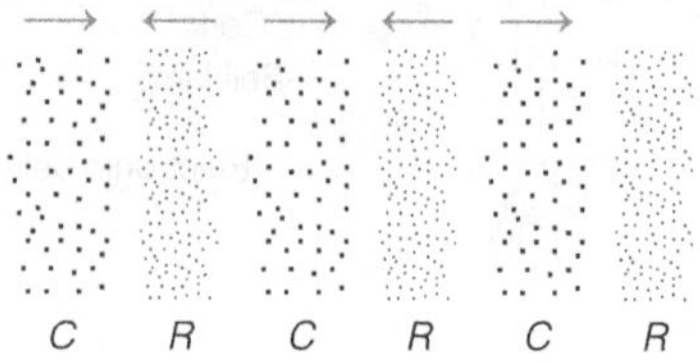

Density variations

Pressure variations

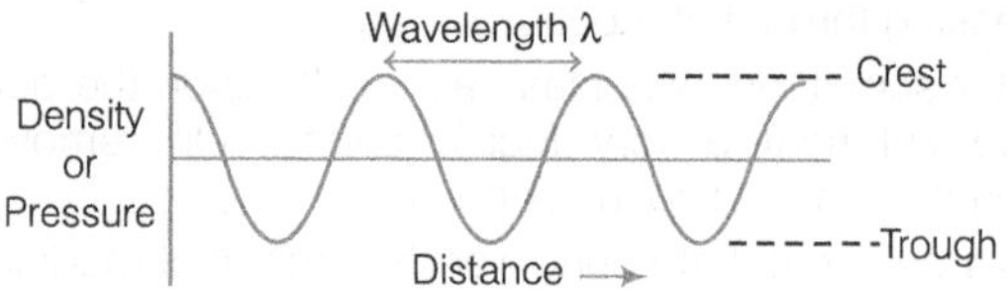

Q.4 Describe in details with the help of a diagram, how compressions and rarefactions are produced in air near a source of sound?

Ans. Sound waves are the longitudinal waves, so they move in the air in the form of compression and rarefaction. When a vibrating object moves forward in air, it pushes and compresses the air in front of it, creating a compression that starts to move away from the vibrating object. When the vibrating object moves backwards, it creates rarefaction.

Compression is the part of a longitudinal wave in which the particles of the medium are closer to one another than they normally are and it is the region of high pressure. It is denoted by C.

Rarefaction is the part of a longitudinal wave in which the particles of the medium are farther apart than they normally are and it is the region of low pressure. It is denoted by R.

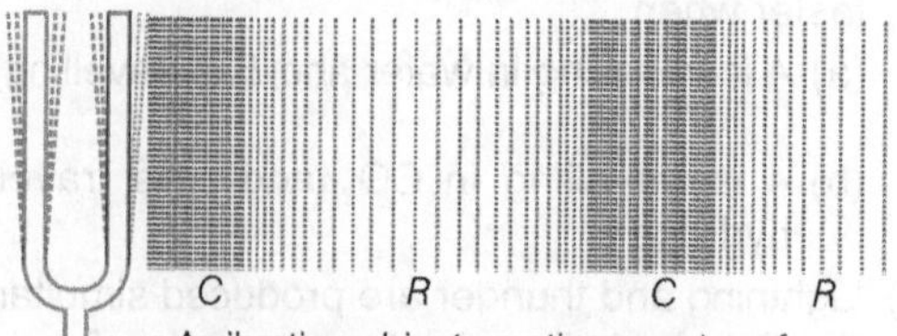

A vibrating object creating a series of compressions (C) and rarefactions (R) in the medium

As the object moves back and forth rapidly, then a series of compressions and rarefactions are created in air. These form sound waves that propagate through the medium.

Q.5 State the factors on which the speed of sound in a gas depend.

Ans. The speed of sound in a gas depends on the following factors

(a) **Density** At constant pressure, the speed of sound in a gas is inversely proportional to the square root of its density.

i.e. Speed of sound $\propto \frac{1}{\sqrt{\text{Density of gas}}}$

(b) **Temperature** The speed of sound in a gas is directly proportional to the square root of its absolute temperature.

i.e. Speed of sound $\propto \sqrt{\text{Absolute temperature of gas}}$

(c) **Humidity** Speed of sound is greater in humid or moist air than in dry air.

(d) **Pressure** Pressure has no effect on the speed of sound in a gas.

Q.6 Shows how ultrasound is used to produce an image of the heart ?

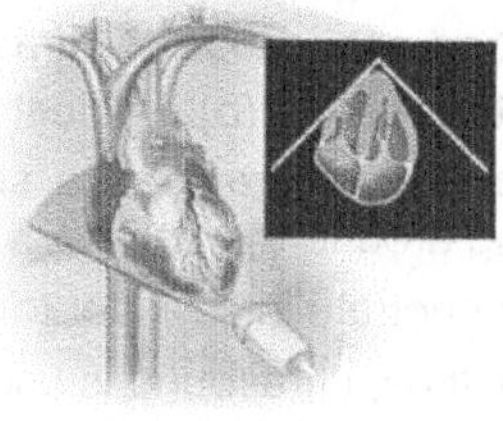

(i) Define ultrasound. **[1]**

(ii) The ultrasound has a wavelength of 1.2×10^{-3} m. The speed of the ultrasound in the human body is 1500 m/s. Calculate the frequency of the ultrasound. **[1]**

(iii) Ultrasound is a longitudinal wave. Describe how particles in the body move as the ultrasound passes.

You may draw a diagram if you wish. **[1]**

(iv) There are small bubbles of gas in the body.

Explain why these bubbles expand and contract as the ultrasound passes. **[1]**

Ans. (i) A sound of frequency above 20 kHz is called the ultrasound.

(ii) $v = f \times \lambda \Rightarrow 1500 = f \times 12 \times 10^{-3}$

$f = 1250{,}000 \text{ Hz} = 125 \times 10^{6} \text{ Hz}$

(iii) The particles in the body oscillate forward and backward, parallel to the direction of motion of the ultrasound wave.

(iv) The pressure increases and decreases alternately along the path of the ultrasound in the body, which causes the gas bubbles in the body to expand and contract.

TYPE - 7 03/04 Marks

Case Based Questions

Q.1 Two friends Shefali and Anuj make a toy telephone by joining two plastic cups through a long string. They both stand apart. Anuj speaks softly into one cup and Shefali hears by putting her ear in the other cup. Now, Shefali speaks and Anuj listens.

Read the given passage carefully and give the answer of the following questions.

(i) What type of waves are produced by voice of Anuj and Shefali in the air inside the plastic cup? **[1]**

(ii) Give one difference between these types of waves. **[1]**

(iii) Why is sound wave called a longitudinal wave? **[1]**

(iv) Waves of frequency 100 Hz are produced in a string as shown in figure. Given its amplitude and wavelength. **[1]**

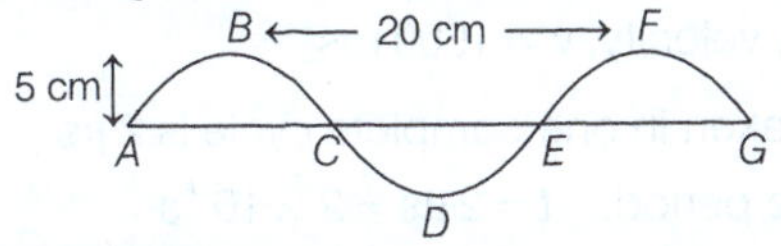

Ans. (i) Longitudinal waves

(ii) In longitudinal wave, particles vibrate parallel to the direction of wave propagation.

In transverse wave, particles vibrate perpendicular to the direction of wave propagation.

(iii) The sound wave is called a longitudinal wave because in a sound wave, the particles of the medium move in a direction parallel to the direction of propagation of the disturbance.

(iv) Amplitude = 5 cm (maximum displacement from mean position)

Wavelength = 20 cm (Distance between two crests or troughs)

Q.2 A density *versus* time graph for a longitudinal wave represents how the density of the medium varies with time at a fixed point as the wave passes through, as shown in figure. **[3]**

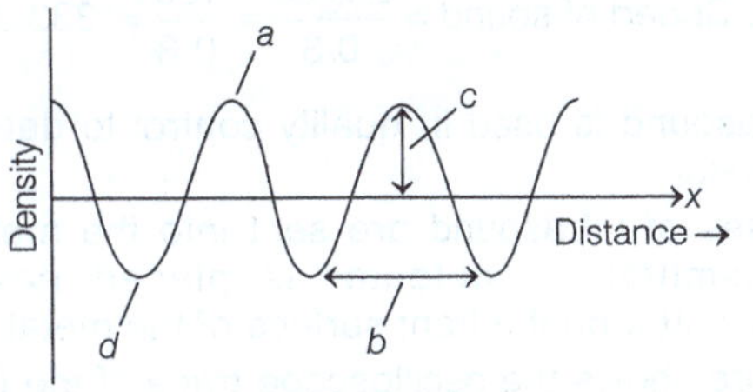

Sr. No.	Description	Label
(a)	The height of a wave	c
(b)	The point of compression	
(c)	The point of rarefaction	
(d)	One complete wavelength	

Ans.

Sr. No.	Description	Label
(a)	The height of a wave	c
(b)	The point of compression	a
(c)	The point of rarefaction	d
(d)	One complete wavelength	b

Q.3 A student conducts an experiment of measure the speed of sound in air. They strike a tuning fork and hold it at different distances from a wall. The time taken for the sound to travel to the wall and back is measured. The student observes that the speed of sound can be calculated using the formula

$$\text{Speed of sound} = \frac{2d}{t}$$

where d is the distance to the wall and t is the time taken.

(i) What phenomenon is demonstrated by the student's experiment? **[1]**

(ii) Why is the distance d multiplied by 2 in the formula? **[1]**

(iii) If the distance to the wall is 50 m and the time taken for the echo is 0.3 seconds, what is the speed of sound in air? **[1]**

Ans. (i) The phenomenon demonstrated is reflection of sound. The sound waves reflect off the wall and return to the source, creating an echo.

(ii) The distance d is multiplied by 2 because the sound travels to the wall and then reflects back to the source. The total distance covered is twice the distance to the wall.

(iii) Using the formula,

$$\text{Speed of sound} = \frac{2d}{t}$$

Substituting $d = 50$ m and $t = 0.3$ s

$$\therefore \text{Speed of sound} = \frac{2 \times 50}{0.3} = \frac{100}{0.3} = 333.33 \text{ m/s}$$

Q.4 Ultrasound is used in quality control to detect cracks in metal.

Pulses of ultrasound are sent into the metal from a transmitter. A detector is placed next to the transmitter on the front surface of the metal.

Figure shows the oscilloscope trace of the ultrasound pulses produced if the metal contains no cracks.

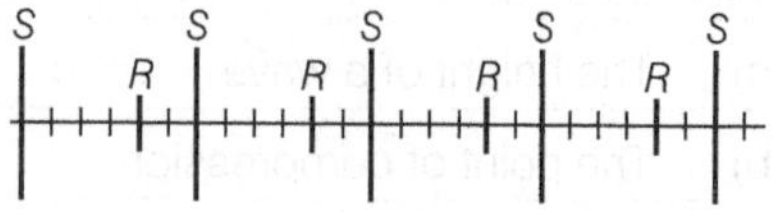

One division along the X-axis represents 1.0×10^{-6} s.

Pulses labelled S are the pulses initially sent out from the transmitter. Each pulse labelled R is the reflection from the back surface of the metal of the previous pulse S.

(i) Use Fig. to calculate the number of pulses sent out by the source in one second. **[1]**

(ii) Suggest two reasons why the amplitude of R is less than the amplitude of S? **[1]**

(iii) Some time later, the piece of metal is tested again. It now has a small crack half-way between the front surface and the back surface.

On Fig. draw the position and size of the pulses produced by this crack. Label each of these pulses C. **[1]**

(iv) A second beam of ultrasound has a frequency of 8.0×10^6 Hz and a speed of 4000 m/s in the metal.

Calculate the wavelength of this ultrasound in the metal. **[1]**

Ans. (i) Given,

The time period is the time between two successive pulse and it is 6×10^{-6} s.

The number of pluses is

$$f = \frac{1}{T} = \frac{1}{6.0 \times 10^{-6}} = 1.7 \times 10^5$$

(ii) (a) Some energy is absorbed in the metal.

(b) Not all the sound is reflected back from the back surface but some passes out of the back of the metal.

(iii)

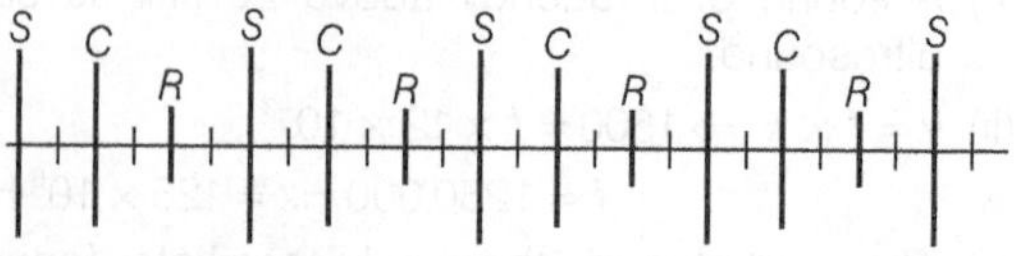

(iv) $\lambda = \frac{v}{f} = \frac{4000}{8.0 \times 10^6} = 5.0 \times 10^{-4}$ m

TYPE - 8

Numerical Questions

Q.1 A source of wave produces 50 crests and 50 troughs in 0.5s. What is the frequency of the wave? **[2]**

Sol. 50 crests and 50 troughs means 50 waves.

$$\text{Frequency of wave} = \frac{\text{Number of waves}}{\text{Time}}$$

$$\text{or frequency} = \frac{50}{0.5}$$

$\therefore$ Frequency = 100 Hz

Q.2 If sound wave of frequency 500 Hz and wavelength 0.88 m is travelling in a medium. Calculate the velocity of the wave in the medium. **[2]**

Sol. Given, Frequency = 500 Hz

Wavelength = 0.88 m

Applying formula,

Velocity = Frequency × Wavelength

$\therefore$ Velocity $= 500 \times 0.88 = 440$ m/s

Q.3 The given graph shows the displacement *versus* time relation for a disturbance travelling with velocity of 1500 ms^{-1}. Calculate the wavelength of the disturbance. **[2]**

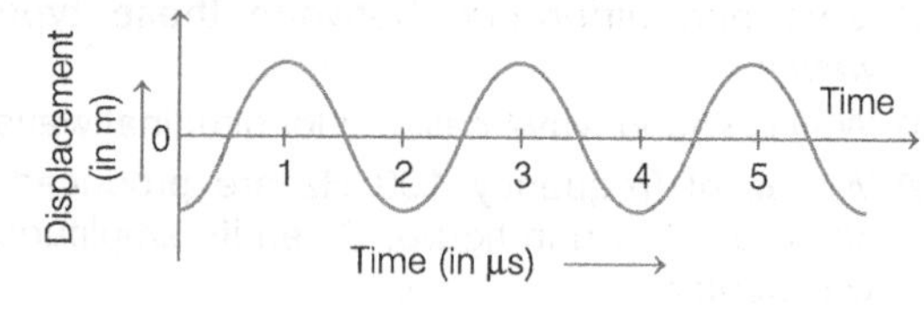

Sol. Given, velocity, $v = 1500$ ms^{-1}

Time taken in one complete cycle is 2 μs.

$\therefore$ Time period, $t = 2\ \mu s = 2 \times 10^{-6}$s

$\therefore$ Wavelength, $\lambda = vt$

$$= 1500 \times 2 \times 10^{-6} = 3 \times 10^{-3} \text{ m}$$

Q.4 Waves of frequency 100 Hz are produced in a string as shown in the figure. Give its **[4]**

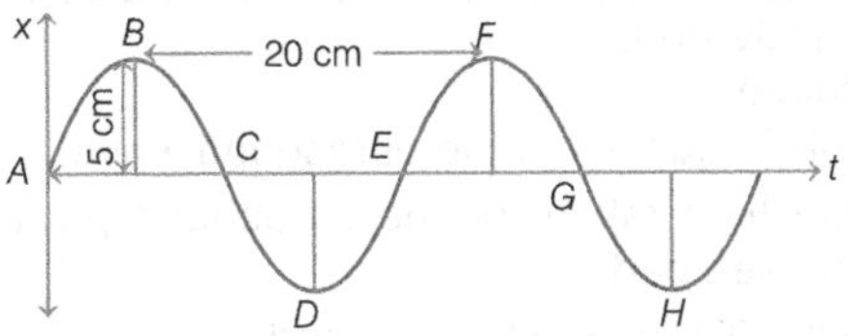

(i) amplitude (ii) wavelength
(iii) velocity (iv) nature

Sol. (i) Amplitude = 5 cm

(ii) Wavelength = 20 cm

(iii) Velocity, $v = \nu\lambda = 100 \times 20 \times 10^{-2} = 20 \text{ ms}^{-1}$

(iv) It is a transverse wave.

Q.5 The time interval between a lightning flash and the first sound of thunder was found to be 6s. If the speed of sound in air is 330 ms^{-1}, then find the distance of flash from the observer. **[2]**

Sol. Speed of sound in air, $v = 330 \text{ ms}^{-1}$

Time is which thunder is heard after lightning is seen,

$t = 6$ s

So, distance between flash and observer = $v \times t$

$= 330 \times 6 = 1980$ m

Q.6 A sound wave travels at a speed of 339 ms^{-1}. If its wavelength is 1.5 cm, then what is the frequency of the wave? Will it be audible? **[2]**

Sol. Given, speed, $v = 339 \text{ ms}^{-1}$

Wavelength, $\lambda = 1.5 \text{cm} = 1.5 \times 10^{-2}\text{m}$

$\therefore$ Frequency, $\nu = \frac{v}{\lambda} = \frac{339}{1.5 \times 10^{-2}} = 22600$ Hz

This frequency is greater than 20000 Hz, so it will not be audible. Audible range for human ear is 20 Hz to 20000 Hz.

Q.7 A wave travels at a speed of 0.4 ms^{-1} and the frequency of wave is 20 Hz. Find the separation between two consecutive compressions. **[2]**

Sol. Wave velocity = 0.4 ms^{-1}

Frequency = 20 Hz

Separation between two consecutive compressions

= Wavelength of a wave

Wave velocity = Frequency × Wavelength

or, $0.4 = 20 \times \lambda$

or $\lambda = \frac{0.4}{20} = 0.02$ m

So, separation between two consecutive compressions is 0.02 m.

Q.8 An observer notices flashes from two tanks firing at each other simultaneously. He hears the sounds 2 seconds and 3.5 seconds after observing the flashes. If the distance between the tanks is 540 m, determine the speed of sound in air. **[3]**

Sol.

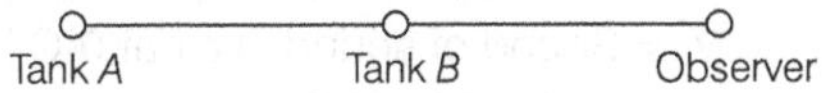

Time taken by the sound of the first tank A to reach observer = 3.5 s

Time taken by the sound of the second tank B to reach observer = 2 s

Time taken by the sound of tank A to reach tank B

$= (3.5 - 2)\text{s} = 1.5 \text{s}$

If speed of sound = $v \text{ ms}^{-1}$

Then, distance between tank A and B is $1.5v$ m

Distance between two tanks = 540 m

$\therefore$ $1.5v = 540$ or $v = 540 / 1.5$

$\Rightarrow$ $v = 360 \text{ ms}^{-1}$

Q.9 A radar signal is received 2×10^{-5}s. After it was sent and reflected by an aeroplane. How far is the aeroplane, if speed of waves is 3×10^8 m/s? **[3]**

Sol. Given, Speed of wave, $v = 3 \times 10^8$ m/s

Time taken for receiving the radar signal $t = 2 \times 10^{-5}$ s

Distance travelled by the wave

$= v \times t = 3 \times 10^8 \times 2 \times 10^{-5} = 6 \times 10^3$ m

Since, the signal travels to the aeroplane and back, we divide the total distance by 2 to get the one-way distance.

Hence, the distance from aeroplane = 3×10^3 m

Q.10 Assuming the speed of sound in air equal to 330 m/s and in water equal to 1360 m/s. Find the time taken to travel a distance 2700 m by sound in

(i) air (ii) water **[3]**

Ans. Given, distance (d) = 2100 m

speed of sound in air, $v_{air} = 330$ m/s

speed of sound in water $v_{water} = 1360$ m/s

(i) Time taken by sound in air,

$$t_{air} = \frac{d}{v_{air}}$$

$$t_{air} = \frac{2700}{330} = 8.81 \text{s}$$

(ii) Time taken by sound in water,

$$t_{water} = \frac{d}{v_{water}}$$

$$t_{water} = \frac{2700}{1360} = 1.98 \text{ s}$$

Q.11 What is the speed of sound at temperature 25°C? **[2]**

Ans. Given, $T = 25°$ C

We know that,

$$v_T = v_o + 0.61T$$

where, v_T = Speed of sound at given temperature

v_0 = Speed of sound in air at 0°C i.e. 330 m/s.

$$v_{25} = 330 + 0.61 \times 25$$

$$v_{25} = 345.25 \text{ m/s}$$

Q.12 **Figure below is a cathode ray oscilloscope (CRO) trace of the pulses of ultrasound sent from the ship and the reflected pulses.**

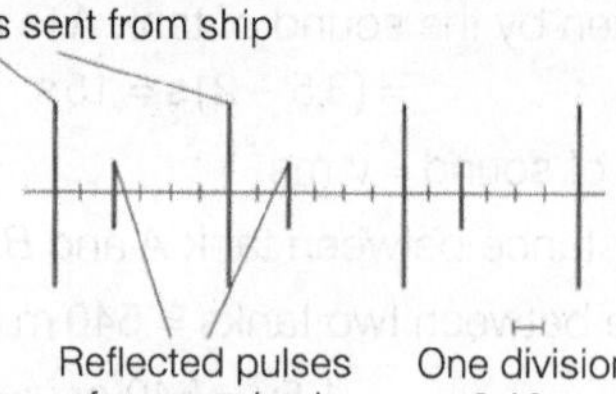

The speed of ultrasound in water is 1500 m/s and the wavelength of the ultrasound wave is 0.030 m. The time-base setting for the *X*-axis on the C.R.O is 0.10 s/division.

Calculate

(i) the frequency of the ultrasound wave. **[1]**

(ii) the time taken for the ultrasound pulse to reach the sea bed. **[1]**

(iii) The distance to the sea bed. **[1]**

Sol. (i) $\text{Frequency} = \frac{v}{\lambda} = \frac{1500}{0.030}$

$$= 50000 \text{ Hz}$$

The pulse travels to the sea bed and back in (2 × 0.10) s. So, we divide the total time by 2 to get the time taken to each the sea bed.

(ii) $\text{Time taken} = \frac{2 \times 0.10}{2} = 0.10 \text{ s}$

(iii) Distance = Speed × Time = (1500) (0.10) = 150 m

10

CURRENT ELECTRICITY

Electric Current

- It is defined as the **rate of flow of electric charge** through any cross-section of a conductor. It is denoted by *I*.
- If *q* amount of charge flows through a conductor in time *t*, then

$$\text{Electric current, } I = \frac{\text{Charge } (q)}{\text{Time } (t)} = \frac{ne}{t}$$

Here, *n* is number of electrons passing through the conductor and *e* is charge on one electron equals 1.6×10^{-19} coulomb.

- It is a **scalar quantity** and its SI unit is **ampere** (A).
- When 1 coulomb of charge flows through any cross-section of a conductor in 1s, then the electric current flowing through it, is said to be 1 ampere.

i.e. $$1 \text{ ampere} = \frac{1 \text{ coulomb}}{1 \text{ second}} \Rightarrow 1\text{ A} = \frac{1\text{C}}{1\text{s}}$$

- Smaller units of current are **milliampere** ($1\text{mA} = 10^{-3}$ A) and **microampere** ($1\,\mu\text{A} = 10^{-6}$ A).

Direction of Current : Conventional and Electronic

- The direction of the flow of positive charges is taken to be the direction of electric current. Conventionally, the direction of electric current is taken as opposite to the direction of flow of electrons.

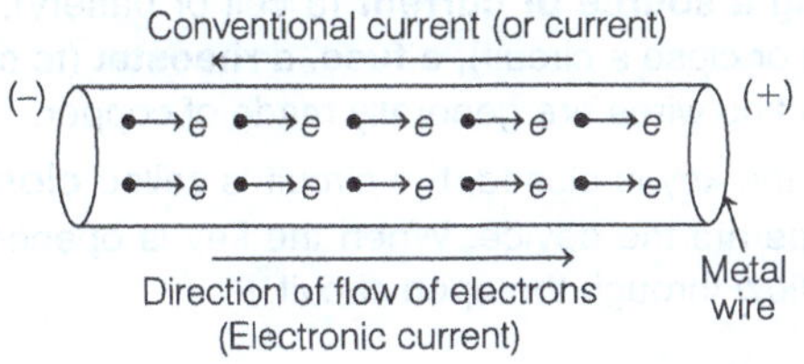

- The direction of conventional current (or current) is opposite to the direction of electronic current.

Direct Current (DC)

- The electric current whose direction and magnitude do not change with time is called direct current (DC). Current obtained from an electric cell is direct current.
- The sources which provide direct current (DC) are called sources of direct current. e.g. Cells, batteries, etc.

Electric Potential

- If work done in moving a positive charge *q* from infinity to the point is *W*, then electric potential *V* of that point is

$$V = \frac{W}{q}$$

- The SI unit of electric potential is **volt (V)**.
- It is a **scalar quantity**.

Electric Potential Difference (ΔV)

- It is defined as the work done per unit charge in moving a unit positive charge from point B to point A (or one point to other point).
- The SI unit of electric potential difference is **volt** (V) and is named after Italian physicist **Alessandro Volta**.
  It is a **scalar quantity**.
- Let W be the work done in moving a charge Q from point B to point A, then the potential difference ($V_B - V_A$) between these two points is given by

$$\Delta V = V_B - V_A = \frac{W}{Q}$$

It can be also given by, $V = \frac{W}{Q}$

Electrical Cell

- It is a device which converts **chemical energy into electrical energy** by maintaining a constant potential difference between its electrodes through chemical reaction.
  - A good cell should fulfill following requirements
    (i) It should provide a constant current.
    (ii) It should be cheap and portable.
    (iii) It should have low internal resistance.
- There are mainly two types of cells
  (i) **Primary Cells** The cells which give electric current as a result of **irreversible chemical reaction** are called primary cells. These cells cannot be used again and again. e.g. Dry cell, voltaic cell, leclanche cell, etc.
  (ii) **Secondary Cells or Accumulator** These type of cells give electric current by **reversible chemical reaction**. The electric energy can be stored in the cell and can be used anytime. Secondary cells can be recharged, i.e. can be used again and again. e.g. Lead or acid accumulator, Ni-Fe or alkali accumulator, Li-H battery, etc.

Electric Circuit

- A **closed** and **continuous** path through which **electric current** flows is known as electric circuit.
- It has various components including a **source of current** (a cell or battery), **a load** (a bulb, heater or any other appliances), a **switch/key** (to open or close a circuit), **a fuse**, a **rheostat** (to control the current through the circuit) and **connecting wires**. The connecting wires are generally made of copper.
- **Closed and Open Circuits** When the key is closed, the circuit is called **closed circuit**. This means that current would flow through the circuit to operate the device. When the key is opened, the circuit is called **open circuit**. This means that current would not flow through the open circuit.

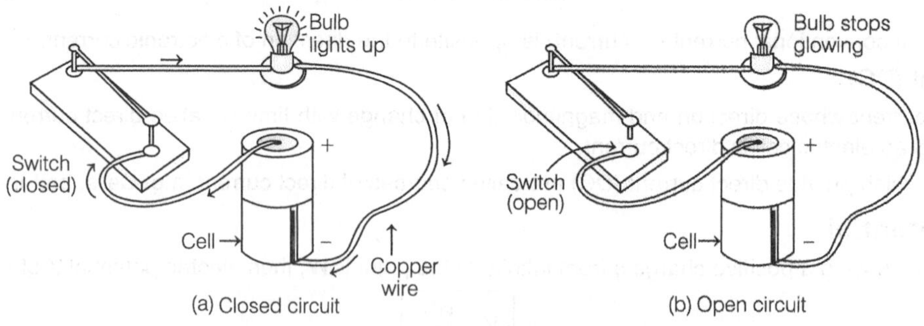

The electric circuit showing actual components like bulb, cell, switch, etc.

Symbols used in Electric Circuit

Circuit Component	Description	Symbol
Cell	Provides potential difference between two points	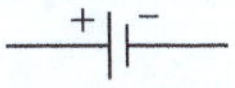
Battery	A combination of two or more cells connected in series	
Connecting wire	Connects different circuit components	
Bulb	Circuit components	
Resistance	Controls current flowing through circuit	
Rheostat	Variable resistance	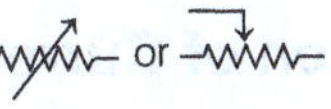
Ammeter	Measures current flowing through circuit	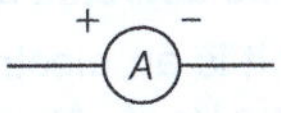
Voltmeter	Measures potential difference between two points	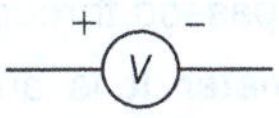
Key open	Open the circuit	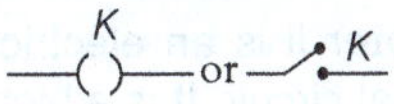
Key closed	Close the circuit	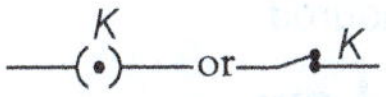
Tapping key	Open	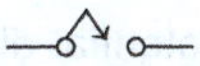
Tapping key	Closed	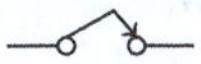
Fuse	Safety device	
Wires joints		
Wires crossing without joining		
Galvanometer	Detects presence and direction of current in a wire	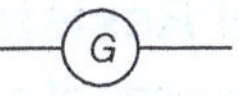
DC generator	Converts mechanical energy into electrical energy (direct current)	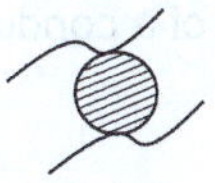
AC generator	Converts mechanical energy into electrical energy (alternating current)	

Simple Circuit Diagram

It is a schematic diagram which represents the relative positions and connections of various circuit components represented by their symbols.

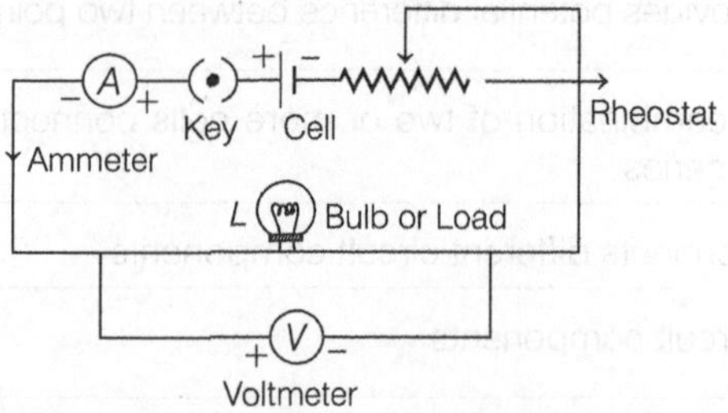

A schematic diagram of an electric circuit comprising of battery, electric bulb, rheostat, ammeter and plug key

Detection of Current

Current can be detected by ammeter and galvanometer as discussed below

- **Ammeter** It is an electrical device used to measure direction and magnitude of electric current. It is connected in series with circuit. An ammeter has negligible resistance, so it does not change the magnitude of current, when current is passed through it.
- **Galvanometer** It is an electrical device which is used to detect the presence of weak current or to find its direction. Galvanometer does not give the magnitude of current.
- **Voltmeter** It is an electrical device used to measure the electrical potential difference between two points in an electrical circuit. It is a high resistance device connected in parallel with the components through which potential to be measured.

Ohm's Law

- If V is the potential difference applied across the ends of conductor through which current I flows, then according to Ohm's law,

$$I \propto V$$

or $$I = \frac{1}{R} \times V$$

or $$I = \frac{V}{R}$$

$$\boxed{V = IR}$$

where, R is the proportionality constant called resistance of the conductor at a given temperature.

Electrical Resistance

- It is that property of a conductor by virtue of which it opposes/resists any flow of charges through it.
- Resistance of a conductor is given by

$$R = \frac{V}{I} \Rightarrow 1\Omega = \frac{1\text{V}}{1\text{A}}$$

i.e., the resistance of a conductor is said to be 1Ω if a current of 1 ampere flows through it when the potential difference across its ends is 1V.

- The SI unit of resistance is **ohm** (Ω).

Factors affecting the resistance of a conductor

(i) The resistance of the conductor is **directly proportional to its length l** or $R \propto l$.

(ii) The resistance of the conductor is **inversely proportional to its cross-section A** or $R \propto \frac{1}{A}$.

(iii) The resistance of the conductor **depends on the nature of the material** of which it is made.

(iv) The resistance of the conductor **increases with increase of its temperature**.

Conductors and Insulators

- The substances or materials which offer very little resistance for the current flowing through them are called conductors. e.g. Almost all metals are good conductors of electric current. They have a large number of free electrons.
- The substances or materials which offer very high resistance to the electric current flowing through them are called insulators. They have almost no free electrons. e.g. Diamond, wood, etc.

Efficient Use of Energy

- The use of energy without wasting is called efficient use of energy.
  e.g. By using LED lights in place of electric bulb, a lot of energy can be saved which goes wasted in the form of heat in electric bulb.
- Some ways to achieve eco-efficient environment are as follows
  (i) **Electric cooker** should be used instead of ordinary vessel.
  (ii) **Saving electricity** (switch OFF the device, when not in use).
  (iii) **By reduction in pollution**, using those fuels which create very little or no pollution.
  (iv) Use of **solar water heater** instead of LPG for heating water.
  (v) Use of solar energy whenever possible.

Social Initiatives

- Due to the rapid growth of industries, demand of energy resources are increasing day-by-day.
- Urbanisation and industrialisation are causing crisis of energy resources and environmental hazards.
- Following initiatives should be taken for efficient use of energy
  (i) Use of **alternative form of energy** such as solar energy, biomass energy, geo-thermal energy, wind energy, etc.
  (ii) **Do not waste energy** Put OFF all the electric devices whenever not in use.
  (iii) **Use of public transport** should be preferred.
  (iv) **Replace the incandescent bulbs** with CFLs and LED bulbs. It reduces approximately 75% of energy in use.

EXAM ORIENTED QUESTIONS

TYPE - 1 01 Mark

Multiple Choice Questions

Q.1 The rate of flow of electric charge is called

(a) voltage (b) resistance

(c) electric current (d) capacitance

Ans. (c) electric current

Q.2 Electrical cell is a device which converts

(a) electrical energy into mechanical energy

(b) mechanical energy into electrical energy

(c) electrical energy into chemical energy

(d) chemical energy into electrical energy

Ans. (d) Electrical cell is a device which converts chemical energy into electrical energy by maintaining a constant potential difference between its electrodes through chemical reaction.

Q.3 Pranati has set up a circuit as shown below.

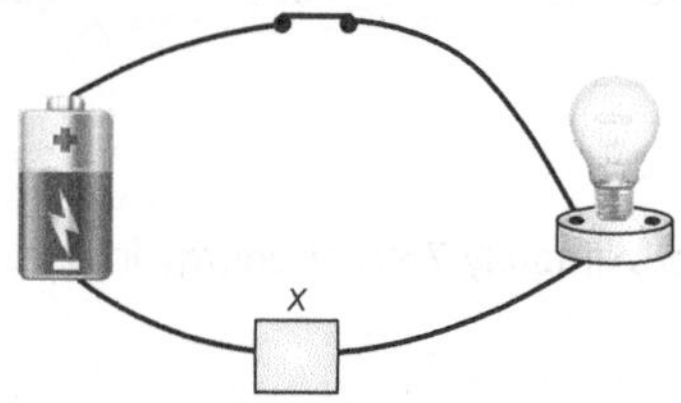

Which of the following should she put in the blank box, marked X to make the bulb glow more brightly?

(a) Bulb (b) Cell

(c) Key (d) Wire

Ans. (b) To make the bulb glow more brightly, adding another cell increases the voltage, which increases the current in the circuit.

Q.4 The bulb in the circuit shown below does not glow.

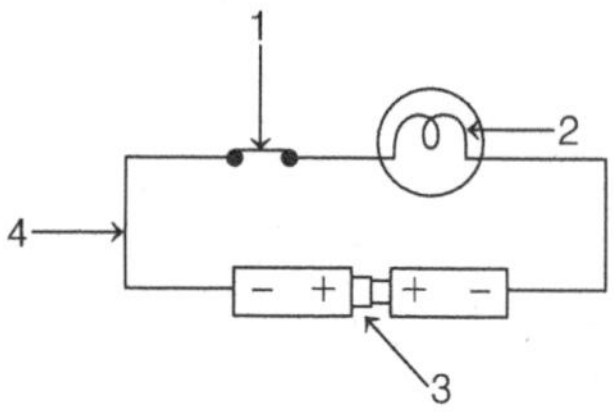

Which of following labelled parts is responsible for this?

(a) 4 (b) 2 (c) 3 (d) 1

Ans. (c) The bulb does not glow because part 3 (cell/battery) is responsible for supplying power. If the battery is dead or not connected properly, no current flows and the bulb remains off.

Q.5 Which of the following cell gives electric current by reversible chemical reaction?

(a) Primary cells

(b) Secondary cells

(c) Both (a) and (b)

(d) Neither (a) nor (b)

Ans. (b) Secondary cells give electric current as a result of reversible chemical reaction, whereas primary cells give electric current as a result of irreversible chemical reaction.

Q.6 Which of the symbol is used for fuse in electrical circuit?

(a) 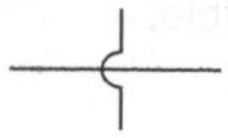 (b) 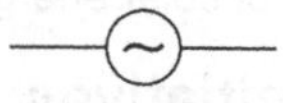

(c)  (d) 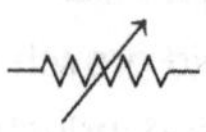

Ans. (c)  ⟶ Fuse

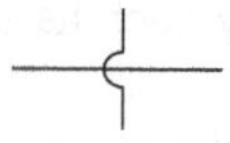 ⟶ Wires crossing without joining

 ⟶ AC generator

 ⟶ Rheostat

Q.7 Identify the circuit in which the electrical components have been properly connected.

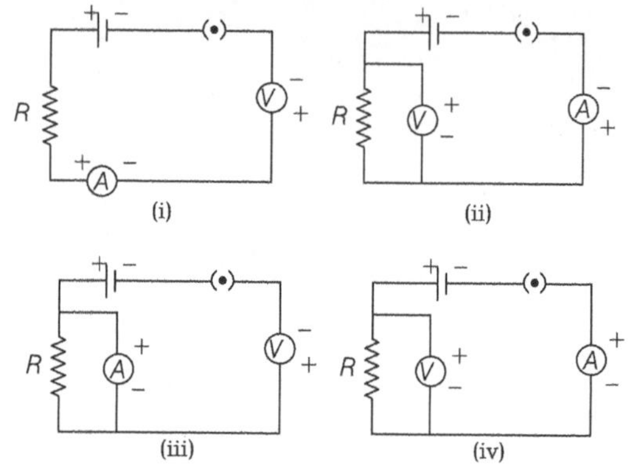

(a) (i) (b) (ii)

(c) (iii) (d) (iv)

Ans. (b) While identifying the circuit, the following conditions must be satisfied.

- An ammeter is always connected in series.
- Voltmeter should be connected in parallel.

- The positive terminals of V and A should be joined to positive terminal of the cell and their negative terminals should be joined to the negative terminal of the cell.

Thus, the above conditions are satisfied in case (ii).

Q.8 Which of the following devices is used to detect the presence of weak current?

(a) Ammeter (b) Galvanometer
(c) Voltmeter (d) None of these

Ans. (b) Galvanometer is an electrical device which is used to detect the presence of weak current.

Q.9 Diagram 1 shows a resistor connected to a battery, an ammeter and a voltmeter. The ammeter reading is 0.5 A and the voltmeter reading is 3.0 V. A second identical resistor is now connected in parallel with the first resistor, as shown in diagram 2.

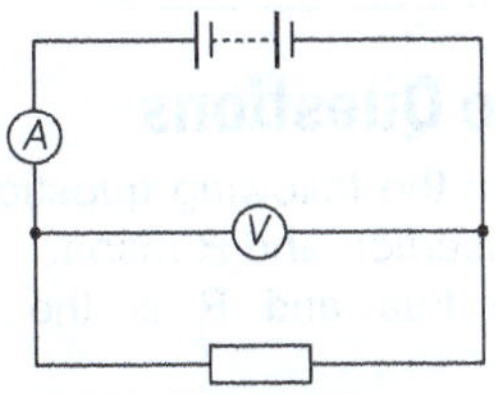

Diagram 1

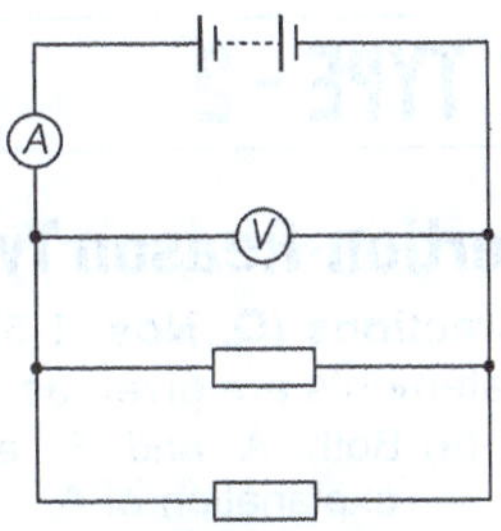

Diagram 2

What are the ammeter and voltmeter readings in the circuit shown in diagram 2?

	ammeter reading/A	voltmeter reading/V
(a)	0.5	3.0
(b)	0.5	6.0
(c)	1.0	1.5
(d)	1.0	3.0

Ans. (d) In diagram 2, the addition of a second resistor does not change, the fact that all components are still connected in parallel to the battery. Hence the potential difference. measured by the voltmeter remains unchanged.

However, the additional resistor draws an extra current and so the current measured by the ammeter

$$= 0.5 + 0.5 = 1.0\text{ A}$$

Q.10 The diagram shows a circuit.

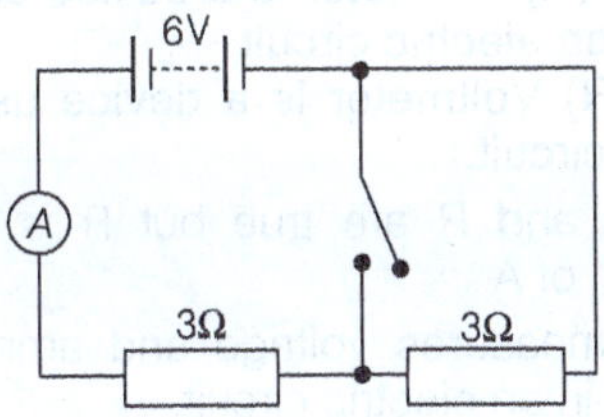

What is the reading on the ammeter when the switch is open, and the reading when it is closed?

	Ammeter reading when open (in A)	Ammeter reading when closed (in A)
(a)	1	1
(b)	1	2
(c)	2	1
(d)	2	2

Ans. (b) When the switch is open, the two resistors are in series and the total resistance in the circuit $= 6\Omega$. Hence, the current in the circuit and the reading of the ammeter $= \frac{V}{R} = \frac{6}{6} = 1.0$ A.

When the switch is closed, the resistor on the right is short-circuited and the current does not pass through it. So, the total resistance in the circuit is then 3 Ω and the value of the current through the ammeter is

$$I = \frac{V}{R} = \frac{6}{3} = 2\text{ A}.$$

Q.11 Voltmeter is an electrical device of

(a) high resistance and always connected in parallel
(b) low resistance and always connected in series
(c) high resistance and always connected in series
(d) low resistance and always connected in parallel

Ans. (a) Voltmeter is an electrical device of high resistance and always connected in parallel to element across which potential difference have to be measured.

Q.12 When length of a conducting wire increases, then its resistance

(a) decreases (b) increases
(c) remains same (d) None of these

Ans. (b) Since, resistance of a conducting wire is directly proportional to its length, hence resistance of a conducting wire increases with increase in its length.

Q.13 A wire of length 1.0 m has a resistance of 2.0 Ω. When connected to a cell, the current in the wire is 3.0 A.

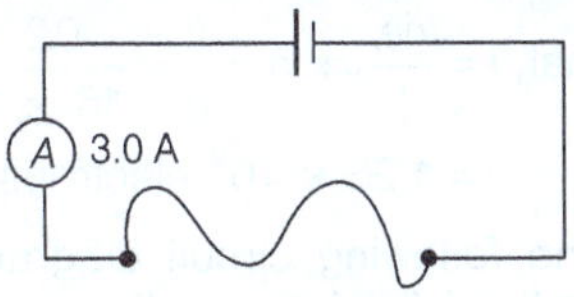

A 2.0 m length of the same wire is connected to the same cell.

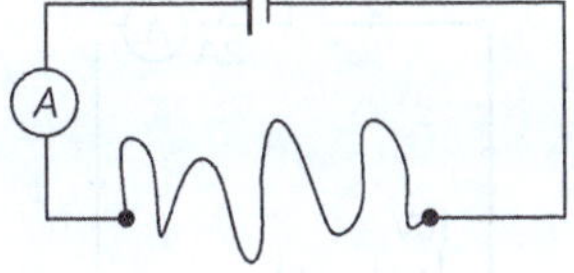

What is the resistance of the wire and the current in it?

Resistance	Current
(a) 1.0 Ω	1.5 A
(b) 1.0 Ω	3.0 A
(c) 4.0 Ω	1.5 A
(d) 4.0 Ω	3.0 A

Ans. (c) The resistance of a wire is proportional to its length. Hence, the 2.0 m wire has a resistance of 2(2.0) = 4.0 Ω. Using Ohm's law, the new current is halved to 1.5 A.

Q.14 By using LED lights in place of incandescent bulb, a lot of

(a) energy can be saved
(b) energy can be wasted
(c) air pollution can be decreased
(d) None of the above

Ans. (a) By using LED lights in place of incandescent bulb, a lot of energy (approximately 75%) can be saved.

Q.15 A current of 4.8 A is flowing in a conductor. The number of electrons passing per second through the conductor will be

(a) 3×10^{20} (b) 76.8×10^{20}
(c) 7.68×10^{-19} (d) 3×10^{19}

Ans. (d) Given, current, $I = 4.8\,A$, $e = 1.6 \times 10^{-19} C$

We know that, $I = \frac{q}{t} = \frac{ne}{t}$

$$\therefore \quad \frac{n}{t} = \frac{I}{e} = \frac{4.8}{1.6 \times 10^{-19}} = 3 \times 10^{19}$$

Q.16 The amount of charge provided by the cell per second into the circuit, if 2 A current flows through the circuit, is

(a) 2 C (b) 1 C (d) 4 C (d) 0.2 C

Ans. (a) Given, $I = 2\,A$, $t = 1s$

$\therefore$ Charge, $q = I \times t = 2 \times 1 = 2\,C$

Q.17 How many electrons enter into the filament of the bulb per second, if current is 0.2 A? (Take, $e = 1.6 \times 10^{-19}$ C)

(a) 6.25×10^{18} (b) 2.5×10^{18}
(c) 1.25×10^{19} (d) 1.25×10^{18}

Ans. (d) Given, $t = 1\,s$, $I = 0.2\,A$

We know that, $I = \frac{ne}{t} \Rightarrow n = \frac{It}{e} = \frac{0.2 \times 1}{1.6 \times 10^{-19}}$

$= 1.25 \times 10^{18}$ electrons/s

Q.18 Consider the following circuit diagram shown below and answer the following questions.

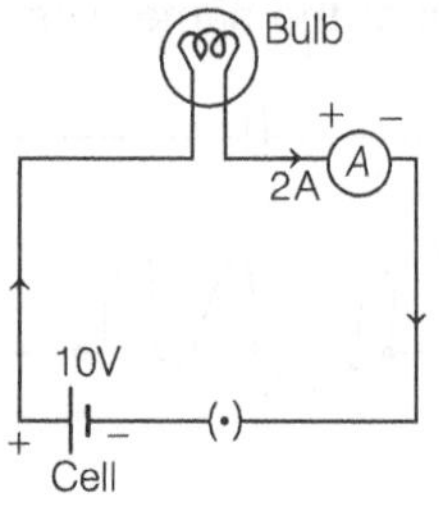

Resistance of the bulb is

(a) 20 Ω (b) 5 Ω (c) 10 Ω (d) 15 Ω

Ans. (b) Given, $V = 10\,V$, $I = 2\,A$

According to Ohm's law, $V = IR$

$$\Rightarrow \quad R = \frac{V}{I} = \frac{10}{2} = 5\,\Omega$$

Q.19 The amount of energy consumed by the bulb per second, if potential difference across battery is 10 V and current in the circuit is 1A is

(a) 15 J (b) 10 J (c) 25 J (d) 20 J

Ans. (b) Given, $I = 1\,A$, $t = 1\,s$, $V = 10\,V$

We know that, $V = \frac{W}{q}$

$$\Rightarrow \quad W = V \cdot q = VIt \quad (\because q = It)$$
$$= 10 \times 1 \times 1 = 10\,J$$

TYPE - 2   01 Mark

Assertion-Reason Type Questions

Directions (Q. Nos. 1-5) In the following questions two statements are given as Assertion and Reason.

(a) Both A and R are true and R is the correct explanation of A.
(b) Both A and R are true but R is not the correct explanation of A.
(c) A is true but R is false.
(d) A is false but R is true.

Q.1 Assertion (A) The direction of conventional current is opposite to the direction of electron flow.

Reason (R) Conventional current assumes that positive charges flow from the positive to the negative terminal.

Ans. (a) Electrons flow from negative to positive, but conventional current is defined as the flow of positive charge, which moves in the opposite direction of electron flow, i.e. (positive to negative).

Q.2 Assertion (A) Direct current flows in only one direction.

Reason (R) Direct current changes its direction periodically.

Ans. (c) Direct current flows in a single, constant direction.

The reason describes alternating current (AC), not direct current (DC).

Q.3 Assertion (A) Ammeter is a device used to measure current in an electric circuit.

Reason (R) Voltmeter is a device used to measure voltage in circuit.

Ans. (b) Both A and R are true but R is not the correct explanation of A.

Voltmeter measures voltage and ammeter measures the current in an electric circuit.

Q.4 Assertion (A) Ammeter reading decreases to one-half when the length of the wire is doubled.

Reason (R) Resistance varies with the length of the wire increases (or decreases).

Ans. (a) We have,

Current, $I = \dfrac{V}{R}$

Resistance of wire is directly proportional to the length.

When the length of the wire is doubled, the resistance of the wire becomes double.

$\therefore$ Current, $I' = \dfrac{V}{2R} \Rightarrow I' = \dfrac{I}{2}$

Therefore, ammeter reading decreases to one-half.

Q.5 Assertion (A) A conductor allows electric current to pass through it easily.

Reason (R) Conductors have free electrons that move under the influence of an electric field.

Ans. (a) Conductors allow electric current to pass through them because they contain free electrons. When an electric field is applied, these electrons move and creating a current.

TYPE - 3 01/02 Marks

Fill in the Blanks

Q.1 Resistance of a conductor is directly proportional to its .... [length/cross-section] **[1]**

Ans. length

Q.2 For a given conductor, resistance ..... [increases/decreases] with an increase in temperature. **[1]**

Ans. increases

Q.3 Energy-efficient appliances consume .... [less/more] electrical energy for the same output. **[1]**

Ans. less

Q.4 Devices like .... [LED/solar light] bulbs are more efficient than in candescent bulbs. **[1]**

Ans. LED

Q.5 The potential difference between two points in a circuit is the work done in moving a unit .... [charge/electric] from one point to another against the .... [charge, magnetic] field. **[2]**

Ans. charge, electric

Q.6 The flow of current in a circuit depends on the .... [potential/current] difference and the .... [potential/resistance] of the circuit. **[2]**

Ans. potential, resistance

TYPE - 4 02 Marks

Very Short Answer Type Questions

Q.1 Draw the symbol of

(i) plug key open (ii) plug key closed

What does each situation mean?

Ans. (i) 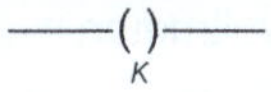 (ii) 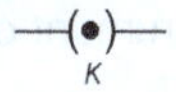

When plug key is opened, no current flows through the circuit and when plug key is closed, current flows through the circuit.

Q.2 What do the following circuit symbols represent?

(i) 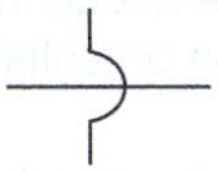 (ii) 

Ans. (i) Wires crossing without joining.

(ii) Fuse

Q.3 Write the name of the symbols used in electric circuits to represent.

(i)  (ii) 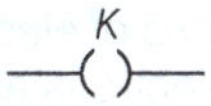

Ans. (i) Bulb (ii) Open plug key

Q.4 (i) What are the values of mA and μA in terms of A? **[1]**

(ii) Draw the symbols of battery and rheostat. **[1]**

Ans. (i) $1\text{ mA} = \dfrac{1}{1000}\text{ A} = 10^{-3}\text{A}$

and $1\mu\text{A} = \dfrac{1}{1000000}\text{ A} = 10^{-6}\text{ A}$

(ii) Symbol of battery

Symbol of rheostat

 or 

Q.5 What is an ammeter? How is it connected in a circuit? Draw a diagram to illustrate your answer.

Ans. An ammeter is an instrument used to measure current. It is always connected in series in a circuit.

This is illustrated in the diagram given below

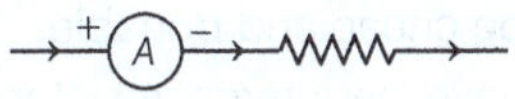

Q.6 Write the use of galvanometer. Draw its symbol also.

Ans. Galvanometer is an electrical device which is used to detect the presence of weak current or to find its direction. It does not give the magnitude of current.

Its symbol is 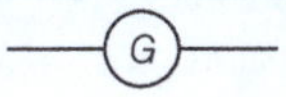

Q.7 **The potential difference between two points in an electric circuit is 1 V. What does it mean? Name a device that helps to measure the potential difference across a conductor.**

Ans. The potential difference between two points is 1 V. It means that, if a charge of 1 coulomb is moved from one point to the other, 1 joule of work is required. The potential difference across a conductor is measured by means of an instrument called the voltmeter.

Q.8 **What happened when two ends of a metallic wire are connected across the terminals of a cell. In which direction electrons are flowing through the conductors?**

Ans. When two ends of a metallic wire are connected across the terminals of a cell, then some potential difference is set up between its ends.

Electrons are flowing through the conductor from its lower potential end to its higher potential end.

Q.9 **What causes the potential difference between the two terminals of a cell?**

Ans. The chemical reaction occurring inside the cell generates excess of electrons at negative terminal and deficiency of electrons at positive terminal.

Q.10 **Let resistance of an electrical component remains constant while the potential difference across the two ends of components decreases to half of its former value. What change will occur in the current through it?**

Ans. By Ohm's law, voltage is directly proportional to the current, i.e. $V \propto I$.

If V becomes half, current flowing through it is also halved.

TYPE - 5 — 03 Marks

Short Answer Type Questions

Q.1 **What are the requirements that a good cell should have?** **[3]**

Ans. A good cell should have the following requirements

(i) It should provide a constant current.

(ii) It should be cheap and portable.

(iii) It should have low internal resistance.

Q.2 **(i) Draw a circuit diagram showing how four bulbs can be lit from a battery of four cells, so that two bulbs are controlled by the same switch while each of the other two bulbs has its own switch.** **[1]**

(ii) Redraw the following circuit using appropriate symbols. **[2]**

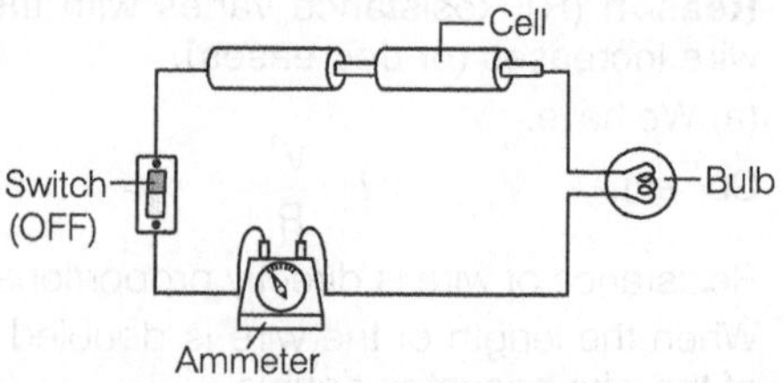

Ans. (i) The circuit diagram is shown as below

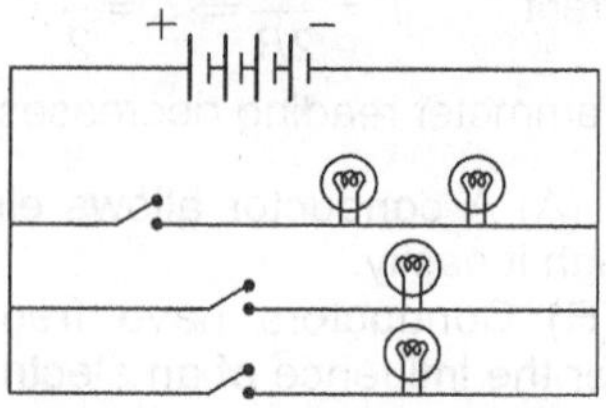

(ii) The circuit redrawn using appropriate symbols is given below.

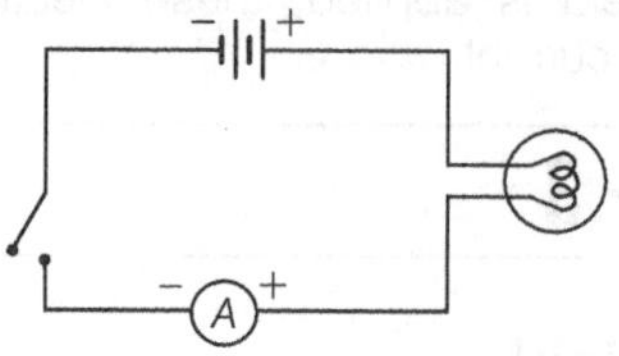

Q.3 **(i) How does the resistance of a wire vary with its area of cross-section?** **[1]**

(ii) Out of the two wires *P* and *Q* shown below, which one has greater resistance? Justify it. **[2]**

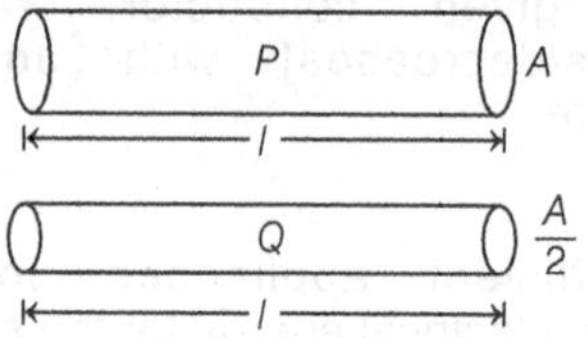

Ans. (i) Resistance is inversely proportional to the area of cross-section of the wire. Thus, if the wire is thick, then resistance is less. If the wire is thin, then resistance is large.

(ii) Smaller the area of cross-section, greater will be resistance as $R \propto \frac{1}{A}$. ($\because$ lengths are same)

So, wire Q has greater resistance.

Q.4 **(i) Complete the circuit given in the figure by inserting an ammeter between the terminals *B* and *C*.** **[1]**

(ii) In the diagram, mark the polarity at the terminals of the ammeter and indicate clearly the direction

of the flow of current in the circuit, when the circuit is complete. **[1]**

(iii) Name and state the purpose of Rh in the circuit. **[1]**

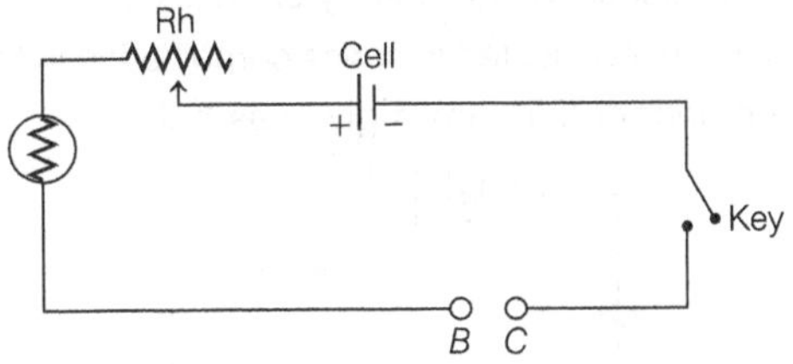

Ans. (i) The circuit is as follows

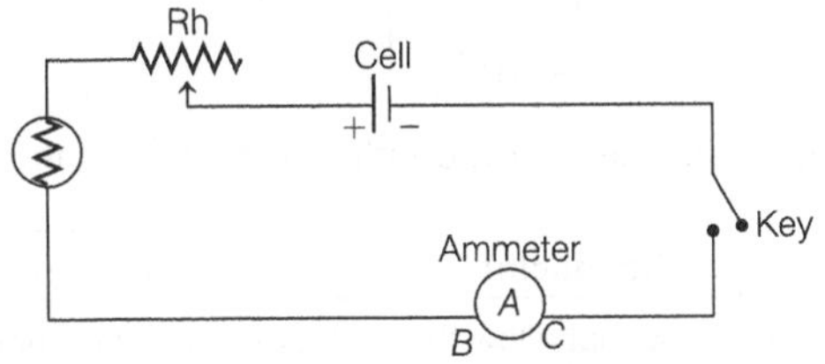

(ii) The circuit is as follows

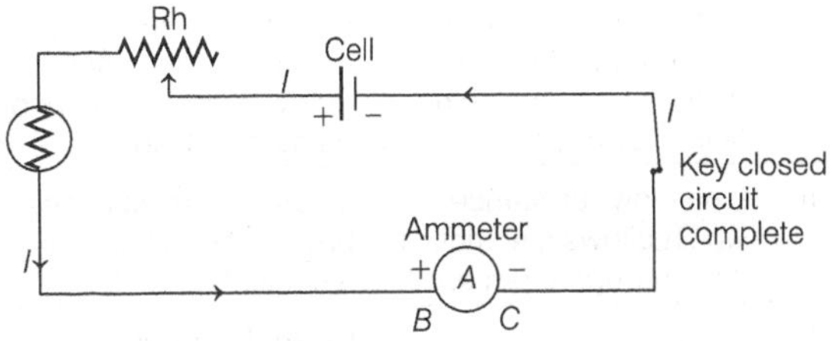

(iii) Rh is the Rheostat. It controls the flow of current in a circuit.

Q.5 Write the three factors on which the resistance of a conductor depends.

Ans. The factors on which the resistance of a conductor depends are as follows

(i) Length of the conductor.

(ii) Area of cross-section of the conductor.

(iii) Nature of the material of the conductor.

Q.6 Two conductors *A* and *B* are joined by a copper wire. State the direction of flow of electrons in each of the following cases

(i) If *A* is positively charged and *B* is negatively charged. **[1]**

(ii) If *A* is negatively charged and *B* is uncharged. **[1]**

(iii) If *A* is negatively charged and *B* is positively charged. **[1]**

Ans. (i) From *B* to *A*

(ii) From *A* to *B*

(iii) From *A* to *B*

TYPE - 6 — 04 Marks

Long Answer Type Questions

Q.1 Differentiate between primary and secondary cells.

Ans.

Primary Cell	Secondary Cell
In this cell, only chemical energy is converted into electrical energy, when current is drawn.	In this cell, chemical energy is converted into electrical energy while discharging and electrical energy can be converted into chemical energy while charging.
This type of cells cannot be recharged again.	This type of cells can be recharged again and again.
In this, chemical reaction is irreversible.	In this, chemical reaction is reversible.

Q.2 Differentiate between closed and open circuits.

Ans.

	Closed Circuit	Open Circuit
(i)	A circuit in which current flows continuously.	A circuit in which current flow is interrupted.
(ii)	Current flows through the circuit.	Current does not flow due to a break in the circuit.
(iii)	The circuit path is complete and continuous.	The circuit path is incomplete or broken.
(iv)	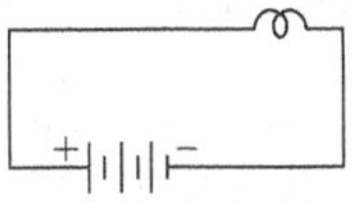	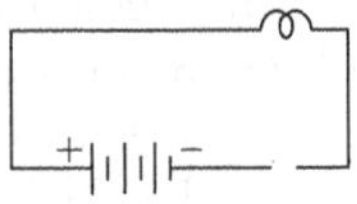

Q.3 In the circuit given below, label the parts *P*, *Q*, *R* and *S*, and state the function of each part.

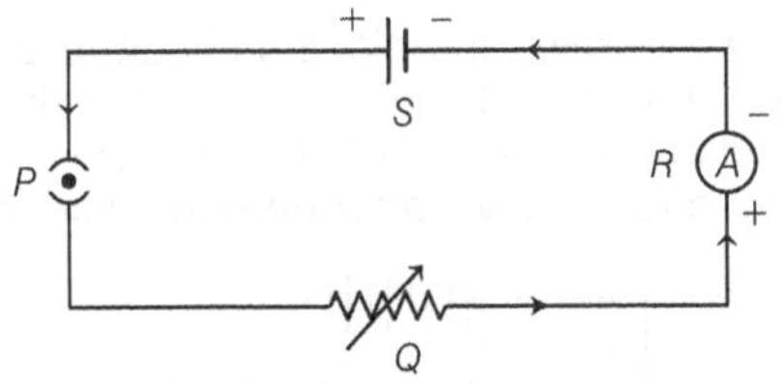

Ans. The circuit components are as follows

$P \rightarrow$ A closed key, which is used to close the circuit.

$Q \rightarrow$ A rheostat, which is used to provide variable resistance in order to control the current flowing through the circuit.

$R \rightarrow$ An ammeter, which measures the current flowing through the circuit.

$S \rightarrow$ A cell, which provides potential difference between two terminals.

Q.4 Consider the points *A, B, C, D, E, F* and *G* in the circuit shown below. Let $V_A, V_B ..., V_G$ be the potentials at *A, B, ..., G* respectively.

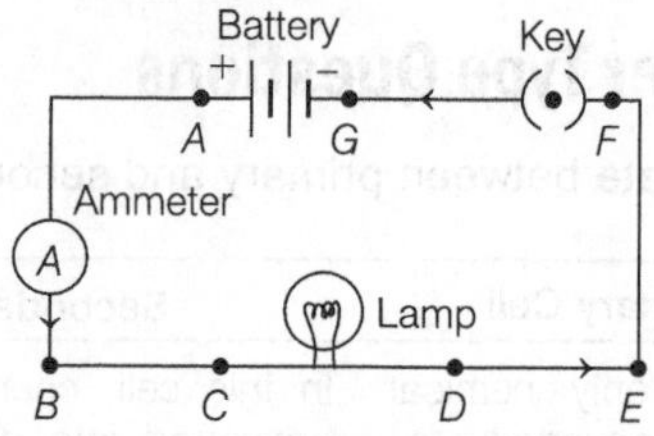

Answer the following questions.

(i) Which point has the highest potential? **[1]**

(ii) Which point has the lowest potential? **[2]**

(iii) Relate the values of $V_A, V_B, ..., V_G$ using the symbols >, = or <. **[1]**

Ans. (i) The highest potential is at the positive terminal of the battery, which is point *A*.

(ii) The lowest potential is at the negative terminal of the battery, which is point *G*.

(iii) $V_A = V_B = V_C > V_D = V_E = V_F = V_G$

Q.5 Write a short note on

(i) voltmeter **[2]**

(ii) ammeter **[2]**

Ans. (i) **Voltmeter** is an electrical device used to measure the electrical potential difference between two points in an electrical circuit. It is a high resistance device connected in parallel with the components through which potential to be measured.

(ii) **Ammeter** is an electrical device used to measure direction and magnitude of electric current. It is connected in series with circuit. An ammeter has negligible resistance, so it does not change the magnitude of current, when current is passed through it.

Q.6 A child has drawn the electric circuit to study Ohm's law as shown in figure. His teacher told that the circuit diagram needs correction. Study the circuit diagram and redraw it after making all corrections.

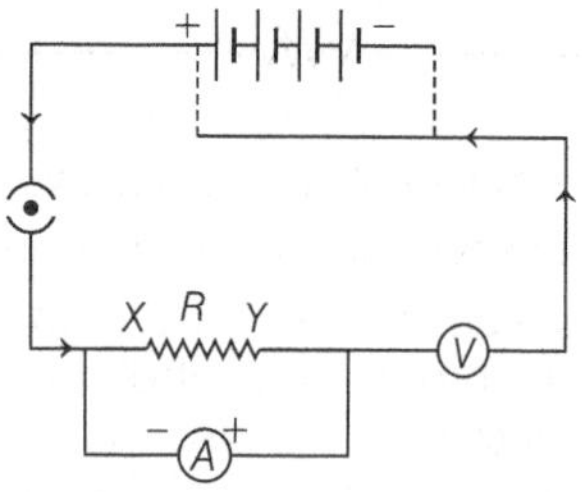

Ans. The circuit diagram is not correct because of the following reasons

(i) Ammeter is connected in parallel with *R* and voltmeter connected in series with it in contrary of the fact that ammeter should be connected in series and voltmeter in parallel. This is so because same current flows in series and same voltage exists in parallel combination.

(ii) The current is drawn from negative terminal and enters into the battery at positive terminal which is not possible in one battery circuit.

(iii) Cells are connected in series combination in the circuit.

The correct diagram is given as below

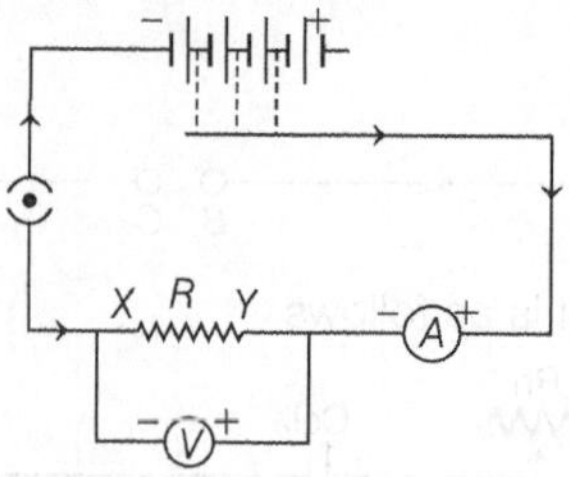

Q.7 Differentiate between conductor and insulator.

Ans.

	Conductor	Insulator
(i)	Materials that allow the flow of electric current easily.	Materials that do not allow the flow of electric current easily.
(ii)	Conductor have free electrons that can move easily when an electric field is applied.	Insulator have tightly bound electrons that cannot move freely under the influence of an electric field.
(iii)	It has low resistance, which allows electricity to flow through them easily.	It has high resistance, preventing the flow of electrical current.
(iv)	Examples : Copper, aluminium, silver, gold.	Examples : Rubber, glass, wood, plastic.

TYPE - 7 03/04 Marks

Case Based Questions

Q.1 The rate of flow of charge is called electric current. The SI unit of electric current is ampere (A). The direction of flow of current is always opposite to the direction of flow of electrons in the circuit. The electric potential is defined as the amount of work done in bringing a unit positive test charge from infinity to a point in an electric field. The amount of work done in bringing an unit positive test charge from one point to another point in an electric field is defined as potential difference.

$$V_{AB} = V_B - V_A = \frac{W_{BA}}{q}$$

The SI unit of potential and potential difference is volt.

(i) Explain, why the direction of conventional current is opposite to the direction of electron flow ? **[1]**

(ii) A charge of 8 C is moved between two points, and 32J of work is done. Calculate the potential difference. **[1]**

(iii) If a current of 5 A flows through a wire for 2 min, calculate the total charge passing through the wire. **[1]**

Ans. (i) In a circuit, electrons move from the negative terminal to the positive terminal because they are negatively charged. However, when electric current was first discovered, it was assumed that current flows from the positive terminal to the negative terminal. This historical convention led to the definition of conventional current, which is always considered to flow opposite to the direction of electron movement.

(ii) Using the formula $V = \frac{W}{q}$

where, $W = 32$ J, $q = 8$ C

$\therefore \quad V = \frac{32}{8} = 4$ V

Thus, the potential difference is 4 V.

(iii) Using the formula $Q = I \times t$

where, $I = 5$A, $t = 120$ s

$\therefore \quad Q = 5 \times 120 = 600$ C

Thus, 600 C of charge passes.

Q.2 A physics teacher sets up a simple circuit to demonstrate Ohm's law. The circuit consists of a 12 V battery, a 4 Ω resistor, and an ammeter in series. A voltmeter is connected across the resistor.

(i) What is the current flowing through the circuit? **[1]**

(ii) Write the mathematical expression of Ohm's law and explain its significance. **[1]**

(iii) Why is it important to connect the ammeter in series and the voltmeter in parallel? **[1]**

Ans. (i) Current, $I = \frac{V}{R} = \frac{12}{4} = 3$ A

(ii) Ohm's law, $V = I \times R$. It states that the potential difference across a conductor is directly proportional to the current flowing through it, provided the temperature remains constant.

(iii) The ammeter measures current and must be in series to measure the flow of electrons. The voltmeter measures potential difference and must be in parallel to measure the voltage across components.

Q.3 It is a simple circuit diagram which represents the relative positions and connections of various circuit. Components represented by their symbols as shown in the diagram below.

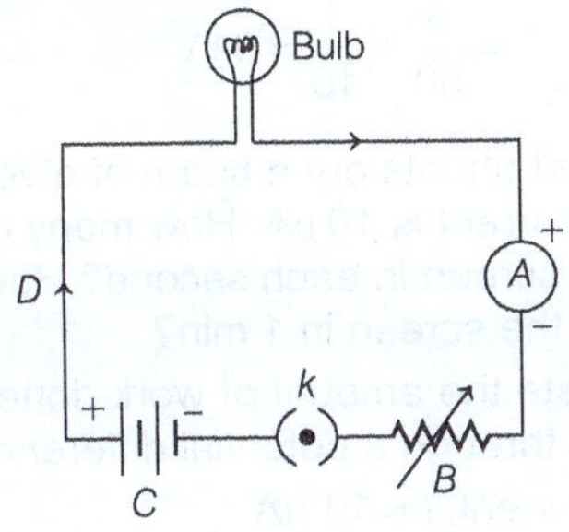

Complete the table, using the labels from the figure. The first label is done for you. **[3]**

S.No.	Description	Label
a.	A device used to measure electric current	A
b.	A group of one or more cells	
c.	A variable resistance to control the current	
d.	Direction of conventional current	

Ans.

S.No.	Description	Label
a.	A device used to measure electric current	A
b.	A group of one or more cells	C
c.	A variable resistance to control the current	B
d.	Direction of conventional current	D

TYPE - 8

Numerical Questions

Q.1 A current of 1 A is drawn by a filament of an electric bulb. Find the number of electrons passing through a cross-section of the filament in 16 s. **[2]**

Sol. Given, $I = 1$ A, $t = 16$ s

Number of electrons = ?

$\because \quad q = It$

and $\quad ne = q$

$\Rightarrow \quad n = \frac{q}{e}$

$\Rightarrow \quad q = 16 \times 1 = 16$ C

and $\quad n = \frac{q}{e} = \frac{16}{1.6 \times 10^{-19}}$

$= 10^{20}$ electrons

Q.2 Calculate the potential difference between two terminals of a battery, if 100 J of work is required to transfer 20 C from one terminal of the battery to the other. **[2]**

Sol. Given, work done, $W = 100$ J

Charge, $\quad q = 20$ C

Potential difference,

$$\therefore \qquad \Delta V = \frac{W}{q}$$

$$= \frac{100}{20} = 5\text{ V}$$

The potential difference between two points is 5 V.

Q.3 The potential difference between the terminals of an electric heater is 75 V, when it draws a current of 5 A from the source. What current will the heater draw, if the potential difference is increased to 150 V? **[2]**

Sol. Given, potential difference, $V = 75\text{ V}$

Current, $I = 5\text{ A}$

We know that, $R = \frac{V}{I}$

$$\Rightarrow \qquad R = \frac{75}{5} = 15\ \Omega$$

When potential difference is increased to 150 V, then current,

$$I' = \frac{V'}{R}$$

$$= \frac{150}{15} = 10\text{ A} \qquad (\because V' = 150\text{ V})$$

So, the current through the heater becomes 10 A.

Q.4 A cell is connected to a bulb which develops a potential difference of 20 V across it. The current in the circuit is measured to be 4 A. Calculate the resistance offered by the filament of the bulb to the flow of current. **[2]**

Sol. Given, potential difference $V = 20\text{ V}$,

Current, $I = 4\text{ A}$

According to Ohm's law, $V = IR$

$$\Rightarrow \qquad R = \frac{V}{I}$$

$$= \frac{20}{4} = 5\ \Omega$$

Q.5 Find the potential difference across the ends of the wire of resistance 5Ω, when a current 2.5 A is flowing through it. **[2]**

Sol. Given, current, $I = 2.5\text{ A}$,

Resistance, $R = 5\ \Omega$

As per Ohm's law, $V = IR$

$$= 2.5 \times 5 = 12.5\text{ V}$$

Q.6 The current flowing through a resistor connected in an electric circuit and the potential difference applied across its ends are shown in figure. **[2]**

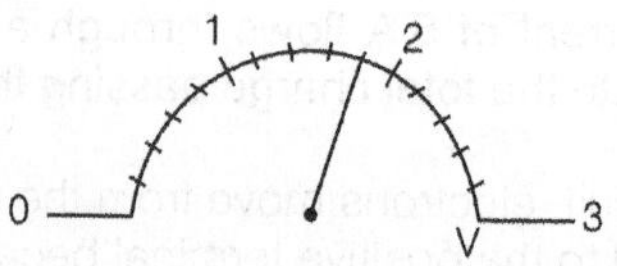

What is the value of the resistance of the resistor?

Sol. Reading from ammeter, $I = 180\text{ mA}$

$$= 0.18\text{ A}$$

Reading from voltmeter,

$$V = 1.8\text{ V}$$

$\therefore$ Resistance of the resistor,

$$R = \frac{V}{I} = \frac{1.8}{0.18} = \frac{180}{18} = 10\Omega$$

Q.7 A resistor allows a current of 0.02 A to flow through it, when there is a potential difference of 10.0 V between its ends. What is its resistance? **[2]**

Sol. Given, current, $I = 0.02\text{ A}$

Potential difference,

$$V = 10.0\text{ V}$$

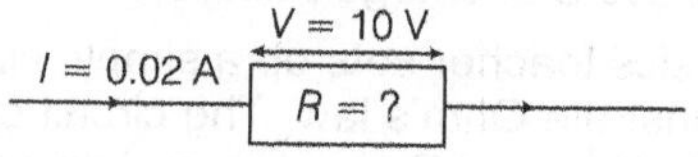

$\therefore$ Resistance, $R = \frac{V}{I}$

$$= \frac{10.0}{0.02} = 500\Omega$$

So, the resistance of the resistor is 500 Ω.

Q.8 When a charge of 50C is moved from infinity to points *X* and *Y*, work is done to do so is 15 J and 20 J, respectively. Calculate potential difference between the points *X* and *Y*. **[2]**

Sol. Given, $W_X = 15\text{ J}$, $W_Y = 20\text{ J}$,

$q = 50\text{C}$, $V_Y - V_X = ?$

$\therefore$ Potential difference between points *X* and *Y*,

$$V_Y - V_X = \frac{W_Y}{q} - \frac{W_X}{q}$$

$$= \frac{(W_Y - W_X)}{q}$$

$$= \frac{20 - 15}{50}$$

$$= \frac{5}{50} = \frac{1}{10} = 0.1\text{ V}$$

Q.9 **(i) A TV set shoots out a beam of electrons. The beam current is 10 μA. How many electrons strike the TV screen in each second? How much charge strikes the screen in 1 min?** **[2]**

(ii) Calculate the amount of work done in moving 4 C charge through a potential difference of 4 V? **[1]**

Sol. (i) Given, current, $I = 10\ \mu\text{A}$

$= 10 \times 10^{-6}$ A

$= 10^{-5}$A

Time, $t = 1$s

Number of electrons per second, $n = ?$

Amount of charges in 1 min, $q = ?$

Using the relation,

$$I = \frac{ne}{t} \qquad (\because q = ne)$$

$$\Rightarrow \quad n = \frac{It}{e} = \frac{10^{-5} \times 1}{1.6 \times 10^{-19}} \qquad (\because e = 1.6 \times 10^{-19}\text{C})$$

$= 6.25 \times 10^{13}$ electrons

$\therefore \quad q = It$

$= 10^{-5} \times 60$

$= 600\,\mu$C

(ii) Given, charge, $q = 4$C

Potential difference,

$V = 4$V

$\therefore$ Work needed to be done,

$W = qV$

$= 4 \times 4 = 16$ J

Q.10 **(i) Calculate the number of electrons constituting 1C of charge.** **[1]**

(ii) What charge is carried by a conductor through which 4.5 A current flows in 1 min? **[1]**

Sol. (i) We know that, charge on 1 electron = 1.6×10^{-19}C

$\Rightarrow$ 1.6×10^{-19} coulomb charge on 1 electron.

$$\therefore \quad 1 \text{ coulomb charge} = \frac{1}{1.6 \times 10^{-19}}$$

$\simeq 6.25 \times 10^{18}$ electrons

(ii) Given, current, $I = 4.5$ A

Time, $t = 1$min

$= 60$ s

$\therefore$ Charge carried by a conductor, $q = It$

$= 4.5 \times 60$

$= 270$ C

MAGNETISM

Magnets

- The substaces having the property of attracting iron pieces are known as magnets.
- Magnets are of two types ; (i) Natural magnets and (ii) Artificial magnets
- The magnet that is found in nature is known as **natural magnet**, e.g. magnetite and lodestone, whereas the magnet that can be made by magnetising the materials like iron, cobalt, nickel etc., is known as **artificial magnet** or **man made magnet. For example** bar magnet, horse shoe magnet, magnetic compass, etc.
- A magnet in the shape of a bar is called **bar magnet**. It has two poles. One pole is designated as **North pole** and the other as **South pole**.
- All magnets have two poles **north pole** and **south pole**, two like poles (both north poles or both south poles) **repel** each other while two unlike poles (one north pole and other south pole) **attract** each other.

Magnetic Field

- The region surrounding a magnet in which **magnetic effect can be experienced** i.e., its force can be detected is called **magnetic field**.
- Magnetic field is a **vector quantity** which has both magnitude and direction.

Magnetism Induced by Bar Magnet

- The temporary magnetic properties acquired by a magnetic material on placing it in contact with magnet, is called **induced magnetism.**
- A magnetic pole induces an opposite polarity on the near end and a similar polarity on the farther end of the iron bar.

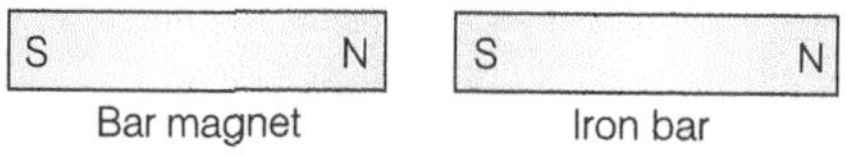

Iron bar becomes induced magnet

Magnetic Field Lines

- Magnetic field lines are imaginary lines around a magnet depicting the field strength of a magnet.

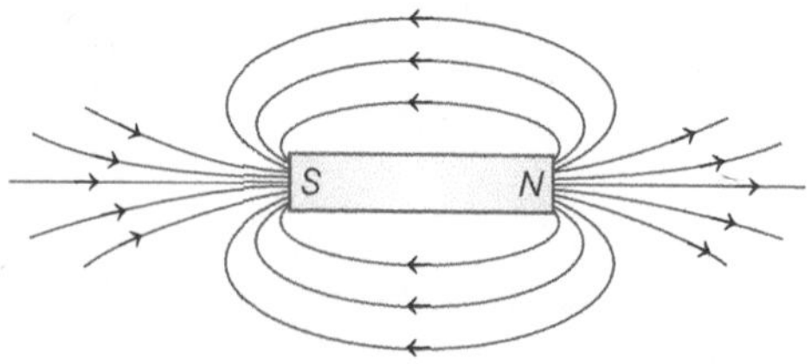

Magnetic field lines around a bar magnet

Properties of Magnetic Field Lines

(i) The magnetic field lines of a magnet form **continuous closed loops**.

(ii) Magnetic field lines originate at the north pole and end at the south pole.

(iii) The **tangent** to the **field lines** at a given **point** represents the **direction** of the **net magnetic field** at that **point**.

REVISION NOTES

(iv) The **larger** the number of field lines crossing per unit area, the **stronger** is the magnitude of the magnetic field.

(v) The magnetic field lines do not **intersect**, or if they did, the direction of the magnetic field would not be unique at the **point of intersection**.

(vi) **Parallel** and **equidistant** magnetic field lines represent a **uniform** magnetic field.

(vii) Magnetic field lines are **crowded** near the **poles** of a magnet, where the magnetic field is strong and are far **separated** near the **middle** of the magnet and far from the magnet, where the magnetic field is **weak**.

(viii) They also **behave** like stretched **elastic rubber strings**.

(ix) These lines emerge **normally** from the **magnetised surface**.

Earth's Magnetism

- Earth acts like a very **big** and **weak** magnet. Earth's magnetism is the magnetic field generated by the motion of molten iron and nickel in its outer core, making earth behave like a giant bar magnet.
- Two places where the magnetic needles becomes vertical are called **magnetic poles**.
- The line joining the places where the magnetic needle becomes horizontal, is called **magnetic equator**.

Evidences of Existence of Earth's Magnetic Field

- The points given below prove the **existence of Earth's magnetic field**

  (i) A freely suspended magnet always rests in **North-South direction**. This is possible only if a magnetic force is applied on the magnet which forces it to always rest in North-South direction.

  (ii) An **iron rod** buried inside the Earth along **North-South direction** becomes a **magnet**. This is possible, if iron rod is kept near a magnet which **induces magnetism** in it.

  (iii) While drawing the magnetic lines of force of a magnet we get neutral points, where the magnetic field is zero. It is possible only if there exists another magnetic field along with the magnetic field of the magnet in opposite direction.

  (iv) A magnetic needles rests with its geometric axis making different angles with horizontal when suspended at different places on earth.

Uniform Magnetic Field of Earth

- The magnetic field of Earth is uniform. The field lines are parallel and equidistant. These lines do not intersect with each other. They are directed from geographic South to geographic North.

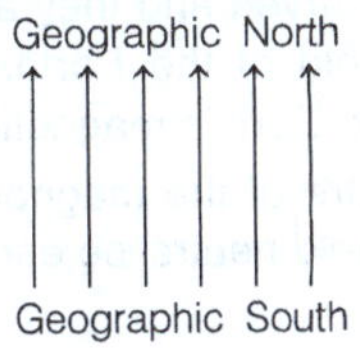

Non-uniform Magnetic Field of a Bar Magnet and Neutral Points

- The magnetic field around a bar magnet is non-uniform. Magnetic lines of force around a bar magnet are not **equispaced** and **parallel**.

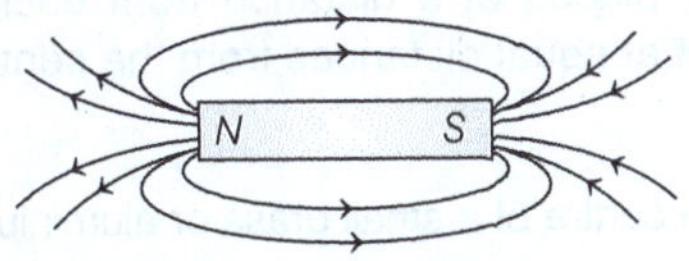

The non-uniform magnetic field lines of a bar magnet placed in the magnetic meridian along with neutral points can be explained for two cases.

(i) **When magnet is placed in magnetic meridian with its North pole pointing towards geographic North** The magnetic field lines obtained in this position are shown in the figure below which are due to the combined effect of the magnetic field of the magnet and the Earth's magnetic field.

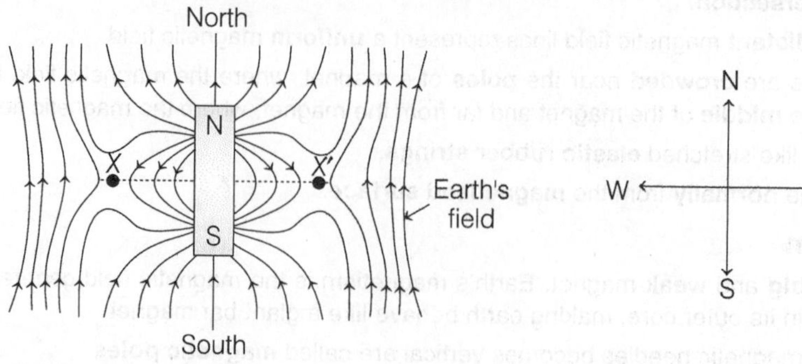

(ii) **When the magnet is placed in magnetic meridian with its South pole points towards geographical North** The magnetic field lines obtained in this position are shown in the figure below which are due to the combined effect of the magnetic field of the magnet and the Earth's magnetic field.

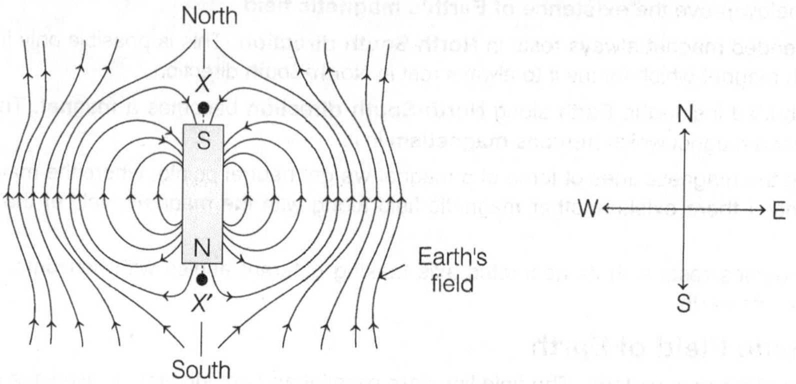

From the above figures, we can conclude that (for both the positions)

- The magnetic field lines near the magnet are curved and they are mainly due to the magnetic field of the magnet which is much stronger than the magnetic field of the Earth. The **magnetic field lines** at distant points are **parallel** to each other and are mainly due to the Earth's magnetic field.
- There are two points equidistant from the centre of the magnet where the magnetic field of the magnet and the horizontal component of the Earth's magnetic field neutralise each other. These are the **neutral points**.

Neutral Points

- **Neutral points** are the points where the magnetic field of a magnet is equal in **magnitude** to the Earth's horizontal magnetic field, but in **opposite** direction. Thus, the resultant magnetic field at neutral points is **zero**. A compass needle if placed at the neutral point will rest in any direction. *X* and *X′* represent neutral point in the above figures.
- When two magnets with like poles are placed at a distance from each other, the neutral point will be located symmetrically on either side of a magnet at equal distances from the centre.

Magnetic Compass

- It is a small magnetic needle pivoted at the centre of a small brass or aluminium box which has a transparent glass top.
- A magnetic compass is used
  (i) to find geographical direction
  (ii) to find direction of a magnetic field
  (iii) to test the polarity of a magnet

Electromagnets

- When an electric current is passed through a conductor, then a magnetic field is produced around the conductor. This phenomena is called **magnetic effect of electric current**. Electromagnet is based on this effect.

- An **electromagnet** is a temporary magnet created by coiling a wire around a metal core and passing a current through the wire. When current flows through the coil, it becomes magnet when current is switched OFF, then its magnetism disappears. It also has a north and sourth poles like permanent magnet.
- The electromagnets can be of any shape but usually, they are of two shapes,
  (i) I-shape (or bar) electromagnet and (ii) U-shape (or horse-shoe) electromagnet

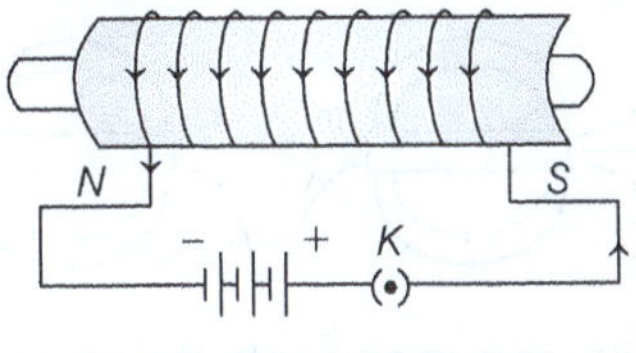

(i) I-shape electromagnet

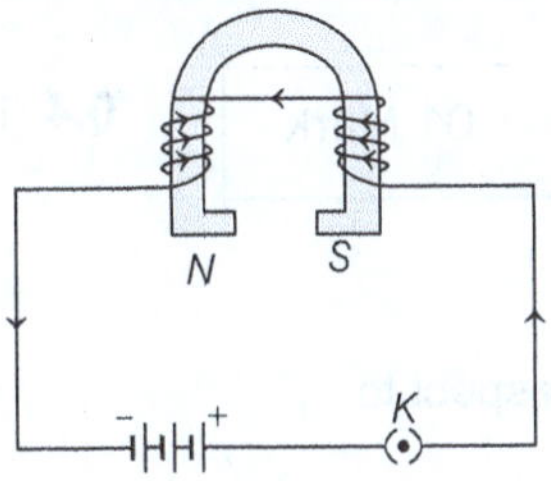

(ii) U-shape electromagnet

Clock Face Rule

- If the **current** is in the **clockwise** direction, the face of the coil will behave like the **south pole.**
- If the **current** is in the **anti-clockwise** direction, the face of the coil will north magnetic pole behave like the **north pole.**

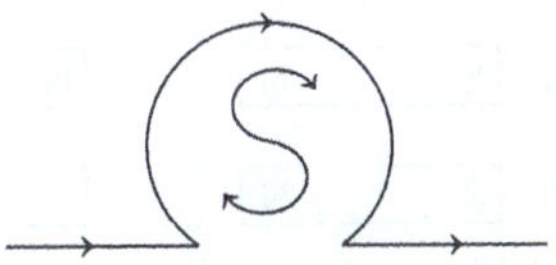
South magnetic pole

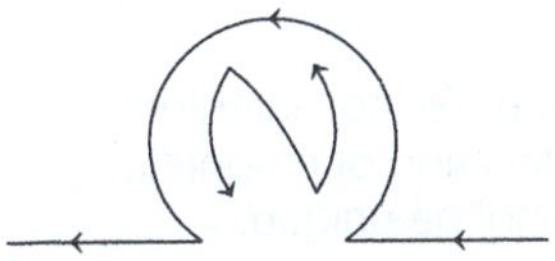
North magnetic pole

Factors Affecting the Strength of Electromagnets

(i) **The core material** Those materials are used as a core materials which allows magnetic field lines to pass through them, such as soft iron.

(ii) **The number of turn in the coil** If number of turns increases the magnetic field produced by it, will also increases.

(iii) **The current flowing through the coil** When the current flowing through a coil increases, the magnetic field strength of the electromagnet also increases.

Uses of Electromagnets

- It is used in electric bells, electric motors, telephone, diaphragms, loudspeakers and for sorting scrap metal and for extraction in hospitals.
- Giant electromagnets are used for lifting and transporting heavy iron scrap, girders, plates, etc.
- For loading furnaces with iron.
- For removing pieces of iron from wounds.
- In scientific research, to study the magnetic properties of a substance in a magnetic field.
- For separating iron pieces from debris and ores, where iron exists as impurities.

Difference between Electromagnet and Permanent Magnet

Electromagnet	Permanent magnet
It is made of soft iron.	It is made of steel.
The magnetic field strength can be changed.	The magnetic field strength cannot be changed.
It produces temporary magnetic field.	It produces a permanent magnetic field.
It produces strong magnetic field.	Magnetic field of a permanent magnet is not so strong.
The polarity of electromagnet can be reversed.	The polarity of a permanent magnet cannot be reversed.
It can easily be demagnetised.	It cannot be easily demagnetised.

EXAM ORIENTED QUESTIONS

TYPE - 1 01 Mark

Multiple Choice Questions

Q.1 Which of the following is not true with respect to magnetic field lines?

(a) Magnetic field lines of force are closed and continuous curve.

(b) Parallel and equidistant magnetic field lines represent a uniform magnetic field.

(c) Two magnetic field lines of force can intersect only at a single point.

(d) None of the above

Ans. (c) The magnetic field lines of force do not intersect each other, if they intersect, then direction of magnetic field at the point of intersection will not be unique.

Q.2 Which of the region (*A*, *B* and *C*) represents region of a uniform magnetic field?

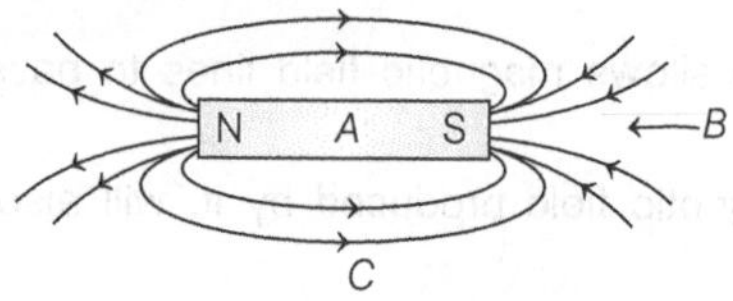

(a) *A* Only (b) *B* Only (c) *A* and *C* both (d) *A*, *B* and *C*

Ans. (a) In the region of a uniform magnetic field, field lines are parallel and equidistant.

Q.3 The diagram shows the magnetic field around the wire *X* which carries a current into the paper.
The arrows on the field lines show the direction of the force on

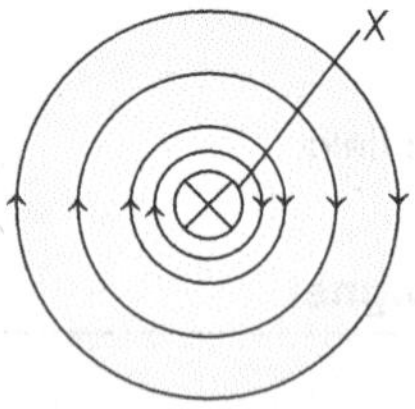

(a) N-pole (b) S-pole

(c) a small negative charge (d) a small positive charge

Ans. (a) The direction of a magnetic field at any point is found by placing a N-pole at that point. The direction in which the N-pole experiences a force and moves, is the direction of the magnetic field.

Q.4 The magnetic field around two bar magnets is shown.

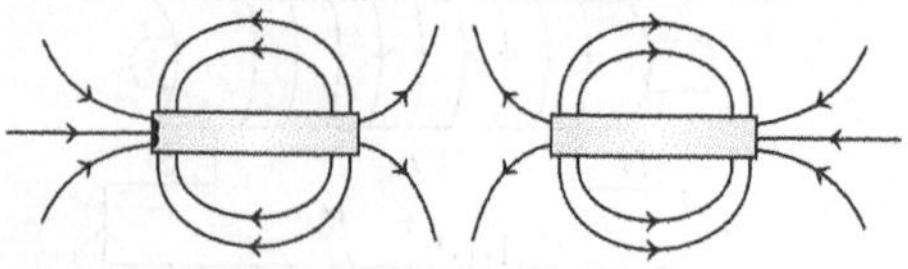

Which diagram represents the correct arrangement of magnetic poles?

(a) [N S] [N S]

(b) [N S] [S N]

(c) [S N] [N S]

(d) [S N] [S N]

Ans. (c) The pattern of the combined magnetic field of the two bar magnets and the direction of the field lines show that N-poles of the two bar magnets are facing each other which results in the repulsive magnetic field between them.

Q.5 Magnetic field pattern due to a bar magnet is shown below in the diagram. This bar magnet is placed at a place where Earth's magnetic field exists.

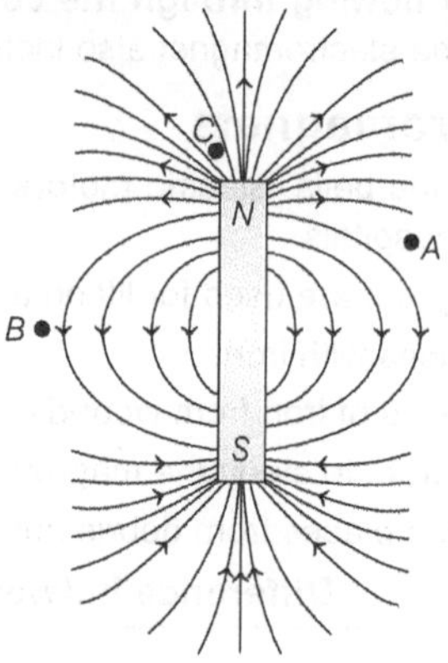

Magnetic field strength is maximum at point

(a) *A* (b) *B*

(c) *C* (d) *A* and *B*

Ans. (c) Magnetic field strength is maximum at point *C* because maximum number of magnetic field lines passes through this point.

Q.6 A bar magnet is used to pick up an iron nail.

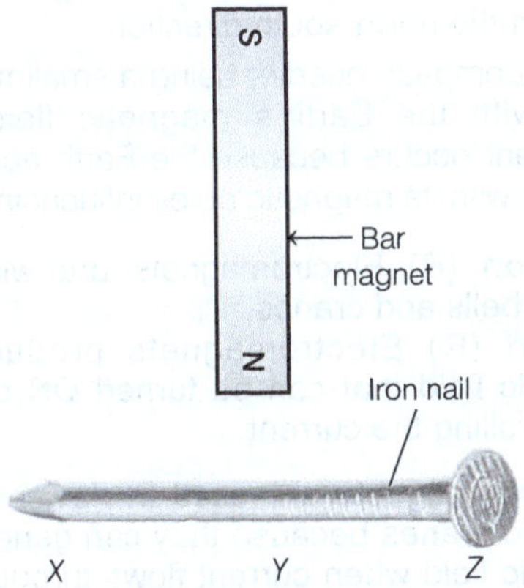

At which parts *X*, *Y* and *Z* is the easiest for the magnet to pick up the iron nail?

(a) At X (b) At Y
(c) At Z (d) It makes no different

Ans. (c) The region with the highest density of magnetic field lines has the greatest strength.

Q.7 The Earth's magnetic field exists due to

(a) rotation of Earth.
(b) convective motion of metallic fluids.
(c) Both (a) and (b)
(d) a huge bar magnet inside the Earth.

Ans. (c) Due to rotation of Earth, electrical currents are produced by convective motion of metallic fluids (consisting mostly of iron and nickel) in inner core of Earth which is responsible for Earth's magnetism.

Q.8 The material used for making the permanent magnet should be such that, its magnetic property is not erased by

(a) temperature variations
(b) minor mechanical damage
(c) stray magnetic field
(d) All of the above

Ans. (d) The material used for making the permanent magnet should be such that, its magnetic property is not erased by temperature variations or minor mechanical damage or stray magnetic fields.

Q.9 Electromagnets are used in

(a) electric bells (b) electric motors
(c) loudspeakers (d) All of these

Ans. (d) Electromagnet is a temporary strong magnet made from a piece of soft iron when current flows in the coil wound around it. It is used in electric bells, electric motors, loudspeakers, etc.

Q.10 Electromagnets are normally have the shapes of

(a) *U* (b) *I*
(c) *L* (d) both (a) and (b)

Ans. (d) Electromagnets are normally in the shape of *I* and *U*.

Q.11 A scrap metal dealer uses a large electromagnet. Which pair of metals will it pick up?

(a) aluminium and brass (b) brass and copper
(c) copper and iron (d) iron and steel

Ans. (d) Iron and steel are magnetic materials and will be attracted by the electromagnet. The rest of the given metals are non-magnetic.

Q.12 Four metal rods are placed, in turn, inside a coil of copper wire.

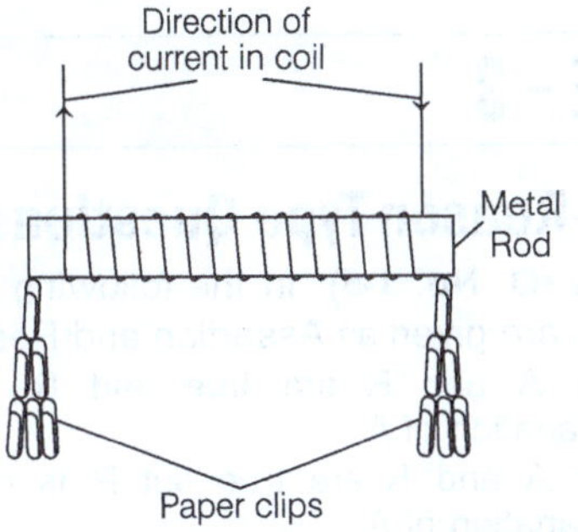

The table below gives the results of the experiment. Which rod would be the most suitable to use for the core of a coil in a circuit breaker?

	No. of paper clips picked up when there is a current in the coil	No. of paper clips still attracted when the current is switched off
(a)	1	0
(b)	20	2
(c)	35	0
(d)	35	30

Ans. (c) The core of a circuit breaker must be made of a soft iron type magnetic material which can be strongly magnetised but does not retain induced magnetism. Hence, *C* attracts the greatest number of clips when there is a current in the coil but the least number of clips when the current in the coil is removed.

TYPE - 2 01/02 Mark

Fill in the Blanks

Q.1 A freely suspended magnet always points in the ……… [North-South/South-East] direction.

Ans. North-East

Q.2 The Earth's magnetic field resembles that of a …… [Horse-shoe magnet/Bar magnet] magnet.

Ans. Bar magnet

Q.3 The instrument used to detect the presence of a magnetic field is …… [Magnetic compass/Ball ended magnet]

Ans. Magnetic compass

Q.4 Like poles of a magnet .... [repel/ attract] each other, while unlike poles .... [repel/ attract] each other.

Ans. repel, attract

Q.5 The space around a magnet where its influence can be felt is called the .... [magnetic field/poles] and its strength is strongest at the .... [magnetic field/poles].

Ans. magnetic field, poles

TYPE - 3 — 01/02 Marks

Assertion-Reason Type Questions

Directions (Q. No. 1-5) In the following questions two statements are given as Assertion and Reason.

(a) Both A and R are true and R is the correct explanation of A.

(b) Both A and R are true but R is not the correct explanation of A.

(c) A is true but R is false.

(d) A is false but R is true.

Q.1 Assertion (A) Magnetic field lines never intersect each other.

Reason (R) If two magnetic field lines intersect, it would mean that the compass needle point in two different directions at the point of intersection, which is impossible.

Ans. (a) Magnetic field lines indicate the direction of the magnetic field. At any given point, there can only be one direction for the magnetic field. If the lines intersect, it implies two directions for the magnetic field, which is not physically possible.

Q.2 Assertion (A) Magnetic field lines are closer near the poles of a bar magnet.

Reason (R) Magnetic field strength is maximum near the poles of a bar magnet.

Ans. (a) The closeness of the magnetic field lines indicated the strength of the magnetic field. Near the poles of a bar magnet, the field strength is maximum and therefore the lines are closer together.

Q.3 Assertion (A) The Earth's magnetic field resembles that of a bar magnet with its south pole near the geographic north pole.

Reason (R) The Earth's magnetic field is caused by the motion of molten iron in its outer core.

Ans. (a) The Earth behaves like a giant bar magnet due to the dynamo effect in its molten outer core, where circulating currents generate the magnetic field. The magnetic south pole of the Earth lies near the geographic north pole.

Q.4 Assertion (A) A compass needle aligns itself along the magnetic field lines of Earth.

Reason (R) A freely suspended magnet always aligns in the north-south direction.

Ans. (a) The compass needle, being a small magnet, aligns itself with the Earth's magnetic field lines. This alignment occurs because the Earth acts like a giant magnet with its magnetic poles influencing the needle.

Q.5 Assertion (R) Electromagnets are widely used in electric bells and cranes.

Reason (R) Electromagnets produce a strong magnetic field that can be turned ON or OFF easily by controlling the current.

Ans. (a) Electromagnets are used in devices like electric bells and cranes because they can generate a strong magnetic field when current flows through them. This field can be easily controlled by switching the current ON or OFF.

TYPE - 4 — 02 Marks

Very Short Answer Type Questions

Q.1 What are artificial magnets? How is it usually made? Why are they required?

Ans. Magnets made by man using elements like iron, nickel, cobalt or their mixture with other elements are called artificial magnets.

We require artificial magnet, due to the following qualities

(i) We can design any shape of artificial magnet as per desire.

(ii) Its magnetism can be obtained as per requirement.

Q.2 How does the magnetic pole strength of a magnet vary when

(i) it is cut into two equal parts parallel to its length **[1]**

(ii) it is cut perpendicular to its length **[1]**

Ans. (i) The magnetic pole strength of new broken magnet is half of the strength of original magnet because both broken parts are identical and equal.

(ii) There is no change in magnetic pole strength of new magnet because new magnet is magnetically identical.

Q.3 You are given two identical rods in which one is magnet and the other is not. How can you tell which one is magnet or not, without suspending it or use of any other apparatus?

Ans. Take one rod on the table and the other in your hand and touch the first rod (lying on the table) at the ends and also in the centre. If there is attraction at all the three points (i.e., both ends and centre), then rod in your hand is a simple rod. If there is a attraction only at the ends but no attraction at the centre, then the rod on the table is a magnet.

Q.4 You are provided two similar bars in which one is a magnet and other is a soft iron. How will you distinguish between them without the use of any other magnet?

Ans. Suspend these bars separately at its centre of gravity, so that they can move freely in horizontal plane. After sometime, when they come to rest, if the bar stays in North-South direction, then it will be a magnet and the other which (points some other direction) is a soft iron bar.

Q.5 How does an iron bar acquire magnetism when it is brought near to the North pole of bar magnet? Draw a diagram of an iron bar to show its polarity. What will happen when magnet is removed?

Ans. When an iron bar is brought near to the North pole of a bar magnet, it gets magnetised in such a way that the nearer end of iron bar becomes South pole and other end becomes North pole.

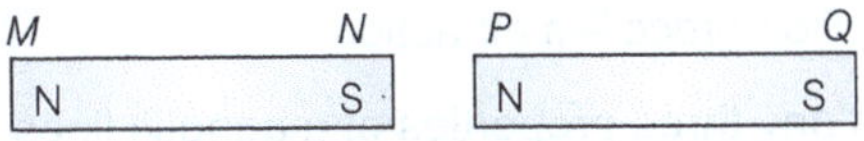

The iron bar *PQ* is placed near a bar magnet *MN*. When magnet is removed the induced magnetism in iron vanishes, then it becomes an ordinary piece of iron bar.

Q.6 Following figure shows that several soft iron pins can be hung one below the other from the pole of a magnet. What will happen when magnet is removed? Explain.

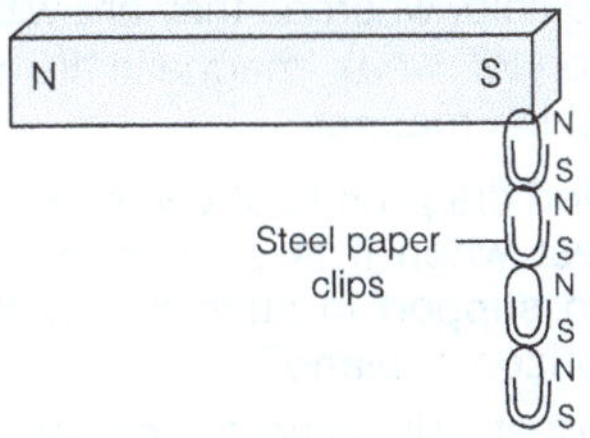

Ans. Soft iron pins are hung with each other by induced magnetism. When magnet is removed, the other pins will fall down because the magnetism in pins vanishes to zero when magnet is removed.

Q.7 Explain, why two magnetic field lines can never intersect each other?

Ans. Two magnetic field lines can never intersect each other because in this condition, there would be two directions of magnetic field at the point of intersection, which can never be possible.

Q.8 Two pairs of magnets are arranged in different ways as shown in the figure. In which of the arrangements do the magnets lose magnetism and why?

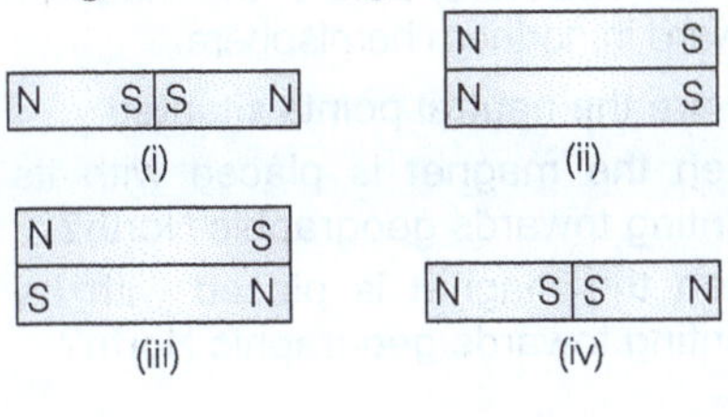

Ans. In (i) and (ii) arrangements, the magnets can lose their property. Since, two bar magnets are placed with their like poles facing each other, so the repulsive force between the like poles can reduce the magnetic strength over time.

Q.9 Plot the Earth's magnetic field lines in a horizontal plane as obtained by a limited space.

Ans. Magnetic field lines in a horizontal plane due to Earth's magnetic field in a limited place is uniform and parallel running from geographic South to geographic North direction.

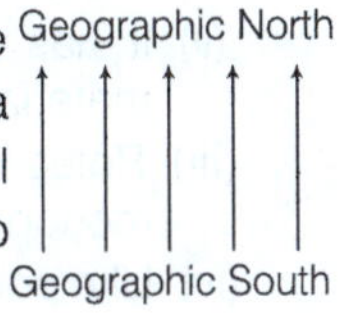

Q.10 How does a compass help in detecting magnetic field around a magnet?

Ans. When the magnetic compass is placed near the magnet, then it gets deflection. This illustrates the presence of magnetic field around a magnet.

Q.11 What is an electromagnet? Give one use of it.

Ans. An electromagnet is a temporary strong magnet. It consists of a long insulated copper wire wound around a soft iron core, which attains magnetism due to the flow of current. Giant electromagnets are used in cranes to lift machinery and other parts.

Q.12 Draw a labelled diagram to make an electromagnet from a soft iron bar *AB*. Mark the polarity at its ends. Write its uses.

Ans. The labelled diagram is shown below

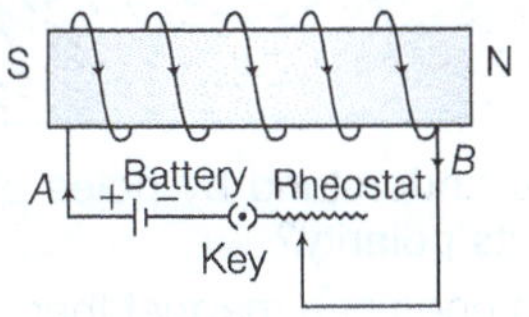

Here, the polarity at the end *A*, where the current is clockwise, is South (S), while at the end *B*, where the current is anti-clockwise, is North (N).

The uses of electromagnet are

(i) For separating the iron pieces from debris and ores.

(ii) In several electrical devices such as telegraph, microphone, loudspeaker, etc.

Q.13 Differentiate between permanent magnets and electromagnets.

Ans.

Electromagnet	Permanent magnet
It is a temporary magnet.	It is a permanent magnet. i.e., it cannot be demagnetised easily.
Its strength can be changed.	Its strength cannot be changed.
Its polarity can be changed.	Its polarity is fixed.

TYPE - 5 03 Marks

Short Answer Type Questions

Q.1 State the properties of a bar magnet.

Ans. The properties of a bar magnet are

(i) A bar magnet has directive property.

(ii) It has attractive property i.e., it attracts magnetic materials.

(iii) Poles exist only in pairs i.e., non-existence of monopole.

(iv) Like poles repel and unlike poles attract each other.

Q.2 Show that iron filings which are sprinkled on a sheet of cardboard over a bar magnet take up a definite pattern.

Ans. When we place a bar magnet below a sheet of cardboard and spread some iron filings uniformly over it. Then, the iron filings arrange themselves along the curved lines when cardboard is slightly taped which is shown in the figure below.

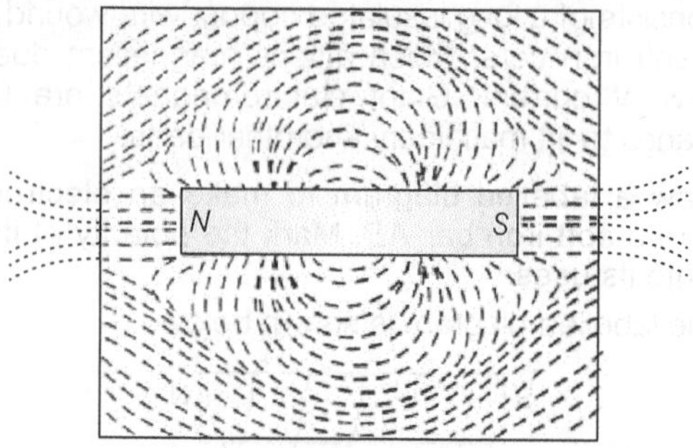

Q.3 What do you understand by poles of a magnet? How will you test its polarity?

Ans. Near the two ends of a magnet there are points, where the magnetic strength is maximum. These are called poles of a magnet.

To test polarity of a magnet, suspend it with a thread through its centre of gravity. So that, it can move freely in horizontal plane. After sometime, it comes to rests. The end directing towards North direction is called North pole and other is South pole.

Q.4 State the evidences of the existence of Earth's magnetic field.

Ans. The existence of Earth's magnetic field is based on the following facts

(i) A freely suspended magnet always rests in geographic North-South direction.

(ii) An iron rod burried inside the Earth along North-South direction, after some days becomes a magnet.

(iii) Neutral points are obtained near a magnet on plotting the magnetic field lines between the Earth's magnet and a bar magnet.

Q.5 Comment upon the statement induced magnetism is temporary.

Ans. When an unmagnetised bar is placed near a magnet, the bar becomes a magnet i.e., it acquires the property of attracting iron filings when they are brought near its ends. This is called induced magnetism.

If the magnet is removed, it is seen that all the iron filings which was clung to it falls down. That means the bar loses its magnetism. Hence, we can say that induced magnetism is temporary.

Q.6 Explain the statement, induction precedes attraction.

Ans. When a piece of iron is brought near one end of a magnet, the nearer end of the piece acquires the opposite polarity. Since, unlike poles attract each other, the iron piece is attracted towards the end of the magnet. So, the piece of iron first becomes a magnet and then it is attracted. This explains the statement induction precedes attraction.

Q.7 Write any three properties of magnetic lines of force.

Ans. Three properties of magnetic field lines are

(i) They leave from N-pole and enter at S-pole and continue inside magnet upto N-pole making closed curves.

(ii) The tangent at any point on the lines of field give the direction of magnetic field at that point.

(iii) Lines of field are crowded in the region of strong magnetic field, whereas they are widely separated in the region of weak magnetic field i.e., usually at middle of the magnet.

Q.8 Draw labelled diagram to show, how will a bar magnet come to rest when it is suspended by a silk thread from a rigid support in such a way that it can freely swing in horizontal plane?

Ans. A bar magnet will come to rest along geographical North-South direction. With North pole of the magnet towards geographical North direction and South pole of magnet towards geographical South direction.

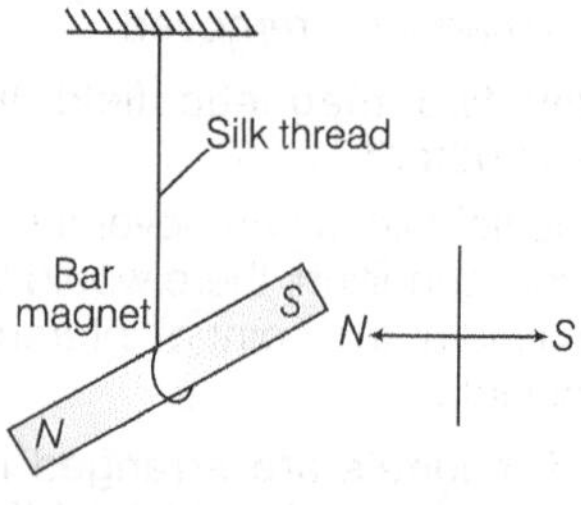

According to diagram, the magnet is not exactly horizontal. The North pole of the magnet is slightly dip downward in northern hemisphere.

Q.9 Where are the neutral points situated

(i) when the magnet is placed with its North pole pointing towards geographic North? **[1]**

(ii) when the magnet is placed with its South pole pointing towards geographic North? **[2]**

Ans. (i) If the North pole of bar magnet pointing towards geographic North, the neutral points are situated symmetrical on either side of a magnet at equal distance from the centre in East-West directions.

(ii) If South pole of a bar magnet pointing towards geographic North, the neutral points are on either side of the magnet at equal distance from the centre in North-South directions.

Q.10 A diagram of the magnetic field lines near a bar magnet with its north pole pointing towards the geographical north pole is shown below.

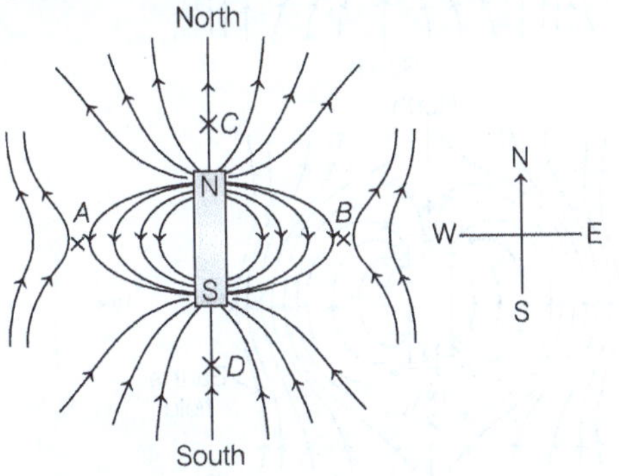

(a) Identify the neutral points in the diagram.

(b) What is the magnitude of the magnetic field lines at each neutral points.

(c) Describe the nature of the magnetic field lines of the bar magnet in the diagram.

Ans. (a) Only *A* and *B* represents the neutral points.

(b) Zero

(c) The magnetic field lines of a bar magnet form continuous closed loops, originating from the north pole and ending at the south pole.

TYPE - 6 — 04 Marks

Long Answer Type Questions

Q.1 What do you mean by the following terms. **[4 × 1 = 1]**

(i) Magnetism (ii) Magnet

(iii) Pole

(iv) Magnetic or effective length of magnet

Ans. (i) **Magnetism** It is the property by virtue of which a substance can attract magnetic materials e.g., soft iron, iron filings, etc.

(ii) **Magnet** Materials which have the property of magnetism are called magnet.

(iii) **Pole** The points inside the magnet near the ends, where the magnetic strength is maximum are called poles of the magnet.
The two poles are equal in strength. They are not situated exactly at the ends of the magnet but slightly inside.

(iv) **Magnetic or Effective Length** The distance between two poles of a magnet is called magnetic length or effective length.

Q.2 (a) (i) Define a magnetic field.

(ii) Draw the magnetic field lines of a bar magnet.

(b) State the effects that the poles of a magnet have on the poles of another magnet placed near to it.

(c) Complete the following magnetic field patterns with N-pole, S-pole and arrowheads. If there is a neutral point, mark with a cross 'X'.

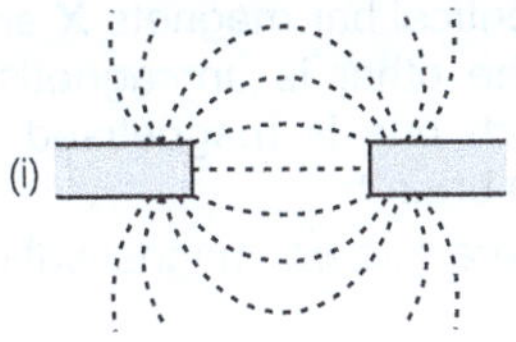

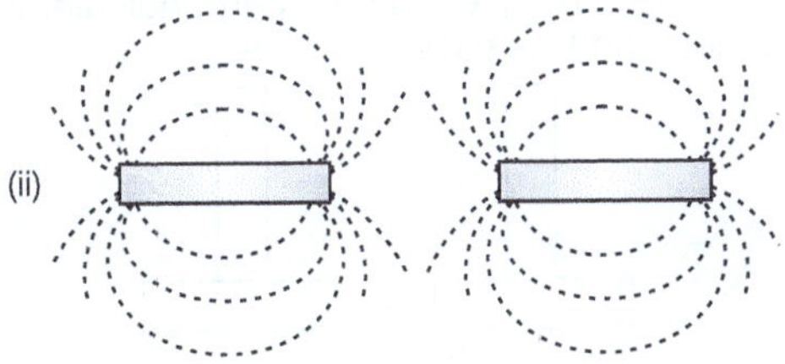

Ans. (a) (i) A magnetic field refers to the region around a magnet where the magnetic force can be experienced by another magnetic material.

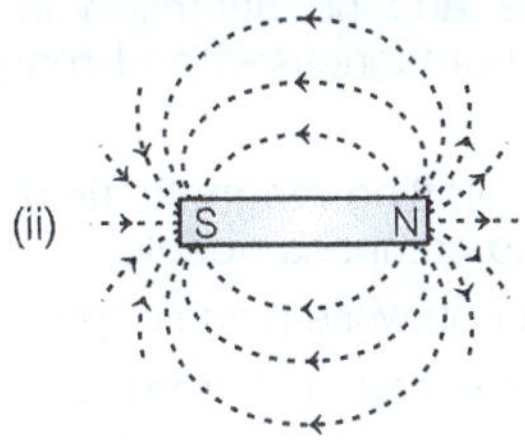

(b) Two like poles repel and two unlike poles attract.

(c)

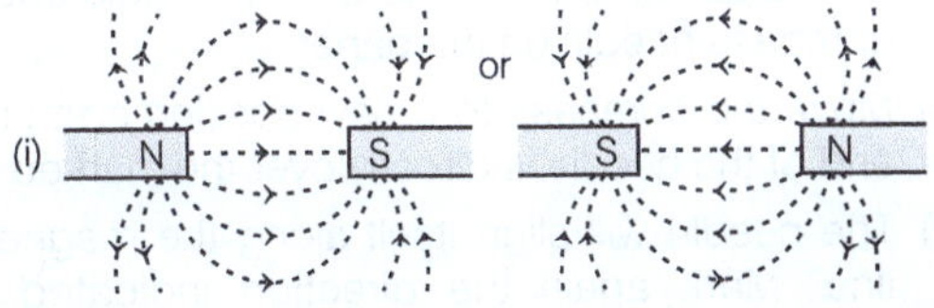

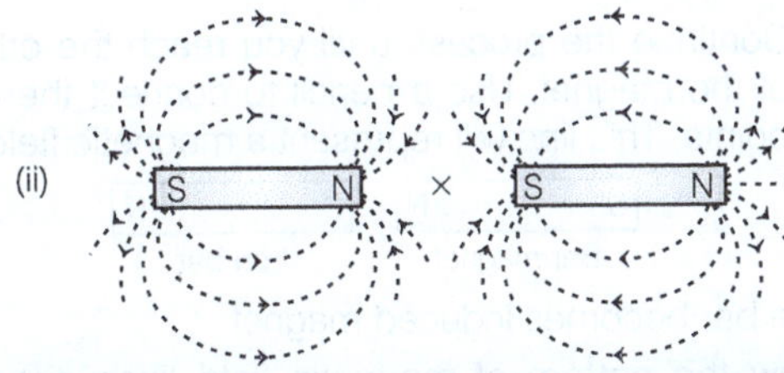

Q.3 In a class room, an ordinary piece of iron bar is placed on the top of a wooden table. Teacher has a bar in his hand and moves her hand below the table near the iron bar. It is observed that ordinary bar moves magically on the table. What conclusion do you draw from this magic?

Ans. The conclusion from this activity are as following

(i) Teacher has strong magnet in his hand.

(ii) Induced magnetism is produced in soft iron bar.

(iii) Opposite poles of magnet attract the bar.

(iv) There is a small force of friction between small iron bar and table top.

(v) Due to induction opposite poles of magnet and iron come close to each other.

Q.4 You are given two identical bar magnets *X* and *Y*, one is magnetised and the other is unmagnetised. How can you identify which one is magnetised by using your hands, eyes and brain?

Ans. As we know that, there is zero magnetisation at the centre of the magnet.

Firstly, place magnet X and Y perpendicularly and then magnet Y on X as shown in figure.

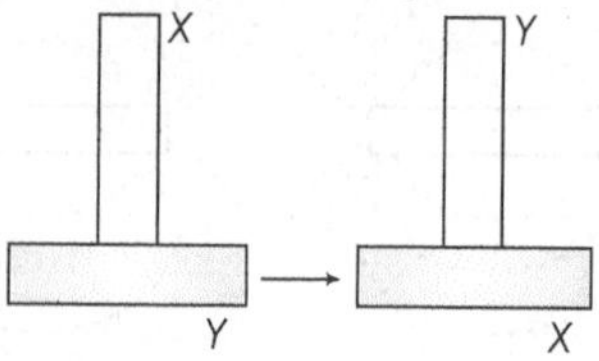

If there is no attraction in first case and there is attraction in second case, then magnet *Y* is magnetised and *X* is unmagnetised. If there is attraction in first case and no attraction in second case, then magnet *X* is magnetised and magnet *Y* is unmagnetised.

Q.5 Explain the method of plotting magnetic field lines by using a bar magnet and compass needle.

Ans. (i) Place the bar magnet on white piece of paper.

(ii) Position the compass near the north pole of the magnet.

(iii) Use a pencil to mark the direction indicated by the compass needle on the paper.

(iv) Move the compass to a new position so that the '*S*' end of the needle is directly over the marked point.

(v) The needle will align itself along the magnetic field line. Mark again the direction indicated by the compass needle.

(vi) Continue the process until you reach the other end of the magnet. Use a pencil to connect the marked points. This line will represent a magnetic field line.

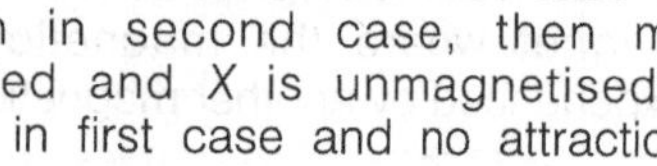

Iron bar becomes induced magnet.

Q.6 Draw the pattern of magnetic field lines near a bar magnet with the help of compass needle

(i) when magnet is placed with its North pole pointing towards geographic North. **[2]**

(ii) when the magnet is placed with its South pole pointing towards geographic North.

Also, indicate the position of neutral point by marking *X*.

Ans. (i)

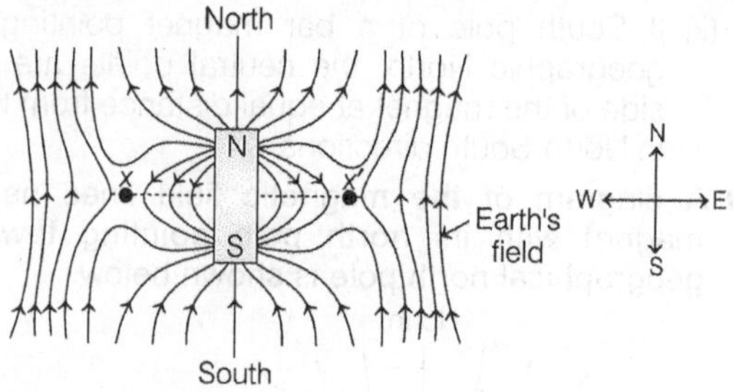

(ii)

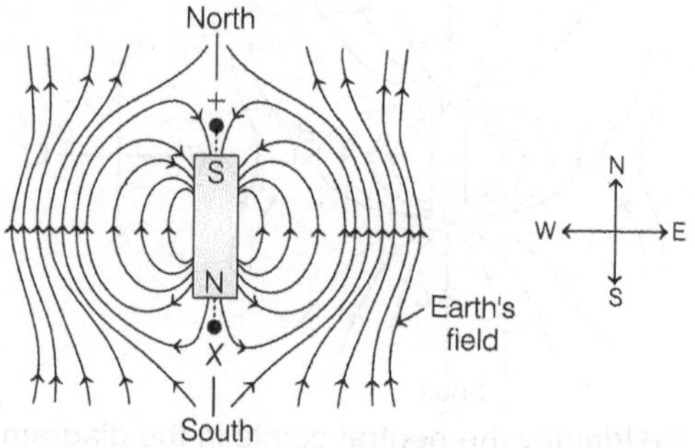

Q.7 **(i) What are the properties of an electromagnet?** **[2]**

(ii) How can we increase the strength of an electromagnet? **[2]**

Ans. (i) The properties of an electromagnet are

(a) It is a temporary magnet.

(b) Its strength can be changed.

(c) Its polarity can be changed.

(ii) The strength of an electromagnet can be increased by increasing the current through the coil.

TYPE - 7

03/04 Marks

Case Based Questions

Q.1 A bar magnet is placed on a table. When iron nails are brought near the ends of the bar magnet, they get attracted. However, at the centre of the bar magnet, the attraction is weak. A compass needle placed near the north pole of the magnet gets deflected significantly.

(i) Why do iron nails get strongly attracted to the ends of the bar magnet? **[1]**

(ii) Why is attraction weak at the centre of the magnet? **[1]**

(iii) If the bar magnet is broken into two pieces, will each retain its magnetic properties ? **[1]**

Ans. (i) The magnetic poles (North and South) are located at the ends of a bar magnet, where the magnetic field is strongest.

(ii) The magnetic field at the centre of the bar magnet is weaker because the poles are located at the ends, not in the middle.

(iii) Yes, each piece will become a smaller magnet with its own north and south poles.

Q.2 **A student places a bar magnet vertically on a table and sprinkles iron filings around it. The filings arrange themselves in distinct patterns around the magnet.**

(i) What do the patterns of the iron filings indicate about the magnetic field of a bar magnet? [1]

(ii) Why the patterns are denser near the poles of the bar magnet? [1]

(iii) What are the neutral points and how can they be identified in this experiment? [1]

Ans. (i) The patterns of the iron filings indicate the magnetic field lines around the bar magnet. They show the direction and strength of the magnetic field.

(ii) The patterns are denser near the poles because the magnetic field is strongest at the poles of the bar magnet.

(iii) The neutral points are the points where the magnetic field of the bar magnet cancels out the Earth's horizontal magnetic field. They can be identified as the regions where no iron filings align themselves.

Q.3 **The south pole of a bar magnet is placed pointing towards the geographical north pole as shown in the diagram below.**

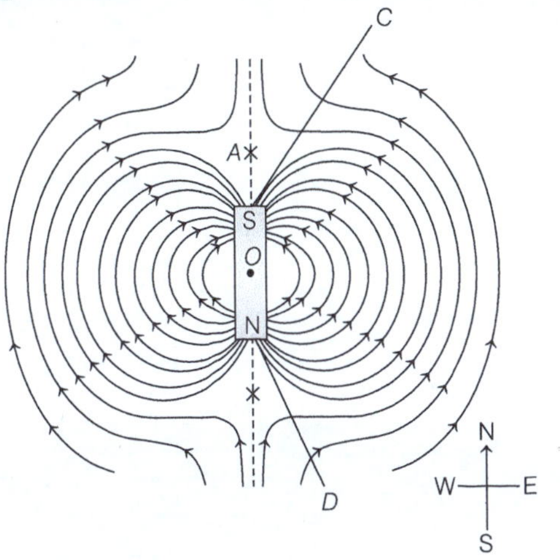

Complete the table, using the labels from the figure. The first label is done for you.

S.No.	Description	Label
a.	The magnetic field lines emerge from	*D*
b.	The magnetic field is zero at	
c.	The geometric centre of bar magnet lies at	
d.	The magnetic field lines converge at	

Ans.

S.No.	Description	Label
a.	The magnetic field lines emerge from	*D*
b.	The magnetic field is zero at	*A* and *B*
c.	The geometric centre of bar magnet lies at	0
d.	The magnetic field lines converge at	*C*

Q.4 **A student builds an electromagnet by winding a copper wire around an iron nail and connecting it to a battery. When the circuit is completed, the nail attracts small pins and paper clips.**

(i) What is the role of the copper wire in the electromagnet? [1]

(ii) What will happen if the current is switched off ? [1]

(iii) Why is a soft iron core preferred over a steel core ? [1]

Ans. (i) The copper wire conducts electricity, creating a magnetic field around the iron nail when current flows through it.

(ii) The iron nail will lose its magnetism, and the pins will not longer be attracted.

(iii) Soft iron quickly gains and loses magnetism, making it more suitable for temporary magnets like electromagnets.

Sample Question Paper

SAMPLE QUESTION PAPER
PHYSICS

General Instructions

Maximum Marks : 80

Time allowed : Two hours

Answer to this paper must be written on the paper provided separately.

You will not be allowed to write during first 15 minutes. This time is to be spent in reading the question paper.

The time given at the head of this paper is the time allowed for writing the answers.

Section A is compulsory. Attempt any four questions from Section B.

The intended marks for questions or parts of questions are given in brackets [].

Section A

(Attempt all questions from this section) **(40 Marks)**

Question 1

Choose the correct answer to the questions from the given options. **(15)**

(i) The diameter of a thin wire can be measured by a **(1)**

(a) vernier calliper (b) metre rule

(c) screw gauge (d) None of these

(ii) The velocity-time graph for one-dimensional motion is shown in the figure. **(1)**

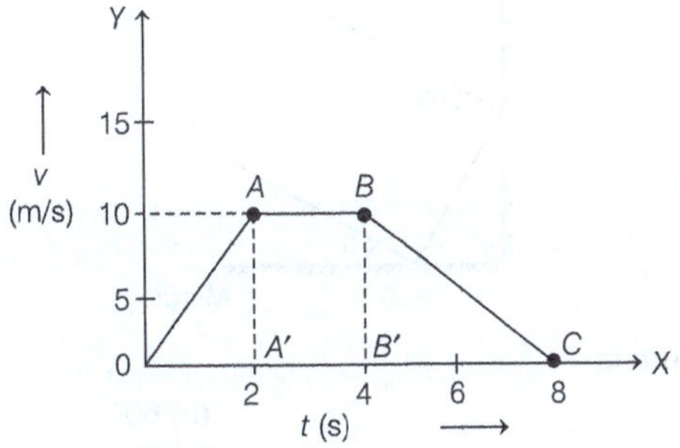

The acceleration of the body from point B to point C is

(a) $-2.5\ m/s^2$ (b) $5\ m/s^2$ (c) 0 (d) $2.5\ m/s^2$

(iii) A truck is moving with a speed of 54 km/ h. Truck driver applies brakes suddenly and brings the truck to rest in 5 s, then the average retarding force on truck, if the total mass of the truck and driver is 400 kg, will be **(1)**

(a) 1200 N (b) 600 N

(c) 800 N (d) 500 N

(iv) As we go from the equator to the poles, the value of g **(1)**

(a) remains the same
(b) decreases
(c) increases
(d) decreases upto a latitude of 45°

(v) At which point of vessel, pressure is minimum? **(1)**

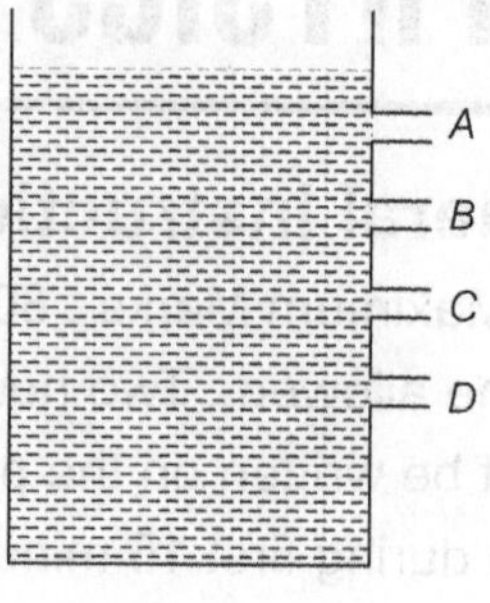

(a) A
(b) B
(c) C
(d) D

(vi) Why the dam of water reservoir is thick at the bottom? **(1)**

(a) Quantity of water increases with depth
(b) Density of water increases with depth
(c) Pressure of water increases with depth
(d) Temperature of water increases with depth

(vii) **Assertion (A)** Hope's experiment demonstrates the anomalous expansion of water.

Reason (R) Water contracts when cooled from 10°C to 4°C and expands below 4°C. **(1)**

(a) Both A and R are true and R is the correct explanation of A.
(b) Both A and R are true but R is not the correct explanation of A.
(c) A is true but R is false.
(d) A is false but R is true.

(viii) Energy enters in a food chain through

(a) producers
(b) primary consumers
(c) secondary consumers
(d) tertiary consumers

(ix)

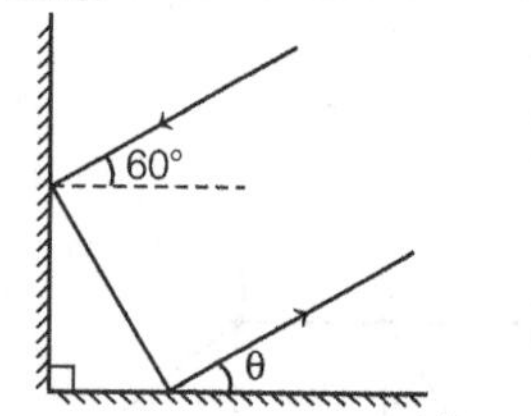

The value of θ in the above figure is **(1)**

(a) 45°
(b) 60°
(c) 90°
(d) 30°

(x) The image formed by a concave mirror is observed to be virtual, erect and larger than the object, where should be the position of the object? **(1)**

(a) Between principal focus and centre of curvature
(b) Centre of curvature
(c) Beyond centre of curvature
(d) Between pole of the mirror and its principal focus

(xi) Sound travels in air, if **(1)**

(a) particles of medium travel from one place to another
(b) there is no moisture in the atmosphere
(c) disturbance moves
(d) both particles as well as disturbance travel from one place to another

(xii) Find the value of wavelength, when frequency of vibration is changed to 300 Hz. Take, $v = 450$ m/s. **(1)**

(a) 1.8 m (b) 0.5 m
(c) 1.5 m (d) 2.5 m

(xiii) Electrical cell is a device which converts **(1)**

(a) electrical energy into mechanical energy
(b) mechanical energy into electrical energy
(c) electrical energy into chemical energy
(d) chemical energy into electrical energy

(xiv) Consider the following circuit diagram shown below and answer the following questions. **(1)**

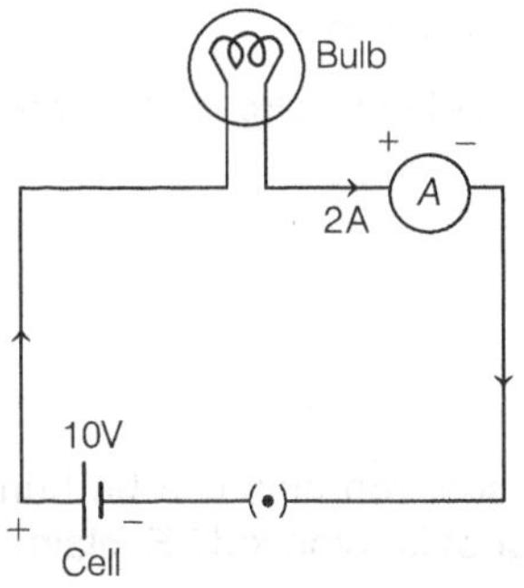

Resistance of the bulb is

(a) 20 Ω (b) 5 Ω
(c) 10 Ω (d) 15 Ω

(xv) Polarity and strength always remain unchanged for a **(1)**

(a) temporary magnet (b) permanent magnet
(c) Both (a) and (b) (d) Neither (a) nor (b)

Question 2 **(25)**

(i) Complete the following by choosing the correct answers from the bracket.

(a) The smallest measurement that can be made accurately by an instrument is called ……… [Least count/pitch]
(b) The rate of change of ………[mass/momentum] is ………[directly/inversely] proportional to the external force applied on it.
(c) The length of water column that exert 1 atm pressure is …………[10.336 m/0.76 m]
(d) The zero of kelvin scale is called………[null point/absolute zero]
(e) At a neutral point, the resultant magnetic field is …………[maximum, zero]

(ii) Draw a graph of density of water *versus* temperature in the range from 0°C to 10°C. **(2)**

(iii) How is time period of a simple pendulum affected in the situations given below. **(2)**

(a) The length is made three times.
(b) The acceleration due to gravity is reduced to one-third.

Question 3

(i) Why is it advised to tie the luggage kept on the roof of a bus with a rope? **(2)**

(ii) (a) Define vector quantities?

(b) Give two examples of vector quantity. **(2)**

(iii) (a) Complete the following ray diagram given below. **(2)**

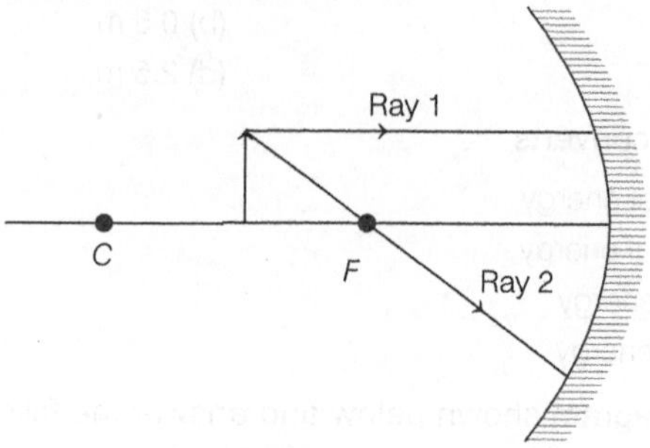

(b) Write the nature, position and size of the image.

(iv) Write the name of the symbols used in electric circuits to represent **(2)**

(a) 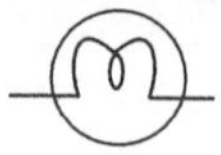

(b) 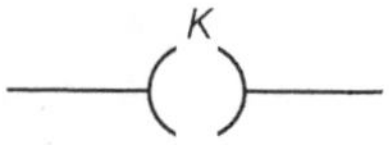

(v) Following figure shows that several soft iron pins can be hung one below the other from the pole of a magnet. What will happen when magnet is removed? Explain. **(2)**

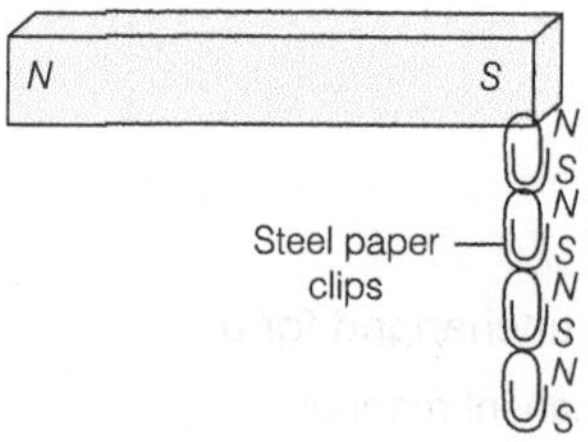

(vi) Name two important hydroelectric power projects in India. **(2)**

(vii) Two cyclists, A and B starts a race on a straight track from the same point at time $t = 0$s.

Cyclist A accelerates uniformly for the first 15 s and reaches a speed of 20 m/s. He then continues at this speed for the next 25 s before decelerating uniformly to rest. Cyclist A takes 50 s to complete the race.

Cyclist B is travelling in parallel to cyclist A with zero initial speed at $t = 0$ and then accelerates uniformly to first 10 s to reach a speed of 25 m/s and travels at this speed for next 20 s, before decelerating uniformly to rest. Cyclist B takes 10 s, to complete the race.

Answer the following questions. **(3)**

(a) What is the initial speed of cyclist A and B?

(b) What is the deceleration of cyclist A as he comes to rest?

(c) In which time interval, speed of cyclist B is constant?

Section B

(Attempt **any four** questions from this section) **(40 Marks)**

Question 4

(i) The velocity-time graph of an ascending passengers lift is shown in figure below. What is the acceleration of the lift **(3)**

(a) during the first two seconds?

(b) between 2nd and 10th second?

(c) during the last two seconds?

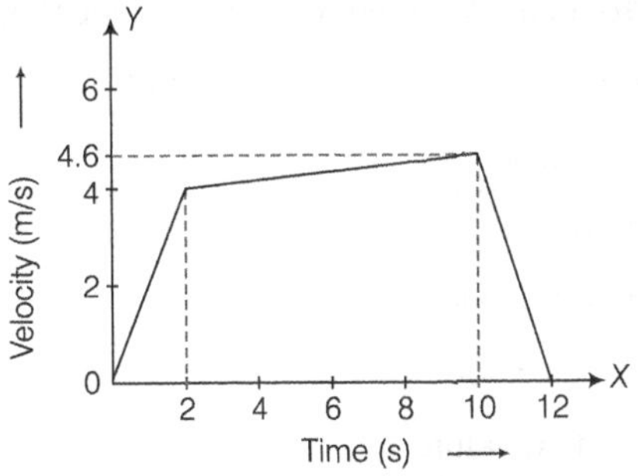

(ii) Look at the diagram below and answer the following questions. **(3)**

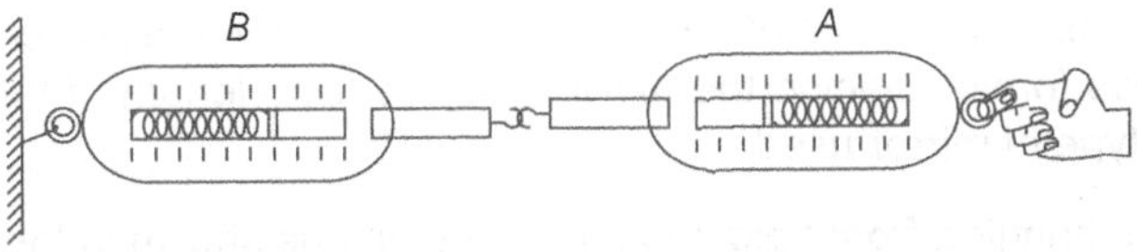

(a) When a force is applied through the free end of the spring balance *A*, the reading on the spring balance *A* is 15 g-wt. What will be the measure of the reading shown by spring balance *B* ?

(b) Write reasons for your answer.

(c) Name the force which balance *A* exerts on balance *B* and the force of balance *B* on balance *A*.

(iii) A student has three concave mirrors *A, B* and *C* of focal lengths 20 cm, 15 cm and 10 cm, respectively. For each concave mirror, he performs the experiment of image formation for three values of object distance of 30 cm, 10 cm and 20 cm. **(4)**

Give reasons for the following.

(a) For the three object distances, identify the mirror which will form an image equal in size to that of object. Find at least one value of object distance.

(b) Out of the three mirrors, identify the mirror which would be preferred to be used for shaving purpose.

(c) For the mirror *B*, draw a ray diagram for image formation for any two given values of object distance.

Question 5

(i) Interpret force in terms of momentum. Represent the following graphically **(3)**

(a) Momentum *versus* velocity, when mass is fixed.

(b) Momentum *versus* mass, when velocity is constant.

(ii) A boy complete one round of a circular race track of diameter 300m in 50 s. Calculate, **(3)**

(a) The distance covered by a body

(b) The displacement

(c) The average speed

(d) The average velocity

(iii) A ray diagram is given for an object located beyond the centre of curvature in front of concave mirror as shown in figure. **(4)**

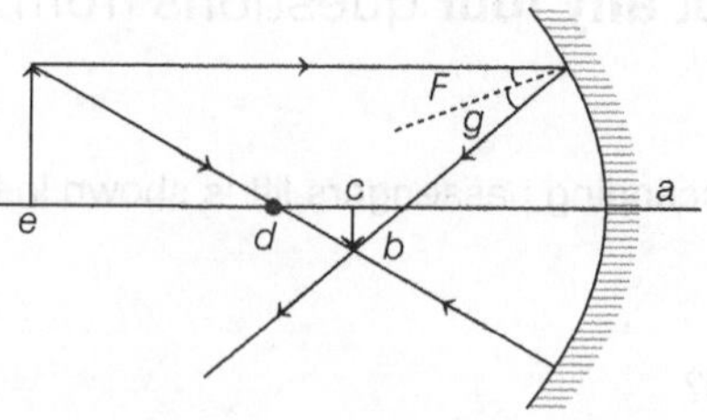

Complete the table, using the labels from the figure. The first label is done for you.

S.No.	Description	Label
(a)	Location of object	e
(b)	Location of image	
(c)	An angle of incidence	
(d)	An angle of reflection	
(e)	The centre of curvature	

Question 6

(i) An object 5 cm tall was placed in front of a spherical mirror at 20 cm distance from the mirror. If a virtual image of 10 cm tall was formed behind the mirror, find the focal length of the mirror and the position of the image. Name the type of mirror used. **(3)**

(ii) A block of mass 5 kg is hanging from rigid support by a string as shown in the figure. **(4)**

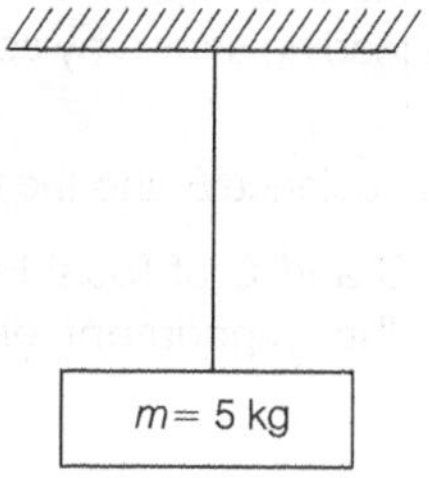

(a) Determine the force exerted by the block on the string.

(b) Determine the force exerted by the string on the block.

(c) Draw the diagram and show the direction of both forces in it.

(iii) Plastic production is increasing day-by-day despite of the fact that plastic is harmful for the environment. Based on the above statement, answer the following. **(3)**

(a) What are the harmful effects of plastic usage?

(b) In our day-to-day situation, what are the alternative that we can use instead of plastics?

(c) What can we learn as a good citizen as in concern for this issue?

Question 7

Figure shows the displacement-time graph of four children *A, B, C* and *D*. Which child has the (i) highest velocity (ii) lowest velocity? **(3)**

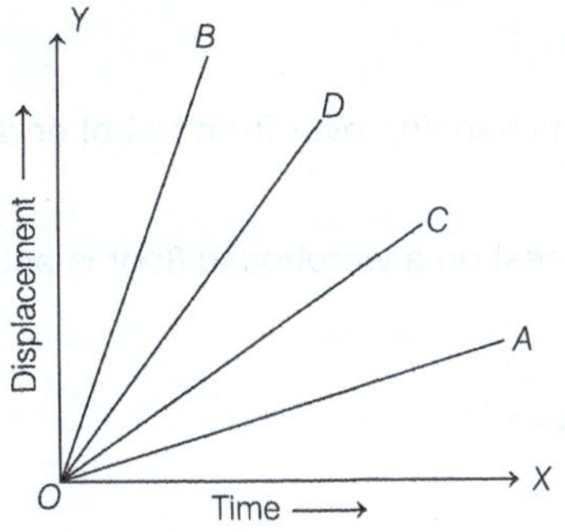

(ii) Answer the following questions.

(a) Two particles are placed at some distance. If the mass of each particle is doubled, keeping the distance between them unchanged, what will be the value of gravitational force between them?

(b) An apple falls from a tree because of gravitational attraction between the Earth and apple. If F_1 is the magnitude of force exerted by the Earth on the apple and F_2 is the magnitude of force exerted by apple on Earth, then find the relation between F_1 and F_2.

(iii) (a) Will a sheet of paper fall slower than one that is crumpled into a ball in vacuum? Why?

(b) Show mathematically that acceleration experienced by an object is independent of its mass.

(c) Show that value of $g = 9.8\ \text{m/s}^2$. (Take, $G = 6.7 \times 10^{-11}\ \text{N-m}^2/\text{kg}^2$, $M = 6 \times 10^{24}\ \text{kg}$, $R = 6.4 \times 10^6\ \text{m}$) **(4)**

Question 8

(i) A body covers a distance *s* in time *t* as follows **(3)**

$t(s)$	0	10	20	30	40	50	60
$s(m)$	0	5	10	15	20	25	30

(a) Plot s - t graph.

(b) What is the slope s - t graph?

(c) Determine the displacement of the body at time $t = 16$ s.

(ii) What does the weather forecast states, if **(3)**

(a) air is humid and Hg falls suddenly?

(b) air pressure rises steeply?

(c) air pressure falls gradually?

(iii) The diagram below shows a curve for a anomalous expansion of water. **(3)**

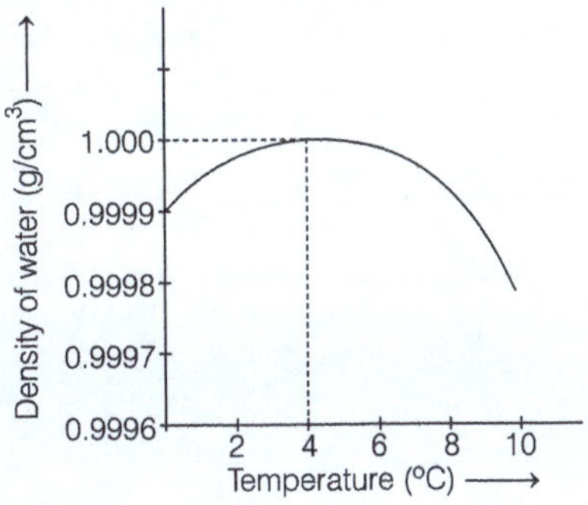

(a) What experiment is used to study the anomalous behaviour of water?

(b) At what temperature the density of water is maximum?

(c) Name any other two substances which shows anomalous behaviour.

Question 9

(i) Why is there so much empasis on changing over from petrol or diesel driver automobiles to CNG driven vehicles? **(3)**

(ii) A crate with mass 32kg initially at rest on a werehouse floor is acted on by a net horizontal force of 140 N. **(3)**

(a) What acceleration is produced?

(b) How for does the crate travel in 13 s?

(c) What is its speed at the end of 10 s.

(iii) Diagram shows a coil wound around a soft material. **(4)**

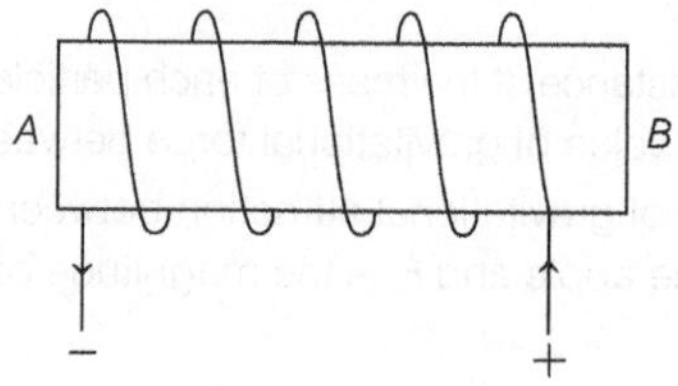

(a) Which material's rod is usually used to make electromagnet?

(b) State the polarity at the end *A* and *B*.

(c) Suggest two ways of increasing the strength of the electromagnet.

Answers

1.(i) (c) A screw gauge is used to measure the diameter of a thin wire because the least count of screw gauge is 0.001 cm. However, the least count of a micrometer screw gauge is 1 μm (0.0001 cm).

(ii) (a) From point B to C, the body undergoes uniform retardation.

Time taken by the body = 8 − 4 = 4 s

Now, acceleration of body = slope of line BC

$$= \frac{0 - 10}{4} = -\frac{10}{4} = -2.5 \ m/s^2$$

(iii) (a) Given, $u = 54 \ km/h = 54 \times \frac{5}{18} \ m/s = 15 \ m/s$

$v = 0$ and $t = 5$ s

∴ Retardation, $a = \frac{v - u}{t} = \frac{0 - 15}{5} = -3 \ m/s^2$

Average retarding force, $F = ma = 400 \times 3 = 1200$ N

(iv) (c) As we move from the equator to the poles, the value of g increases because the distance from the Earth's centre to the surface is smaller at the poles than at equator.

(v) (a) As we know, pressure exerted by liquid is directly proportional to the height of the vertical column. Therefore, pressure at point A is minimum and at point D, pressure is maximum.

(vi) (c) The dam of water is thick at the bottom because due to maximum depth, the pressure of water is maximum at bottom and to bear this maximum pressure dam should be thick at the bottom.

(vii) (a) Hope's experiment is used to study the behaviour of water when it is cooled. The experiment shows that water contracts as it cools from a higher temperature to 4°C but then starts expanding when cooled further below 4°C.

(viii) (a) Energy enters in a food chain through producers.

(ix) (b) According to question,

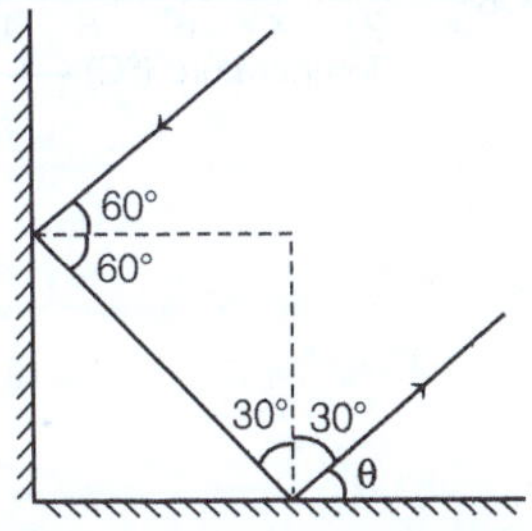

∴ The value of θ is 60°.

(x) (d) If the object is placed between the pole of the mirror and its principal focus, then virtual, erect and magnified image will be formed.

(xi) (c) When sound travels in air, then only disturbance created by the vibration of particle moves from one place to another.

(xii) (c) According to given condition, $v = 450$ m/s and $f = 300$ Hz

$$\therefore \quad \lambda = \frac{v}{f} \qquad [\because v = f\lambda]$$

$$= \frac{450}{300} = 1.5 \text{ m}$$

(xiii) (d) Electrical cell is a device which converts chemical energy into electrical energy by maintaining a constant potential difference between its electrodes through chemical reaction.

(xiv) (b) Given, $V = 10$ V, $I = 2$ A

According to Ohm's law, $V = IR \Rightarrow R = \frac{V}{I} = \frac{10}{2} = 5\ \Omega$

(xv) (d) Polarity and strength always remain same for a permanent magnet.

2. (i) (a) Least count

(b) momentum, directly

(c) 10.336 m

(d) absolute zero

(e) zero

(ii) The curve given below shows the variation of density of water with respect to temperature from 0°C to 10°C.

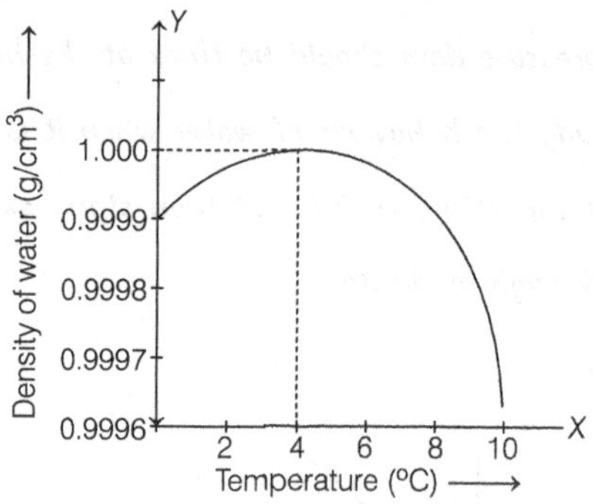

(iii) We know that, $T = 2\pi\sqrt{\frac{l}{g}}$

(a) If $l' = 3l$

$$T' = 2\pi\sqrt{\frac{3l}{g}}$$

$$T' = \sqrt{3}\,T$$

(b) If $g' = \frac{g}{3}$

$$T' = 2\pi\sqrt{\frac{l}{\frac{g}{3}}}$$

$$T' = 2\pi\sqrt{\frac{3l}{g}}$$

$$T' = \sqrt{3}\,T$$

3. (i) It is advised to tie any luggage kept on the roof of a bus because, when the bus stops suddenly, then bus comes in the state of rest but the luggage remains in the state of motion. So, due to inertia of motion, the luggage moves forward and falls down from the roof of the bus. If the bus starts suddenly, then bus comes in the state of motion but luggage remains in the state of rest. Due to inertia of rest, the luggage moves in the backward direction and falls down.

(ii) (a) A vector quantity is defined as the physical quantity that has both directions as well as magnitude.

(b) Two examples of vector quantities are velocity and force.

(iii) (a) Image formation when object is placed between centre of curvature C and focus F.

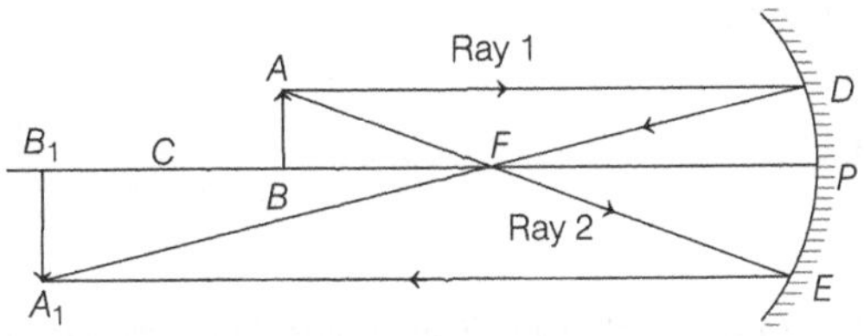

(b) The nature and size of image - Real, inverted and magnified.

The position of image - Beyond the centre of curvature.

(iv) (a) Bulb

(b) Open plug key

(v) Soft iron pins are hung with each other by induced magnetism. When magnet is removed, the pins will fall down because the magnetism in pins vanishes when magnet is removed.

(vi) Two important hydroelectric power projects in India are

(a) Bhakra - Nangal Project (Satluj river)

(c) Hirakund Project (Mahanadi river)

(vii) (a) Initial speed of cyclist A and B is zero as both cyclist start from rest.

(b) Given, initial velocity, $u = 20$ m/s

Final velocity, $v = 0$ m/s

Time $t = 10$ s

From first equation of motion, $a = \frac{v - u}{t} = \frac{0 - 20}{10} = -2\ m/s^2$

So, the deceleration is $2\ m/s^2$.

(c) Speed of cyclist B is constant during the time interval 10 s to 30 s.

4. (i) **Case I**

$\Delta v = 4 - 0 = 4\ m/s, \quad \Delta t = 2 - 0 = 2\ s, \quad a_1 = ?$

$\therefore a_1 = \frac{\Delta v}{\Delta t} = \frac{4}{2} = 2\ m/s^2$

(ii) **Case II**

$\Delta v = 4.6 - 4 = 0.6\ m/s, \quad \Delta t = 10 - 2 = 8\ s, \quad a_2 = ?$

$\therefore \quad a_2 = \frac{\Delta v}{\Delta t} = \frac{0.6}{8} = 0.075\ m/s^2$

(iii) **Case III**

$\Delta v = 0 - 4.6 = -4.6\ m/s,$

$\Delta t = 12 - 10 = 2\ s, \quad a_3 = ?$

$\therefore \quad a_3 = \frac{\Delta v}{\Delta t} = \frac{-4.6}{2} = -2.3\ m/s^2$

Negative sign shows retardation.

(ii) (a) 15 g-wt.

(b) From Newton's third law, the force exerted by B on A and force exerted by A on B are equal.

(c) Force of reaction and force of action.

(iii) (a) When an object is placed at the centre of curvature (i.e., double the distance of focal length) of concave mirror, the image formed is equal in size to that of object. So, for object distance 20 cm, the mirror C with focal length 10 cm is used as

$u = R = 2f = 2 \times 10\ cm = 20\ cm.$

(b) For shaving purpose, mirror B ($f = 15$ cm) would be preferred to form an enlarged and erect image of the face at distance 10 cm.

(c) (I) For $u = 30$ cm

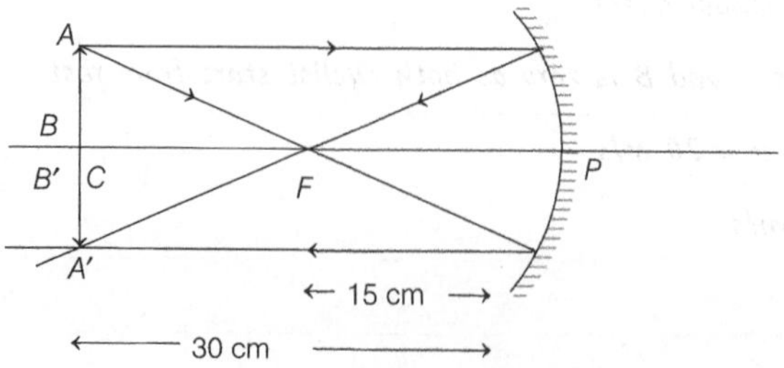

(ii) For $u = 10$ cm

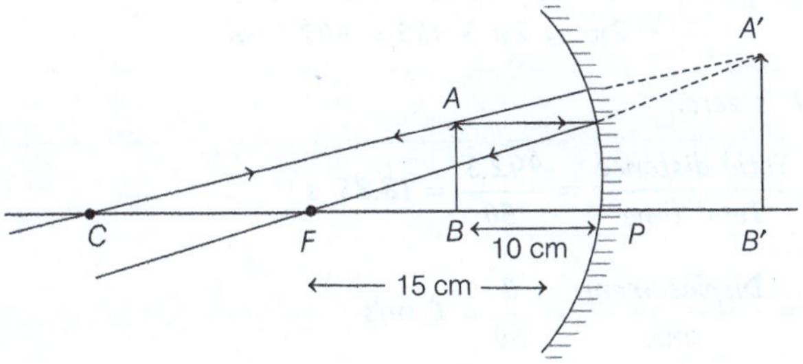

5. As we know, force = rate of change of momentum per unit time

$$\Rightarrow \quad F = \frac{\Delta p}{\Delta t}$$

(a) Graph of momentum versus velocity

As, $p = mv$

if m = constant

$\Rightarrow \quad p \propto v$

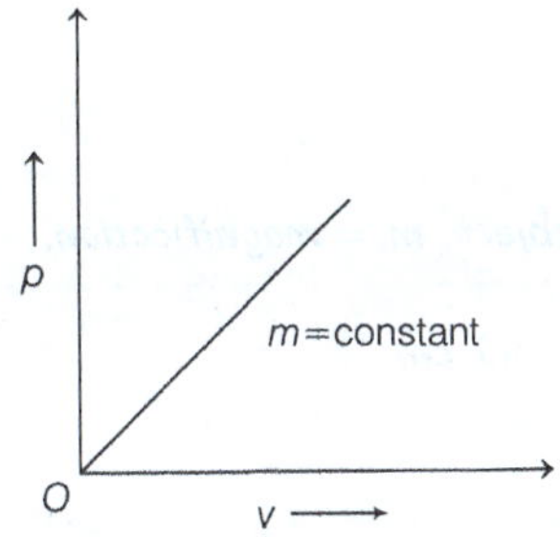

(b) Graph of momentum versus mass.

As, $p = mv$

if v = constant $\Rightarrow \quad p \propto m$

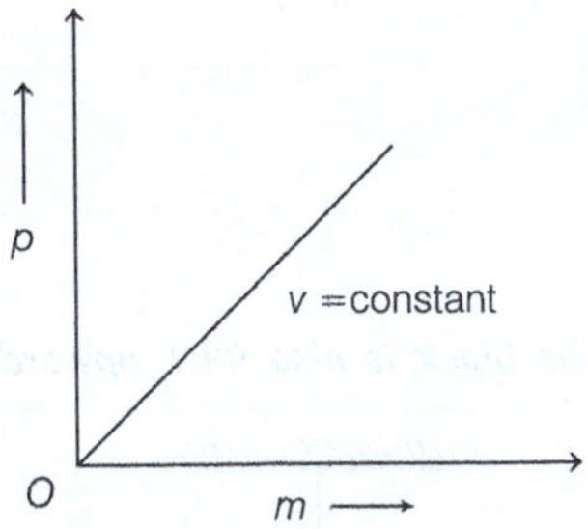

(ii) Given, diameter $D = 300$ m

$\therefore$ radius, $r = \frac{300}{2} = 150$ m

Time, $t = 50$ s

(a) Distance covered by a body = Circumference of circle

$$= 2\pi r = 2\pi \times 150 = 942.5 \text{ m}$$

(b) The displacement is zero.

(c) Average speed $= \dfrac{\text{Total distance}}{\text{Total time}} = \dfrac{942.5}{50} = 18.85$ s

(d) Average velocity $= \dfrac{\text{Displacement}}{\text{time}} = \dfrac{0}{50} = 0$ m/s

(iii)

S. No.	Description	Label
(a)	Location of object	e
(b)	Location of image	c
(c)	An angle of incidence	f
(d)	An angle of reflection	g
(e)	The centre of curvature	d

6. (i) Given, $u = -20$ cm, $h_i = 10$ cm and $h_o = 5$ cm

As we know, $m = \dfrac{h_i}{h_o} = \dfrac{10}{5} = 2$

where, h_i = size of image, h_o = size of object, m = magnification.

Also, $m = -\dfrac{v}{u} \Rightarrow 2 = \left(\dfrac{-v}{-20}\right) \Rightarrow v = 40$ cm

From mirror formula, $\dfrac{1}{f} = \dfrac{1}{v} + \dfrac{1}{u}$

where, u = object distance, v = image distance

and f = focal length.

$$\frac{1}{f} = \frac{1}{40} + \frac{1}{(-20)} = \frac{1-2}{40} = \frac{-1}{40} \Rightarrow f = -40 \text{ cm}$$

So, mirror is concave.

(ii) (a) Force, $F = mg = 5 \times 9.8 = 49$ N

(b) The force exerted by the string on the block is also 49N, upward in direction.

(c)

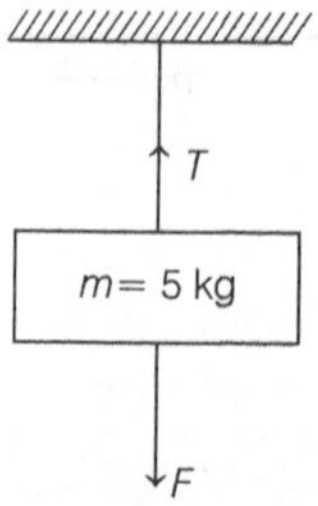

(iii) (a) Burning of plastics cause pollution. Plastics cause harm to the cattle/animals, if it enters inside their alimentary canal.

(b) Paper bags/jute bags can be used instead of plastic bag.

(c) Every citizen should be discouraged to use plastics as a source of packaging and storing as it is non-biodegradable.

7. (i) Velocity = Slope of displacement-time

Since, slope of child B is greater than all other children. Hence, child B has the highest velocity.

Similarly, the slope of child A is smallest, so it has lowest velocity.

(ii) (a) Gravitational force, $F_1 = G\dfrac{Mm}{r^2}$

If mass of each particle is doubled, then

$$F_2 = G\frac{(2M)(2m)}{r^2}$$

$$\text{or } F_2 = 4G\frac{Mm}{r^2}$$

$$\text{or} \qquad F_2 = 4F_1 \qquad \left(\because F_1 = G\frac{Mm}{r^2}\right)$$

(b) From third law of motion, to every action, there is an equal and opposite reaction and they act on two different bodies, so magnitudes of F_1 and F_2 are equal.

$$\Rightarrow \qquad F_1 = -F_2$$

(iii) (a) Both of them will fall at the same speed because acceleration produced in freely falling bodies is the same for all bodies, irrespective of their shapes or masses.

(b) Consider a body of mass m on the surface of the Earth, M be mass of the Earth, R be the distance between the body and centre of the Earth (radius of the Earth) and g is the acceleration due to gravity.

Let F be the force acting on the body.

According to Newton's second law of motion,

$$F = mg \qquad \text{...(i)}$$

According to Newton's law of gravitation,

$$F = G\frac{M \times m}{R^2} \qquad \text{...(ii)}$$

From Eqs. (i) and (ii), we get

$$mg = G\frac{M \times m}{R^2}$$

$\therefore\ g = \dfrac{GM}{R^2}$, thus g is independent of the mass of the body.

(c) $\therefore\ g = \frac{GM}{R^2} = \frac{6.7 \times 10^{-11} N - m^2\ kg^{-2} \times 6 \times 10^{24} kg}{(6.4 \times 10^6 m)^2}$

$= \frac{6.7 \times 6}{6.4 \times 6.4} \times \frac{10^{-11+24}}{10^{12}} = 0.981 \times N / kg$

$= 9.81\ m/s^2 \approx 9.8\ m/s^2$

Thus, the value of $g = 9.8\ m / s^2$.

8. (i) (a)

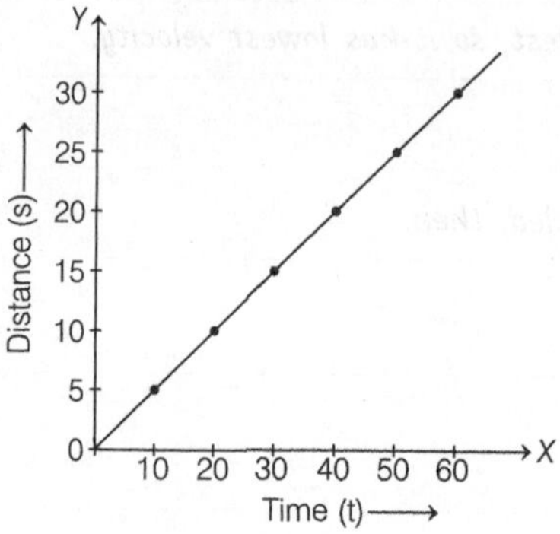

(b) Slope of the graph is

$slope = \frac{30}{60} = 0.5$

(c) Displacement at $t = 16$ s

First, solve for velocity of body

Velocity = slope of the graph

$= \frac{30}{60} = 0.5\ m/s$

Displacement $= v \times t$

$= 0.5 \times 16 = 8\ m$

(ii) (a) It indicates storm or cyclone.

(b) It indicates weather is dry.

(c) It indicates the possibility of rain.

(iii) (a) Hope's experiment

(b) 4°C

(c) Silver Iodide and Silica

9. (i) There is so much emphasis on changing over from petrol or diesel driven automobiles to CNG driven vehicles because of the following reasons.

(a) It does not produce smoke.

(b) On burning CNG it produces CO_2 and water.

(c) It does not leave unburnt hydrocarbons, lead particulates, etc., which pollute the environment.

(ii) Given, initial velocity, $u = 0$ m/s

Force, $F = 140$ N

Mass, $m = 32$ kg

(a) From Newton's second law,

$$F = ma$$

$$\text{or } a = \frac{F}{m}$$

$$a = \frac{140}{32} = 4.37 \text{ m/s}$$

(b) From second equation of motion,

$$s = ut + \frac{1}{2}at^2$$

$$s = 0 \times 13 + \frac{1}{2} \times 4.37 \times 13^2$$

$$s = 369.26 \text{ m}$$

(c) From first equation of motion,

$$v = u + at$$

$$v = 0 + 4.37 \times 10$$

$$v = 4.37 \text{ m/s}$$

(iii) (a) Soft iron

(b) The polarity at the end A when the current is anti-clockwise, is north (N), while at the end B where the current is clockwise, is south (S).

(c) Two ways to increasing the strength of the electromagnet.

- Increase the number of turns in the wire.
- Increase the current in the wire.